Book of Psalms

Book of Psalms

Translated by

Daniel A. Elias

Tzeruf Co.

Author: *Daniel A. Elias, J.D.*

Publisher: Tzeruf Co (tzeruf.com)
235 S. Lyon Ave #39
Hemet, CA 92543   USA
mail@tzeruf.com

SAN Number   853-0203

First Edition Published 2013

Publisher's Cataloging-in-Publication data

Elias, Daniel A..

Book of Psalms

English Paperback   ISBN   978-0-9792826-5-2

1. Religion 2. Bible Studies 3. Old Testament 4. Psalms 5. Hebrew..

Table of Contents

The objective of this book is to;

1) make the reader more fluent in the reading of the Hebrew Language,

2) to feed the soul with the effects of reading the hebrew letters and the bible code,

3) to learn the Hebrew vocabulary,

4) to help memorize verses that are interesting to a person,

5) to foster kavanah.

One Hebrew word of a verse contains so much subtle information. There is the root, the prefix, the affix, dropped weak letters, gutturals, dagesh lene, dagesh forte, it's sentence grammatical name, etc. There is only space for a one word translation. Much of the English grammar has been left out by necessity; ie. the translation "the" was put in only when there was a specific prefix letter Heh.

Every expression in the [ongoing] present tense can variably be expressed in the future tense as well as in the past tense. This is because anything that is ongoing is in the present and has already happened and will continue to happen.

I would have preferred to translate the tenses of the verbs as they actually appear instead of looking to the sentence meaning to infer the past, present or future. However in order to make the translations simple to understand for the majority of people who do not understand this concept I have inferred verb tenses to optimize understanding.

The vast majority of the Hebrew words in the Bible are very easy to translate. Generally everyone agrees on their meanings and these words are used in everyday life in Israel. But many the hard Hebrew words with uncertain roots are such that even experts question their meanings and translations.

The Eskimos have 20 words for snow. This same principle applies to the Hebrew words found in the Torah. There may be 20 Hebrew words that

Psalms Intro

FIVE BOOKS

The Book of Psalms is divided, after the analogy of the Pentateuch, into five books, each closing with a doxology or benediction (For the Orthodox Christian division into twenty kathismata, see Eastern Orthodox usage, below):

FIRST BOOK comprises the first 41 Psalms. All of these are ascribed to David except Psalms 1, 2, 10, and 33, which, though untitled in the Hebrew, were also traditionally ascribed to David. While Davidic authorship cannot be confirmed, this probably is the oldest section of the Psalms.

SECOND BOOK consists of the next 31 Psalms (42–72). Eighteen of these are ascribed to David. Psalm 72 begins "For Solomon", but is traditionally understood as being written by David as a prayer for his son. The rest are anonymous.

THIRD BOOK contains seventeen Psalms (73–89), of which Psalm 86 is ascribed to David, Psalm 88 to Heman the Ezrahite, and Psalm 89 to Ethan the Ezrahite.

FOURTH BOOK also contains seventeen Psalms (90–106), of which Psalm 90 is ascribed to Moses, and Psalms 101 and 103 to David.

FIFTH BOOK contains the remaining 44 Psalms. Of these, 15 are ascribed to David, one (Psalm 127) as a charge to Solomon.

There is a concluding note at the end of Psalms 41, 72, 89, and 106, which suggests that the book is in five separate sections.

TYPES OF PSALMS

There are ten types of Psalms (Tehillim in Hebrew) according to the Talmud (Pesachim 117a);

Nitzuach, Nigun, Maskil, Mizmor, Shir, Ashrey, Tehilah, Tefilah, Hoda'ah, and Haleluyah.

ASCRIBING

Jewish tradition posits that the Psalms are the work of David (seventy-three Psalms are with David's name),

Additionally, thirteen Psalms have headings that refer to some event in the life of David. These Psalms are 3, 7, 18, 34, 51, 52, 54, 56, 57, 59, 60, 63 and 142. Some of the references involved are quite ambiguous or obscure.

Psalms 39, 62, and 77 are linked with Jeduthun, to be sung after his manner or in his choir.

Psalms 50 and 73–83 are the Psalms of Asaph, associated with Asaph, as the master of his choir, to be sung in the worship of God.

The ascriptions of Psalms 42, 44–49, 84, 85, 87, and 88 assert that the "sons of Korah" were entrusted with arranging and singing them; 2 Chronicles 20:19 suggests that this group formed a leading part of the Korathite singers.

Hebraist Joel M. Hoffman suggests that Psalm 49 may be an anti-corruption Psalm, not "for Korah" but "against Korah."

LEVITIES SONG OF THE DAY

Traditionally, a different "Psalm for the Day" is read after the morning service each day of the week (starting Sunday, Psalms: 24, 48, 82, 94, 81, 93, 92). This is described in the Mishnah (the initial codification of the Jewish oral tradition) in the tractate "Tamid". According to the Talmud, these daily Psalms were originally recited on that day of the week by the Levites in the Temple in Jerusalem.

INDIVIDUAL PSALMS

HALLEL. Psalm 136 is generally called "the great Hallel", but the Talmud also includes Psalms   120–135.

Psalms 113–118 constitute the Hallel, which is recited on the three great feasts; Peasach (Passover), Shavuot (Weeks), and Succot (Tabernacles); at the new moon; and on the eight days of Hanukkah. A version of Psalm 136 with slightly different wording appears in the Dead Sea Scrolls.

SONGS OF ASCENTS.   Psalms 120–134 are referred to as, and are thought to have been used as hymns of approach by pilgrims to the Temple in Jerusalem.

PSALM 119 is the longest Psalm. It is composed of 176 verses, in sets of eight verses, each set beginning with one of the 22 Hebrew letters. Several other Psalms also have alphabetical arrangements.

Psalm 117 is the shortest Psalm, containing but two verses.

These psalms are believed to be written (rather than oral) compositions from the first, and thus of a relatively late date.

- Songs of Zion – Psalms 48, 76, 84, 87, 122, 134;
- Historical Litanies – Psalms 78, 105, 106, 135, 136;
- Pilgrim Liturgies – Psalms 81, 21;
- Entrance Liturgies – Psalms 15, 24;
- Judgment Liturgies – Psalms 50, 82;
- Mixed Types – 36, 40, 41, 68

Psalm forms or types also include:

 * Songs of Zion – Psalms 48, 76, 84, 87, 122, 134;

 * Historical Litanies – Psalms 78, 105, 106, 135, 136;

 * Pilgrim Liturgies – Psalms 81, 21;

 * Entrance Liturgies – Psalms 15, 24;

 * Judgment Liturgies – Psalms 50, 82;

 * Mixed Types – 36, 40, 41, 68

TEMPLE

Psalms were actually sung in front of the Tabernacle, and then later during the reign of King Solomon, when the Temple was completed, they were sung from the steps of the Temple. The singers all came from the tribe of Levi (Levites), and it was exclusively their privilege - no non-Levites were allowed to sing in that area of the Temple. Levites played musical accompaniment on various instruments, some mentioned within the Psalms themselves.

TALMUDIC PERIOD

In the Talmudic period no Psalms were recited as part of the service except for the Hallel psalms (psalms of praise, Psalms 113 to Psalm 118) on the festival.

POST TALMUDIC PERIOD

As the post-Talmudic liturgy developed, a large number of further psalms were incorporated into the Prayer Book, not all at once but gradually over the centuries. To the daily morning service were added: Psalms 100, 145 and 150. To the Sabbath and festival services were added Psalms 19, 34, 90, 91, 135, 136, 33, 92, 93 in this order, since on these days people, not having to go out to work, did not have to hurry from the synagogue.

At the end of the morning service, a special psalm for each day is recited, prefaced with the words:"This is the first [second, third, and so on] day of the week, on which the Levites in the Temple used to say . . ." Psalm 24 is recited when the Sefer Torah is returned to the Ark after the reading on weekdays, and Psalm 29 on the Sabbath.

SPECIAL PSALMS FOR SPECIAL DAYS

The penitential Psalm 27 is recited at the end of the morning and evening service during the penitential season from the beginning of the month of Elul until the final day of Sukkot [Hoshanah Rabbah].

Before the evening service at the termination of the Sabbath Psalms 144 and 67 are read.

Psalm 104 is read during the morning service on Rosh Hodesh, the New Moon, and during the afternoon service on winter Sabbaths.

WELCOMING SHABBATH

As part of their ritual for welcoming the Sabbath, the Safed Kabbalists [mystics who lived in Safed, Israel in the sixteenth century) introduced the Psalms 95-99 and 29, corresponding to the six days of creation, on the eve of the Sabbath, and this is now the universal custom at the Friday night service. Verses from Psalms are scattered through other parts of the Prayer Book.

Psalms 95–99, 29, 92, and 93, along with some later readings, comprise the introduction ("Kabbalat Shabbat") to the Friday night service.

DEATH

When a Jew dies, a watch is kept over the body and Tehillim (Psalms) are recited constantly by sun or candlelight, until the burial service.

II. Book One (1:1 - 41:14)

I. Book One (1:1-41:13)

A. The righteous way - wisdom (1:1-6)

B. God establishes his anointed - royal (2:1-11)

C. Trust when surrounded by enemies - individual lament (3:1-8)

D. Confidence in need - individual lament (4:1-8)

E. God will deal with enemies - individual lament (5:1-12)

F. Prayer for healing - individual lament (6:1-10)

G. Plea for deliverance from persecutors - individual lament (7:1-17)

H. Praise of God's majesty and human worth - hymn (8:1-9)

I. Prayer for oppressed - individual lament (9:1-10:18)

J. Refuge in God - song of trust (11:1-7)

K. People's plea for protection - community lament (12:1-8)

L. How long? - individual lament (13:1-6)

M. No one seeks God - individual lament (14:1-7)

N. Who can live before God? - liturgy (15:1-5)

O. Trust in God - song of trust (16:1-11)

P. May God deal with enemies - individual lament (17:1-15)

Q. God, our Rock - individual song of thanksgiving (18:1-50)

R. Creation witnesses to God - hymn (19:1-6)

S. God's perfect law - wisdom (19:7-14)

T. Prayer for the king - royal (20:1-9)

U. A king's praise to God - royal (21:1-13)

V. Why has God forsaken? - individual lament (22:1-31)

W. The Lord as shepherd - song of trust (23:1-6)

X. Who can stand vefore God? - liturgy (24:1-10)

Y. Teach and forgive - individual lament (25:1-22)

Z. Vindicate me - individual lament (26:1-12)

AA. No need to fear - song of trust (27:1-6)

BB. Do not turn aside, God - individual lament (27:7-14)

CC. God is my strength - individual lament (28:1-9)

DD. God's voice - hymn (29:1-11)

EE. Praise for deliverance from enemies - individual song of thanksgiving (30:1-12)

FF. Prayer for help in great distress - individual lament (31:1-24)

GG. Joy of confession and forgiveness - individual song of thanksgiving (32:1-11)

HH. Faithful God - hymn (33:1-22)

II. Praise for rescue from trouble - individual song of thanksgiving (34:1-22)

JJ. Prayer for deliverance from enemies - individual lament (35:1-28)

KK. Human evil - wisdom (36:1-4)

LL. Divine good - hymn (36:5-9)

MM. Request for deliverance - individual lament (36:10-12)

NN. Be patient and trust God - wisdom (37:1-40)

OO. Prayer for healing from terrible illness - individual lament (38:1-22)

PP. Prayer for wisdom and forgiveness - individual lament (39:1-13)

QQ. Praise for rescue - individual song of thanksgiving (40:1-10)

RR. Prayer for rescue - individual lament (40:11-17)

SS. Prayer for healing - individual lament (41:1-13)

II. Book Two (42:1-72:20)

A. Thirsting for God - individual lament (42:1-43:5)

B. Prayer for national deliverance - community lament (44:1-26)

C. For the king's wedding - royal (45:1-17)

D. God, our refuge and strength - song of Zion (46:1-11)

E. God rules the nations - hymn (47:1-9)

F. Praise for Zion - song of Zion (48:1-14)

G. Do not trust in wealth - wisdom (49:1-20)

H. Correct sacrifice - liturgy (50:1-23)

I. Create a clean heart - individual lament (51:1-19)

J. Deceit cannot win - individual lament (52:1-9)

K. No one seeks God - individual lament (53:1-6)

L. Seeking vindication - individual lament (54:1-7)

M. Betrayed by a friend - individual lament (55:1-23)

N. Trust in God - individual lament (56:1-13)

O. Be merciful - individual lament (57:1-11)

P. Let the nation be avenged - community lament (58:1-11)

Q. Deliver from enemies - individual lament (59:1-17)

R. Prayer after military defeat - community lament (60:1-12)

S. Request for God's protection - individual lament (61:1-8)

T. God, my rock and salvation - song of trust (62:1-12)

U. Praise for God's presence - song of trust (63:1-11)

V. Prayer for protection from enemies - individual lament (64:1-10)

W. Praise for the productive earth - community song of thanksgiving (65:1-13)

X. God's goodness - hymn (66:1-12)

Y. Praise for God's intercession - individual song of thanksgiving (66:13-20)

Z. Praise for harvest - community song of thanksgiving (67:1-7)

AA. Triumphant God - hymn (68:1-35)

BB. Prayer for rescue from enemies - individual lament (69:1-36)

CC. Prayer for rescue from enemies - individual lament (70:1-5)

DD. Prayer for protection - individual lament (71:1-24)

EE. Prayer for king - royal (72:1-20)

III. Book Three (73:1-89:52)

A. Trust despite appearances - wisdom (73:1-28)

B. Prayer for a humiliated nation - community lament (74:1-23)

C. Praise for God;s vindication - community song of thanksgiving (75:1-10)

D. God's glory - song of Zion (76:1-12)

E. God's past acts - individual lament (77:1-20)

F. God's care and Israel's sin - historical (78:1-72)

G. Prayer for conquered Jerusalem - community lament (79:1-13)

H. Prayer for forsaken Israel - community lament (80:1-19)

I. Appeal for faithfulness - liturgy (81:1-16)

J. Judge the earth - individual lament (82:1-8)

K. Punish our enemies - community lament (83:1-18)

L. God's lovely dwelling place - song of Zion (84:1-12)

M. Prayer for restoration - community lament (85:1-13)

N. Prayer for rescue from enemies - individual lament (86:1-17)

O. City of God - song of Zion (87:1-7)

P. Complaint - individual lament (88:1-18)

Q. Blessing of God and king - royal (89:1-37)

R. Prayer for rescue of king and nation - royal lament (89:38-52)

IV. Book Four (90:1-106:48)

A. Plea for God to remove His anger - community lament (90:1-17)

B. God's protection - song of trust (91:1-16)

C. Praise for God's actions - individual song of thanksgiving (92:1-15)

D. God is king - hymn (93:1-5)

E. Prayer for God's vengeance on wicked - community lament (94:1-23)

F. Enthronement songs (95:1-99:9)

1. Let us worship - hymn (95:1-11)

2. Sing to the Lord - hymn (96:1-13)

3. The Lord is king - hymn (97:1-12)

4. Victorious Lord - hymn (98:1-9)

5. God is enthroned - hymn (99:1-9)

G. Make a joyful noise - hymn (100:1-5)

H. King's pledge - royal (101:1-8)

I. Prayer for help in affliction - individual lament (102:1-28)

J. Bless the Lord - hymn (103:1-22)

K. God, Creator and Provider - hymn (104:1-35)

L. God's love toward Israel - hymn (105:1-45)

M. Confession of sins - hymn (106:1-48)

V. Book Five (107:1-150:6)

A. Deliverance from many difficulties - community song of thanksgiving (107:1-43)

B. Steadfast heart - hymn (108:1-9)

C. Prayer for victory over enemy - community lament (108:10-13)

D. Prayer for help - individual lament (109:1-31)

E. Sit at my right hand - royal (110:1-7)

F. God's great works - hymn (111:1-10)

G. Blessed are those who fear God - wisdom (112:1-10)

H. God helps the needy - hymn (113:1-9)

I. God's deeds in the exodus - hymn (113:1-9)

J. God vs. worthless idols - liturgy (115:1-18)

K. Praise for deliverance - individual song of thanksgiving (116:1-19)

L. Praise the Lord - hymn (117:1-2)

M. Trust in God was not disappointed - individual song of thanksgiving (118:1-29)

N. God's good law - wisdom (119:1-176)

O. Songs of Ascent (120:1-134:3)

1. Deliver from slander - individual lament (120:1-7)

2. I lift my eyes to the hills - song of trust (121:1-8)

3. Pray for the peace of Jerusalem - song of Zion (122:1-9)

4. Have mercy on us - community lament (123:1-4)

5. Our help is God - community song of thanksgiving (124:1-8)

6. God's protection - song of trust (125:1-5)

7. Restore our fortunes - community lament (126:1-6)

8. God's blessings in a family - wisdom (127:1-5)

9. The blessed home - wisdom (128:1-6)

10. God destroyed enemies - community song of thanksgiving (129:1-

8)

11. Out of the depths - individual lament (130:1-8)

12. Humble trust - song of trust (131:1-3)

13. God's promises - royal (132:1-18)

14. Harmony - wisdom (133:1-3)

15. Bless the Lord - liturgy (134:1-3)

P. God above all gods - hymn (135:1-21)

Q. For his steadfast love endures forever - liturgical hymn (136:1-26)

R. By the rivers of Babylon - community lament (137:1-9)

S. Praise for deliverance - individual song of thanksgiving (138:1-8)

T. God, you have searched me - individual lament (139:1-24)

U. Prayer for deliverance from slandering enemies - individual lament (140:1-13)

V. Keep me from evil - individual lament (141:1-10)

W. Prayer for deliverance from persecutors - individual lament (142:1-7)

X. Prayer for rescue from enemies - individual lament (143:1-12)

Y. Blessed be the Rock - royal lament (144:1-11)

Z. Prayer for God's blessing - blessing/hymn (144:12-15)

AA. Great is the Lord - hymn (145:1-21)

BB. Happy are those who serve God - hymn (146:1-10)

CC. Good acts of God - hymn (147:1-20)

DD. Let creation praise God - hymn (148:1-14)

EE. Praise God for His salvation - hymn (149:1-9)

FF. All creation and instruments should praise God - hymn (150:1-6)

Psalms Readings

There are two ways to read through the book of psalms.

The first way is to read through the entire book of psalms every week. Thus the book is divided into seven parts, one part read each day. The portions are assigned as follows:

Sun	1-29
Mon	30-50
Tue	51-72
Wed	73-89
Thur	90-106
Fri	107-119
Sat	120-150

The second way is to say the entire book over a thirty day period. The portions are assigned as follows:

First Week

Day	Psalms
01	1-9
02	10-17
03	18-22
04	23-28
05	29-34
06	35-38
07	39-43

Second Week

Day	Psalms
08	44-48
09	49-54
10	55-59
11	60-65
12	66-68
13	69-71
14	72-76

Third Week

Day	Psalms
15	77-78
16	79-82
17	83-87
18	88-89
19	90-96
20	97-103
21	104-105

Fourth Week

Day	Psalms
22	106-107
23	108-112
24	113-118
25	119:1-96
26	119:97-176
27	120-134
28	135-139

Fifth week

Day	Psalms
29	140-144
30	145-150

BOOK OF PSALMS

PSALM 1

ספר תהילים פרק א

אַשְׁרֵי־הָאִישׁ אֲשֶׁר לֹא הָלַךְ בַּעֲצַת רְשָׁעִים
wicked ones   in counsel   walks   not which the man - praiseworthy

וּבְדֶרֶךְ חַטָּאִים לֹא עָמָד וּבְמוֹשַׁב לֵצִים לֹא יָשָׁב:
he sits   not   scorner ones   and in session stands not sinner ones and in way

1 Blessed is the man that walketh not in the counsel of the ungodly, nor standeth in the
way of sinners, nor sitteth in the seat of the scornful.

כִּי אִם־בְּתוֹרַת יְהֹוָה חֶפְצוֹ וּבְתוֹרָתוֹ יֶהְגֶּה יוֹמָם וָלָיְלָה:
and night by day he meditates and in his Torah his delight ihvh in Torah – with like

2 But his delight is in the law of the LORD; and in his law doth he meditate day and
night.

וְהָיָה כְּעֵץ שָׁתוּל עַל־פַּלְגֵי מָיִם אֲשֶׁר פִּרְיוֹ יִתֵּן בְּעִתּוֹ
in its season it gives its fruit which water brooks – upon planted like tree and it will be

וְעָלֵהוּ לֹא יִבּוֹל וְכֹל אֲשֶׁר־יַעֲשֶׂה יַצְלִיחַ:
he will prosper he does – which and all will wither not and its leaf

3 And he shall be like a tree planted by the rivers of water, that bringeth forth his fruit
in his season; his leaf also shall not wither; and whatsoever he doeth shall prosper.

לֹא־כֵן הָרְשָׁעִים כִּי אִם־כַּמֹּץ אֲשֶׁר־תִּדְּפֶנּוּ רוּחַ:
wind it driven away – which like chaff – with like the wicked ones thus – not

4 The ungodly are not so: but are like the chaff which the wind driveth away.

עַל־כֵּן לֹא־יָקֻמוּ רְשָׁעִים בַּמִּשְׁפָּט
in judgment wicked ones they rise up – not thus – upon

וְחַטָּאִים בַּעֲדַת צַדִּיקִים:
righteous ones in congregation and sinner ones

5 Therefore the ungodly shall not stand in the judgment, nor sinners in the
congregation of the righteous.

כִּי־יוֹדֵעַ יְהֹוָה דֶּרֶךְ צַדִּיקִים
righteous ones way ihvh knows – like

וְדֶרֶךְ רְשָׁעִים תֹּאבֵד:
it will perish wicked and way

6 For the LORD knoweth the way of the righteous: but the way of the ungodly shall
perish.

PSALM 2

ספר תהילים פרק ב

לָמָה רָגְשׁוּ גוֹים וּלְאֻמִּים יֶהְגּוּ־רִיק׃

vain thing – they reveal   and to peoples   nations   rage   why

1 Why do the heathen rage, and the people imagine a vain thing?

יִתְיַצְּבוּ מַלְכֵי־אֶרֶץ

earth – kings   they come out

וְרוֹזְנִים נוֹסְדוּ־יָחַד עַל־יְהוָה וְעַל־מְשִׁיחוֹ׃

his anointed – and upon   ihvh - upon   together – they deliberate   and chancellors

2 The kings of the earth set themselves, and the rulers take counsel together, against the LORD, and against his anointed, saying,

נְנַתְּקָה אֶת־מוֹסְרוֹתֵימוֹ וְנַשְׁלִיכָה מִמֶּנּוּ עֲבֹתֵימוֹ׃

his ropes   from us   and we cast off   his bonds – that   let us pull away

3 Let us break their bands asunder, and cast away their cords from us.

יוֹשֵׁב בַּשָּׁמַיִם יִשְׂחָק אֲדֹנָי יִלְעַג־לָמוֹ׃

to them - he mocks   Adoni   he laughs   in heavens   he sits

4 He that sitteth in the heavens shall laugh: the Lord shall have them in derision.

אָז יְדַבֵּר אֵלֵימוֹ בְאַפּוֹ וּבַחֲרוֹנוֹ יְבַהֲלֵמוֹ׃

he troubles them   and in his wrath   in his anger   unto them   he speaks   then

5 Then shall he speak unto them in his wrath, and vex them in his sore displeasure.

וַאֲנִי נָסַכְתִּי מַלְכִּי עַל־צִיּוֹן הַר־קָדְשִׁי׃

my holy – mountain   Zion – upon   my king   have set firm   and I

6 Yet have I set my king upon my holy hill of Zion.

אֲסַפְּרָה אֶל חֹק יְהוָה אָמַר אֵלַי

unto me   said   ihvh   statute   unto   I declare

בְּנִי אַתָּה אֲנִי הַיּוֹם יְלִדְתִּיךָ׃

begotten you   the day   I   you   my son

7 I will declare the decree: the LORD hath said unto me, Thou art my Son; this day have I begotten thee.

שְׁאַל מִמֶּנִּי וְאֶתְּנָה גוֹים נַחֲלָתֶךָ וַאֲחֻזָּתְךָ אַפְסֵי־אָרֶץ׃

earth – end parts   and your possessions   your inheritance   nations   and I give   from me   ask

8 Ask of me, and I shall give thee the heathen for thine inheritance, and the uttermost parts of the earth for thy possession.

תְּרֹעֵם בְּשֵׁבֶט בַּרְזֶל כִּכְלִי יוֹצֵר תְּנַפְּצֵם׃

you will shatter them   potter   like vessel   iron   in rod   you will break them

9 Thou shalt break them with a rod of iron; thou shalt dash them in pieces like a potter's vessel.

וְעַתָּה מְלָכִים הַשְׂכִּילוּ הִוָּסְרוּ שֹׁפְטֵי אָרֶץ׃

and now	kings	the you be instructed	you admonish	judges	earth

10 Be wise now therefore, O ye kings: be instructed, ye judges of the earth.

עִבְדוּ אֶת־יְהֹוָה בְּיִרְאָה וְגִילוּ בִּרְעָדָה׃

you serve	ihvh – that	in fear	and you rejoice	in trembling

11 Serve the LORD with fear, and rejoice with trembling.

נַשְּׁקוּ־בַר פֶּן־יֶאֱנַף וְתֹאבְדוּ דֶרֶךְ

son - kiss	he angry - lest	and you perish	way

כִּי־יִבְעַר כִּמְעַט אַפּוֹ אַשְׁרֵי כָּל־חוֹסֵי בוֹ׃

he kindle – like	like little	his anger	praiseworthy	ones taking refuge – all	in him

12 Kiss the Son, lest he be angry, and ye perish from the way, when his wrath is kindled but a little. Blessed are all they that put their trust in him.

PSALM 3

ספר תהילים פרק ג

מִזְמוֹר לְדָוִד בְּבָרְחוֹ מִפְּנֵי אַבְשָׁלוֹם בְּנוֹ׃

his son   Absalom   from face   in his fleeing   to David   psalm

יְהֹוָה מָה־רַבּוּ צָרָי   רַבִּים קָמִים עָלָי׃

upon me   rising ones   many ones   my adversaries   many – how   ihvh

1. A Psalm of David, when he fled from Absalom his son. LORD, how are they increased that trouble me! many are they that rise up against me.

רַבִּים אֹמְרִים לְנַפְשִׁי אֵין יְשׁוּעָתָה לֹּו בֵאלֹהִים סֶלָה׃

Selah   in Elohim   to him   salvation   isn't   to my soul   saying ones   many ones

2 Many there be which say of my soul, There is no help for him in God. Selah.

וְאַתָּה יְהֹוָה מָגֵן בַּעֲדִי כְּבוֹדִי וּמֵרִים רֹאשִׁי׃

my head   and lifting ones   my glory   in my being   shield   ihvh   and you

3 But thou, O LORD, art a shield for me; my glory, and the lifter up of mine head.

קוֹלִי אֶל־יְהֹוָה אֶקְרָא וַיַּעֲנֵנִי מֵהַר קָדְשׁוֹ סֶלָה׃

Selah   his holiness   from mountain   and he answers me   I cry   ihvh – unto   my voice

4 I cried unto the LORD with my voice, and he heard me out of his holy hill. Selah.

אֲנִי שָׁכַבְתִּי וָאִישָׁנָה הֱקִיצוֹתִי כִּי יְהֹוָה יִסְמְכֵנִי׃

he sustained me   ihvh   like   the I awoke   and I slept   I lay down   I

5 I laid me down and slept; I awaked; for the LORD sustained me.

לֹא־אִירָא מֵרִבְבוֹת עָם אֲשֶׁר סָבִיב שָׁתוּ עָלָי׃

upon me   they set   around   which   people   from myriads   I will fear - not

6 I will not be afraid of ten thousands of people, that have set themselves against me round about.

קוּמָה יְהֹוָה הוֹשִׁיעֵנִי אֱלֹהַי

my Elohim   save me   ihvh   arise

כִּי־הִכִּיתָ אֶת־כָּל־אֹיְבַי לֶחִי שִׁנֵּי רְשָׁעִים שִׁבַּרְתָּ׃

you broke   wicked ones   teeth   to cheek bone   my enemies - all – that   struck - like

7 Arise, O LORD; save me, O my God: for thou hast smitten all mine enemies upon the cheek bone; thou hast broken the teeth of the ungodly.

לַיהֹוָה הַיְשׁוּעָה עַל־עַמְּךָ בִרְכָתֶךָ סֶּלָה׃

Sela   your blessing   your people - upon   the salvation   to ihvh

8 Salvation belongeth unto the LORD: thy blessing is upon thy people. Selah.

PSALM 4

ספר תהילים פרק ד

לַמְנַצֵּחַ   בִּנְגִינוֹת   מִזְמוֹר   לְדָוִד:

to David   Psalm   in Neginoth   to him that is over

1 To the chief Musician on Neginoth, A Psalm of David.

בְּקָרְאִי   עֲנֵנִי   אֱלֹהֵי   צִדְקִי   בַּצָּר   הִרְחַבְתָּ   לִי

to me   you enlarge   in distress   my righteousness   my Elohim   answer me   in my calling

חָנֵּנִי   וּשְׁמַע   תְּפִלָּתִי:

my prayer   and hear   be gracious

Hear me when I call, O God of my righteousness: thou hast enlarged me when I was in distress; have mercy upon me, and hear my prayer.

בְּנֵי־אִישׁ   עַד־מֶה   כְבוֹדִי   לִכְלִמָּה

to confound   my glory   what – until   man - sons

תֶּאֱהָבוּן   רִיק   תְּבַקְשׁוּ   כָזָב   סֶלָה:

Sela   lie   you seek it   empty   you will love

2 O ye sons of men, how long will ye turn my glory into shame? how long will ye love vanity, and seek after leasing? Selah.

וּדְעוּ   כִּי־הִפְלָה   יְהוָה   חָסִיד   לוֹ

to him   pious   ihvh   set apart – like   and you know

יְהוָה   יִשְׁמַע   בְּקָרְאִי   אֵלָיו:

unto him   in my call   he will hear   ihvh

3 But know that the LORD hath set apart him that is godly for himself: the LORD will hear when I call unto him.

רִגְזוּ   וְאַל־תֶּחֱטָאוּ   אִמְרוּ   בִלְבַבְכֶם   עַל־מִשְׁכַּבְכֶם

your beds – upon   in your hearts   you say   you sin it - and don't   you tremble

וְדֹמּוּ   סֶלָה:

Sela   and be still

4 Stand in awe, and sin not: commune with your own heart upon your bed, and be still. Selah.

זִבְחוּ   זִבְחֵי־צֶדֶק   וּבִטְחוּ   אֶל־יְהוָה:

ihvh - unto   and you trust   righteous - my offerings   you offer

5 Offer the sacrifices of righteousness, and put your trust in the LORD.

רַבִּים   אֹמְרִים   מִי־יַרְאֵנוּ   טוֹב   נְסָה־עָלֵינוּ   אוֹר   פָּנֶיךָ   יְהוָה:

ihvh   your face   light   upon us - lift up   good   will see us – who   sayings   many

6 There be many that say, Who will shew us any good? LORD, lift thou up the light of thy countenance upon us.

נָתַתָּה שִׂמְחָה בְלִבִּי מֵעֵת דְּגָנָם וְתִירוֹשָׁם רָבּוּ׃

it multiplied   and their grape juice   their grain   from season   in my heart   happiness   you gave

7 Thou hast put gladness in my heart, more than in the time that their corn and their wine increased.

בְּשָׁלוֹם יַחְדָּו אֶשְׁכְּבָה וְאִישָׁן

and sleep   I lie down   together   in peace

כִּי־אַתָּה יְהֹוָה לְבָדָד לָבֶטַח תּוֹשִׁיבֵנִי׃

you dwell me   to security   alone   ihvh   you – like

8 I will both lay me down in peace, and sleep: for thou, LORD, only makest me dwell in safety.

PSALM 5

ספר תהילים פרק ה

לַמְנַצֵּחַ   אֶל־הַנְּחִילוֹת   מִזְמוֹר לְדָוִד:

to him that is over   the allotments – unto   Psalm   to David

1. To the chief Musician for the flutes, A Psalm of David.

אֲמָרַי   הַאֲזִינָה   יְהֹוָה   בִּינָה   הֲגִיגִי:

my words   the towards ear   ihvh   understand   the my soliloquy

2. Give ears to my words, O Lord, consider my meditation.

הַקְשִׁיבָה לְקוֹל שַׁוְעִי מַלְכִּי וֵאלֹהָי   כִּי־אֵלֶיךָ אֶתְפַּלָּל:

the attend   to voice   my cry   my king   and my Elohim   like – unto you   I will pray

3. Listen to the voice of my cry, my King, and my God; for to you I will pray.

יְהֹוָה בֹּקֶר תִּשְׁמַע קוֹלִי בֹּקֶר אֶעֱרָךְ־לְךָ וַאֲצַפֶּה:

ihvh   morning   you hear   my voice   morning   I will direct - to you   and I will watch

4. You shall hear my voice in the morning, O Lord; in the morning will I direct my prayer to you, and will look up.

כִּי לֹא אֵל חָפֵץ רֶשַׁע אָתָּה לֹא יְגֻרְךָ   רָע:

like   not   El   delight   wicked   you   not   be your dwelling   bad

5. For you are not a God who has pleasure in wickedness; nor shall evil dwell with you.

לֹא־יִתְיַצְּבוּ הוֹלְלִים לְנֶגֶד עֵינֶיךָ   שָׂנֵאתָ כָּל־פֹּעֲלֵי אָוֶן:

they stand firm - not   boaster ones   to in front   your eye   you hate   all – workers   affliction

6. The foolish shall not stand in your sight; you hate all evil doers.

תְּאַבֵּד דֹּבְרֵי כָזָב אִישׁ־דָּמִים וּמִרְמָה יְתָעֵב   יְהֹוָה:

you destroy   speakers   lie   man –blood ones   and deceit   he abhorring   ihvh

7. You shall destroy those who speak falsehood; the Lord will loathe the bloody and deceitful man.

וַאֲנִי בְּרֹב   חַסְדְּךָ   אָבוֹא בֵיתֶךָ

and I   in much   your kindness   I will come   your house

אֶשְׁתַּחֲוֶה אֶל־הֵיכַל קָדְשְׁךָ בְּיִרְאָתֶךָ:

I will bow down   temple – unto   your holiness   in your fear

8. But as for me, I will come into your house in the multitude of your love; and in your fear I will worship toward your holy temple.

יְהֹוָה נְחֵנִי בְצִדְקָתֶךָ לְמַעַן שׁוֹרְרָי

ihvh   lead me   in your righteousness   to end   my controllers

הַוֹשַׁר [הַיְשַׁר] לְפָנַי דַּרְכֶּךָ:

make straight   before me   your way

9. (K) Lead me, O Lord, in your righteousness because of my enemies; make your way straight before my face.

כִּי אֵין בְּפִיהוּ נְכוֹנָה קִרְבָּם הַוּוֹת

destructions   their inward thought   correctness   in their mouth   isn't   like

קֶבֶר־פָּתוּחַ גְּרוֹנָם לְשׁוֹנָם יַחֲלִיקוּן׃

they make smooth   their tongue   their throat   opened - tomb

10. For there is no truth in their mouth; in their heart there is wickedness; their throat is an open sepulcher; they flatter with their tongue.

הַאֲשִׁימֵם אֱלֹהִים יִפְּלוּ מִמֹּעֲצוֹתֵיהֶם בְּרֹב פִּשְׁעֵיהֶם

their transgressions   in much   from their schemes   they fall   Elohim   the guilty

הַדִּיחֵמוֹ כִּי מָרוּ בָךְ׃

in you   they rebelled   like   the expel them

11. Condemn them, O God; let them fall by their own counsels; cast them out in the multitude of their transgressions; for they have rebelled against you.

וְיִשְׂמְחוּ כָל־חוֹסֵי בָךְ לְעוֹלָם יְרַנֵּנוּ

they shout joy   forever   in you   ones taking refuge – all   and they be happy

וְתָסֵךְ עָלֵימוֹ וְיַעְלְצוּ בְךָ אֹהֲבֵי שְׁמֶךָ׃

your name   lovers   in you   and they exult   upon them   and you will overshadow

12. But let all those who put their trust in you rejoice; let them always shout for joy, because you defend them; let those who love your name be joyful in you.

כִּי־אַתָּה תְּבָרֵךְ צַדִּיק יְהֹוָה כַּצִּנָּה רָצוֹן תַּעְטְרֶנּוּ׃

you surround him   favor   like buckler   ihvh   righteous   you bless   you - like

13. For you, Lord, will bless the righteous; with favor you will cover him as with a shield.

PSALM 6

ספר תהילים פרק ו

לַמְנַצֵּחַ　בִּנְגִינוֹת　עַל־הַשְּׁמִינִית　מִזְמוֹר　לְדָוִד׃

to David　Psalm　the stringed harp - upon　in Neginoth　to him that is over

1. To the chief Musician for stringed instruments, according to the Sheminith, a psalm of David.

יְהוָה אַל־בְּאַפְּךָ　תוֹכִיחֵנִי　וְאַל־בַּחֲמָתְךָ　תְיַסְּרֵנִי׃

you chasten me　in your wrath - and don't　rebuke me　in your anger - don't　ihvh

2. O Lord, do not rebuke me in your anger, nor chasten me in your hot displeasure.

חָנֵּנִי　יְהוָה　כִּי　אֻמְלַל　אָנִי　רְפָאֵנִי　יְהוָה　כִּי　נִבְהֲלוּ　עֲצָמָי׃

my bones　terror it　like　ihvh　heal me　I　languishing　like　ihvh　be gracious to me

3. Have mercy upon me, O Lord; for I am weak; O Lord, heal me; for my bones shudder.

וְנַפְשִׁי　נִבְהֲלָה　מְאֹד　וְאַתְּ [וְאַתָּה] יְהוָה　עַד־מָתָי׃

when - until　ihvh　and you　greatly　troubled　and my soul

4. My soul is also much troubled. And you, O Lord, how long?

שׁוּבָה יְהוָה　חַלְּצָה נַפְשִׁי　הוֹשִׁיעֵנִי לְמַעַן חַסְדֶּךָ׃

your kindness　to end　save me　my soul　deliver　ihvh　return

5. Return, O Lord, deliver my soul. Oh save me for the sake of your loving kindness!

כִּי אֵין בַּמָּוֶת זִכְרֶךָ　בִּשְׁאוֹל מִי יוֹדֶה־לָּךְ׃

to you - thanks　who　in Shoel　your remembrance　in death　isn't　like

6. For in death there is no remembrance of you. In Sheol who shall give you thanks?

יָגַעְתִּי בְּאַנְחָתִי אַשְׂחֶה בְכָל־לַיְלָה מִטָּתִי

my bed　night - in all　I drench　in my groaning　I weary

בְּדִמְעָתִי עַרְשִׂי אַמְסֶה׃

I soak　my couch　in my tears

7. I am weary with my moaning; all night I make my bed swim; I drench my couch with my tears.

עָשְׁשָׁה מִכַּעַס עֵינִי עָתְקָה בְּכָל־צוֹרְרָי׃

my adversaries - in all　aged　my eyes　from anger　wastes

8. My eye wastes away because of grief; it grows weak because of all my enemies.

סוּרוּ　מִמֶּנִּי כָּל־פֹּעֲלֵי אָוֶן כִּי־שָׁמַע יְהוָה קוֹל בִּכְיִי׃

my weeping　voice　ihvh　heard - like　iniquity　doers - all　from me　you depart

9. Depart from me, all you evil doers; for the Lord has heard the voice of my weeping.

שָׁמַע יְהוָה תְּחִנָּתִי　יְהוָה תְּפִלָּתִי יִקָּח׃

he will take　my prayer　ihvh　my supplication　ihvh　heard

10. The Lord has heard my supplication; the Lord will receive my prayer.

יֵבֹשׁוּ   וְיִבָּהֲלוּ   מְאֹד   כָּל־אֹיְבָי   יָשֻׁבוּ   יֵבֹשׁוּ   רָגַע׃

moment   ashamed   they return   my enemies - all   greatly   and they troubled   they ashamed

11. Let all my enemies be ashamed and much troubled; let them return and be ashamed in a moment.

PSALM 7

ספר תהילים פרק ז

שִׁגָּיוֹן לְדָוִד אֲשֶׁר־שָׁר לַיהוָה עַל־דִּבְרֵי־כוּשׁ בֶּן־יְמִינִי׃

Yamite – son   Cush - speakings – upon   to ihvh   sung - which   to David   an ecstasy

1 Shiggaion of David, which he sang unto the LORD, concerning the words of Cush
the Benjamite.

יְהוָה אֱלֹהַי בְּךָ חָסִיתִי הוֹשִׁיעֵנִי מִכָּל־רֹדְפַי וְהַצִּילֵנִי׃

and deliver me   my pursuers - from all   save me   I took refuge   in you   my Elohim   ihvh

O LORD my God, in thee do I put my trust: save me from all them that persecute me,
and deliver me:

פֶּן־יִטְרֹף כְּאַרְיֵה נַפְשִׁי פֹּרֵק וְאֵין מַצִּיל׃

rescuer   and isn't   renderer   my soul   like lion   he tear – lest

2 Lest he tear my soul like a lion, rending it in pieces, while there is none to deliver.

יְהוָה אֱלֹהַי אִם־עָשִׂיתִי זֹאת אִם־יֶשׁ־עָוֶל בְּכַפָּי׃

in my palms   inequity - there is – if   this   I have done – if   my Elohim   ihvh

3 O LORD my God, if I have done this; if there be iniquity in my hands;

אִם־גָּמַלְתִּי שׁוֹלְמִי רָע וָאֲחַלְּצָה צוֹרְרִי רֵיקָם׃

causelessly   my foe   and I delivered   bad   my peace   I rewarded – if

4 If I have rewarded evil unto him that was at peace with me; (yea, I have delivered him
that without cause is mine enemy:)

יִרַדֹּף אוֹיֵב נַפְשִׁי וְיַשֵּׂג וְיִרְמֹס לָאָרֶץ חַיָּי

my life   to earth   and he tramples   and he overtakes   my soul   enemy   he pursues

וּכְבוֹדִי לֶעָפָר יַשְׁכֵּן סֶלָה׃

Selah   it dwells   to dust   and my honor

5 Let the enemy persecute my soul, and take it; yea, let him tread down my life upon the
earth, and lay mine honour in the dust. Selah.

קוּמָה יְהוָה בְּאַפֶּךָ הִנָּשֵׂא בְּעַבְרוֹת צוֹרְרָי

my adversaries   in rages   be lifted   in your anger   ihvh   arise

וְעוּרָה אֵלַי מִשְׁפָּט צִוִּיתָ׃

you commanded   judgment   unto me   and awake

6 Arise, O LORD, in thine anger, lift up thyself because of the rage of mine enemies:
and awake for me to the judgment that thou hast commanded.

וַעֲדַת לְאֻמִּים תְּסוֹבְבֶךָּ וְעָלֶיהָ לַמָּרוֹם שׁוּבָה׃

return   to high   and upon it   surrounds you   to peoples   and congregation

7 So shall the congregation of the people compass thee about: for their sakes therefore
return thou on high.

יְהוָה יָדִין עַמִּים שָׁפְטֵנִי יְהוָה כְּצִדְקִי   וּכְתֻמִּי   עָלָי:
upon me   and like my integrity   like my righteousness   ihvh   judge me   peoples   he judge   ihvh

8 The LORD shall judge the people: judge me, O LORD, according to my righteousness, and according to mine integrity that isin me.

יִגְמָר־נָא רַע רְשָׁעִים וּתְכוֹנֵן צַדִּיק
righteous   and you establish   wicked ones   bad   now - put

וּבֹחֵן לִבּוֹת וּכְלָיוֹת אֱלֹהִים צַדִּיק:
righteous   Elohim   and reins   hearts   and searcher

9 Oh let the wickedness of the wicked come to an end; but establish the just: for the righteous God trieth the hearts and reins.

מָגִנִּי עַל־אֱלֹהִים מוֹשִׁיעַ יִשְׁרֵי־לֵב:
heart – upright   messiah   Elohim – upon   my shield

10 My defence is of God, which saveth the upright in heart.

אֱלֹהִים שׁוֹפֵט צַדִּיק וְאֵל זֹעֵם בְּכָל־יוֹם:
day - in all   indignant   and El   righteous   judger   Elohim

11 God judgeth the righteous, and God is angry with the wicked every day.

אִם־לֹא יָשׁוּב חַרְבּוֹ יִלְטוֹשׁ קַשְׁתּוֹ דָרַךְ וַיְכוֹנְנֶהָ:
and established it   he bent   his bow   he sharpens   his sword   he returns   not – if

12 If he turn not, he will whet his sword; he hath bent his bow, and made it ready.

וְלוֹ הֵכִין כְּלֵי־מָוֶת חִצָּיו לְדֹלְקִים יִפְעָל:
he works   to flaming ones   his arrows   death - instruments   prepared   and to him

13 He hath also prepared for him the instruments of death; he ordaineth his arrows against the persecutors.

הִנֵּה יְחַבֶּל־אָוֶן וְהָרָה עָמָל וְיָלַד שָׁקֶר:
lie   and begets   mischief   and conceives   inequity - he travails   here

14 Behold, he travaileth with iniquity, and hath conceived mischief, and brought forth falsehood.

בּוֹר כָּרָה וַיַּחְפְּרֵהוּ וַיִּפֹּל בְּשַׁחַת יִפְעָל:
he works   in pit   and he falls   and dug deep   he dug   pit

15 He made a pit, and digged it, and is fallen into the ditch which he made.

יָשׁוּב עֲמָלוֹ בְרֹאשׁוֹ וְעַל־קָדְקֳדוֹ חֲמָסוֹ יֵרֵד:
descends   his violence   his crown - and upon   in his head   his mischief   he returns

16 His mischief shall return upon his own head, and his violent dealing shall come down upon his own pate.

אוֹדֶה יְהוָה כְּצִדְקוֹ וַאֲזַמְּרָה שֵׁם־יְהוָה עֶלְיוֹן:
most high   ihvh – name   and I sing psalms   like his righteousness   ihvh   I give thanks

17 I will praise the LORD according to his righteousness: and will sing praise to the name of the LORD most high.

PSALM 8

ספר תהילים פרק ח

לַמְנַצֵּחַ　　עַל־הַגִּתִּית　מִזְמוֹר　לְדָוִד:
to him that is over　upon - the Gittith　psalm　to David

1 To the chief Musician upon Gittith, A Psalm of David.

יְהוָה　אֲדֹנֵינוּ　מָה־אַדִּיר　שִׁמְךָ　בְּכָל־הָאָרֶץ
ihvh　our Adoni　what - excellent　your name　in all - the earth

אֲשֶׁר־תְּנָה　הוֹדְךָ　עַל־הַשָּׁמָיִם:
which - you set　your majesty　upon the heavens

O LORD our Lord, how excellent is thy name in all the earth! who hast set thy glory above the heavens.

מִפִּי　עוֹלְלִים　וְיֹנְקִים　יִסַּדְתָּ　עֹז　לְמַעַן　צוֹרְרֶיךָ
from mouth　babes　you founded　strength　and sucklings　to end　your adversaries

לְהַשְׁבִּית　אוֹיֵב　וּמִתְנַקֵּם:
to the cease　enemy　and avenger ones

2 Out of the mouth of babes and sucklings hast thou ordained strength because of thine enemies, that thou mightest still the enemy and the avenger.

כִּי־אֶרְאֶה　שָׁמֶיךָ　מַעֲשֵׂי　אֶצְבְּעֹתֶיךָ
like - I see　your heavens　works　your fingers

יָרֵחַ　וְכוֹכָבִים　אֲשֶׁר　כּוֹנָנְתָּה:
moon　and stars　which　you established

3 When I consider thy heavens, the work of thy fingers, the moon and the stars, which thou hast ordained;

מָה־אֱנוֹשׁ　כִּי־תִזְכְּרֶנּוּ　וּבֶן־אָדָם　כִּי　תִפְקְדֶנּוּ:
what - Enosh　like - you remember him　and son - Adam　like　you visit him

4 What is man, that thou art mindful of him? and the son of man, that thou visitest him?

וַתְּחַסְּרֵהוּ　מְּעַט　מֵאֱלֹהִים　וְכָבוֹד　וְהָדָר　תְּעַטְּרֵהוּ:
and you made him lack　little　from Elohim　and glory　and honor　you crowned him

5 For thou hast made him a little lower than the angels, and hast crowned him with glory and honour.

תַּמְשִׁילֵהוּ　בְּמַעֲשֵׂי　יָדֶיךָ　כֹּל　שַׁתָּה　תַחַת־רַגְלָיו:
you make him rule　in works　your hands　all　you put　under - his feet

6 Thou madest him to have dominion over the works of thy hands; thou hast put all things under his feet:

צֹנֶה　וַאֲלָפִים　כֻּלָּם　וְגַם　בַּהֲמוֹת　שָׂדָי:
sleep　and oxen　all them　and also　beasts　field

7 All sheep and oxen, yea, and the beasts of the field;

צִפּוֹר שָׁמַיִם וּדְגֵי הַיָּם עֹבֵר אָרְחוֹת יַמִּים:

seas   roads   passes   the sea   and fishes   heavens   bird

8 The fowl of the air, and the fish of the sea, and whatsoever passeth through the paths of the seas.

יְהֹוָה אֲדֹנֵינוּ מָה־אַדִּיר שִׁמְךָ בְּכָל־הָאָרֶץ:

the earth - in all   your name   excellent - what   our Adoni   ihvh

9 O LORD our Lord, how excellent is thy name in all the earth!

PSALM 9

ספר תהילים פרק ט

לַמְנַצֵּחַ   עַל   מוּת   לַבֵּן   מִזְמוֹר   לְדָוִד:

to him that is over upon Muth Laben psalm to David

1 To the chief Musician upon Muthlabben, A Psalm of David.

אוֹדֶה   יְהֹוָה   בְּכָל־לִבִּי   אֲסַפְּרָה   כָּל־נִפְלְאוֹתֶיךָ:

I will give thanks ihvh my heart - in all I declare your wondrous works - all

I will praise thee, O LORD, with my whole heart; I will shew forth all thy marvellous works.

אֶשְׂמְחָה   וְאֶעֶלְצָה   בָךְ   אֲזַמְּרָה   שִׁמְךָ   עֶלְיוֹן:

I will be glad and I will exalt in you I will sing psalms your name most high

2 I will be glad and rejoice in thee: I will sing praise to thy name, O thou most High.

בְּשׁוּב־אוֹיְבַי   אָחוֹר   יִכָּשְׁלוּ   וְיֹאבְדוּ   מִפָּנֶיךָ:

my enemies - in returning backward they stumble and perish from your face

3 When mine enemies are turned back, they shall fall and perish at thy presence.

כִּי־עָשִׂיתָ   מִשְׁפָּטִי   וְדִינִי   יָשַׁבְתָּ   לְכִסֵּא   שׁוֹפֵט   צֶדֶק:

you done - like my judgment and my cause you sat to throne judging righteousness

4 For thou hast maintained my right and my cause; thou satest in the throne judging right.

גָּעַרְתָּ   גוֹיִם   אִבַּדְתָּ   רָשָׁע   שְׁמָם   מָחִיתָ   לְעוֹלָם   וָעֶד:

you rebuked nation's you destroyed wicked their names you blotted out to forever and time

5 Thou hast rebuked the heathen, thou hast destroyed the wicked, thou hast put out their name for ever and ever.

הָאוֹיֵב   תַּמּוּ   חֳרָבוֹת   לָנֶצַח

the enemy they consumed desolations to victory

וְעָרִים   נָתַשְׁתָּ   אָבַד   זִכְרָם   הֵמָּה:

and cities you plucked up has perished their remembrance they are

6 O thou enemy, destructions are come to a perpetual end: and thou hast destroyed cities; their memorial is perished with them.

וַיהֹוָה   לְעוֹלָם   יֵשֵׁב   כּוֹנֵן   לַמִּשְׁפָּט   כִּסְאוֹ:

and ihvh to forever he set he established to judgment his throne

7 But the LORD shall endure for ever: he hath prepared his throne for judgment.

וְהוּא   יִשְׁפֹּט־תֵּבֵל   בְּצֶדֶק   יָדִין   לְאֻמִּים   בְּמֵישָׁרִים:

and he inhabited world - will judge in righteousness he will judge to peoples in upright ones

8 And he shall judge the world in righteousness, he shall minister judgment to the people in uprightness.

וַיְהִי יְהֹוָה מִשְׂגָּב לַדָּךְ מִשְׂגָּב לְעִתּוֹת בַּצָּרָה:

| in trouble | to seasons | high place | to oppressed | high place | ihvh | and it be |

9 The LORD also will be a refuge for the oppressed, a refuge in times of trouble.

וְיִבְטְחוּ בְךָ יוֹדְעֵי שְׁמֶךָ כִּי לֹא־עָזַבְתָּ דֹרְשֶׁיךָ יְהֹוָה:

| ihvh | your seekers | you forsaken – not | like | your name | those knowers | in you | and they trust |

10 And they that know thy name will put their trust in thee: for thou, LORD, hast not forsaken them that seek thee.

זַמְּרוּ לַיהֹוָה יֹשֵׁב צִיּוֹן הַגִּידוּ בָעַמִּים עֲלִילוֹתָיו:

| his deeds | in peoples | the declare | Zion | dwellers | to ihvh | you sing psalms |

11 Sing praises to the LORD, which dwelleth in Zion: declare among the people his doings.

כִּי־דֹרֵשׁ דָּמִים אוֹתָם זָכָר

| he remembers | to them | bloods | inquiring - like |

לֹא־שָׁכַח צַעֲקַת עֲנִיִּים [עֲנָוִים]:

| afflicted ones | the cry | he forgot - not |

12 When he maketh inquisition for blood, he remembereth them: he forgetteth not the cry of the humble.

חָנְנֵנִי יְהֹוָה רְאֵה עָנְיִי מִשֹּׂנְאָי מְרוֹמְמִי מִשַּׁעֲרֵי מָוֶת:

| death | from my gates | and you lift me up | from my haters | my affliction | see | ihvh | be gracious to me |

13 Have mercy upon me, O LORD; consider my trouble which I suffer of them that hate me, thou that liftest me up from the gates of death:

לְמַעַן אֲסַפְּרָה כָּל־תְּהִלָּתֶיךָ בְּשַׁעֲרֵי בַת־צִיּוֹן

| Zion - daughter | in my gates | your praise - all | I declare | to end |

אָגִילָה בִּישׁוּעָתֶךָ:

| in your salvation | I rejoice |

14. That I may shew forth all thy praise in the gates of the daughter of Zion: I will rejoice in thy salvation.

טָבְעוּ גוֹיִם בְּשַׁחַת עָשׂוּ בְּרֶשֶׁת־זוּ טָמָנוּ נִלְכְּדָה רַגְלָם:

| their feet | ensnared | they concealed | this - in net | they made | in pit | nation's | you sunk |

15 The heathen are sunk down in the pit that they made: in the net which they hid is their own foot taken.

נוֹדַע יְהֹוָה מִשְׁפָּט עָשָׂה בְּפֹעַל כַּפָּיו נוֹקֵשׁ רָשָׁע

| wicked | snared | his palm | in works | he made | judgment | ihvh | became known |

הִגָּיוֹן סֶלָה:

| sela | meditation |

16 The LORD is known by the judgment which he executeth: the wicked is snared in the work of his own hands. Higgaion. Selah.

יָשׁוּבוּ רְשָׁעִים לִשְׁאוֹלָה כָּל־גּוֹיִם שְׁכֵחֵי אֱלֹהִים׃

Elohim   forgetting   nations – all   to Shoel   wicked ones   they return

17 The wicked shall be turned into hell, and all the nations that forget God.

כִּי לֹא לָנֶצַח יִשָּׁכַח אֶבְיוֹן

needy   it be forgotten   to victory   not   like

תִּקְוַת עֲנָוִים [עֲנִיִּים] תֹּאבַד לָעַד׃

to time   it will perish   afflicted ones   expectations

18 For the needy shall not alway be forgotten: the expectation of the poor shall not perish for ever.

קוּמָה יְהוָה אַל־יָעֹז אֱנוֹשׁ יִשָּׁפְטוּ גוֹיִם עַל־פָּנֶיךָ׃

your face – upon   nations   they be judged   Enosh   it be strong– don't   ihvh   rise

19 Arise, O LORD; let not man prevail: let the heathen be judged in thy sight.

שִׁיתָה יְהוָה מוֹרָה לָהֶם יֵדְעוּ גוֹיִם אֱנוֹשׁ הֵמָּה סֶּלָה׃

Sela   they are   Enosh   nations   they know   to them   fear   ihvh   set you

20 Put them in fear, O LORD: that the nations may know themselves to be but men. Selah.

Psalm 10

ספר תהילים פרק י

לָמָה יְהוָה תַּעֲמֹד בְּרָחוֹק תַּעְלִים לְעִתּוֹת בַּצָּרָה:

| in trouble | to seasons | you hiding ones | in far | you stand | ihvh | why |

1 Why standest thou afar off, O LORD? why hidest thou thyself in times of trouble?

בְּגַאֲוַת־רָשָׁע יִדְלַק עָנִי יִתָּפְשׂוּ בִּמְזִמּוֹת זוּ חָשָׁבוּ:

| they devise | this | in devices | they be taken | poor | hotly pursue | wicked - in pride |

2 The wicked in his pride doth persecute the poor: let them be taken in the devices that they have imagined.

כִּי־הִלֵּל רָשָׁע עַל־תַּאֲוַת נַפְשׁוֹ וּבֹצֵעַ בֵּרֵךְ נִאֵץ יְהוָה:

| ihvh | despised | blesses | and covetous | his soul | desire – upon | wicked | has boasted - like |

3 For the wicked boasteth of his heart's desire, and blesseth the covetous, whom the LORD abhorreth.

רָשָׁע כְּגֹבַהּ אַפּוֹ בַּל־יִדְרֹשׁ אֵין אֱלֹהִים כָּל־מְזִמּוֹתָיו:

| his schemes – all | Elohim | isn't | he will seek - in not | his looks | like pride | wicked |

4 The wicked, through the pride of his countenance, will not seek after God: God is not in all his thoughts.

יָחִילוּ דְרָכָו [דְּרָכָיו] בְּכָל־עֵת מָרוֹם מִשְׁפָּטֶיךָ מִנֶּגְדּוֹ

| from before him | your judgments | high | time - in all | his ways | they be profane |

כָּל־צוֹרְרָיו יָפִיחַ בָּהֶם:

| in them | he puffs | his foes – all |

5 His ways are always grievous; thy judgments are far above out of his sight: as for all his enemies, he puffeth at them.

אָמַר בְּלִבּוֹ בַּל־אֶמּוֹט לְדֹר וָדֹר אֲשֶׁר לֹא־בְרָע:

| in evil – not | which | and generation | to generation | I will bemoved – not | in his heart | he said |

6 He hath said in his heart, I shall not be moved: for I shall never be in adversity.

אָלָה פִּיהוּ מָלֵא וּמִרְמוֹת וָתֹךְ תַּחַת לְשׁוֹנוֹ עָמָל וָאָוֶן:

| inequity | mischief | his tongue | under | and oppression | and deceits | full | his mouth | cursing |

7 His mouth is full of cursing and deceit and fraud: under his tongue is mischief and vanity.

יֵשֵׁב בְּמַאְרַב חֲצֵרִים בַּמִּסְתָּרִים יַהֲרֹג נָקִי

| innocent | he murders | in secret places | villages | in ambush | he sits |

עֵינָיו לְחֵלְכָה יִצְפֹּנוּ:

| they lurking | to pauper | his eyes |

8 He sitteth in the lurking places of the villages: in the secret places doth he murder the innocent: his eyes are privily set against the poor.

יָאֱרֹב בַּמִּסְתָּר כְּאַרְיֵה בְסֻכֹּה יֶאֱרֹב לַחֲטוֹף עָנִי

poor   to ensnare   he ambushes   in his covert   like lion   in secret places   he ambushes

יַחְטֹף עָנִי בְּמָשְׁכוֹ בְרִשְׁתּוֹ:

in his net   in his drawing   poor   he catches

9 He lieth in wait secretly as a lion in his den: he lieth in wait to catch the poor: he doth catch the poor, when he draweth him into his net.

וְדָכֹה [יִדְכֶּה] יָשֹׁחַ וְנָפַל בַּעֲצוּמָיו חֵלְכָּאִים [חֵיל כָּאִים]:

sore ones   by his strong ones   and fallen   he bows down   and crouches

10 He croucheth, and humbleth himself, that the poor may fall by his strong ones.

אָמַר בְּלִבּוֹ שָׁכַח אֵל הִסְתִּיר פָּנָיו בַּל־רָאָה לָנֶצַח:

to victory   see – in not   his face   has hid   El   forgotten   in his heart   he said

11 He hath said in his heart, God hath forgotten: he hideth his face; he will never see it.

קוּמָה יְהוָה אֵל נְשָׂא יָדֶךָ אַל־תִּשְׁכַּח עֲנָיִים [עֲנָוִים]:

poor ones   forget - don't   your hand   lift   El   ihvh   arise

12 Arise, O LORD; O God, lift up thine hand: forget not the humble.

עַל־מֶה נִאֵץ רָשָׁע אֱלֹהִים אָמַר בְּלִבּוֹ לֹא תִּדְרֹשׁ:

he will require   not   in his heart   he said   Elohim   wicked   spurns   what - upon

13 Wherefore doth the wicked contemn God? he hath said in his heart, Thou wilt not require it.

רָאִתָה כִּי־אַתָּה עָמָל וָכַעַס תַּבִּיט

you observe   and anger   mischief   you – like   you saw

לָתֵת בְּיָדֶךָ עָלֶיךָ יַעֲזֹב חֵלְכָה יָתוֹם אַתָּה הָיִיתָ עוֹזֵר:

helper   were   you   orphan   pauper   he entrusts   upon you   in your hand   to give

14 Thou hast seen it: for thou beholdest mischief and spite, to requite it with thy hand: the poor committeth himself unto thee; thou art the helper of the fatherless.

שְׁבֹר זְרוֹעַ רָשָׁע וָרָע תִּדְרוֹשׁ־רִשְׁעוֹ בַל־תִּמְצָא:

you find – till not   his wickedness - you seek   and evil   wicked   arm   breaker

15 Break thou the arm of the wicked and the evil man: seek out his wickedness till thou find none.

יְהוָה מֶלֶךְ עוֹלָם וָעֶד אָבְדוּ גוֹיִם מֵאַרְצוֹ:

from his land   nations   perished   and again   forever   king   ihvh

16 The LORD is King for ever and ever: the heathen are perished out of his land.

תַּאֲוַת עֲנָוִים שָׁמַעְתָּ יְהוָה תָּכִין לִבָּם תַּקְשִׁיב אָזְנֶךָ:

your ear   you will attend   their hearts   prepare   ihvh   you have heard   humble ones   desire

17 LORD, thou hast heard the desire of the humble: thou wilt prepare their heart, thou wilt cause thine ear to hear:

לִשְׁפֹּט יָתוֹם וָדָךְ בַּל־יוֹסִיף עוֹד לַעֲרֹץ אֱנוֹשׁ מִן־הָאָרֶץ:

the earth – from   Enosh   to terrify   again   will add – till not   and oppressed   orphan   to judge

18 To judge the fatherless and the oppressed, that the man of the earth may no more oppress.

PSALM 11

ספר תהילים פרק יא

לַמְנַצֵּחַ   לְדָוִד   בַּיהוָה   חָסִיתִי

I took refuge   in ihvh   to David   to him that is over

אֵיךְ   תֹּאמְרוּ   לְנַפְשִׁי   נוּדוּ [נוּדִי]   הַרְכֶם צִפּוֹר׃

bird   your mountain   flee   to my soul   you say it   how

1. (K) To the chief Musician of David. In the Lord I put my trust; how can you say to
my soul, Flee like a bird to your mountain?

כִּי הִנֵּה הָרְשָׁעִים יִדְרְכוּן קֶשֶׁת

bow   they bend   the wicked ones   here   like

כּוֹנְנוּ חִצָּם   עַל־יֶתֶר   לִירוֹת בְּמוֹ־אֹפֶל לְיִשְׁרֵי־לֵב׃

heart - to upright   darkness – in them   to shoot   string – upon   their arrow   they fixed

2. For, behold, the wicked bend their bow, they make ready their arrow on the string,
that they may shoot in darkness at the upright in heart.

כִּי־הַשָּׁתוֹת יֵהָרֵסוּן   צַדִּיק מַה־פָּעָל׃

act – what   righteous   they pulled down   the settled - like

3. If the foundations are destroyed, what can the righteous do?

יְהוָה בְּהֵיכַל קָדְשׁוֹ יְהוָה בַּשָּׁמַיִם כִּסְאוֹ

his throne   in heavens   ihvh   his holiness   in temple   ihvh

עֵינָיו יֶחֱזוּ עַפְעַפָּיו יִבְחֲנוּ בְּנֵי אָדָם׃

Adam   sons   they test   his eyelids   behold   his eyes

4. The Lord is in his holy temple, the Lord's throne is in heaven; his eyes behold, his
eyelids test the children of men.

יְהוָה צַדִּיק יִבְחָן   וְרָשָׁע וְאֹהֵב חָמָס שָׂנְאָה נַפְשׁוֹ׃

his soul   hated   violence   and lover   and wicked   he tests   righteous   ihvh

5. The Lord tests the righteous; but his soul hates the wicked and he who loves violence.

יַמְטֵר עַל־רְשָׁעִים פַּחִים אֵשׁ וְגָפְרִית

and brimstone   fire   coals   wicked ones – upon   it rain

וְרוּחַ זִלְעָפוֹת מְנָת כּוֹסָם׃

their cup   portion   hot sandstorm   and wind

6. Upon the wicked he shall rain coals, fire and brimstone, and a scorching wind shall be
the portion of their cup.

כִּי־צַדִּיק יְהוָה צְדָקוֹת אָהֵב יָשָׁר   יֶחֱזוּ   פָּנֵימוֹ׃

his face   they perceive   upright   loves   righteousness   ihvh   righteous - like

7. For the Lord is righteous; he loves righteousness; the upright shall behold his face.

Psalm 12

ספר תהילים פרק יב

לַמְנַצֵּחַ עַל־הַשְּׁמִינִית מִזְמוֹר לְדָוִד׃

to him that is over	Sheminith – upon	psalm	to David

1 To the chief Musician upon Sheminith, A Psalm of David.

הוֹשִׁיעָה יְהוָה כִּי־גָמַר חָסִיד כִּי־פַסּוּ אֱמוּנִים מִבְּנֵי אָדָם׃

save	ihvh	ceased – like	pious	vanished – like	faithful ones	from sons	Adam

Help, LORD; for the godly man ceaseth; for the faithful fail from among the children of men.

שָׁוְא יְדַבְּרוּ אִישׁ אֶת־רֵעֵהוּ שְׂפַת חֲלָקוֹת בְּלֵב וָלֵב יְדַבֵּרוּ׃

vanity	they speak	man	his neighbors - that	lip	smoothnesses	in heart	and heart	they speak

2 They speak vanity every one with his neighbour: with flattering lips and with a double heart do they speak.

יַכְרֵת יְהוָה כָּל־שִׂפְתֵי חֲלָקוֹת לָשׁוֹן מְדַבֶּרֶת גְּדֹלוֹת׃

he cuts off	ihvh	lips – all	smoothnesses	tongue	from speakings	great ones

3 The LORD shall cut off all flattering lips, and the tongue that speaketh proud things:

אֲשֶׁר אָמְרוּ לִלְשֹׁנֵנוּ נַגְבִּיר שְׂפָתֵינוּ אִתָּנוּ מִי אָדוֹן לָנוּ׃

which	said	to our tongues	we will prevail	our lips	with us	who	master	to us

4 Who have said, With our tongue will we prevail; our lips are our own: who is lord over us?

מִשֹּׁד עֲנִיִּים מֵאַנְקַת אֶבְיוֹנִים עַתָּה אָקוּם

from oppression	poor ones	from sighings	needy ones	now	I will rise

יֹאמַר יְהוָה אָשִׁית בְּיֵשַׁע יָפִיחַ לוֹ

I say	ihvh	I will set them	in safety	he will puff	to it

5 For the oppression of the poor, for the sighing of the needy, now will I arise, saith the LORD; I will set him in safety from him that puffeth at him.

אִמְרוֹת יְהוָה אֲמָרוֹת טְהֹרוֹת כֶּסֶף צָרוּף בַּעֲלִיל

words	ihvh	words	pure ones	silver	smelted	in furnace

לָאָרֶץ מְזֻקָּק שִׁבְעָתָיִם׃

to earth	refined	seven times

6 The words of the LORD are pure words: as silver tried in a furnace of earth, purified seven times.

אַתָּה יְהוָה תִּשְׁמְרֵם תִּצְּרֶנּוּ מִן־הַדּוֹר זוּ לְעוֹלָם׃

you	ihvh	will heed them	will preserve them	the generation - from	this	to forever

7 Thou shalt keep them, O LORD, thou shalt preserve them from this generation for ever.

סָבִיב רְשָׁעִים יִתְהַלָּכוּן כְּרֻם זֻלֻּת לִבְנֵי אָדָם:
surround   wicked ones   they will walk   exalting   squandering   to sons   Adam

8 The wicked walk on every side, when the vilest men are exalted.

Psalm 13

ספר תהילים פרק יג

לַמְנַצֵּחַ   מִזְמוֹר   לְדָוִד׃
to him that is over   psalm   to David

1. To the chief Musician, A Psalm of David.

עַד־אָנָה יְהֹוָה תִּשְׁכָּחֵנִי נֶצַח עַד־אָנָה
now - until   victory   you forget me   ihvh   now - until

תַּסְתִּיר אֶת־פָּנֶיךָ מִמֶּנִּי׃
you hide   your face - that   from me

2. How long will you forget me, O Lord? For ever? How long will you hide your face from me?

עַד־אָנָה אָשִׁית עֵצוֹת בְּנַפְשִׁי יָגוֹן בִּלְבָבִי יוֹמָם
now - until   I set   plans   in my soul   sorrow   in my heart   days

עַד־אָנָה יָרוּם אֹיְבִי עָלָי׃
now - until   be exalted   my enemy   upon me

3. How long shall I take counsel in my soul, having sorrow in my heart daily? How long shall my enemy be exalted over me?

הַבִּיטָה עֲנֵנִי יְהֹוָה אֱלֹהָי הָאִירָה עֵינַי פֶּן־אִישַׁן הַמָּוֶת׃
the look   answer me   ihvh   my Elohim   the shine   my eyes   thus - I sleep   the death

4. Look and answer me, O Lord my God; lighten my eyes, lest I sleep the sleep of death;

פֶּן־יֹאמַר אֹיְבִי יְכָלְתִּיו צָרַי יָגִילוּ כִּי אֶמּוֹט׃
he says - thus   enemy   I overcame him   my adversaries   like they rejoice   I falter

5. Lest my enemy say, I have prevailed against him; and those who trouble me rejoice when I am moved.

וַאֲנִי בְּחַסְדְּךָ בָטַחְתִּי יָגֵל לִבִּי בִּישׁוּעָתֶךָ
and I   in your kindness   I trust   will rejoice   my heart   in your salvation

אָשִׁירָה לַיהֹוָה כִּי גָמַל עָלָי׃
I will sing   to ihvh   like   dealt kindly   upon me

6. But I have trusted in your loving kindness; my heart shall rejoice in your salvation. I will sing to the Lord, because he has dealt bountifully with me.

Psalm 14

ספר תהילים פרק יד

לַמְנַצֵּחַ   לְדָוִד

to David   to him that is over

אָמַר נָבָל בְּלִבּוֹ אֵין אֱלֹהִים

Elohim   isn't   in his heart   fool   said

הִשְׁחִיתוּ הִתְעִיבוּ עֲלִילָה אֵין עֹשֵׂה־טוֹב:

good – doing   isn't   cursing   they abominable   they corrupt

1. To the chief Musician of David. The fool has said in his heart, There is no God. They are corrupt, they have done abominable deeds, there is none that does good.

יְהוָה מִשָּׁמַיִם הִשְׁקִיף עַל־בְּנֵי־אָדָם

Adam - sons - upon   looked down   from heavens   ihvh

לִרְאוֹת הֲיֵשׁ מַשְׂכִּיל דֹּרֵשׁ אֶת־אֱלֹהִים:

Elohim – that   seeker   proverb person   the there is?   to see

2. The Lord looked down from heaven upon the children of men, to see if there were any who understand, and seek God.

הַכֹּל סָר יַחְדָּו נֶאֱלָחוּ אֵין עֹשֵׂה־טוֹב אֵין גַּם־אֶחָד:

one – also   isn't   good – doer   isn't   they corrupted   together   departed   the all

3. They have all gone astray, they have all become corrupted; there is none that does good, no, not one.

הֲלֹא יָדְעוּ כָּל־פֹּעֲלֵי אָוֶן אֹכְלֵי עַמִּי

my people   eating   inequity   workers – all   they know   the not?

אָכְלוּ לֶחֶם יְהוָה לֹא קָרָאוּ:

they call   not   ihvh   bread   they ate

4. Do all the evil doers have no knowledge? Who eat up my people like they eat bread, and call not on the Lord.

שָׁם פָּחֲדוּ פָחַד כִּי־אֱלֹהִים בְּדוֹר צַדִּיק:

righteous   in generation   Elohim – like   dread   they greatly afraid   there

5. They were in great fear; for God is in the generation of the righteous.

עֲצַת־עָנִי תָבִישׁוּ כִּי יְהוָה מַחְסֵהוּ:

his refuge   ihvh   like   you shame   poor - counsel

6. You shame the counsel of the poor, because the Lord is his refuge.

מִי־יִתֵּן מִצִּיּוֹן יְשׁוּעַת יִשְׂרָאֵל בְּשׁוּב יְהוָה שְׁבוּת עַמּוֹ

his people   captivity   ihvh   in returning   Israel   salvation   from Zion   he gives - who

יָגֵל יַעֲקֹב יִשְׂמַח יִשְׂרָאֵל:

Israel   he be happy   Jacob   rejoice

7. Oh, that the salvation of Israel would come out of Zion! When the Lord shall bring

back the exile of his people, Jacob shall rejoice, and Israel shall be glad.

PSALM 15

ספר תהילים פרק טו

מִזְמוֹר לְדָוִד יְהוָה מִי־יָגוּר בְּאָהֳלֶךָ מִי־יִשְׁכֹּן בְּהַר קָדְשֶׁךָ׃

<small>your holy · in mountain · will dwell – who · in your tent · will sojourn – who · ihvh · to David · Psalm</small>

1. A Psalm of David. Lord, who shall abide in your tent? Who shall dwell in your holy mountain?

הוֹלֵךְ תָּמִים וּפֹעֵל צֶדֶק וְדֹבֵר אֱמֶת בִּלְבָבוֹ׃

<small>in his heart · truth · and speaker · righteousness · and worker · perfect ones · he walks</small>

2. He who walks uprightly, and does what is right, and speaks the truth in his heart.

לֹא־רָגַל עַל־לְשֹׁנוֹ לֹא־עָשָׂה לְרֵעֵהוּ רָעָה

<small>evil · to his neighbor · done - not · his tongue - upon · slander - not</small>

וְחֶרְפָּה לֹא־נָשָׂא עַל־קְרֹבוֹ׃

<small>his near - upon · casts – not · and disgrace</small>

3. He who does not slander with his tongue, nor does evil to his neighbor, nor takes up a reproach against his neighbor.

נִבְזֶה בְּעֵינָיו נִמְאָס וְאֶת־יִרְאֵי יְהוָה יְכַבֵּד

<small>he honors · ihvh · fearing - and that · reproach · in his eyes · despised</small>

נִשְׁבַּע לְהָרַע וְלֹא יָמִר׃

<small>he change · and not · to the evil · he swears</small>

4. In whose eyes a vile person is despised; but he honors those who fear the Lord. He who swears to his own hurt, and does not change.

כַּסְפּוֹ לֹא־נָתַן בְּנֶשֶׁךְ וְשֹׁחַד עַל־נָקִי לֹא־לָקָח

<small>takes – not · innocent – upon · and bribe · in interest · he gives - not · his money</small>

עֹשֵׂה אֵלֶּה לֹא יִמּוֹט לְעוֹלָם׃

<small>to forever · he be moved · not · these · doer</small>

5. He who does not put out his money at interest, nor takes a bribe against the innocent. He who does these things shall never be moved.

Psalm 16

ספר תהילים פרק טז

מִכְתָּם לְדָוִד שָׁמְרֵנִי אֵל כִּי־חָסִיתִי בָךְ:

in you · I took refuge - like · El · heed me · to David · Miktam

1. A Miktam of David. Preserve me, O God; for in you I put my trust.

אָמַרְתְּ לַיהוָה אֲדֹנָי אָתָּה טוֹבָתִי בַּל־עָלֶיךָ:

upon you - it not · my goodness · you · Adoni · to ihvh · I said

2. I have said to the Lord, You are my Lord; I have no good apart from you;

לִקְדוֹשִׁים אֲשֶׁר־בָּאָרֶץ הֵמָּה וְאַדִּירֵי כָּל־חֶפְצִי־בָם:

in them – my delighting – all · and excellent · they are · in earth -which · to holy ones

3. As for the holy ones who are in the earth, they are the excellent, in whom is all my delight.

יִרְבּוּ עַצְּבוֹתָם אַחֵר מָהָרוּ

they rush · other gods · their sorrows · they increase

בַּל־אַסִּיךְ נִסְכֵּיהֶם מִדָּם

from blood · their drink offerings · I libate– in not

וּבַל־אֶשָּׂא אֶת־שְׁמוֹתָם עַל־שְׂפָתָי:

my lips – upon · their names - that · I lift - and in not

4. And for those who choose another god, their sorrows shall be multiplied; their drink offerings of blood I will not offer, nor take up their names upon my lips.

יְהוָה מְנָת־חֶלְקִי וְכוֹסִי אַתָּה תּוֹמִיךְ גּוֹרָלִי:

my lot · you maintain · you · and my glass · my portion – serving · ihvh

5. The Lord is the portion of my inheritance and of my cup; you maintain my lot.

חֲבָלִים נָפְלוּ־לִי בַּנְּעִמִים אַף־נַחֲלָת שָׁפְרָה עָלָי:

upon me · been beautiful · inheritance - then · in pleasant ones · to me – they fallen · lines

6. The lines are fallen for me in pleasant places; I have a goodly heritage.

אֲבָרֵךְ אֶת־יְהוָה אֲשֶׁר יְעָצָנִי אַף־לֵילוֹת יִסְּרוּנִי כִלְיוֹתָי:

like night seasons · admonishes me · nights - then · counsels me · which · ihvh – that · I bless

7. I will bless the Lord, who has given me counsel; my insides also instruct me in the night seasons.

שִׁוִּיתִי יְהוָה לְנֶגְדִּי תָמִיד כִּי מִימִינִי בַּל־אֶמּוֹט:

I will falter - in not · from my right hand · like · always · to before me · ihvh · I have set

8. I have set the Lord always before me; because he is at my right hand, I shall not be moved.

לָכֵן שָׂמַח לִבִּי וַיָּגֶל כְּבוֹדִי אַף־בְּשָׂרִי יִשְׁכֹּן לָבֶטַח:

to safety · dwells · my flesh - then · my honor · and rejoiced · my heart · happy · to thus

9. Therefore my heart is glad, and my glory rejoices; my flesh also dwells secure.

כִּי לֹא־תַעֲזֹב נַפְשִׁי לִשְׁאוֹל לֹא־תִתֵּן חֲסִידְךָ לִרְאוֹת שָׁחַת׃

like	you abandon - not	my soul	to Shoel	you give - not	your pious	to seeings	pit

10. (K) For you will not abandon my soul to Sheol; nor will you suffer your pious one to see the pit.

תּוֹדִיעֵנִי אֹרַח חַיִּים

you make me know	path	life

שֹׂבַע שְׂמָחוֹת אֶת־פָּנֶיךָ נְעִמוֹת בִּימִינְךָ נֶצַח׃

full	happiness	your presence – that	pleasures	in your right hand	victory

11. You will show me the path of life; in your presence is fullness of joy; at your right hand there are pleasures for evermore.

PSALM 17

ספר תהילים פרק יז

תְּפִלָּה לְדָוִד שִׁמְעָה יְהֹוָה צֶדֶק

righteousness · ihvh · hear · to David · prayer

הַקְשִׁיבָה רִנָּתִי הַאֲזִינָה תְפִלָּתִי בְּלֹא שִׂפְתֵי מִרְמָה׃

deceit · lips · in not · my prayer · the towards ear · my appeal · the attend

1. A prayer of David. Hear the right, O Lord, attend to my cry, give ear to my prayer from lips free of deceit.

מִלְּפָנֶיךָ מִשְׁפָּטִי יֵצֵא עֵינֶיךָ תֶּחֱזֶינָה מֵישָׁרִים׃

uprightness · will behold · your eyes · it goes out · my judgment · from your presence

2. Let my sentence come forth from your presence; let your eyes behold the right.

בָּחַנְתָּ לִבִּי פָּקַדְתָּ לַּיְלָה צְרַפְתַּנִי

you have tested me · night · you have visited · my heart · you have proved

בַל־תִּמְצָא זַמֹּתִי בַּל־יַעֲבָר־פִּי׃

my mouth - will transgress – nothing · my purpose · you found - nothing

3. You have tested my heart; you have visited me in the night; you have tested me, and found nothing; let my mouth not transgress.

לִפְעֻלּוֹת אָדָם בִּדְבַר שְׂפָתֶיךָ אֲנִי שָׁמַרְתִּי אָרְחוֹת פָּרִיץ׃

[the] violent · roads · have heeded · I · your lips · in speak · Adam · to works

4. Concerning the works of men, by the word of your lips I have kept away from the paths of the violent.

תָּמֹךְ אֲשֻׁרַי בְּמַעְגְּלוֹתֶיךָ בַּל־נָמוֹטוּ פְעָמָי׃

my steps · moved - in not · in your tracks · my goings · held fast

5. My steps have held fast to your paths, my feet have not slipped.

אֲנִי קְרָאתִיךָ כִי־תַעֲנֵנִי אֵל הַט־אָזְנְךָ לִי שְׁמַע אִמְרָתִי׃

my word · hear · to me · your ear - incline · El · you will answer me - like · called you · I

6. I have called upon you, for you will answer me, O God; incline your ear to me, and hear my speech.

הַפְלֵה חֲסָדֶיךָ מוֹשִׁיעַ חוֹסִים מִמִּתְקוֹמְמִים בִּימִינֶךָ׃

in your right hand · from ones rising up · fleeing ones · who saves · your mercies · make wonderful

7. Show your marvelous loving kindness, O you who save from their enemies, by your right hand, those who seek refuge.

שָׁמְרֵנִי כְּאִישׁוֹן בַּת־עָיִן בְּצֵל כְּנָפֶיךָ תַּסְתִּירֵנִי׃

you hide me · your wings · in shadow · eye - daughter · like the pupil · heed me

8. Keep me as the apple of the eye, hide me under the shadow of your wings,

מִפְּנֵי רְשָׁעִים זוּ שַׁדּוּנִי אֹיְבַי בְּנֶפֶשׁ יַקִּיפוּ עָלָי׃

upon me · they will enclose · in my soul · enemies · did me violence · who · wicked ones · from face

9. From the wicked who oppress me, from my deadly enemies who surround me.

חֶלְבָּמוֹ סָגְרוּ פִּימוֹ דִּבְּרוּ בְגֵאוּת׃

in pride   they have spoken   their mouth   they shut   their fat

10. They are enclosed in their own fat; with their mouth they speak arrogantly.

אַשֻּׁרֵינוּ עַתָּה סְבָבוּנִי [סְבָבוּנוּ] עֵינֵיהֶם יָשִׁיתוּ לִנְטוֹת בָּאָרֶץ׃

in the earth   to tread   they have set   their eyes   they surround us   now   are goings

11. (K) They dog our steps; they surround us; they have set their eyes to tread us down to the earth;

דִּמְיֹנוֹ כְּאַרְיֵה יִכְסוֹף לִטְרוֹף וְכִכְפִיר יֹשֵׁב בְּמִסְתָּרִים׃

in secret places   sitting   and as young lion   to tear   is greedy   like a lion   his likeness

12. He is like a lion that is greedy for its prey, and like a young lion lurking in secret places.

קוּמָה יְהֹוָה קַדְּמָה פָנָיו הַכְרִיעֵהוּ פַּלְּטָה נַפְשִׁי מֵרָשָׁע חַרְבֶּךָ׃

your sword   from wicked   my soul   deliver   cast him down   his face   confront   ihvh   arise

13. Arise, O Lord, confront him, cast him down; save my soul from the wicked, by your sword;

מִמְתִים יָדְךָ יְהֹוָה מִמְתִים מֵחֶלֶד חֶלְקָם בַּחַיִּים

in life   their portion   from old time   from mortals   ihvh   your hand   from mortals

וּצְפִינְךָ [וּצְפוּנְךָ] תְּמַלֵּא בִטְנָם יִשְׂבְּעוּ בָנִים

sons   they satisfied   their belly   you fill   and your treasure

וְהִנִּיחוּ יִתְרָם לְעוֹלְלֵיהֶם׃

to their children   their plenty   and they will bestow

14. (K) From men, by your hand, O Lord, from men whose portion in life is of the world, and whose belly you fill with your treasure; who have many children, and who leave their abundance to their babes.

אֲנִי בְּצֶדֶק אֶחֱזֶה פָנֶיךָ אֶשְׂבְּעָה בְהָקִיץ תְּמוּנָתֶךָ׃

your likeness   in awakening   I will be satisfied   your face   will behold   in righteousness   I

15. As for me, I will behold your face in righteousness; I shall be satisfied, when I awake, with beholding your likeness.

PSALM 18

ספר תהילים פרק יח

לַמְנַצֵּחַ לְעֶבֶד יְהוָה לְדָוִד אֲשֶׁר דִּבֶּר
spoke   which   to David ihvh to servant to him that is over

לַיהוָה אֶת־דִּבְרֵי הַשִּׁירָה הַזֹּאת בְּיוֹם
in day   the this   the song speakings - that   to ihvh

הִצִּיל־יְהוָה אוֹתוֹ מִכַּף כָּל־אֹיְבָיו וּמִיַּד שָׁאוּל:
Saul and from hand his enemies-all from palm to him ihvh - delivered

1. To the chief Musician of David, the servant of the Lord, who spoke to the Lord the words of this song in the day that the Lord saved him from the hand of all his enemies, and from the hand of Saul;

וַיֹּאמַר אֶרְחָמְךָ יְהוָה חִזְקִי:
my strength ihvh I will exult you and he said

2. And he said, I will love you, O Lord, my strength.

יְהוָה סַלְעִי וּמְצוּדָתִי וּמְפַלְטִי אֵלִי צוּרִי
my rock my El and my deliverance and my fortress my crag ihvh

אֶחֱסֶה־בּוֹ מָגִנִּי וְקֶרֶן יִשְׁעִי מִשְׂגַּבִּי:
my high place my salvation and horn my shield in him - I take refuge

3. The Lord is my rock, and my fortress, and my savior; my God, my strength, in whom I will trust; my shield, and the horn of my salvation, and my high tower.

מְהֻלָּל אֶקְרָא יְהוָה וּמִן־אֹיְבַי אִוָּשֵׁעַ:
I will be saved enemies – and from ihvh I will call from praised

4. I will call on the Lord, who is worthy to be praised; so shall I be saved from my enemies.

אֲפָפוּנִי חֶבְלֵי־מָוֶת וְנַחֲלֵי בְלִיַּעַל יְבַעֲתוּנִי:
terrify me in cursing men and streams death – chords compressed me

5. The sorrows of death surround me, and the floods of ungodly men make me afraid.

חֶבְלֵי שְׁאוֹל סְבָבוּנִי קִדְּמוּנִי מוֹקְשֵׁי מָוֶת:
death snares confronted me surrounded me Shoel chords

6. The cords of Sheol surround me; the snares of death took me by surprise.

בַּצַּר־לִי אֶקְרָא יְהוָה
ihvh I called to me - in the distress

וְאֶל־אֱלֹהַי אֲשַׁוֵּעַ יִשְׁמַע מֵהֵיכָלוֹ קוֹלִי
my voice from his temple he heard I cry my Elohim - and unto

וְשַׁוְעָתִי לְפָנָיו תָּבוֹא בְאָזְנָיו:
in his ears it comes to before him and my cry

7. In my distress I called upon the Lord, and cried to my God; from his temple he heard

my voice, and my cry to him reached his ears.

וַתִּגְעַשׁ וַתִּרְעַשׁ הָאָרֶץ וּמוֹסְדֵי הָרִים

mountains and foundations the earth and the quaked and the shook

יִרְגָּזוּ וַיִּתְגָּעֲשׁוּ כִּי חָרָה לוֹ׃

to him wrath like and they shook they trembled

8. Then the earth shook and trembled; and the foundations of the mountains moved and were shaken, because he was angry.

עָלָה עָשָׁן בְּאַפּוֹ וְאֵשׁ מִפִּיו תֹּאכֵל גֶּחָלִים בָּעֲרוּ מִמֶּנּוּ׃

from it kindled coals devouring from his mouth and fire in his nostrils smoke went up

9. Smoke went out from his nostrils, and a devouring fire from his mouth; coals were kindled by it.

וַיֵּט שָׁמַיִם וַיֵּרַד וַעֲרָפֶל תַּחַת רַגְלָיו׃

his feet under and utter darkness and descended heavens and he bowed

10. And he bowed the heavens, and came down; and darkness was under his feet.

וַיִּרְכַּב עַל־כְּרוּב וַיָּעֹף וַיֵּדֶא עַל־כַּנְפֵי־רוּחַ׃

wind - wings - upon he swooped and he flew cherub – upon and he rode

11. And he rode on a kerub, and flew; he flew on the wings of the wind.

יָשֶׁת חֹשֶׁךְ סִתְרוֹ סְבִיבוֹתָיו סֻכָּתוֹ חֶשְׁכַת־מַיִם עָבֵי שְׁחָקִים׃

skies cloud waters - dark his pavilion · around him his hiding darkness he set

12. He made darkness his secret place; his pavilion around him was dark with waters and thick clouds of the skies.

מִנֹּגַהּ נֶגְדּוֹ עָבָיו עָבְרוּ בָּרָד וְגַחֲלֵי־אֵשׁ׃

fire - and coals hail they passed his clouds passed before him out of brightness

13. Out of the brightness that was before him his thick clouds passed, hail stones and coals of fire.

וַיַּרְעֵם בַּשָּׁמַיִם יְהוָה וְעֶלְיוֹן יִתֵּן קֹלוֹ בָּרָד וְגַחֲלֵי־אֵשׁ׃

fire - and coals hail his voice he gave and most high ihvh in heavens and thundered

14. The Lord also thundered in the heavens, and the Highest gave his voice; hail stones and coals of fire.

וַיִּשְׁלַח חִצָּיו וַיְפִיצֵם וּבְרָקִים רָב וַיְהֻמֵּם׃

and he discomforted them much and lightnings and shattered them his arrows and he sent

15. And he sent out his arrows, and scattered them; and he shot out lightnings, and confounded them.

וַיֵּרָאוּ אֲפִיקֵי מַיִם וַיִּגָּלוּ מוֹסְדוֹת תֵּבֵל

world foundations and were discovered water channels and were seen

מִגַּעֲרָתְךָ יְהוָה מִנִּשְׁמַת רוּחַ אַפֶּךָ׃

your nostrils wind from blast ihvh from your rebuke

16. Then the channels of waters were seen, and the foundations of the world were laid bare at your rebuke, O Lord, at the blast of the breath of your nostrils.

יִשְׁלַ֣ח מִמָּר֑וֹם יִ֭קָּחֵנִי יַֽמְשֵׁ֗נִי מִמַּ֥יִם רַבִּֽים׃

many | from waters | he drew me | he took me | from on high | he sent

17. He sent from above, he took me, he drew me out of many waters.

יַ֭צִּילֵנִי מֵאֹיְבִ֣י עָ֑ז וּ֝מִשֹּׂנְאַ֗י כִּֽי־אָמְצ֥וּ מִמֶּֽנִּי׃

than I | they stronger - like | and from my haters | strong | from my enemies | he delivered me

18. He saved me from my strong enemy, and from those who hated me; for they were too strong for me.

יְקַדְּמ֥וּנִי בְיוֹם־אֵידִ֑י וַֽיְהִי־יְהוָ֖ה לְמִשְׁעָ֣ן לִֽי׃

to me | to [a] stay | ihvh | and was | my calamity | in day | they confronted me

19. They surprised me in the day of my calamity; but the Lord was my stay.

וַיּוֹצִיאֵ֥נִי לַמֶּרְחָ֑ב יְ֝חַלְּצֵ֗נִי כִּ֘י חָ֥פֵֽץ בִּֽי׃

in me | he delighted | like | he delivered me | to the broad place | and he brought me out

20. He brought me forth also into a large place; he saved me, because he delighted in me.

יִגְמְלֵ֣נִי יְהוָ֣ה כְּצִדְקִ֑י כְּבֹ֥ר יָ֝דַ֗י יָשִׁ֥יב לִֽי׃

to me | he restores | my hands | like pureness | like my righteousness | ihvh | he rewards me

21. The Lord rewards me according to my righteousness; according to the cleanness of my hands he recompenses me.

כִּֽי־שָׁ֭מַרְתִּי דַּרְכֵ֣י יְהוָ֑ה וְלֹֽא־רָ֝שַׁ֗עְתִּי מֵאֱלֹהָֽי׃

from my Elohim | I behaved wickedly - and not | ihvh | ways | I heeded - like

22. For I have kept the ways of the Lord, and have not wickedly departed from my God.

כִּ֣י כָל־מִשְׁפָּטָ֣יו לְנֶגְדִּ֑י וְ֝חֻקֹּתָ֗יו לֹא־אָסִ֥יר מֶֽנִּי׃

from me | I put away - not | and his statutes | to before me | his judgments - all | like

23. For all his judgments were before me, and I did not put away his statutes from me.

וָאֱהִ֣י תָמִ֣ים עִמּ֑וֹ וָ֝אֶשְׁתַּמֵּ֗ר מֵעֲוֹנִֽי׃

from my inequity | and I kept | with him | perfect | and I was

24. I was also upright before him, and I kept myself from my iniquity.

וַיָּֽשֶׁב־יְהוָ֣ה לִ֣י כְצִדְקִ֑י כְּבֹ֥ר יָ֝דַ֗י לְנֶ֣גֶד עֵינָֽיו׃

his eyes | to before | my hand | honor | like my righteousness | to me | ihvh - and he returned

25. Therefore has the Lord recompenses me according to my righteousness, according to the cleanness of my hands in his eyesight.

עִם־חָסִ֥יד תִּתְחַסָּ֑ד עִם־גְּבַ֖ר תָּמִ֣ים תִּתַּמָּֽם׃

you will show upright | perfect | gentleman-with | you will show mercy | merciful - with

26. With the merciful you will show yourself merciful; with an upright man you will show yourself upright;

עִם־נָבָ֥ר תִּתְבָּרָ֑ר וְעִם־עִ֝קֵּ֗שׁ תִּתְפַּתָּֽל׃

you will show subtle | perverse - and with | you will show yourself pure | purified - with

27. With the pure you will show yourself pure; and with the perverse you will show

yourself subtle.

כִּי־אַתָּה עַם־עָנִי תוֹשִׁיעַ וְעֵינַיִם רָמוֹת תַּשְׁפִּיל:

you will make low   exalted   and eyes   you will save   afflicted-people   you - like

28. For you will save the afflicted people; but will bring down haughty looks.

כִּי־אַתָּה תָּאִיר נֵרִי יְהֹוָה אֱלֹהַי יַגִּיהַּ חָשְׁכִּי:

my darkness   will brighten   my Elohim   ihvh   my lamp   will make shine   you - like

29. For you will light my candle; the Lord my God will enlighten my darkness.

כִּי־בְךָ אָרֻץ גְּדוּד וּבֵאלֹהַי אֲדַלֶּג־שׁוּר:

wall - I leap over   and in my Elohim   through troop   I run   in you - like

30. For by you I can run through a troop; and by my God I can leap over a wall.

הָאֵל תָּמִים דַּרְכּוֹ אִמְרַת יְהֹוָה צְרוּפָה

purified   ihvh   word   his way   upright   the El

מָגֵן הוּא לְכֹל הַחוֹסִים בּוֹ:

to him   the fleeing ones   to all   he   shield

31. As for God, his way is perfect; the word of the Lord is proven; he is a shield to all those who trust in him.

כִּי מִי אֱלוֹהַּ מִבַּלְעֲדֵי יְהֹוָה וּמִי־צוּר זוּלָתִי אֱלֹהֵינוּ:

our Elohim   except   rock - and who   ihvh   from besides   Elohim   who   like

32. For who is God but the Lord? Who is a rock but our God?

הָאֵל הַמְאַזְּרֵנִי חָיִל וַיִּתֵּן תָּמִים דַּרְכִּי:

my way   perfect   and he gave   strength   who girded me   the El

33. It is God who girds me with strength, and makes my way perfect.

מְשַׁוֶּה רַגְלַי כָּאַיָּלוֹת וְעַל בָּמֹתַי יַעֲמִידֵנִי:

he stands me   my high place   and upon   like hinds   my feet   setting

34. He makes my feet to be like hinds' feet, and sets me upon my heights.

מְלַמֵּד יָדַי לַמִּלְחָמָה וְנִחֲתָה קֶשֶׁת־נְחוּשָׁה זְרוֹעֹתָי:

my arms   brass – bow   and press down   the war   my hands   teaching

35. He teaches my hands to war, so that a bow of bronze is bent by my arms.

וַתִּתֶּן־לִי מָגֵן יִשְׁעֶךָ

your salvation   shield   and you gave me

וִימִינְךָ תִסְעָדֵנִי וְעַנְוָתְךָ תַרְבֵּנִי:

you make me great   and your humility   you supported me   and your right hand

36. You have also given me the shield of your salvation; and your right hand has supported me, and your gentleness has made me great.

תַּרְחִיב צַעֲדִי תַחְתָּי וְלֹא מָעֲדוּ קַרְסֻלָּי:

my ankles   tottered   and not   under me   my step   you enlarged

37. You have enlarged my steps under me, so that my feet did not slip.

אֶרְדּוֹף אוֹיְבַי וָאַשִּׂיגֵם וְלֹא־אָשׁוּב עַד־כַּלּוֹתָם׃

consumed them – until   I return - and not   and overtaken them   my enemies   I pursued

38. I have pursued my enemies, and overtaken them; and did not turn back till they were consumed.

אֶמְחָצֵם וְלֹא־יֻכְלוּ קוּם יִפְּלוּ תַּחַת רַגְלָי׃

my feet   under   they fell   rise   they able - and not   I shattered them

39. I have crashed them so that they were not able to rise; they have fallen under my feet.

וַתְּאַזְּרֵנִי חַיִל לַמִּלְחָמָה תַּכְרִיעַ קָמַי תַּחְתָּי׃

under me   my arisers   you subdued   to war   strength   and you girded me

40. For you have girded me with strength to the battle; you have subdued under me those who rose up against me.

וְאֹיְבַי נָתַתָּה לִּי עֹרֶף וּמְשַׂנְאַי אַצְמִיתֵם׃

I will exterminate them   and from my haters   back   to me   you gave   and my enemies

41. You have also my enemies turn their backs to me; that I might destroy those who hate me.

יְשַׁוְּעוּ וְאֵין מוֹשִׁיעַ עַל־יְהוָה וְלֹא עָנָם׃

he answered them   and not   ihvh - upon   saving   and isn't   they cried

42. They cried, but there was none to save them; they cried to the Lord, but he did not answer them.

וְאֶשְׁחָקֵם כְּעָפָר עַל־פְּנֵי־רוּחַ כְּטִיט חוּצוֹת אֲרִיקֵם׃

I empty them   outside   like dirt   wind – face – upon   like dust   and I grind them

43. And I beat them small as the dust before the wind; I cast them as the dirt in the streets.

תְּפַלְּטֵנִי מֵרִיבֵי עָם תְּשִׂימֵנִי לְרֹאשׁ גּוֹיִם

nations   to head   you set me   people   from strivings   you delivered me

עַם לֹא־יָדַעְתִּי יַעַבְדוּנִי׃

will serve me   I known – not   people

44. You have saved me from the strivings of the people; and you have made me the head of nations; a people whom I have not known shall serve me.

לְשֵׁמַע אֹזֶן יִשָּׁמְעוּ לִי בְּנֵי־נֵכָר יְכַחֲשׁוּ־לִי׃

to me – they submit   strange - sons   to me   they will heed   ear   to hearing

45. As soon as they hear of me, they shall obey me; the strangers shall submit themselves to me.

בְּנֵי־נֵכָר יִבֹּלוּ וְיַחְרְגוּ מִמִּסְגְּרוֹתֵיהֶם׃

from their holds   and they come trembling   will fade   stranger - sons

46. The strangers shall fade away, and come trembling out of their close places.

חַי־יְהוָה וּבָרוּךְ צוּרִי וְיָרוּם אֱלוֹהֵי יִשְׁעִי׃

my salvation   my Elohim   and exalted   my rock   and blessed   ihvh - life

47. The Lord lives; and blessed is my rock; and let the God of my salvation be exalted.

הָאֵל הַנּוֹתֵן נְקָמוֹת לִי וַיַּדְבֵּר עַמִּים תַּחְתָּי׃

under me   peoples   and he speaks   to me   avengements   the giver   the El

48. It is God who avenges me, and subdues the peoples under me.

מְפַלְּטִי מֵאֹיְבָי אַף מִן־קָמַי תְּרוֹמְמֵנִי

you exalt me   my arising - from   then   from my enemies   he who delivers me

מֵאִישׁ חָמָס תַּצִּילֵנִי׃

you deliver me   violence   from man

49. He saves me from my enemies; you lift me up above those who rise up against me; you save me from the violent man.

עַל־כֵּן אוֹדְךָ בַגּוֹיִם יְהֹוָה וּלְשִׁמְךָ אֲזַמֵּרָה׃

I sing psalms   to your name   ihvh   in nations   I will give thanks   thus upon

50. Therefore I will give thanks to you, O Lord, among the nations, and sing praises to your name.

מַגְדִּל [מַגְדִּיל] יְשׁוּעוֹת מַלְכּוֹ וְעֹשֶׂה חֶסֶד לִמְשִׁיחוֹ

to his anointed   kindness   and doing   his king   salvations   magnified

לְדָוִד וּלְזַרְעוֹ עַד־עוֹלָם׃

forever – till   and to his seed   to David

51. Great deliverance he gives to his king; and shows loving kindness to his anointed, to David, and to his seed for evermore.

PSALM 19

ספר תהילים פרק יט

לַמְנַצֵּחַ   מִזְמוֹר   לְדָוִד:
to David   Psalm   to him that is over

1 To the chief Musician, A Psalm of David.

הַשָּׁמַיִם מְסַפְּרִים כְּבוֹד־אֵל וּמַעֲשֵׂה יָדָיו מַגִּיד הָרָקִיעַ:
the firmament   telling   his hands   and works   El – glory   declaring ones   the heavens

The heavens declare the glory of God; and the firmament sheweth his handiwork.

יוֹם לְיוֹם יַבִּיעַ אֹמֶר וְלַיְלָה לְּלַיְלָה יְחַוֶּה־דָּעַת:
knowledge – conveys   to night   and night   saying   utters   to day   day

2 Day unto day uttereth speech, and night unto night sheweth knowledge.

אֵין אֹמֶר וְאֵין דְּבָרִים בְּלִי נִשְׁמָע קוֹלָם:
their voice   heard   without   speakings   and isn't   saying   isn't

3 There is no speech nor language, where their voice is not heard.

בְּכָל־הָאָרֶץ יָצָא קַוָּם וּבִקְצֵה תֵבֵל מִלֵּיהֶם
their words   inhabited world   and in end   their measuring tape   came out   the earth – in all

לַשֶּׁמֶשׁ שָׂם אֹהֶל בָּהֶם:
in them   tent   put   to sun

4 Their line is gone out through all the earth, and their words to the end of the world. In them hath he set a tabernacle for the sun,

וְהוּא כְּחָתָן יֹצֵא מֵחֻפָּתוֹ יָשִׂישׂ כְּגִבּוֹר לָרוּץ אֹרַח:
road   to run   like mighty man   he joyful   from his canopy   comer out   like bridegroom   and he

5 Which is as a bridegroom coming out of his chamber, and rejoiceth as a strong man to run a race.

מִקְצֵה הַשָּׁמַיִם מוֹצָאוֹ וּתְקוּפָתוֹ עַל־קְצוֹתָם וְאֵין נִסְתָּר מֵחַמָּתוֹ:
from his heat   hidden   and isn't   their ends – upon   and his circuit   his going out   the heavens   from end

6 His going forth is from the end of the heaven, and his circuit unto the ends of it: and there is nothing hid from the heat thereof.

תּוֹרַת יְהֹוָה תְּמִימָה מְשִׁיבַת נָפֶשׁ עֵדוּת יְהֹוָה
ihvh   testimony   soul   from returning   perfect   ihvh   Torah

נֶאֱמָנָה מַחְכִּימַת פֶּתִי:
simple   wise making   trustworthy

7 The law of the LORD is perfect, converting the soul: the testimony of the LORD is sure, making wise the simple.

פִּקּוּדֵי יְהֹוָה יְשָׁרִים מְשַׂמְּחֵי־לֵב
heart – from happy   upright ones   ihvh   precepts

מִצְוַת יְהֹוָה בָּרָה מְאִירַת עֵינָיִם:

eyes   enlightenings   clean   ihvh   commandment

8 The statutes of the LORD *are* right, rejoicing the heart: the commandment of the
LORD *is* pure, enlightening the eyes.

יִרְאַת יְהֹוָה טְהוֹרָה עוֹמֶדֶת לָעַד

to ever   standing   pure   ihvh   fear

מִשְׁפְּטֵי־יְהֹוָה אֱמֶת צָדְקוּ יַחְדָּו:

together   they righteous   truth   ihvh – judgments

9 The fear of the LORD *is* clean, enduring for ever: the judgments of the LORD *are*
true *and* righteous altogether.

הַנֶּחֱמָדִים מִזָּהָב וּמִפַּז רָב

many   and from pure gold   from gold   the desirable ones

וּמְתוּקִים מִדְּבַשׁ וְנֹפֶת צוּפִים:

honey comb   and droppings   from honey   and sweet ones

10 More to be desired *are they* than gold, yea, than much fine gold: sweeter also than
honey and the honeycomb.

גַּם־עַבְדְּךָ נִזְהָר בָּהֶם בְּשָׁמְרָם עֵקֶב רָב:

much   very end   in their heeding   in them   warned   your servant – also

11 Moreover by them is thy servant warned: *and* in keeping of them *there is* great reward.

שְׁגִיאוֹת מִי־יָבִין מִנִּסְתָּרוֹת נַקֵּנִי:

clean me   from hidden ones   he understand – who   errors

12 Who can understand *his* errors? cleanse thou me from secret *faults*.

גַּם מִזֵּדִים חֲשֹׂךְ עַבְדֶּךָ אַל־יִמְשְׁלוּ־בִי אָז אֵיתָם

I will be perfect   then   in me - they rule - don't   your servant   restrain   from proud ones   also

וְנִקֵּיתִי מִפֶּשַׁע רָב:

many   from transgressions   and I will be innocent

13 Keep back thy servant also from presumptuous *sins*; let them not have dominion
over me: then shall I be upright, and I shall be innocent from the great transgression.

יִהְיוּ לְרָצוֹן אִמְרֵי־פִי וְהֶגְיוֹן לִבִּי לְפָנֶיךָ

before you   my heart   and the meditation   my mouth – sayings   to favor   they be

יְהֹוָה צוּרִי וְגֹאֲלִי:

and my redeemer   my rock   ihvh

14 Let the words of my mouth, and the meditation of my heart, be acceptable in thy
sight, O LORD, my strength, and my redeemer.

Psalm 20

ספר תהילים פרק כ

לַמְנַצֵּחַ   מִזְמוֹר   לְדָוִד׃
to him that is over   Psalm   to David

1. To the chief Musician, A Psalm of David.

יַעַנְךָ   יְהֹוָה   בְּיוֹם   צָרָה   יְשַׂגֶּבְךָ   שֵׁם   אֱלֹהֵי   יַעֲקֹב׃
he answer you   ihvh   in day   distress   he totally defends you   name   Elohim   Jacob

2. May the Lord hear you in the day of trouble! May the name of the God of Jacob defend you!

יִשְׁלַח־עֶזְרְךָ   מִקֹּדֶשׁ   וּמִצִּיּוֹן   יִסְעָדֶךָ׃
your help - he sends   from holy   and from Zion   he braces you

3. May he send you help from the sanctuary, and strengthen you out of Zion!

יִזְכֹּר   כָּל־מִנְחֹתֶךָ   וְעוֹלָתְךָ   יְדַשְּׁנֶה   סֶלָה׃
he will remember   your offerings - all   and your burnt sacrifices   he find faults   Sela

4. May he remember all your offerings, and accept with favor your burnt sacrifice! Selah.

יִתֶּן־לְךָ   כִלְבָבֶךָ   וְכָל־עֲצָתְךָ   יְמַלֵּא׃
to you – he gives   like your heart   your counsel - and all   he fills

5. May he grant you your heart's desire, and fulfil all your plans!

נְרַנְּנָה   בִּישׁוּעָתֶךָ   וּבְשֵׁם־אֱלֹהֵינוּ   נִדְגֹּל
shout joy   in your salvation   our Elohim - and in name   set up banners

יְמַלֵּא   יְהֹוָה   כָּל־מִשְׁאֲלוֹתֶיךָ׃
he fill   ihvh   your petitions - all

6. May we rejoice in your salvation, and in the name of our God set up our banners! May the Lord fulfil all your petitions!

עַתָּה   יָדַעְתִּי   כִּי   הוֹשִׁיעַ   יְהֹוָה   מְשִׁיחוֹ
now   I know   like   saver   ihvh   his anointed

יַעֲנֵהוּ   מִשְּׁמֵי   קָדְשׁוֹ   בִּגְבֻרוֹת   יֵשַׁע   יְמִינוֹ׃
he will answer him   from heavens   his holiness   in mighty acts   he does   his right hand

7. Now I know that the Lord saves his anointed; he will answer him from his holy heaven with the saving strength of his right hand.

אֵלֶּה   בָרֶכֶב   וְאֵלֶּה   בַסּוּסִים
these   in chariot   and these   in horses

וַאֲנַחְנוּ   בְּשֵׁם־יְהֹוָה   אֱלֹהֵינוּ   נַזְכִּיר׃
and we   ihvh – in name   our Elohim   we will remember

8. Some trust in chariots, and some in horses; but we will remember the name of the Lord our God.

הֵמָּה כָּרְעוּ   וְנָפָלוּ וַאֲנַחְנוּ קַמְנוּ וַנִּתְעוֹדָד:
<small>and stand upright   will rise   and we   and they fallen   bowed down   they are</small>

9. They are brought down and fall; but we shall rise, and stand upright.

יְהֹוָה הוֹשִׁיעָה הַמֶּלֶךְ יַעֲנֵנוּ   בְיוֹם־קָרְאֵנוּ:
<small>our calling - in day   he will answer us   the king   saver   ihvh</small>

10. Save, Lord; the king will answer us on the day when we call.

PSALM 21

ספר תהילים פרק כא

לַמְנַצֵּחַ   מִזְמוֹר   לְדָוִד:
to David   psalm   to him that is over

יהוה   בְּעָזְּךָ   יִשְׂמַח־מֶלֶךְ   וּבִישׁוּעָתְךָ   מַה־יָּגֶיל   [יָגֵל]   מְאֹד:
very   he exult – what   and in your salvation   king – he happy   in your strength   ihvh

1. To the chief Musician, A Psalm of David. The king has joy in your strength, O Lord; and in your salvation how greatly he rejoices!

תַּאֲוַת   לִבּוֹ   נָתַתָּה   לּוֹ   וַאֲרֶשֶׁת   שְׂפָתָיו   בַּל־מָנַעְתָּ   סֶּלָה:
Sela   you withheld – in not   his lips   and requests   to him   you gave   his heart   desire

2 Thou hast given him his heart's desire, and hast not withholden the request of his lips. Selah.

כִּי־תְקַדְּמֶנּוּ   בִּרְכוֹת   טוֹב   תָּשִׁית   לְרֹאשׁוֹ   עֲטֶרֶת   פָּז:
pure gold   crown   to his head   you set   good   blessings   you anticipate him - like

3 For thou preventest him with the blessings of goodness: thou settest a crown of pure gold on his head.

חַיִּים   שָׁאַל   מִמְּךָ   נָתַתָּה   לּוֹ   אֹרֶךְ   יָמִים   עוֹלָם   וָעֶד:
and ever   forever   days   length   to him   you gave   from you   he asked   life

4 He asked life of thee, and thou gavest it him, even length of days for ever and ever.

גָּדוֹל   כְּבוֹדוֹ   בִּישׁוּעָתֶךָ   הוֹד   וְהָדָר   תְּשַׁוֶּה   עָלָיו:
upon him   you set   and majesty   honor   in your salvation   his glory   great

5 His glory is great in thy salvation: honour and majesty hast thou laid upon him.

כִּי־תְשִׁיתֵהוּ   בְרָכוֹת   לָעַד   תְּחַדֵּהוּ   בְשִׂמְחָה   אֶת־פָּנֶיךָ:
your presence – that   in happiness   you gladdened him   to ever   blessings   you set him - like

6 For thou hast made him most blessed for ever: thou hast made him exceeding glad with thy countenance.

כִּי־הַמֶּלֶךְ   בֹּטֵחַ   בַּיהוָה   וּבְחֶסֶד   עֶלְיוֹן   בַּל־יִמּוֹט:
he falter – in not   most high   and in kindness   in ihvh   trusts   the king - like

7 For the king trusteth in the LORD, and through the mercy of the most High he shall not be moved.

תִּמְצָא   יָדְךָ   לְכָל־אֹיְבֶיךָ   יְמִינְךָ   תִּמְצָא   שֹׂנְאֶיךָ:
your haters   you will find   your right hand   your enemies – to all   your hand   will find

8 Thine hand shall find out all thine enemies: thy right hand shall find out those that hate thee.

תְּשִׁיתֵמוֹ   כְּתַנּוּר   אֵשׁ   לְעֵת   פָּנֶיךָ   יהוה   בְּאַפּוֹ   יְבַלְּעֵם:
swallow them up   in his anger   ihvh   your presence   to season   fire   like furnace   you put them

וְתֹאכְלֵם אֵשׁ:

fire   and will eat them

9 Thou shalt make them as a fiery oven in the time of thine anger: the LORD shall swallow them up in his wrath, and the fire shall devour them.

פִּרְיָמוֹ מֵאֶרֶץ תְּאַבֵּד וְזַרְעָם מִבְּנֵי אָדָם:

Adam   from sons   and their seed   destroy   from earth   their fruit

10 Their fruit shalt thou destroy from the earth, and their seed from among the children of men.

כִּי־נָטוּ   עָלֶיךָ רָעָה חָשְׁבוּ מְזִמָּה בַּל־יוּכָלוּ:

they prevail – in not   device   they thought   evil   upon you   they directed - like

11 For they intended evil against thee: they imagined a mischievous device, which they are not able to perform.

כִּי תְּשִׁיתֵמוֹ שֶׁכֶם בְּמֵיתָרֶיךָ תְּכוֹנֵן   עַל־פְּנֵיהֶם:

their faces – upon   you will establish   in your strings   back   you will set them   like

12 Therefore shalt thou make them turn their back, when thou shalt make ready thine arrows upon thy strings against the face of them.

רוּמָה יְהֹוָה בְּעֻזֶּךָ נָשִׁירָה וּנְזַמְּרָה גְּבוּרָתֶךָ:

your might   and sing psalms   we will sing   in your strength   ihvh   exalted

13 Be thou exalted, LORD, in thine own strength: so will we sing and praise thy power.

PSALM 22

ספר תהילים פרק כב

לַמְנַצֵּחַ   עַל־אַיֶּלֶת הַשַּׁחַר מִזְמוֹר לְדָוִד:
to David   psalm   the dawn   hind – upon   to him that is over

1. To the chief Musician, according to Ayeleth HaShahar, a Psalm of David.

אֵלִי אֵלִי לָמָה עֲזַבְתָּנִי   רָחוֹק מִישׁוּעָתִי דִּבְרֵי שַׁאֲגָתִי:
my roaring   speakings   from my salvation   far   you foresaken me   why   Eli   Eli

2. My God, my God, why have you forsaken me? Why are you so far from helping me, from the words of my loud complaint?

אֱלֹהַי אֶקְרָא יוֹמָם וְלֹא תַעֲנֶה   וְלַיְלָה וְלֹא־דוּמִיָּה לִי:
to me   repose – and not   and night   you answer   and not   by day   I call   my Elohim

3. O my God, I cry in the daytime, but you do not hear; and in the night, and I have no rest.

וְאַתָּה קָדוֹשׁ יוֹשֵׁב תְּהִלּוֹת יִשְׂרָאֵל:
Israel   praises   inhabits   holy   and you

4. But you are holy, O you who are enthroned on the praises of Israel.

בְּךָ בָּטְחוּ אֲבֹתֵינוּ בָּטְחוּ   וַתְּפַלְּטֵמוֹ:
and you delivered them   they confided   our fathers   confided   in you

5. Our fathers trusted in you; they trusted, and you saved them.

אֵלֶיךָ זָעֲקוּ וְנִמְלָטוּ   בְּךָ   בָטְחוּ וְלֹא־בוֹשׁוּ:
they ashamed – and not   they trusted   in you   and they escaped   they cried   unto you

6. They cried to you, and were saved; they trusted in you, and were not disappointed.

וְאָנֹכִי תוֹלַעַת וְלֹא־אִישׁ חֶרְפַּת אָדָם וּבְזוּי   עָם:
people   and despised   Adam   reproach   man- and not   worm   and I

7. But I am a worm, and not a man; scorned by men, and despised by the people.

כָּל־רֹאַי יַלְעִגוּ לִי יַפְטִירוּ בְשָׂפָה יָנִיעוּ רֹאשׁ:
head   they shake   in lip   they open   to me   they mock   seeing me - all

8. All those who see me mock me; they move the lip, they shake their head, saying,

גֹּל אֶל־יְהוָֹה יְפַלְּטֵהוּ יַצִּילֵהוּ כִּי חָפֵץ בּוֹ:
in him   he delighted   like   he rescues him   he delivers him   ihvh – upon   roll

9. He trusted on the Lord that he would save him; let him save him, seeing he delights in him.

כִּי־אַתָּה גֹחִי   מִבָּטֶן   מַבְטִיחִי עַל־שְׁדֵי אִמִּי:
my mother   breast – upon   from my trust   from womb   taking me out   you - like

10. But you are he who took me out of the womb; you made me hope when I was upon my mother's breasts.

עָלֶיךָ הָשְׁלַכְתִּי מֵרָחֶם מִבֶּטֶן אִמִּי אֵלִי אָתָּה׃

you   my El   my mother   from belly   from womb   I was the cast   unto you

11. I was cast upon you from the womb; you are my God from my mother's belly.

אַל־תִּרְחַק מִמֶּנִּי כִּי־צָרָה קְרוֹבָה כִּי־אֵין עוֹזֵר׃

helper   isn't – like   near   trouble – like   from me   you far - don't

12. Do not be far from me; for trouble is near; for there is none to help.

סְבָבוּנִי פָּרִים רַבִּים אַבִּירֵי בָשָׁן כִּתְּרוּנִי׃

compressed me   Bashan   mighty bulls   many   bulls   surrounded me

13. Many bulls surround me; strong bulls of Bashan surround me.

פָּצוּ עָלַי פִּיהֶם אַרְיֵה טֹרֵף וְשֹׁאֵג׃

and roaring   tearing   lion   their mouths   upon me   they opened

14. They open wide their mouths at me, like a ravening and a roaring lion.

כַּמַּיִם נִשְׁפַּכְתִּי וְהִתְפָּרְדוּ כָּל־עַצְמוֹתָי הָיָה

it was   my bones – all   and separated   I poured out   like water

לִבִּי כַּדּוֹנָג נָמֵס בְּתוֹךְ מֵעָי׃

my bowels   in midst   melted   like wax   my heart

15. I am poured out like water, and all my bones are out of joint; my heart is like wax; it is melted in the midst of my bowels.

יָבֵשׁ כַּחֶרֶשׂ כֹּחִי וּלְשׁוֹנִי מֻדְבָּק מַלְקוֹחָי

my palate   from cleaving   and my tongue   my strength   like potsherd   has dried

וְלַעֲפַר־מָוֶת תִּשְׁפְּתֵנִי׃

you lay down me   death – and to dust

16. My strength is dried up like a potsherd; and my tongue cleaves to my jaws; and you lay me down in the dust of death.

כִּי־סְבָבוּנִי כְּלָבִים עֲדַת מְרֵעִים הִקִּיפוּנִי כָּאֲרִי יָדַי וְרַגְלָי׃

and my feet   my hand   like lion   they seize   from wicked   assembly   like dogs   surrounded me – like

17. For dogs surround me; the assembly of the wicked encircle me; they seize my hands and my feet like a lion.

אֲסַפֵּר כָּל־עַצְמוֹתָי הֵמָּה יַבִּיטוּ יִרְאוּ־בִי׃

upon me - they see   they look   they   my bones –all   I count

18. I can count all my bones; they look and stare at me.

יְחַלְּקוּ בְגָדַי לָהֶם וְעַל־לְבוּשִׁי יַפִּילוּ גוֹרָל׃

a lot   they cast   my clothing – and upon   to them   my garments   they divide

19. They divide my garments among them, and cast lots for my clothing.

וְאַתָּה יְהוָה אַל־תִּרְחָק אֱיָלוּתִי לְעֶזְרָתִי חוּשָׁה׃

make haste   to my help   my strength   you be far – don't   ihvh   and you

20. But you, O Lord, be not far from me; O my strength, hasten to my help.

הַצִּילָה מֵחֶרֶב נַפְשִׁי מִיַּד־כֶּלֶב יְחִידָתִי׃

my only one   dog - from hand   my soul   from sword   deliver

21. Save my soul from the sword; my only one from the power of the dog.

הוֹשִׁיעֵנִי מִפִּי אַרְיֵה וּמִקַּרְנֵי רֵמִים עֲנִיתָנִי׃

you answered me   wild oxen   and from horns   lion   from mouth   save me

22. Save me from the lion's mouth; for you have answered me from the horns of the wild oxen.

אֲסַפְּרָה שִׁמְךָ לְאֶחָי בְּתוֹךְ קָהָל אֲהַלְלֶךָּ׃

I praise you   congregation   in midst   to my brethren   your name   I declare

23. I will declare your name to my brothers; in the midst of the congregation will I praise you.

יִרְאֵי יְהֹוָה הַלְלוּהוּ כָּל־זֶרַע יַעֲקֹב כַּבְּדוּהוּ

glorify him   Jacob   seed – all   praise him   ihvh   you that fear

וְגוּרוּ מִמֶּנּוּ כָּל־זֶרַע יִשְׂרָאֵל׃

Israel   seed – all   from him   and you fear

24. You who fear the Lord, praise him; all you the seed of Jacob, glorify him; and fear him, all you the seed of Israel.

כִּי לֹא־בָזָה וְלֹא שִׁקַּץ עֱנוּת עָנִי

poor   poverty   abhorred   and not   he despised - not   like

וְלֹא־הִסְתִּיר פָּנָיו מִמֶּנּוּ וּבְשַׁוְּעוֹ אֵלָיו שָׁמֵעַ׃

he heard   unto him   and in his crying   from him   his face   the hidden – and not

25. For he has not despised nor loathed the affliction of the afflicted; nor has he hidden his face from him; but when he cried to him, he heard.

מֵאִתְּךָ תְהִלָּתִי בְּקָהָל רָב נְדָרַי אֲשַׁלֵּם נֶגֶד יְרֵאָיו׃

his fearing   before   I pay   my vows   many   in congregation   my praise   from thee

26. My praise shall be of you in the great congregation; I will pay my vows before those who fear him.

יֹאכְלוּ עֲנָוִים וְיִשְׂבָּעוּ יְהַלְלוּ יְהֹוָה דֹּרְשָׁיו

his seekers   ihvh   they praise   and they satisfied   humble ones   they eat

יְחִי לְבַבְכֶם לָעַד׃

forever   your hearts   live

27. The humble shall eat and be satisfied; those who seek him shall praise the Lord. May your heart live for ever!

יִזְכְּרוּ וְיָשֻׁבוּ אֶל־יְהֹוָה כָּל־אַפְסֵי־אָרֶץ

earth – far ends – all   ihvh unto   and they will return   they will remember

וְיִשְׁתַּחֲווּ לְפָנֶיךָ כָּל־מִשְׁפְּחוֹת גּוֹיִם׃

nations   families – all   before you   and bow down

28. All the ends of the world shall remember and turn to the Lord; and all the families

of the nations shall worship before you.

כִּי לַיהוָֹה הַמְּלוּכָה וּמֹשֵׁל בַּגּוֹיִם׃

like   to ihvh   the kingdom   and ruler   in nations

29. For the kingdom is the Lord's; and he is ruler over the nations.

אָכְלוּ וַיִּשְׁתַּחֲווּ כָּל־דִּשְׁנֵי־אֶרֶץ לְפָנָיו יִכְרְעוּ כָּל־יוֹרְדֵי עָפָר

you eat   and bowed down   earth – fat ones – all   before him   they bend   descenders - all   dust

וְנַפְשׁוֹ לֹא חִיָּה׃

and his soul   not   alive

30. All the fat ones of the earth shall eat and worship; all those who go down to the dust, and he who cannot keep alive his own soul, shall bow before him.

זֶרַע יַעַבְדֶנּוּ יְסֻפַּר לַאדֹנָי לַדּוֹר׃

seed   they serve him   I be storied   to Adonai   to generation

31. Their seed shall serve him; it shall be told of the Lord to the coming generation.

יָבֹאוּ וְיַגִּידוּ צִדְקָתוֹ לְעַם נוֹלָד כִּי עָשָׂה׃

they come   and they tell   his righteousness   to peoples   will be born   like   he did

32. They shall come, and shall declare his righteousness to a people that shall be born, that he has done this.

PSALM 23

ספר תהילים פרק כג

מִזְמוֹר לְדָוִד יְהוָה רֹעִי לֹא אֶחְסָר׃

I will lack · not · my shepherd · ihvh · to David · Psalm

The LORD is my shepherd; I shall not want.

בִּנְאוֹת דֶּשֶׁא יַרְבִּיצֵנִי עַל־מֵי מְנֻחוֹת יְנַהֲלֵנִי׃

he leads me · from still ones · waters - upon · he lays me down · grass · in lush

2 He maketh me to lie down in green pastures: he leadeth me beside the still waters.

נַפְשִׁי יְשׁוֹבֵב יַנְחֵנִי בְמַעְגְּלֵי־צֶדֶק לְמַעַן שְׁמוֹ׃

his name · to end · righteous - in steps · he leads me · he restores · my soul

3 He restoreth my soul: he leadeth me in the paths of righteousness for his name's sake.

גַּם כִּי־אֵלֵךְ בְּגֵיא צַלְמָוֶת לֹא־אִירָא רָע כִּי־אַתָּה עִמָּדִי

with me · you - like · evil · I will fear - not · deadly gloom · in valley · I walk - like · also

שִׁבְטְךָ וּמִשְׁעַנְתֶּךָ הֵמָּה יְנַחֲמֻנִי׃

my comfort · they are · and your staff · your rod

4 Yea, though I walk through the valley of the shadow of death, I will fear no evil: for thou art with me; thy rod and thy staff they comfort me.

תַּעֲרֹךְ לְפָנַי שֻׁלְחָן נֶגֶד צֹרְרָי

my foes · beside · table · before me · you prepare

דִּשַּׁנְתָּ בַשֶּׁמֶן רֹאשִׁי כּוֹסִי רְוָיָה׃

overflowing · my glass · my head · in oil · you have made fat

5 Thou preparest a table before me in the presence of mine enemies: thou anointest my head with oil; my cup runneth over.

אַךְ טוֹב וָחֶסֶד יִרְדְּפוּנִי כָּל־יְמֵי חַיָּי

my life · days - all · will peruse me · and mercy · good · surely

וְשַׁבְתִּי בְּבֵית־יְהוָה לְאֹרֶךְ יָמִים׃

days · to length · ihvh - in house · and I will dwell

6 Surely goodness and mercy shall follow me all the days of my life: and I will dwell in the house of the LORD for ever.

PSALM 24

ספר תהילים פרק כד

לְדָוִד מִזְמוֹר לַיהֹוָה הָאָרֶץ וּמְלוֹאָהּ תֵּבֵל וְיֹשְׁבֵי בָהּ׃

| in it | and dwellers | world | and fullness | the earth | to ihvh | Psalm | to David |

1 A Psalm of David. The earth is the LORD'S, and the fulness thereof; the world, and they that dwell therein.

הוּא עַל־יַמִּים יְסָדָהּ וְעַל־נְהָרוֹת יְכוֹנְנֶהָ׃

| he established | rivers - and upon | he founded | seas – upon | he |

2 For he hath founded it upon the seas, and established it upon the floods.

מִי־יַעֲלֶה בְהַר יְהֹוָה וּמִי־יָקוּם בִּמְקוֹם קָדְשׁוֹ׃

| his holy | in place | will rise - and who | ihvh | in mountain | will ascend - who |

3 Who shall ascend into the hill of the LORD? or who shall stand in his holy place?

נְקִי כַפַּיִם וּבַר לֵבָב אֲשֶׁר לֹא־נָשָׂא לַשָּׁוְא נַפְשִׁי

| my soul | to vanity | lifted – not | which | heart | and pure | palms | clean |

וְלֹא נִשְׁבַּע לְמִרְמָה׃

| to deceit | sworn | and not |

4 He that hath clean hands, and a pure heart; who hath not lifted up his soul unto vanity, nor sworn deceitfully.

יִשָּׂא בְרָכָה מֵאֵת יְהֹוָה וּצְדָקָה מֵאֱלֹהֵי יִשְׁעוֹ׃

| his salvation | from my Elohim | and righteousness | ihvh | from that | blessing | he will receive |

5 He shall receive the blessing from the LORD, and righteousness from the God of his salvation.

זֶה דּוֹר דֹּרְשׁוֹ [דֹּרְשָׁיו] מְבַקְשֵׁי פָנֶיךָ יַעֲקֹב סֶלָה׃

| Selah | Jacob | your face | from asking | his seekers | generation | this |

6 This is the generation of them that seek him, that seek thy face, O Jacob. Selah.

שְׂאוּ שְׁעָרִים רָאשֵׁיכֶם וְהִנָּשְׂאוּ פִּתְחֵי עוֹלָם

| forever | openings | and be lifted up | your heads | gates | lift up |

וְיָבוֹא מֶלֶךְ הַכָּבוֹד׃

| the glory | king | and will come |

7 Lift up your heads, O ye gates; and be ye lift up, ye everlasting doors; and the King of glory shall come in.

מִי זֶה מֶלֶךְ הַכָּבוֹד יְהֹוָה עִזּוּז וְגִבּוֹר יְהֹוָה גִּבּוֹר מִלְחָמָה׃

| war | mighty | ihvh | and mighty | strong | ihvh | the glory | king | this | who |

8 Who is this King of glory? The LORD strong and mighty, the LORD mighty in battle.

שְׂאוּ שְׁעָרִים רָאשֵׁיכֶם וּשְׂאוּ פִּתְחֵי עוֹלָם

| forever | doors | and lift up | your heads | gates | lift up |

וְיָבֹא   מֶלֶךְ   הַכָּבוֹד:
the glory   king   and will come

9 Lift up your heads, O ye gates; even lift them up, ye everlasting doors; and the King of glory shall come in.

מִי   הוּא   זֶה   מֶלֶךְ   הַכָּבוֹד   יְהֹוָה   צְבָאוֹת
legions   ihvh   the glory   king   this   he   who

הוּא   מֶלֶךְ   הַכָּבוֹד   סֶלָה:
Selah   the glory   king   he

10 Who is this King of glory? The LORD of hosts, he is the King of glory. Selah.

PSALM 25

ספר תהילים פרק כה

לְדָוִד אֵלֶיךָ יְהֹוָה נַפְשִׁי אֶשָּׂא׃

to David   unto you   ihvh   my soul   I lift

1. A Psalm of David. To you, O Lord, I lift up my soul.

אֱלֹהַי בְּךָ בָטַחְתִּי אַל־אֵבוֹשָׁה אַל־יַעַלְצוּ אֹיְבַי לִי׃

my Elohim   in you   I confided   I be ashamed – don't   they exult – don't   my enemies   to me

2. O my God, I trust in you; let me not be ashamed, let not my enemies triumph over me.

גַּם כָּל־קֹוֶיךָ לֹא יֵבֹשׁוּ יֵבֹשׁוּ הַבּוֹגְדִים רֵיקָם׃

also   waits for you – all   not   they be ashamed   they be ashamed   transgress ones   causelessly

3. Also, let none who waits on you be ashamed; let those who transgress without cause be ashamed.

דְּרָכֶיךָ יְהֹוָה הוֹדִיעֵנִי אֹרְחוֹתֶיךָ לַמְּדֵנִי׃

your way   ihvh   make me know   your path   teach me

4. Make me know your ways, O Lord; teach me your paths.

הַדְרִיכֵנִי בַאֲמִתֶּךָ וְלַמְּדֵנִי כִּי־אַתָּה

the direct me   in your truth   and teach me   you – like

אֱלֹהֵי יִשְׁעִי אוֹתְךָ קִוִּיתִי כָּל־הַיּוֹם׃

my Elohim   my salvation   to you   I wait   the day – all

5. Lead me in your truth, and teach me; for you are the God of my salvation; for you I wait all the day.

זְכֹר־רַחֲמֶיךָ יְהֹוָה וַחֲסָדֶיךָ כִּי מֵעוֹלָם הֵמָּה׃

your mercies - remember   ihvh   and your kindness   like   from of old   they were

6. Remember, O Lord, your compassion and your loving kindness; for they have been from of old.

חַטֹּאות נְעוּרַי וּפְשָׁעַי אַל־תִּזְכֹּר כְּחַסְדְּךָ

sins   my youth   and my transgressions   remember – don't   like your kindness

זְכָר־לִי־אַתָּה לְמַעַן טוּבְךָ יְהֹוָה׃

remember - to me - you   to end   your goodness   ihvh

7. Remember not the sins of my youth, nor my transgressions; according to your loving kindness remember me for your goodness' sake, O Lord.

טוֹב וְיָשָׁר יְהֹוָה עַל־כֵּן יוֹרֶה חַטָּאִים בַּדָּרֶךְ׃

good   and upright   ihvh   thus – upon   he instructs   sinner ones   in way

8. Good and upright is the Lord; therefore he instructs sinners in the way.

יַדְרֵךְ עֲנָוִים בַּמִּשְׁפָּט וִילַמֵּד עֲנָוִים דַּרְכּוֹ׃

he leads   humble ones   in judgment   and he teaches   humble ones   his way

9. He guides the humble in judgment; and he teaches the humble his way.

כָּל־אָרְחוֹת יְהֹוָה חֶסֶד וֶאֱמֶת לְנֹצְרֵי בְרִיתוֹ וְעֵדֹתָיו׃

and his testimonies   his covenant   to keepers   and truth   kindness   ihvh   roads - all

10. All the paths of the Lord are loving kindness and truth to those who keep his covenant and his testimonies.

לְמַעַן־שִׁמְךָ יְהֹוָה וְסָלַחְתָּ לַעֲוֹנִי כִּי רַב־הוּא׃

it – much   like   to my inequity   and pardon   ihvh   your name – to end

11. For your name's sake, O Lord, pardon my iniquity; for it is great.

מִי זֶה הָאִישׁ יְרֵא יְהֹוָה יוֹרֶנּוּ בְּדֶרֶךְ יִבְחָר׃

he will choose   in way   he will instruct him   ihvh   fearing   the man   this   who

12. Who is the man who fears the Lord? Him shall he teach in the way that he should choose.

נַפְשׁוֹ בְּטוֹב תָּלִין וְזַרְעוֹ יִירַשׁ אָרֶץ׃

earth   will inherit   and his seed   will lodge   in good   his soul

13. His soul shall abide in prosperity, and his seed shall inherit the earth.

סוֹד יְהֹוָה לִירֵאָיו וּבְרִיתוֹ לְהוֹדִיעָם׃

to reveal   and his covenant   to those who fear him   ihvh   foundation

14. The counsel of the Lord is with those who fear him; and he will reveal to them his covenant.

עֵינַי תָּמִיד אֶל־יְהֹוָה כִּי הוּא־יוֹצִיא מֵרֶשֶׁת רַגְלָי׃

my feet   from net   he bring out – he   like   ihvh - unto   continually   my eyes

15. My eyes are always toward the Lord; for he shall pluck my feet out of the net.

פְּנֵה־אֵלַי וְחָנֵּנִי כִּי־יָחִיד וְעָנִי אָנִי׃

I   and afflicted   alone – like   and gracious   unto me - turn your face

16. Turn to me, and be gracious to me; for I am desolate and afflicted.

צָרוֹת לְבָבִי הִרְחִיבוּ מִמְּצוּקוֹתַי הוֹצִיאֵנִי׃

bring me out   from my distresses   enlarged   my heart   distresses

17. The troubles of my heart are enlarged; O bring me out of my distresses!

רְאֵה־עָנְיִי וַעֲמָלִי וְשָׂא לְכָל־חַטֹּאותָי׃

my sins – to all   and forgive   and my travail   my affliction - see

18. Look upon my affliction and my pain; and forgive all my sins.

רְאֵה אוֹיְבַי כִּי־רָבּוּ וְשִׂנְאַת חָמָס שְׂנֵאוּנִי׃

they hated me   violence   and hatred   they multiply – like   my enemies   see

19. Consider my enemies; for they are many; and they hate me with a cruel hatred.

שָׁמְרָה נַפְשִׁי וְהַצִּילֵנִי אַל־אֵבוֹשׁ כִּי־חָסִיתִי בָךְ׃

in you   I took refuge - like   ashame me – don't   and deliver me   my soul   keep

20. O keep my soul, and save me; let me not be ashamed; for I put my trust in you.

תֹּם־וָיֹשֶׁר   יִצְּרוּנִי כִּי קִוִּיתִיךָ׃

I awaited you   like   preserves me   and upright - integrity

21. Let integrity and uprightness preserve me; for I wait on you.

פְּדֵה־אֱלֹהִים אֶת־יִשְׂרָאֵל מִכֹּל צָרוֹתָיו׃

its distresses   from all   Israel – that   Elohim - redeem

22. Redeem Israel, O God, out of all his troubles.

PSALM 26

ספר תהילים פרק כו

לְדָוִד שָׁפְטֵנִי יְהֹוָה כִּי־אֲנִי בְּתֻמִּי הָלַכְתִּי
to David | judge me | ihvh | I – like | in my integrity | I walked

וּבַיהֹוָה בָּטַחְתִּי לֹא אֶמְעָד:
and in ihvh | I trusted | not | I will waiver

1 *A Psalm* of David. Judge me, O LORD; for I have walked in mine integrity: I have trusted also in the LORD; therefore I shall not slide.

בְּחָנֵנִי יְהֹוָה וְנַסֵּנִי צָרוֹפָה [צָרְפָה] כִלְיוֹתַי וְלִבִּי:
examine me | ihvh | and test me | scrutinize | my kidneys | and my heart

2 Examine me, O LORD, and prove me; try my reins and my heart.

כִּי־חַסְדְּךָ לְנֶגֶד עֵינָי וְהִתְהַלַּכְתִּי בַּאֲמִתֶּךָ:
your mercy – like | to before | my eyes | and I walked | in your truth

3 For thy loving kindness is before mine eyes: and I have walked in thy truth.

לֹא־יָשַׁבְתִּי עִם־מְתֵי־שָׁוְא וְעִם־נַעֲלָמִים לֹא אָבוֹא:
I sat – not | vanity – persons - with | dissemblers – and with | not | I will come

4 I have not sat with vain persons, neither will I go in with dissemblers.

שָׂנֵאתִי קְהַל מְרֵעִים וְעִם־רְשָׁעִים לֹא אֵשֵׁב:
I hated | assembly | from wicked ones | wicked ones – and with | not | I will sit

5 I have hated the congregation of evildoers; and will not sit with the wicked.

אֶרְחַץ בְּנִקָּיוֹן כַּפָּי וַאֲסֹבְבָה אֶת־מִזְבַּחֲךָ יְהֹוָה:
I wash | in innocence | my palms | and I will surround | that – your altar | ihvh

6 I will wash mine hands in innocency: so will I compass thine altar, O LORD:

לַשְׁמִעַ בְּקוֹל תּוֹדָה וּלְסַפֵּר כָּל־נִפְלְאוֹתֶיךָ:
to hear | in voice | thanksgiving | and story | all – your mysticals

7 That I may publish with the voice of thanksgiving, and tell of all thy wondrous works.

יְהֹוָה אָהַבְתִּי מְעוֹן בֵּיתֶךָ וּמְקוֹם מִשְׁכַּן כְּבוֹדֶךָ:
ihvh | I love | shelter | your house | and place | place | your honor

8 LORD, I have loved the habitation of thy house, and the place where thine honour dwelleth.

אַל־תֶּאֱסֹף עִם־חַטָּאִים נַפְשִׁי וְעִם־אַנְשֵׁי דָמִים חַיָּי:
gather - don't | sinner ones – with | my soul | men – and with | blood ones | my life

9 Gather not my soul with sinners, nor my life with bloody men:

אֲשֶׁר־בִּידֵיהֶם זִמָּה וִימִינָם מָלְאָה שֹּׁחַד:
in their hands – which | mischief | and their right hand | full | bribe

10 In whose hands is mischief, and their right hand is full of bribes.

וַאֲנִי בְּתֻמִּי אֵלֵךְ פְּדֵנִי וְחָנֵּנִי:

and revive me　　redeem me　　will walk　in my integrity　　and I

11 But as for me, I will walk in mine integrity: redeem me, and be merciful unto me.

רַגְלִי עָמְדָה בְמִישׁוֹר בְּמַקְהֵלִים אֲבָרֵךְ יְהוָה:

ihvh　　I will bless　　in congregations　　in level place　　stands　　my foot

12 My foot standeth in an even place: in the congregations will I bless the LORD.

PSALM 27

לְדָוִד יְהֹוָה אוֹרִי וְיִשְׁעִי
to David   ihvh   my light   and my salvation

מִמִּי אִירָא יְהֹוָה מָעוֹז חַיַּי מִמִּי אֶפְחָד׃
from who   I will fear   ihvh   fortress   my life   from who   I will dread fear

1. A Psalm of David. The Lord is my light and my salvation. Whom shall I fear? The
Lord is the strength of my life. Of whom shall I be afraid?

בִּקְרֹב עָלַי מְרֵעִים לֶאֱכֹל אֶת־בְּשָׂרִי
in near   upon me   from wicked ones   to eat   my flesh – that

צָרַי וְאֹיְבַי לִי הֵמָּה כָּשְׁלוּ וְנָפָלוּ׃
my adversaries   and my enemies   to me   they   they stumbled   and they fall

2. When the wicked, my enemies and my adversaries, came upon me to eat up my flesh,
they stumbled and fell.

אִם־תַּחֲנֶה עָלַי מַחֲנֶה לֹא־יִירָא לִבִּי
if – will encamp   upon me   encampment   not – will fear   my heart

אִם־תָּקוּם עָלַי מִלְחָמָה בְּזֹאת אֲנִי בוֹטֵחַ׃
if – will rise   upon me   war   in this   I   trust

3. Though a host should encamp against me, my heart shall not fear; though war should
rise against me, even then I will be confident.

אַחַת שָׁאַלְתִּי מֵאֵת־יְהֹוָה אוֹתָהּ אֲבַקֵּשׁ
you   I ask   ihvh – from that   to it   I will seek

שִׁבְתִּי בְּבֵית־יְהֹוָה כָּל־יְמֵי חַיַּי
my dwelling   ihvh - in house   days – all   my life

לַחֲזוֹת בְּנֹעַם־יְהֹוָה וּלְבַקֵּר בְּהֵיכָלוֹ׃
to behold   ihvh - in pleasant   and to inquire   in his temple

4. One thing have I desired of the Lord, that I will seek after; that I may dwell in the
house of the Lord all the days of my life, to behold the beauty of the Lord, and to
inquire in his temple.

כִּי יִצְפְּנֵנִי בְּסֻכֹּה בְּיוֹם רָעָה
like   he will hide me   in his pavilion   in day   bad

יַסְתִּרֵנִי בְּסֵתֶר אָהֳלוֹ בְּצוּר יְרוֹמְמֵנִי׃
he will hide me   in concealment   his tent   in rock   he will lift high me

5. For in the time of trouble he shall hide me in his pavilion; under the cover of his tent
shall he hide me; he shall set me up upon a rock.

וְעַתָּה יָרוּם רֹאשִׁי עַל־אֹיְבַי סְבִיבוֹתַי
and now   will lift high   my head   my enemies - upon   around me

וְאֶזְבְּחָה בְאָהֳלוֹ זִבְחֵי תְרוּעָה אָשִׁירָה וַאֲזַמְּרָה לַיהוָה׃

<small>to ihvh   and I will sing psalms   I will sing   alarm sound   offerings   in his tent   and I will offering</small>

6. And now shall my head be lifted up above my enemies around me; therefore I will offer in his tent sacrifices of joy; I will sing, I will make music to the Lord.

שְׁמַע־יְהוָה קוֹלִי אֶקְרָא וְחָנֵּנִי וַעֲנֵנִי׃

<small>and answer me   and be gracious to me   I call   my voice   ihvh – hear</small>

7. Hear, O Lord, when I cry with my voice; be gracious to me, and answer me.

לְךָ אָמַר לִבִּי בַּקְּשׁוּ פָנָי אֶת־פָּנֶיךָ יְהוָה אֲבַקֵּשׁ׃

<small>I will seek   ihvh   your face – that   my face   you seek   my heart   I said   to you</small>

8. Of you my heart said, Seek my face; Your face, O Lord, will I seek!

אַל־תַּסְתֵּר פָּנֶיךָ מִמֶּנִּי אַל־תַּט בְּאַף עַבְדֶּךָ

<small>your servant   in anger   turn away – don't   from me   your face   you hide – don't</small>

עֶזְרָתִי הָיִיתָ אַל־תִּטְּשֵׁנִי

<small>abandon me – don't   you were   my help</small>

וְאַל־תַּעַזְבֵנִי אֱלֹהֵי יִשְׁעִי׃

<small>my salvation   my Elohim   forsake me – and don't</small>

9. Hide not your face from me; put not your servant away in anger; you have been my help; do not abandon me, nor forsake me, O God of my salvation.

כִּי־אָבִי וְאִמִּי עֲזָבוּנִי וַיהוָה יַאַסְפֵנִי׃

<small>will gather me in   and ihvh   foresook me   and my mother   my father – like</small>

10. For my father and my mother have forsaken me, but the Lord will take me up.

הוֹרֵנִי יְהוָה דַּרְכֶּךָ וּנְחֵנִי בְּאֹרַח מִישׁוֹר לְמַעַן שׁוֹרְרָי׃

<small>my watchers   to end   evenness   in road   and lead me   your path   ihvh   teach me</small>

11. Teach me your way, O Lord, and lead me on a level path, because of my enemies.

אַל־תִּתְּנֵנִי בְּנֶפֶשׁ צָרָי

<small>my adversaries   in soul   give me – don't</small>

כִּי קָמוּ־בִי עֵדֵי־שֶׁקֶר וִיפֵחַ חָמָס׃

<small>violence   and breathes out   lies – witnesses   in me – they have risen   like</small>

12. Do not give me up to the will of my enemies; for false witnesses have risen up against me, and they breathe out violence.

לוּלֵא הֶאֱמַנְתִּי לִרְאוֹת בְּטוּב־יְהוָה בְּאֶרֶץ חַיִּים׃

<small>life   in earth   ihvh – in good   to seeings   the my belief   perhaps</small>

13. Were it not that I believe I should see the goodness of the Lord in the land of the living.

קַוֵּה אֶל־יְהוָה חֲזַק וְיַאֲמֵץ לִבֶּךָ וְקַוֵּה אֶל־יְהוָה׃

<small>ihvh – unto   and wait   your heart   and encourage   be strong   ihvh – unto   place hope</small>

14. Wait on the Lord; be of good courage, and he shall strengthen your heart; and wait on the Lord.

PSALM 28

לְדָוִד אֵלֶיךָ יְהֹוָה אֶקְרָא צוּרִי אַל־תֶּחֱרַשׁ מִמֶּנִּי
from me   be silent – don't   my rock   I call   ihvh   unto you   to David

פֶּן־תֶּחֱשֶׁה מִמֶּנִּי
from me   you hushing – lest

וְנִמְשַׁלְתִּי עִם־יוֹרְדֵי בוֹר׃
pit   descenders – with   and I comparable

1. A Psalm of David. To you I will cry, O Lord my rock. Do not be silent to me, lest, if you are silent to me, I become like those who go down into the pit.

שְׁמַע קוֹל תַּחֲנוּנַי בְּשַׁוְּעִי אֵלֶיךָ בְּנָשְׂאִי יָדַי אֶל־דְּבִיר קָדְשֶׁךָ
your holy   sanctuary – unto   my hand   in my lifting up   unto you   in my crying   my pleadings   voice   hear

2. Hear the voice of my supplications, when I cry to you, when I lift up my hands toward your holy sanctuary.

אַל־תִּמְשְׁכֵנִי עִם־רְשָׁעִים
wicked ones – with   draw me – don't

וְעִם־פֹּעֲלֵי אָוֶן דֹּבְרֵי שָׁלוֹם עִם־רֵעֵיהֶם וְרָעָה בִּלְבָבָם׃
in their hearts   and evil   their neighbors – with   peace   speakers   inequity   workers – and with

3. Do not take me away with the wicked, and with the evil doers, who speak peace to their neighbors, but there is evil in their hearts.

תֶּן־לָהֶם כְּפָעֳלָם
like their works   to them - give

וּכְרֹעַ מַעַלְלֵיהֶם כְּמַעֲשֵׂה יְדֵיהֶם תֵּן לָהֶם הָשֵׁב גְּמוּלָם לָהֶם׃
to them   their reward   the return   to them   give   their hands   like works   from their actions   and like evil

4. Give them according to their works, and according to the wickedness of their deeds; give them according to the work of their hands; render to them their due reward.

כִּי לֹא יָבִינוּ אֶל־פְּעֻלֹּת יְהֹוָה וְאֶל־מַעֲשֵׂה
work – and unto   ihvh   works – unto   they understand   not   like

יָדָיו יֶהֶרְסֵם וְלֹא יִבְנֵם׃
he build them   and not   he will tear down them   his hands

5. Because they do not regard the works of the Lord, nor the operation of his hands, he shall destroy them, and not build them up.

בָּרוּךְ יְהֹוָה כִּי־שָׁמַע קוֹל תַּחֲנוּנָי׃
my supplications   voice   he heard - like   ihvh   blessed

6. Blessed be the Lord, because he has heard the voice of my supplications.

יְהֹוָה עֻזִּי וּמָגִנִּי בּוֹ בָטַח לִבִּי וְנֶעֱזָרְתִּי

and I helped   my heart   trusted   in him   and my shield   my strength   ihvh

וַיַּעֲלֹז לִבִּי וּמִשִּׁירִי אֲהוֹדֶנּוּ׃

I will praise him   and from my song   my heart   and exulted

7. The Lord is my strength and my shield; my heart trusted in him, and I am helped; therefore my heart greatly rejoices; and with my song I will praise him.

יְהֹוָה עֹז־לָמוֹ וּמָעוֹז יְשׁוּעוֹת מְשִׁיחוֹ הוּא׃

he   his anointed   salvations   and stronghold   to them – strength   ihvh

8. The Lord is their strength, and he is the saving strength of his anointed.

הוֹשִׁיעָה אֶת־עַמֶּךָ וּבָרֵךְ אֶת־נַחֲלָתֶךָ

your inheritance – that   and bless   your peoples – that   save

וּרְעֵם וְנַשְּׂאֵם עַד־הָעוֹלָם׃

the forever – till   and raise them   and shepherd them

9. Save your people, and bless your inheritance; be their shepherd, and carry them forever.

Psalm 29

ספר תהילים פרק כט

מִזְמוֹר　לְדָוִד
Psalm　to David

הָבוּ לַיהֹוָה בְּנֵי אֵלִים　הָבוּ לַיהֹוָה כָּבוֹד וָעֹז:
ascribe　to ihvh　son　Elohim　ascribe　to ihvh　glory　and strength

1. A Psalm of David. Ascribe to the Lord, O you mighty, give to the Lord glory and strength.

הָבוּ לַיהֹוָה כְּבוֹד שְׁמוֹ　הִשְׁתַּחֲווּ לַיהֹוָה בְּהַדְרַת־קֹדֶשׁ:
ascribe　to ihvh　glory　his name　worship　to ihvh　holy - in beauty

2. Give to the Lord the glory due to his name; worship the Lord in the beauty of holiness.

קוֹל יְהֹוָה עַל־הַמָּיִם אֵל־הַכָּבוֹד הִרְעִים יְהֹוָה עַל־מַיִם רַבִּים:
voice　ihvh　the waters – upon　the glory – El　thundering　ihvh　waters – upon　many

3. The voice of the Lord is upon the waters; the God of glory thunders; the Lord is upon many waters.

קוֹל־יְהֹוָה בַּכֹּחַ　קוֹל יְהֹוָה בֶּהָדָר:
ihvh - voice　in powerful　voice　ihvh　in magnificence

4. The voice of the Lord is powerful; the voice of the Lord is full of majesty.

קוֹל יְהֹוָה שֹׁבֵר אֲרָזִים　וַיְשַׁבֵּר יְהֹוָה אֶת־אַרְזֵי הַלְּבָנוֹן:
voice　ihvh　breaks　cedar trees　and breaks　ihvh　cedar – that　the Lebanon

5. The voice of the Lord breaks the cedars; the Lord breaks the cedars of Lebanon.

וַיַּרְקִידֵם　כְּמוֹ־עֵגֶל לְבָנוֹן וְשִׂרְיֹן כְּמוֹ בֶן־רְאֵמִים:
and he make skip them　calf – like　Lebanon　and Sirion　like　ox - son

6. He makes them skip like a calf; Lebanon and Sirion like a young wild ox.

קוֹל־יְהֹוָה חֹצֵב לַהֲבוֹת אֵשׁ:
ihvh - voice　divides　to flames　fire

7. The voice of the Lord divides the flames of fire.

קוֹל יְהֹוָה יָחִיל מִדְבָּר יָחִיל יְהֹוָה מִדְבַּר קָדֵשׁ:
voice　ihvh　he shakes　desert　he shakes　ihvh　desert　kadesh

8. The voice of the Lord shakes the wilderness; the Lord shakes the wilderness of Kadesh.

קוֹל יְהֹוָה יְחוֹלֵל אַיָּלוֹת
voice　ihvh　he makes calf　hinds

וַיֶּחֱשֹׂף יְעָרוֹת וּבְהֵיכָלוֹ כֻּלּוֹ אֹמֵר כָּבוֹד:
and strips　forests　and in his temple　his all　say　honor

9. The voice of the Lord makes the hinds to calve, and strips the forests bare; and in his

temple every one speaks of his glory.

יְהֹוָה לַמַּבּוּל יָשָׁב וַיֵּשֶׁב יְהֹוָה מֶלֶךְ לְעוֹלָם:

forever   king   ihvh   and he sits   he sits   to flood   ihvh

10. The Lord sits enthroned at the flood; and the Lord sits enthroned as King forever.

יְהֹוָה עֹז לְעַמּוֹ יִתֵּן יְהֹוָה יְבָרֵךְ אֶת־עַמּוֹ בַשָּׁלוֹם:

in peace   people – that   he will bless   ihvh   he gives   to his people   strength   ihvh

11. The Lord will give strength to his people; the Lord will bless his people with peace.

PSALM 30

ספר תהילים פרק ל

מִזְמוֹר שִׁיר חֲנֻכַּת הַבַּיִת לְדָוִד:

to David   the house   dedication   song   psalm

1 A Psalm and Song at the dedication of the house of David.

אֲרוֹמִמְךָ יְהוָה כִּי דִלִּיתָנִי וְלֹא־שִׂמַּחְתָּ אֹיְבַי לִי:

to me   my enemies   he happy - and not   you drawn me up   like   ihvh   I will exalt you

I will extol thee, O LORD, for thou hast lifted me up, and hast not made my foes to rejoice over me.

יְהוָה אֱלֹהָי שִׁוַּעְתִּי אֵלֶיךָ וַתִּרְפָּאֵנִי:

and you healed me   unto you   I cried out   my Elohim   ihvh

2 O LORD my God, I cried unto thee, and thou hast healed me.

יְהוָה הֶעֱלִיתָ מִן־שְׁאוֹל נַפְשִׁי חִיִּיתַנִי מִיּוֹרְדִי־ [מִיָּרְדִי] בוֹר:

pit   from descending me   you gave me life   my soul   Shoel – from   the you raised   ihvh

3 O LORD, thou hast brought up my soul from the grave: thou hast kept me alive, that I should not go down to the pit.

זַמְּרוּ לַיהוָה חֲסִידָיו וְהוֹדוּ לְזֵכֶר קָדְשׁוֹ:

his holiness   to remembrance   and you give thanks   his devout   to ihvh   you sing psalms

4 Sing unto the LORD, O ye saints of his, and give thanks at the remembrance of his holiness.

כִּי רֶגַע בְּאַפּוֹ חַיִּים בִּרְצוֹנוֹ

in his favor   life   in his anger   moment   like

בָּעֶרֶב יָלִין בֶּכִי וְלַבֹּקֶר רִנָּה:

shouting joy   and to morning   weeping   he spends night   in evening

5 For his anger endureth but a moment; in his favour is life: weeping may endure for a night, but joy cometh in the morning.

וַאֲנִי אָמַרְתִּי בְשַׁלְוִי בַּל־אֶמּוֹט לְעוֹלָם:

to forever   I will falter - in not   in my serenity   I said   and I

6 And in my prosperity I said, I shall never be moved.

יְהוָה בִּרְצוֹנְךָ הֶעֱמַדְתָּה לְהַרְרִי עֹז

strength   to my mountain   the you stand   in your favor   ihvh

הִסְתַּרְתָּ פָנֶיךָ הָיִיתִי נִבְהָל:

troubled   I was   your face   you hid

7 LORD, by thy favour thou hast made my mountain to stand strong: thou didst hide thy face, and I was troubled.

אֵלֶיךָ יְהוָה אֶקְרָא וְאֶל־אֲדֹנָי אֶתְחַנָּן:

I appealed   Adoni - and unto   I called   ihvh   unto you

8 I cried to thee, O LORD; and unto the LORD I made supplication.

מַה־בֶּצַע בְּדָמִי בְּרִדְתִּי אֶל־שָׁחַת

you ditch – unto	in my descent	in my blood	gain - what

הֲיוֹדְךָ עָפָר הֲיַגִּיד אֲמִתֶּךָ׃

your truth	the he will tell	dust	thanking you

9 What profit is there in my blood, when I go down to the pit? Shall the dust praise thee? shall it declare thy truth?

שְׁמַע־יְהֹוָה וְחָנֵּנִי יְהֹוָה הֱיֵה עֹזֵר לִי׃

to me	helper	you be	ihvh	and be gracious	ihvh - hear

10 Hear, O LORD, and have mercy upon me: LORD, be thou my helper.

הָפַכְתָּ מִסְפְּדִי לְמָחוֹל לִי פִּתַּחְתָּ שַׂקִּי וַתְּאַזְּרֵנִי שִׂמְחָה׃

happiness	and have girded me	my sackcloth	you opened	to me	to dancing	from my mourning	you transformed

11 Thou hast turned for me my mourning into dancing: thou hast put off my sackcloth, and girded me with gladness;

לְמַעַן יְזַמֶּרְךָ כָבוֹד

glory	I will sing psalms to you	to end

וְלֹא יִדֹּם יְהֹוָה אֱלֹהַי לְעוֹלָם אוֹדֶךָ׃

I will give you thanks	to forever	my Eloha	ihvh	will be silent	and not

12 To the end that *my* glory may sing praise to thee, and not be silent. O LORD my God, I will give thanks unto thee for ever.

Psalm 31

ספר תהילים פרק לא

לַמְנַצֵּחַ מִזְמוֹר לְדָוִד:
to him that is over   psalm   to David

1. To the chief Musician, A Psalm of David.

בְּךָ יְהוָה חָסִיתִי אַל־אֵבוֹשָׁה לְעוֹלָם בְּצִדְקָתְךָ פַלְּטֵנִי:
in you ihvh I ashamed – don't to ever in your righteousness deliver me my refuge

2. In you, O Lord, I take refuge; never let me be ashamed; save me in your righteousness.

הַטֵּה אֵלַי אָזְנְךָ מְהֵרָה הַצִּילֵנִי
incline unto me your ears speedily deliver me

הֱיֵה לִי לְצוּר־מָעוֹז לְבֵית מְצוּדוֹת לְהוֹשִׁיעֵנִי:
be you to me to rock – from strength to house fortress to save me

3. Incline your ear to me; save me speedily; be you my strong rock, a fortress of defense to save me.

כִּי־סַלְעִי וּמְצוּדָתִי אָתָּה וּלְמַעַן שְׁמְ־ תַּנְחֵנִי וּתְנַהֲלֵנִי:
my crag – like and my fortress you and to end your name you lead me and you guide me

4. For you are my rock and my fortress; therefore for your name's sake lead me, and guide me.

תּוֹצִיאֵנִי מֵרֶשֶׁת זוּ טָמְנוּ לִי כִּי־אַתָּה מָעוּזִי:
my bringer from net this they buried to me like – you my stronghold

5. Pull me out of the net that they have laid secretly for me; for you are my stronghold.

בְּיָדְךָ אַפְקִיד רוּחִי פָּדִיתָה אוֹתִי יְהוָה אֵל אֱמֶת:
in your hand I commit my spirit you redeemed me ihvh El truth

6. Into your hand I commit my spirit; you have redeemed me, O Lord God of truth.

שָׂנֵאתִי הַשֹּׁמְרִים הַבְלֵי־שָׁוְא וַאֲנִי אֶל־יְהוָה בָּטָחְתִּי:
I hated the heeding ones emptiness – vanities and I ihvh – unto I confided

7. I hate those who regard lying vanities; but I trust in the Lord.

אָגִילָה וְאֶשְׂמְחָה בְּחַסְדֶּךָ אֲשֶׁר
I rejoice and I happy in your mercy which

רָאִיתָ אֶת־עָנְיִי יָדַעְתָּ בְּצָרוֹת נַפְשִׁי:
I saw my affliction – that you knew in distress my soul

8. I will be glad and rejoice in your loving kindness; for you have considered my affliction; you have known the troubles of my soul;

וְלֹא הִסְגַּרְתַּנִי בְּיַד־אוֹיֵב הֶעֱמַדְתָּ בַמֶּרְחָב רַגְלָי:
and not you locked up me enemy – in hand the you set in broad place my feet

9. And you have not delivered into the hand of the enemy; you have set my feet in a

broad place.

חָנֵּנִי יְהוָה כִּי צַר־לִי עָשְׁשָׁה בְכַעַס עֵינִי נַפְשִׁי וּבִטְנִי׃

and my body   my soul   my eye   in vexation   done   to me – distress   like   ihvh   be gracious

10. Be gracious to me, O Lord, for I am in distress; my eye is consumed with grief, my soul and my body.

כִּי כָלוּ בְיָגוֹן חַיַּי וּשְׁנוֹתַי בַּאֲנָחָה

in sighing   and my years   my life   in sorrow   consumed   like

כָּשַׁל בַּעֲוֹנִי כֹחִי וַעֲצָמַי עָשֵׁשׁוּ׃

waste away   and my bones   my strength   in my inequity   stumbled

11. For my life is spent with grief, and my years with sighing; my strength fails because of my iniquity, and my bones waste away.

מִכָּל־צֹרְרַי הָיִיתִי חֶרְפָּה וְלִשֲׁכֵנַי מְאֹד

greatly   and to my neighbors   reproach   I am   my adversaries   from all

וּפַחַד לִמְיֻדָּעָי רֹאַי בַּחוּץ נָדְדוּ מִמֶּנִּי׃

from me   they flee   in outside   see me   to my acquaintances   and dread

12. I am the scorn of all my enemies, and exceedingly of my neighbors, and a dread to my acquaintances; those who see me in the street flee from me.

נִשְׁכַּחְתִּי כְּמֵת מִלֵּב הָיִיתִי כִּכְלִי אֹבֵד׃

lost   like vessel   I am   from heart   as dead   I am forgotten

13. I am forgotten out of mind like one who is dead; I am like a broken vessel.

כִּי שָׁמַעְתִּי דִּבַּת רַבִּים מָגוֹר מִסָּבִיב בְּהִוָּסְדָם יַחַד עָלַי

upon me   together   in their conspiring   around   terror   many   muttering   I heard   like

לָקַחַת נַפְשִׁי זָמָמוּ׃

they schemed   my soul   to take

14. For I have heard the slander of many; fear was on every side; while they took counsel together against me, they schemed to take away my life.

וַאֲנִי עָלֶיךָ בָטַחְתִּי יְהוָה אָמַרְתִּי אֱלֹהַי אָתָּה׃

you   my Elohim   I said   ihvh   I confided   upon you   and I

15. But I trusted in you, O Lord; I said, You are my God.

בְּיָדְךָ עִתֹּתָי הַצִּילֵנִי מִיַּד־אוֹיְבַי וּמֵרֹדְפָי׃

and from my pursuers   my enemy - from hand   deliver me   my time   in your hand

16. My times are in your hand; save me from the hand of my enemies, and from those who persecute me.

הָאִירָה פָנֶיךָ עַל־עַבְדֶּךָ הוֹשִׁיעֵנִי בְחַסְדֶּךָ׃

in your kindness   save me   your servant – upon   your face   the shine

17. Let your face shine upon your servant; save me in your loving kindness.

יְהוָה אַל־אֵבוֹשָׁה כִּי קְרָאתִיךָ יֵבֹשׁוּ רְשָׁעִים יִדְּמוּ לִשְׁאוֹל׃

to Shoel   they silent   wicked   they ashamed   I called you   like   I be shamed - don't   ihvh

18. Let me not be ashamed, O Lord; for I have called on you; let the wicked be ashamed, and let them be silent in Sheol.

תֵּאָלַמְנָה שִׂפְתֵי שָׁקֶר הַדֹּבְרוֹת
the speaking ones   falsehood   lips   you will be muted

עַל־צַדִּיק עָתָק בְּגַאֲוָה וָבוּז׃
and contempt   in pride   arrogance   righteous - upon

19. Let the lying lips be put to silence; which speak insolent words, arrogantly and contemptuously against the righteous.

מָה רַב טוּבְךָ אֲשֶׁר־צָפַנְתָּ לִירֵאֶיךָ
to those who fear you   you hidden - which   your goodness   much   how

פָּעַלְתָּ לַחוֹסִים בָּךְ נֶגֶד בְּנֵי אָדָם׃
Adam   sons   before   in you   to ones seeking refuge   you act

20. Oh how great is your goodness, which you have laid up for those who fear you; which you have done for those who trust in you, in the sight of the sons of men!

תַּסְתִּירֵם בְּסֵתֶר פָּנֶיךָ מֵרֻכְסֵי אִישׁ תִּצְפְּנֵם
you hide them   man   from snares   your face   in concealment   you hide them

בְּסֻכָּה מֵרִיב לְשֹׁנוֹת׃
tongues   from strife   in pavilion

21. You hide them in the covert of your presence from the plots of men; you keep them secretly in a pavilion from the strife of tongues.

בָּרוּךְ יְהֹוָה כִּי־הִפְלִיא חַסְדּוֹ לִי בְּעִיר מָצוֹר׃
siege   in city   to me   his kindness   marvelous – like   ihvh   blessed

22. Blessed be the Lord; for he has marvelously shown me his loving kindness in a besieged city.

וַאֲנִי אָמַרְתִּי בְחָפְזִי נִגְרַזְתִּי מִנֶּגֶד עֵינֶיךָ
your eyes   from before   I axed   in my nervous haste   said   and I

אָכֵן שָׁמַעְתָּ קוֹל תַּחֲנוּנַי בְּשַׁוְּעִי אֵלֶיךָ׃
unto thee   in my crying   my supplications   voice   you heard   surely

23. For I said in my haste, I am cut off from before your eyes; nevertheless you heard the voice of my supplications when I cried to you.

אֶהֱבוּ אֶת־יְהֹוָה כָּל־חֲסִידָיו אֱמוּנִים
faithful ones   his pious – all   ihvh - that   you love

נֹצֵר יְהֹוָה וּמְשַׁלֵּם עַל־יֶתֶר עֹשֵׂה גַאֲוָה׃
pride   he does   surplus – upon   and from paying   ihvh   preserving

24. O love the Lord, all you his pious ones; for the Lord preserves the faithful, and plentifully repays him who acts arrogantly.

חִזְקוּ וְיַאֲמֵץ לְבַבְכֶם כָּל־הַמְיַחֲלִים לַיהֹוָה׃
to ihvh   the long hoping ones – all   your heart   and be valiant   be strong

25. Be of good courage, and let your heart be strong, all you who hope in the Lord.

Psalm 32

ספר תהילים פרק לב

לְדָוִד מַשְׂכִּיל אַשְׁרֵי נְשׂוּי־פֶּשַׁע כְּסוּי חֲטָאָה:
sin   covered transgression - forgiven happy Maskil to David

1. A Psalm of David, A Maskil. Happy is he whose transgression is forgiven, whose sin is covered.

אַשְׁרֵי אָדָם לֹא יַחְשֹׁב יְהוָֹה לוֹ עָוֹן וְאֵין בְּרוּחוֹ רְמִיָּה:
deceit in his spirit and isn't inequity to him ihvh he impute not Adam happy

2. Happy is the man to whom the Lord does not impute iniquity, and in whose spirit there is no guile.

כִּי הֶחֱרַשְׁתִּי בָּלוּ עֲצָמָי בְּשַׁאֲגָתִי כָּל־הַיּוֹם:
the day – all in my roaring my bones deteriorated the my silence like

3. When I kept silence, my bones wasted away through my groaning all day long.

כִּי יוֹמָם וָלַיְלָה תִּכְבַּד עָלַי יָדֶךָ
your hand upon me you heavy and night by day like

נֶהְפַּךְ לְשַׁדִּי בְּחַרְבֹנֵי קַיִץ סֶלָה:
Sela summer in my droughts my moisture changed

4. For day and night your hand was heavy on me; my moisture is turned into the drought of summer. Selah.

חַטָּאתִי אוֹדִיעֲךָ וַעֲוֹנִי לֹא־כִסִּיתִי
I covered – not and my inequity I acknowledge you my sin

אָמַרְתִּי אוֹדֶה עֲלֵי פְשָׁעַי לַיהוָֹה
to ihvh my transgressions upon me I will acknowledge I said

וְאַתָּה נָשָׂאתָ עֲוֹן חַטָּאתִי סֶלָה:
Sela my sin inequity forgave and you

5. I acknowledged my sin to you, and I did not hide my iniquity. I said, I will confess my transgressions to the Lord; and you forgave the iniquity of my sin. Selah.

עַל־זֹאת יִתְפַּלֵּל כָּל־חָסִיד אֵלֶיךָ לְעֵת מְצֹא
found to time unto you righteous – all he prays this - upon

רַק לְשֵׁטֶף מַיִם רַבִּים אֵלָיו לֹא יַגִּיעוּ:
they touch not unto him many ones waters to flood only

6. For this shall every one who is pious pray to you in a time when you may be found; then surely the floods of great waters shall not come near him.

אַתָּה סֵתֶר לִי מִצַּר תִּצְּרֵנִי
you preserve from distress to me hiding place you

רָנֵּי פַלֵּט תְּסוֹבְבֵנִי סֶלָה:
Sela you surround me deliverance my joy shouting

7. You are my hiding place; you shall preserve me from trouble; you shall surround me with songs of deliverance. Selah.

אַשְׂכִּילְךָ וְאוֹרְךָ בְּדֶרֶךְ־זוּ תֵלֵךְ אִיעֲצָה עָלֶיךָ עֵינִי׃

| my eyes | upon you | I will counsel | you walk | this – in way | and your direct | I will instruct you |

8. I will instruct you and teach you in the way which you shall go; I will counsel you with my eye upon you.

אַל־תִּהְיוּ כְּסוּס כְּפֶרֶד אֵין הָבִין

| the understanding | isn't | like mule | like horse | you be - don't |

בְּמֶתֶג וָרֶסֶן עֶדְיוֹ לִבְלוֹם בַּל קְרֹב אֵלֶיךָ׃

| unto you | near | without | to restrain | his ornament | and bridle | in bit |

9. Do not be like the horse, or like the mule, which have no understanding; whose mouth must be held in with bit and bridle, lest they do not come near you.

רַבִּים מַכְאוֹבִים לָרָשָׁע וְהַבּוֹטֵחַ בַּיהוָה חֶסֶד יְסוֹבְבֶנּוּ׃

| it surrounds him | kindness | in ihvh | and the truster | to wicked | sorrows | many ones |

10. Many are the sorrows of the wicked; but loving kindness shall surround him who trusts in the Lord.

שִׂמְחוּ בַיהוָה וְגִילוּ צַדִּיקִים וְהַרְנִינוּ כָּל־יִשְׁרֵי־לֵב׃

| heart – upright – all | and the joy shout | righteous ones | and you rejoice | in ihvh | you happy |

11. Be glad in the Lord, and rejoice, you righteous; and shout for joy, all you who are upright in heart.

PSALM 33

ספר תהילים פרק לג

רַנְּנוּ צַדִּיקִים֮ בַּיהוָ֥ה לַיְשָׁרִ֗ים נָאוָ֥ה תְהִלָּֽה׃
<small>prayer fitting to upright ones in ihvh righteous ones you joy shout</small>

1. Rejoice in the Lord, O you righteous; for praise befits the upright.

הוֹד֣וּ לַיהוָ֣ה בְּכִנּ֑וֹר בְּנֵ֥בֶל עָ֝שׂ֗וֹר זַמְּרוּ־לֽוֹ׃
<small>to him - sing psalms ten string in lyre in harp to ihvh you thank</small>

2. Praise the Lord with a lyre; make music to him with the harp of ten strings.

שִֽׁירוּ־ל֖וֹ שִׁ֣יר חָדָ֑שׁ הֵיטִ֥יבוּ נַ֝גֵּ֗ן בִּתְרוּעָֽה׃
<small>in alarm sounds play you be skillful new song to him you sing</small>

3. Sing to him a new song; play skillfully with loud shouts.

כִּֽי־יָשָׁ֥ר דְּבַר־יְהוָ֑ה וְכָל־מַ֝עֲשֵׂ֗הוּ בֶּאֱמוּנָֽה׃
<small>in faithfulness his works - and all ihvh – speakings upright - like</small>

4. For the word of the Lord is right; and all his works are done in faithfulness.

אֹ֭הֵב צְדָקָ֣ה וּמִשְׁפָּ֑ט חֶ֥סֶד יְ֝הוָ֗ה מָלְאָ֥ה הָאָֽרֶץ׃
<small>the earth full ihvh kindness and judgment righteousness lover</small>

5. He loves righteousness and judgment; the earth is full of the goodness of the Lord.

בִּדְבַ֣ר יְ֭הוָה שָׁמַ֣יִם נַעֲשׂ֑וּ וּבְר֥וּחַ פִּ֝֗יו כָּל־צְבָאָֽם׃
<small>their legions – all his mouth and in spirit made it heavens ihvh in speakings</small>

6. By the word of the Lord were the heavens made; and all the host of them by the breath of his mouth.

כֹּנֵ֣ס כַּ֭נֵּד מֵ֣י הַיָּ֑ם נֹתֵ֖ן בְּאֹצָר֣וֹת תְּהוֹמֽוֹת
<small>deepths in storehouses giver the sea water heap he gathers</small>

7. He gathers the waters of the sea together as a heap; he lays up the depths in storehouses.

יִֽירְא֣וּ מֵ֭יהוָה כָּל־הָאָ֑רֶץ מִמֶּ֥נּוּ יָ֝ג֗וּרוּ כָּל־יֹשְׁבֵ֥י תֵבֵֽל׃
<small>inhabited world dwelling – all they awe from me the earth – all from ihvh they will fear</small>

8. Let all the earth fear the Lord; let all the inhabitants of the world stand in awe of him.

כִּ֤י ה֣וּא אָמַ֣ר וַיֶּ֑הִי הֽוּא־צִוָּ֝֗ה וַֽיַּעֲמֹֽד׃
<small>and it stood commanded – he and it was said he like</small>

9. For he spoke, and it was done; he commanded, and it stood fast.

יְֽהוָ֗ה הֵפִ֥יר עֲצַת־גּוֹיִ֑ם הֵ֝נִ֗יא מַחְשְׁב֥וֹת עַמִּֽים׃
<small>peoples thoughts he frustrates nations counsel voids ihvh</small>

10. The Lord brings the counsel of the nations to naught; he frustrates the schemes of the people.

עֵצַת יְהוָה לְעוֹלָם תַּעֲמֹד מַחְשְׁבוֹת לִבּוֹ לְדֹר וָדֹר׃

and generation · to generation · his heart · thoughts · it stands · to forever · ihvh · counsel

11. The counsel of the Lord stands forever, the thoughts of his heart to all generations.

אַשְׁרֵי הַגּוֹי אֲשֶׁר־יְהוָה אֱלֹהָיו הָעָם בָּחַר לְנַחֲלָה לוֹ׃

to him · to inheritance · he chose · the people · its Elohim · ihvh – which · the nation · happy

12. Happy is the nation whose God is the Lord; and the people whom he has chosen for his own inheritance.

מִשָּׁמַיִם הִבִּיט יְהוָה רָאָה אֶת־כָּל־בְּנֵי הָאָדָם׃

the Adam · sons – all – that · he sees · ihvh · beheld · from heaven

13. The Lord looks down from heaven; he beholds all the sons of men.

מִמְּכוֹן־שִׁבְתּוֹ הִשְׁגִּיחַ אֶל כָּל־יֹשְׁבֵי הָאָרֶץ׃

the earth · dwellers – all · unto · he peers · his dwelling – from place

14. From the place of his habitation he looks upon all the inhabitants of the earth.

הַיֹּצֵר יַחַד לִבָּם הַמֵּבִין אֶל־כָּל־מַעֲשֵׂיהֶם׃

their deeds – all – unto · the understanding · their hearts · together · the former

15. He fashions their hearts alike; he considers all their deeds.

אֵין הַמֶּלֶךְ נוֹשָׁע בְּרָב־חָיִל גִּבּוֹר לֹא־יִנָּצֵל בְּרָב־כֹּחַ׃

power – in much · he rescued – not · mighty · army – in many · saved · the king · isn't

16. A king is not saved by a great army; a mighty man is not saved by great strength.

שֶׁקֶר הַסּוּס לִתְשׁוּעָה וּבְרֹב חֵילוֹ לֹא יְמַלֵּט׃

he will escape · not · his strength · and in much · to salvation · the horse · lie

17. A horse is a vain thing for safety; nor shall he save any by his great strength.

הִנֵּה עֵין יְהוָה אֶל־יְרֵאָיו לַמְיַחֲלִים לְחַסְדּוֹ׃

to his kindness · to hoping ones · his fearing – unto · ihvh · eye · here

18. Behold, the eye of the Lord is upon those who fear him, upon those who hope in his loving kindness;

לְהַצִּיל מִמָּוֶת נַפְשָׁם וּלְחַיּוֹתָם בָּרָעָב׃

in famine · and to sustain them · their soul · from death · to deliver

19. To save their soul from death, and to keep them alive in famine.

נַפְשֵׁנוּ חִכְּתָה לַיהוָה עֶזְרֵנוּ וּמָגִנֵּנוּ הוּא׃

he · and our shield · our help · to ihvh · wait · our souls

20. Our soul waits for the Lord; he is our help and our shield.

כִּי־בוֹ יִשְׂמַח לִבֵּנוּ כִּי בְשֵׁם קָדְשׁוֹ בָטָחְנוּ׃

we trusted · his holiness · in name · like · our hearts · will be happy · in him - like

21. For our heart shall rejoice in him, because we have trusted in his holy name.

יְהִי־חַסְדְּךָ יְהוָה עָלֵינוּ כַּאֲשֶׁר יִחַלְנוּ לָךְ׃

to you · we hoped · when · upon us · ihvh · your kindness - let be

22. Let your loving kindness, O Lord, be upon us, even as we hope in you.

Psalm 34

ספר תהילים פרק לד

לְדָוִד בְּשַׁנּוֹתוֹ אֶת־טַעְמוֹ לִפְנֵי אֲבִימֶלֶךְ וַיְגָרְשֵׁהוּ וַיֵּלַךְ:

| and he went | and he drove away him | Abimelech | before | his behavior – that | in his change | to David |

1. A Psalm of David, when he changed his behavior before Abimelech; who drove him away, and he departed.

אֲבָרְכָה אֶת־יְהוָה בְּכָל־עֵת תָּמִיד תְּהִלָּתוֹ בְּפִי:

| in my mouth | his praise | always | time – in all | ihvh – that | I will bless |

2. I will bless the Lord at all times; his praise shall continually be in my mouth.

בַּיהוָה תִּתְהַלֵּל נַפְשִׁי יִשְׁמְעוּ עֲנָוִים וְיִשְׂמָחוּ:

| and they happy | humble ones | they will hear | my soul | will pray | in ihvh |

3. My soul shall make her boast in the Lord; the humble shall hear of it, and be glad.

גַּדְּלוּ לַיהוָה אִתִּי וּנְרוֹמְמָה שְׁמוֹ יַחְדָּו:

| together | his name | and we exalt | with me | to ihvh | you magnify |

4. O magnify the Lord with me, and let us exalt his name together.

דָּרַשְׁתִּי אֶת־יְהוָה וְעָנָנִי וּמִכָּל־מְגוּרוֹתַי הִצִּילָנִי:

| he delivered me | my terrors – and from all | and he answered me | ihvh – that | I sought |

5. I sought the Lord, and he answered me, and saved me from all my fears.

הִבִּיטוּ אֵלָיו וְנָהָרוּ וּפְנֵיהֶם אַל־יֶחְפָּרוּ:

| will be ashamed – don't | and their faces | and were radiant | unto him | they looked |

6. They looked to him, and were radiant; and their faces shall not be ashamed.

זֶה עָנִי קָרָא וַיהוָה שָׁמֵעַ וּמִכָּל־צָרוֹתָיו הוֹשִׁיעוֹ:

| his savior | his troubles – and from all | hears | and ihvh | calls | poor man | this |

7. This poor man cried, and the Lord heard him, and saved him out of all his troubles.

חֹנֶה מַלְאַךְ־יְהוָה סָבִיב לִירֵאָיו וַיְחַלְּצֵם:

| and he delivered them | to his fearers | surround | ihvh – angel | encamping |

8. The angel of the Lord encamps around those who fear him, and saves them.

טַעֲמוּ וּרְאוּ כִּי־טוֹב יְהוָה אַשְׁרֵי הַגֶּבֶר יֶחֱסֶה־בּוֹ:

| in him - takes refuge | the gentlemen | happy | ihvh | good – like | and you see | you taste |

9. O taste and see that the Lord is good; happy is the man who trusts in him.

יְראוּ אֶת־יְהוָה קְדֹשָׁיו כִּי אֵין מַחְסוֹר לִירֵאָיו:

| to his fearers | from lack | isn't | like | his holy ones | ihvh – that | you fear |

10. O fear the Lord, you his pious ones; for those who fear him have no want.

כְּפִירִים רָשׁוּ וְרָעֵבוּ וְדֹרְשֵׁי יְהוָה לֹא־יַחְסְרוּ כָל־טוֹב:

| good - all | they will lack – not | ihvh | and seek | and hunger | suffering | like young lions |

11. The young lions suffer want and hunger; but those who seek the Lord shall not lack any good thing.

לְכוּ־בָנִים שִׁמְעוּ־לִי יִרְאַת יְהֹוָה אֲלַמֶּדְכֶם:
      I will teach you   ihvh   fear   to me – hear   sons – come

12. Come, you children, listen to me; I will teach you the fear of the Lord.

מִי־הָאִישׁ הֶחָפֵץ חַיִּים אֹהֵב יָמִים לִרְאוֹת טוֹב:
    good   to see   days   loves   life   the desire   the man - who

13. Who is the man who desires life, and loves many days, that he may see good?

נְצֹר לְשׁוֹנְךָ מֵרָע וּשְׂפָתֶיךָ מִדַּבֵּר מִרְמָה:
   deceit   from speaking   and your lips   from bad   your tongue   guard

14. Keep your tongue from evil, and your lips from speaking guile.

סוּר מֵרָע וַעֲשֵׂה־טוֹב בַּקֵּשׁ שָׁלוֹם וְרָדְפֵהוּ:
   and pursue it   peace   ask   good – and do   from bad   depart

15. Depart from evil, and do good; seek peace, and pursue it.

עֵינֵי יְהֹוָה אֶל־צַדִּיקִים וְאָזְנָיו אֶל־שַׁוְעָתָם:
   their cry – unto   and his ears   righteous – unto   ihvh   eyes

16. The eyes of the Lord are upon the righteous, and his ears are open to their cry.

פְּנֵי יְהֹוָה בְּעֹשֵׂי רָע לְהַכְרִית מֵאֶרֶץ זִכְרָם:
   their memory   from earth   to cut off   bad   in doing   ihvh   face

17. The face of the Lord is against those who do evil, to cut off their remembrance from the earth.

צָעֲקוּ וַיהֹוָה שָׁמֵעַ וּמִכָּל־צָרוֹתָם הִצִּילָם:
   he delivers them   troubles - and from all   heard   and ihvh   they cried

18. The righteous cry, and the Lord hears, and saves them out of all their troubles.

קָרוֹב יְהֹוָה לְנִשְׁבְּרֵי־לֵב וְאֶת־דַּכְּאֵי־רוּחַ יוֹשִׁיעַ:
   he saves   spirit – crushed – and that   heart – to broken   ihvh   near

19. The Lord is near to the broken hearted, and saves those of a contrite spirit.

רַבּוֹת רָעוֹת צַדִּיק וּמִכֻּלָּם יַצִּילֶנּוּ יְהֹוָה:
   ihvh   he delivers them   and from all them   righteous   evils   many

20. Many are the afflictions of the righteous; but the Lord saves him out of them all.

שֹׁמֵר כָּל־עַצְמוֹתָיו אַחַת מֵהֵנָּה לֹא נִשְׁבָּרָה:
   broken   not   from them   one   his bones – all   he heeds

21. He keeps all his bones; not one of them is broken.

תְּמוֹתֵת רָשָׁע רָעָה וְשֹׂנְאֵי צַדִּיק יֶאְשָׁמוּ:
   they will be condemned   righteous   and haters   evil   wicked   it killing blow

22. Evil shall slay the wicked; and those who hate the righteous shall be condemned.

פּוֹדֶה יְהֹוָה נֶפֶשׁ עֲבָדָיו וְלֹא יֶאְשְׁמוּ כָּל־הַחֹסִים בּוֹ:
   to him   the refuge ones - all   they condemned   and not   his servants   soul   ihvh   redeemer

23. The Lord redeems the soul of his servants; and none of those who trust in him shall be condemned.

PSALM 35

ספר תהילים פרק לה

לְדָוִד רִיבָה יְהֹוָה אֶת־יְרִיבַי לְחַם אֶת־לֹחֲמָי׃
implead me – that   to heat   my quarrellers - that   ihvh   fight   to David

1. A Psalm of David. Contend, O Lord, with those who contend with me; fight against those who fight against me.

הַחֲזֵק מָגֵן וְצִנָּה   וְקוּמָה בְּעֶזְרָתִי׃
in my help   and arise   and buckler   shield   hold fast

2. Take hold of shield and buckler, and stand up for my help.

וְהָרֵק חֲנִית וּסְגֹר לִקְרַאת רֹדְפָי
my persecutors   to meet   and come close   spear   and draw out

אֱמֹר לְנַפְשִׁי יְשֻׁעָתֵךְ אָנִי׃
I   your salvation   to my soul   say

3. Draw out also the spear and javelin against those who persecute me; say to my soul, I am your salvation.

יֵבֹשׁוּ   וְיִכָּלְמוּ   מְבַקְשֵׁי נַפְשִׁי
my soul   seekers   and they confounded   they ashamed

יִסֹּגוּ   אָחוֹר וְיַחְפְּרוּ חֹשְׁבֵי רָעָתִי׃
me evil   thinkers   and abashed   backward   they turned away

4. Let those who seek after my soul be confounded and put to shame, let those who scheme evil against me be turned back and brought to confusion.

יִהְיוּ כְּמֹץ לִפְנֵי־רוּחַ וּמַלְאַךְ יְהֹוָה דּוֹחֶה׃
chasing   ihvh   and angel   wind – before   like chaff   they be

5. Let them be as chaff before the wind; and let the angel of the Lord chase them.

יְהִי־דַרְכָּם חֹשֶׁךְ וַחֲלַקְלַקּוֹת וּמַלְאַךְ יְהֹוָה רֹדְפָם׃
pursuing them   ihvh   and angel   and slippery   darkness   their way - let be

6. Let their way be dark and slippery; and let the angel of the Lord pursue them.

כִּי־חִנָּם טָמְנוּ־לִי שַׁחַת רִשְׁתָּם חִנָּם חָפְרוּ לְנַפְשִׁי׃
to my soul   they bored   causelessly   their net   slough   to me – they hid   causelessly - like

7. For without cause they hid for me their net; without cause they dug a pit for my soul.

תְּבוֹאֵהוּ שׁוֹאָה לֹא יֵדָע
he know   not   desolation   it come to him

וְרִשְׁתּוֹ אֲשֶׁר־טָמַן תִּלְכְּדוֹ בְּשׁוֹאָה יִפָּל־בָּהּ׃
in it – he fall   in desolation   it his catch   he hid - which   and his net

8. Let destruction come upon him unawares; and let his net that he hid catch himself; into ruin let him fall.

וְנַפְשִׁי תָּגִיל בַּיהוָה תָּשִׂישׂ בִּישׁוּעָתוֹ:
and my soul — you rejoice — in ihvh — it will be joyful — in his salvation

9. And my soul shall be joyful in the Lord; it shall rejoice in his salvation.

כָּל עַצְמֹתַי תֹּאמַרְנָה יְהוָה מִי כָמוֹךָ מַצִּיל עָנִי מֵחָזָק מִמֶּנּוּ
all — my bones — will say now — ihvh — who — like you — delivering — poor — from strong — from he

וְעָנִי וְאֶבְיוֹן מִגֹּזְלוֹ:
and poor — and needy — from his spoils

10. All my bones shall say, Lord, who is like to you, who rescues the poor from him who is too strong for him; the poor and needy from him who robs him.

יְקוּמוּן עֵדֵי חָמָס אֲשֶׁר לֹא־יָדַעְתִּי יִשְׁאָלוּנִי:
they will rise — witnesses — violence — which — not - I know — they ask me

11. False witnesses rise up; they ask me of things that I know not.

יְשַׁלְּמוּנִי רָעָה תַּחַת טוֹבָה שְׁכוֹל לְנַפְשִׁי:
they pay to me — evil — instead — good — bereavement — to my soul

12. They repay me evil for good; a bereavement to my soul.
to my clothing in the sickness and I

וַאֲנִי בַּחֲלוֹתָם לְבוּשִׁי שָׂק עִנֵּיתִי בַצּוֹם נַפְשִׁי
and I — in their sickness — I dressed — sackcloth — I humbled — in fasting — my soul

וּתְפִלָּתִי עַל־חֵיקִי תָשׁוּב:
and my prayer — onto – my bosom — you return

13. But as for me, when they were sick, my clothing was sackcloth; I afflicted my soul with fasting; and as for my prayer may it return to my own bosom.

כְּרֵעַ כְּאָח־לִי הִתְהַלָּכְתִּי כַּאֲבֶל־אֵם קֹדֵר שַׁחוֹתִי:
like friend — like brother – to me — I behaved myself — mourning one – like mourning — mother - like — I bowed down

14. I behaved as though he had been my friend or brother; I bowed down heavily, as one who mourns for his mother.

וּבְצַלְעִי שָׂמְחוּ וְנֶאֱסָפוּ נֶאֶסְפוּ עָלַי נֵכִים
and in my halting — they were glad — and gathered — together — upon me — wretched ones

וְלֹא יָדַעְתִּי קָרְעוּ וְלֹא־דָמּוּ:
and not — I knew — they to me — were silent - and not

15. But when I stumbled they rejoiced, and gathered themselves together; Wretches whom I knew not tear me in pieces without ceasing.

בְּחַנְפֵי לַעֲגֵי מָעוֹג חָרֹק עָלַי שִׁנֵּימוֹ:
in profane — to mockers — cake — gnash — upon me — their teeth

16. Like profane men, scornful mockers, they gnashed at me with their teeth.

אֲדֹנָי כַּמָּה תִרְאֶה
Adoni — how long — you see

הָשִׁיבָה נַפְשִׁי מִשֹּׁאֵיהֶם מִכְּפִירִים יְחִידָתִי׃

| my only one | from young lions | their desolations | my soul | restore |

17. Lord, how long will you look on? Rescue my soul from their destructions, my only one from the lions.

אוֹדְךָ בְּקָהָל רָב בְּעַם עָצוּם אֲהַלְלֶךָּ׃

| I praise you | strong | in nation | much | in congregation | I give you thanks |

18. I will give you thanks in the great congregation; I will praise you among a great many people.

אַל־יִשְׂמְחוּ־לִי אֹיְבַי שֶׁקֶר שֹׂנְאַי חִנָּם יִקְרְצוּ־עָיִן׃

| eye – they wink | causelessly | haters of me | falsehood | my enemies | to me – they be happy - don't |

19. Let not those who are my enemies wrongfully rejoice over me; nor let those who hate me without cause wink their eye.

כִּי לֹא שָׁלוֹם יְדַבֵּרוּ וְעַל רִגְעֵי־אֶרֶץ דִּבְרֵי מִרְמוֹת יַחֲשֹׁבוּן׃

| they devise | deceits | words | earth - lulled | and upon | they speak | peace | not | like |

20. For they do not speak peace; but they plot deceitful schemes against those who are quiet in the land.

וַיַּרְחִיבוּ עָלַי פִּיהֶם אָמְרוּ הֶאָח הֶאָח רָאֲתָה עֵינֵינוּ׃

| our eyes | have seen | aha | aha | they said | their mouth | upon me | and they widened |

21. They opened their mouth wide against me, and said, Aha, aha! Our eye has seen it!

רָאִיתָה יְהוָה אַל־תֶּחֱרַשׁ אֲדֹנָי אַל־תִּרְחַק מִמֶּנִּי׃

| from me | be far – don't | Adoni | be silent - don't | ihvh | you saw |

22. This you have seen, O Lord; do not be silent; O Lord, do not be far from me.

הָעִירָה וְהָקִיצָה לְמִשְׁפָּטִי אֱלֹהַי וַאדֹנָי לְרִיבִי׃

| to my cause | and Adoni | my Elohim | to judgment | and wake | the arouse |

23. Bestir yourself, and awake to my judgment, to my cause, my God and my Lord.

שָׁפְטֵנִי כְצִדְקְךָ יְהוָה אֱלֹהָי וְאַל־יִשְׂמְחוּ־לִי׃

| to me - they be happy - and don't | my Elohim | ihvh | like your righteousness | judge me |

24. Judge me, O Lord my God, according to your righteousness; and do not let them rejoice over me.

אַל־יֹאמְרוּ בְלִבָּם הֶאָח נַפְשֵׁנוּ אַל־יֹאמְרוּ בִּלַּעֲנוּהוּ׃

| we swallowed up him | they say – don't | our soul | the ah | in their hearts | they say – don't |

25. Do not let them say in their hearts, Aha, we have our heart's desire! Do not let them say, We have swallowed him up!

יֵבֹשׁוּ וְיַחְפְּרוּ יַחְדָּו שְׂמֵחֵי רָעָתִי יִלְבְּשׁוּ־בֹשֶׁת

| in shame – they clothed | my evils | happy ones | together | and disgraced | they be ashamed |

וּכְלִמָּה הַמַּגְדִּילִים עָלָי׃

| upon me | the magnifying ones | and dishonor |

26. Let those who rejoice at my calamity be ashamed and brought to confusion; let those who magnify themselves against me be clothed with shame and dishonor.

יָרֹנּוּ　　וְיִשְׂמְחוּ　　חֲפֵצֵי　　צִדְקִי　　וְיֹאמְרוּ　תָמִיד
they joy shout　and they happy　delighting　my righteousness　and they say　continually

יִגְדַּל　יְהֹוָה　הֶחָפֵץ　שְׁלוֹם　עַבְדּוֹ׃
be magnified　ihvh　the delights　peace　his servant

27. Let those who favor my righteous cause shout for joy, and be glad; let them say
continually, Let the Lord be magnified, who delights in the prosperity of his servant.

וּלְשׁוֹנִי　תֶהְגֶּה　צִדְקֶךָ　כָּל־הַיּוֹם　תְּהִלָּתֶךָ׃
and my tongue　it will tell　your righteousness　all – the day　your praise

28. And my tongue shall speak of your righteousness and of your praise all the day long.

Psalm 36

ספר תהילים פרק לו

לַמְנַצֵּחַ   לְעֶבֶד־יְהוָה לְדָוִד׃

to David   ihvh – to servant   to him that is over

1. To the chief Musician, A Psalm of David the servant of the Lord.

נְאֻם־פֶּשַׁע   לָרָשָׁע בְּקֶרֶב לִבִּי אֵין־פַּחַד אֱלֹהִים לְנֶגֶד עֵינָיו׃

his eyes   before   Elohim   fear –isn't   my heart   in near   to wicked   transgression - states

2. Transgression speaks to the wicked in his heart, there is no fear of God before his eyes.

כִּי־הֶחֱלִיק אֵלָיו בְּעֵינָיו לִמְצֹא עֲוֺנוֹ לִשְׂנֹא׃

to hate   his inequity   to find   in his eyes   unto him   he flattered - like

3. For he flatters himself in his own eyes, that his iniquity cannot be found and hated.

דִּבְרֵי־פִיו   אָוֶן   וּמִרְמָה חָדַל לְהַשְׂכִּיל   לְהֵיטִיב׃

to the better   to the intelligent   ceased   and deceit   iniquity   his mouth - speakings

4. The words of his mouth are iniquity and deceit; he has ceased to act wisely, and to do good.

אָוֶן   יַחְשֹׁב עַל־מִשְׁכָּבוֹ יִתְיַצֵּב עַל־דֶּרֶךְ לֹא־טוֹב

good – not   way - upon   he sets himself   his bed – upon   he devises   inequity

רָע לֹא יִמְאָס׃

he loathes   not   evil

5. He plots mischief while on his bed; he sets himself in a way that is not good; he does not loathe evil.

יְהוָה בְּהַשָּׁמַיִם חַסְדֶּךָ   אֱמוּנָתְךָ עַד־שְׁחָקִים׃

clouds – till   your faithfulness   your kindness   in the heavens   ihvh

6. Your loving kindness, O Lord, is in the heavens; and your faithfulness reaches to the clouds.

צִדְקָתְךָ   כְּהַרְרֵי־אֵל מִשְׁפָּטֶךָ תְּהוֹם

depth   your judgments   El – like mountains   your righteousness

רַבָּה אָדָם וּבְהֵמָה תּוֹשִׁיעַ יְהוָה׃

ihvh   you save   and beast   Adon   much

7. Your righteousness is like the great mountains; your judgments are a great deep; O Lord, you preserve man and beast.

מַה־יָּקָר חַסְדְּךָ אֱלֹהִים וּבְנֵי אָדָם בְּצֵל כְּנָפֶיךָ יֶחֱסָיוּן׃

takes refuge   your wings   in shade   Adam   and sons   Elohim   your mercy   precious - how

8. How excellent is your loving kindness, O God! Therefore the children of men take refuge under the shadow of your wings.

יִרְוְיֻן   מִדֶּשֶׁן   בֵּיתֶךָ   וְנַחַל   עֲדָנֶיךָ   תַשְׁקֵם:

they will be satisfied   with fatness   your house   and stream   your luxuries   you make them drink

9. They shall be abundantly satisfied with the fatness of your house; and you shall make them drink of the river of your pleasures.

כִּי־עִמְּךָ   מְקוֹר   חַיִּים   בְּאוֹרְךָ   נִרְאֶה־אוֹר:

like - with you   fountain   life   in your light   we will see - light

10. For with you is the fountain of life; in your light shall we see light.

מְשֹׁךְ   חַסְדְּךָ   לְיֹדְעֶיךָ   וְצִדְקָתְךָ   לְיִשְׁרֵי־לֵב:

prolong   your kindness   to your knowers   and your righteous   to upright - heart

11. O continue your loving kindness to those who know you; and your righteousness to the upright in heart.

אַל־תְּבוֹאֵנִי   רֶגֶל   גַּאֲוָה   וְיַד־רְשָׁעִים   אַל־תְּנִדֵנִי:

don't - bring my   foot   proud   and hand - wicked ones   don't - drive me away

12. Let not the foot of arrogance come against me, and let not the hand of the wicked drive me away.

שָׁם   נָפְלוּ   פֹּעֲלֵי   אָוֶן   דֹּחוּ   וְלֹא־יָכְלוּ   קוּם:

there   they fell   workers   iniquity   they thrust down   and not - able   rise

13. There are the evil doers fallen; they are cast down, and are not able to rise.

Psalm 37

ספר תהילים פרק לז

לְדָוִד אַל־תִּתְחַר בַּמְּרֵעִים אַל־תְּקַנֵּא בְּעֹשֵׂי עַוְלָה:

inequity | in workers | be jealous – don't | in wickedness | fret yourself - don't | to David

1. A Psalm of David. Do not fret because of the wicked, nor be envious against the evil doers.

כִּי כֶחָצִיר מְהֵרָה יִמָּלוּ וּכְיֶרֶק דֶּשֶׁא יִבּוֹלוּן:

they wither | vegetation | and like green | they fade | speedily | like grass | like

2. For they shall soon be cut down like the grass, and wither like the green herb.

בְּטַח בַּיהֹוָה וַעֲשֵׂה־טוֹב שְׁכָן־אֶרֶץ וּרְעֵה אֱמוּנָה:

faithfulness | and see | land - dwell | good – and do | in ihvh | trust

3. Trust in the Lord, and do good; so shall you dwell in the land, and enjoy security.

וְהִתְעַנַּג עַל־יְיָהֹוָה וְיִתֶּן־לְךָ מִשְׁאֲלֹת לִבֶּךָ:

your heart | requests | to you - and he give | ihvh – upon | and celebrate

4. Delight yourself also in the Lord; and he shall give you the desires of your heart.

גּוֹל עַל־יְיָהֹוָה דַּרְכֶּךָ וּבְטַח עָלָיו וְהוּא יַעֲשֶׂה:

will do | and he | upon him | and trust | your way | ihvh – upon | roll

5. Commit your way to the Lord; trust also in him; and he shall bring it to pass.

וְהוֹצִיא כָאוֹר צִדְקֶךָ וּמִשְׁפָּטֶךָ כַּצָּהֳרָיִם:

like noon | and your judgment | your righteousness | like light | and he will bring out

6. And he shall bring forth your righteousness like the light, and your judgment like the noonday.

דּוֹם לַיהֹוָה וְהִתְחוֹלֵל לוֹ

to him | and wait patiently | to ihvh | be silent

אַל־תִּתְחַר בְּמַצְלִיחַ דַּרְכּוֹ בְּאִישׁ עֹשֶׂה מְזִמּוֹת:

schemes | doing | in man | his way | in prospering | you be hot – don't

7. Rest in the Lord, and wait patiently for him; do not fret yourself over him who prospers in his way, over the man who carries out evil schemes.

הֶרֶף מֵאַף וַעֲזֹב חֵמָה אַל־תִּתְחַר אַךְ־לְהָרֵעַ:

to the evil - only | you fret - don't | wrath | and forsake | from anger | cease

8. Cease from anger, and forsake wrath; do not fret yourself; it comes only to evil.

כִּי־מְרֵעִים יִכָּרֵתוּן וְקֹוֵי יְהֹוָה הֵמָּה יִירְשׁוּ־אָרֶץ:

earth - they will inherit | they are | ihvh | and waiters | he will be cut off | wicked ones - like

9. For evil doers shall be cut off; but those who wait upon the Lord shall inherit the earth.

וְעוֹד מְעַט וְאֵין רָשָׁע וְהִתְבּוֹנַנְתָּ עַל־מְקוֹמוֹ וְאֵינֶנּוּ:

and isn't | his place - upon | and you consider | wicked | and isn't | little | and still

10. For yet a little while, and the wicked shall not be; though you look well at his place, he will not be there.

וַעֲנָוִים יִירְשׁוּ־אָרֶץ וְהִתְעַנְּגוּ עַל־רֹב שָׁלוֹם:

peace   much - upon   and will celebrate   earth - will inherit   and humble

11. But the humble shall inherit the earth; and shall delight themselves in the abundance of peace.

זֹמֵם רָשָׁע לַצַּדִּיק וְחֹרֵק עָלָיו שִׁנָּיו:

his teeth   upon him   and gnashing   to righteous   wicked   plotting

12. The wicked plots against the just, and gnashes at him with his teeth.

אֲדֹנָי יִשְׂחַק־לוֹ כִּי־רָאָה כִּי־יָבֹא יוֹמוֹ:

his day   he come – like   he sees – like   to him - he will laugh   Adoni

13. The Lord shall laugh at him; for he sees that his day is coming.

חֶרֶב פָּתְחוּ רְשָׁעִים וְדָרְכוּ קַשְׁתָּם

their bow   and bent   wicked ones   drawn   sword

לְהַפִּיל עָנִי וְאֶבְיוֹן לִטְבוֹחַ יִשְׁרֵי־דָרֶךְ:

ways – upright   to slay   and needy   poor   to the fall

14. The wicked have drawn out the sword, and have bent their bow, to bring down the poor and needy, and to slay those who are of upright ways.

חַרְבָּם תָּבוֹא בְלִבָּם וְקַשְּׁתוֹתָם תִּשָּׁבַרְנָה:

will be broken   and their bows   in their hearts   will come   their sword

15. Their sword shall enter into their own heart, and their bows shall be broken.

טוֹב מְעַט לַצַּדִּיק מֵהֲמוֹן רְשָׁעִים רַבִּים:

many   wicked ones   from crowd   to righteous   little   good

16. A little that a righteous man has is better than the riches of many wicked men.

כִּי זְרוֹעוֹת רְשָׁעִים תִּשָּׁבַרְנָה וְסוֹמֵךְ צַדִּיקִים יְהֹוָה:

ihvh   righteous ones   and holding   will be broken   wicked ones   arms   like

17. For the arms of the wicked shall be broken; but the Lord upholds the righteous.

יוֹדֵעַ יְהֹוָה יְמֵי תְמִימִם וְנַחֲלָתָם לְעוֹלָם תִּהְיֶה:

it will be   to forever   and their inheritance   perfect   days   ihvh   knows

18. The Lord knows the days of the upright; and their inheritance shall be forever.

לֹא־יֵבֹשׁוּ בְּעֵת רָעָה וּבִימֵי רְעָבוֹן יִשְׂבָּעוּ:

they will be satisfied   famine   and in days   bad   in season   they ashamed – not

19. They shall not be ashamed in the evil time; and in the days of famine they shall be satisfied.

כִּי רְשָׁעִים יֹאבֵדוּ וְאֹיְבֵי יְהֹוָה

ihvh   and enemies   they perish   wicked ones   like

כִּיקַר כָּרִים כָּלוּ בֶעָשָׁן כָּלוּ:

they consumed   in smoke   they consumed   pastures   like precious

20. But the wicked shall perish; the enemies of the Lord are like the glory of the meadows; they shall be consumed; they shall pass away like smoke.

לֹוֶה רָשָׁע וְלֹא יְשַׁלֵּם וְצַדִּיק חֹונֵן וְנֹותֵן:

and giver   gracious   and righteous   he pay   and not   wicked   borrows

21. The wicked borrows, and does not pay back; but the righteous man gives with good loving kindness.

כִּי מְבֹרָכָיו יִירְשׁוּ אָרֶץ וּמְקֻלָּלָיו יִכָּרֵתוּ:

they will be cut off   and his cursing ones   earth   they will inherit   from his blessed   like

22. For those blessed by him shall inherit the earth; and those cursed by him shall be cut off.

מֵיְהֹוָה מִצְעֲדֵי־גֶבֶר כֹּונָנוּ וְדַרְכֹּו יֶחְפָּץ:

he delights   and his way   established   gentlemen - steps   from ihvh

23. The steps of a good man are ordered by the Lord; and he delights in his way.

כִּי־יִפֹּל לֹא־יוּטָל כִּי־יְהֹוָה סֹומֵךְ יָדֹו:

his hard   upholds   ihvh - like   he cast forth - not   he fall - like

24. Though he fall, he shall not be utterly cast down; for the Lord upholds him with his hand.

נַעַר הָיִיתִי גַּם־זָקַנְתִּי וְלֹא־רָאִיתִי צַדִּיק נֶעֱזָב

forsaken   righteous   I seen – and not   I old man – also   I was   youth

וְזַרְעֹו מְבַקֶּשׁ־לָחֶם:

bread – seeking   and his seed

25. I have been young, and I am now old; yet have I not seen the righteous forsaken, nor his seed begging bread.

כָּל־הַיֹּום חֹונֵן וּמַלְוֶה וְזַרְעֹו לִבְרָכָה:

to blessed   and his seed   and obligating   gracious   the day - all

26. He lends generously at all times; and his seed is blessed.

סוּר מֵרָע וַעֲשֵׂה־טֹוב וּשְׁכֹן לְעֹולָם:

forever   and dwell   good - and do   from bad   depart

27. Depart from evil, and do good; and you shall abide for ever.

כִּי יְהֹוָה אֹהֵב מִשְׁפָּט

judgment   loves   ihvh   like

וְלֹא־יַעֲזֹב אֶת־חֲסִידָיו לְעֹולָם נִשְׁמָרוּ

they heeded   forever   his devoted – that   he forsake - and not

וְזֶרַע רְשָׁעִים נִכְרָת:

will be cut off   wicked ones   and seed

28. For the Lord loves justice, and does not forsake his pious ones; they are preserved for ever; but the seed of the wicked shall be cut off.

צַדִּיקִים יִירְשׁוּ־אָרֶץ וְיִשְׁכְּנוּ לָעַד עָלֶיהָ׃

upon it   to time   and they dwell   earth – will inherit   righteous ones

29. The righteous shall inherit the land, and dwell in it for ever.

פִּי־צַדִּיק יֶהְגֶּה חָכְמָה וּלְשׁוֹנוֹ תְּדַבֵּר מִשְׁפָּט׃

judgment   it speaks   and his tongue   wisdom   he portends   righteous - mouth

30. The mouth of the righteous speaks wisdom, and his tongue talks of justice.

תּוֹרַת אֱלֹהָיו בְּלִבּוֹ לֹא תִמְעַד אֲשֻׁרָיו׃

his progress   it teeeter   not   in his heart   his Elohim   Torah

31. The Torah of his God is in his heart; none of his steps shall falter.

צוֹפֶה רָשָׁע לַצַּדִּיק וּמְבַקֵּשׁ לַהֲמִיתוֹ׃

to the his slay   and seeks   to righteous   wicked   watcher

32. The wicked man watches the righteous, and seeks to slay him.

יְהוָה לֹא־יַעַזְבֶנּוּ בְיָדוֹ וְלֹא יַרְשִׁיעֶנּוּ בְּהִשָּׁפְטוֹ׃

in his judgment   they condemn   and not   in his hand   he leave him – not   ihvh

33. The Lord will not abandon him to his own hand, nor let him be condemned when he is brought to trial.

קַוֵּה אֶל־יְהוָה וּשְׁמֹר דַּרְכּוֹ

his way   and heed   ihvh – unto   wait

וִירוֹמִמְךָ לָרֶשֶׁת אָרֶץ בְּהִכָּרֵת רְשָׁעִים תִּרְאֶה׃

you will see   wicked ones   in cutting off   earth   to inherit   and he will exalt you

34. Wait on the Lord, and keep his way, and he shall exalt you to inherit the land; when the wicked are cut off, you shall see it.

רָאִיתִי רָשָׁע עָרִיץ וּמִתְעָרֶה כְּאֶזְרָח רַעֲנָן׃

flourishing   like native tree   and spreading himself   ruthless   wicked   I saw

35. I have seen the wicked in great power, and spreading himself like a green tree.

וַיַּעֲבֹר וְהִנֵּה אֵינֶנּוּ וָאֲבַקְשֵׁהוּ וְלֹא נִמְצָא׃

he found   and not   and I sought   they not   and here   and he passed

36. Yet he passed away, and, behold, he was not; I sought him, but he could not be found.

שְׁמָר־תָּם וּרְאֵה יָשָׁר כִּי־אַחֲרִית לְאִישׁ שָׁלוֹם׃

peace   to man   afterwards – like   upright   and see   perfect one - heed

37. Mark the perfect man, and behold the upright; for the end of that man is peace.

וּפֹשְׁעִים נִשְׁמְדוּ יַחְדָּו אַחֲרִית רְשָׁעִים נִכְרָתָה׃

will be cut off   wicked ones   afterwards   together   destroyed   transgressor ones

38. But the transgressors shall be destroyed together; the descendants of the wicked shall be cut off.

וּתְשׁוּעַת צַדִּיקִים מֵיְהוָה מָעוּזָּם בְּעֵת צָרָה׃

distress   in season   their refuge   from ihvh   righteous ones   and salvation

39. And the salvation of the righteous is of the Lord; he is their strength in the time of trouble.

וַיַּעְזְרֵם יְהוָה וַיְפַלְּטֵם יְפַלְּטֵם מֵרְשָׁעִים
from wicked ones · and he deliver them · and he delivered them · ihvh · and helped them

וְיוֹשִׁיעֵם כִּי חָסוּ בוֹ:
in him · they refuge · like · and he saves them

40. And the Lord shall help them, and rescue them; he shall rescue them from the wicked, and save them, because they take refuge in him.

PSALM 38

ספר תהילים פרק לח

מִזְמוֹר לְדָוִד לְהַזְכִּיר:

psalm   to David   to the remembering

1. A Psalm of David, to bring to remembrance.

יְהוָה אַל־בְּקֶצְפְּךָ תוֹכִיחֵנִי וּבַחֲמָתְךָ תְיַסְּרֵנִי:

ihvh   in your rage - don't   you rebuke me   and in your wrath   you chasten me

2. O Lord, rebuke me not in your anger; nor chasten me in your wrath.

כִּי־חִצֶּיךָ נִחֲתוּ־בִי וַתִּנְחַת עָלַי יָדֶךָ:

your arrows - like   have settled – in me   and presses   upon me   your hand

3. For your arrows stick fast in me, and your hand presses me hard.

אֵין־מְתֹם בִּבְשָׂרִי מִפְּנֵי זַעְמֶךָ אֵין־שָׁלוֹם

בַּעֲצָמַי מִפְּנֵי חַטָּאתִי:

soundness – isn't   in my flesh   from my face   your indignation   peace – isn't

in my bones   from my face   my sin

4. There is no soundness in my flesh because of your anger; nor is there any rest in my bones because of my sin.

כִּי־עֲוֹנֹתַי עָבְרוּ רֹאשִׁי כְּמַשָּׂא כָבֵד יִכְבְּדוּ מִמֶּנִּי:

my iniquities - like   they passed over   my head   like burden   heavy   they heavy   from me

5. For my iniquities have gone over my head; like a heavy burden they are too heavy for me.

הִבְאִישׁוּ נָמַקּוּ חַבּוּרֹתָי מִפְּנֵי אִוַּלְתִּי:

they stink   and they festered   my wounds   from my face   my foolishness

6. My wounds grow foul and fester because of my foolishness.

נַעֲוֵיתִי שַׁחֹתִי עַד־מְאֹד כָּל־הַיּוֹם קֹדֵר הִלָּכְתִּי:

I am depraved   I bowed   till – again   all – the day   mourning   I walk

7. I am troubled; I am bowed down greatly; I go mourning all the day long.

כִּי־כְסָלַי מָלְאוּ נִקְלֶה וְאֵין מְתֹם בִּבְשָׂרִי:

my loins - like   they full   burning   and isn't   soundness   in my flesh

8. For my loins are filled with burning; and there is no soundness in my flesh.

נְפוּגֹתִי וְנִדְכֵּיתִי עַד־מְאֹד שָׁאַגְתִּי מִנַּהֲמַת לִבִּי:

I feeble   and crushed   till – again   I roar   from anguish   my heart

9. I am feeble and crushed; I groan because of the tumult of my heart.

אֲדֹנָי נֶגְדְּךָ כָל־תַּאֲוָתִי וְאַנְחָתִי מִמְּךָ לֹא־נִסְתָּרָה:

Adoni   before you   my desire – all   and my sighing   from you   not – hidden

10. Lord, all my desire is before you; and my sighing is not hidden from you.

לִבִּי סְחַרְחַר עֲזָבַנִי כֹחִי וְאוֹר עֵינַי גַּם־הֵם אֵין אִתִּי׃

<small>with me   isn't   them – also   my eyes   and light   my strength   forsaken me   throbs   my heart</small>

11. My heart throbs, my strength fails me; as for the light of my eyes, it also is gone from me.

אֹהֲבַי וְרֵעַי מִנֶּגֶד נִגְעִי יַעֲמֹדוּ וּקְרוֹבַי מֵרָחֹק עָמָדוּ׃

<small>they stand   from far   and my close ones   they stand   my plague   aloof   and my neighbors   my loved ones</small>

12. My lovers and my friends stand aloof from my plague; and my kinsmen stand far away.

וַיְנַקְשׁוּ מְבַקְשֵׁי נַפְשִׁי וְדֹרְשֵׁי רָעָתִי דִּבְּרוּ הַוּוֹת

<small>destruction   they speak   my evil   and seekers   my soul   seekers   and they laid snares</small>

וּמִרְמוֹת כָּל־הַיּוֹם יֶהְגּוּ׃

<small>they mumble   the day – all   and deceits</small>

13. Those who seek after my life lay snares for me; and those who seek my hurt speak mischievous things, and plot deceits all the day long.

וַאֲנִי כְחֵרֵשׁ לֹא אֶשְׁמָע וּכְאִלֵּם לֹא יִפְתַּח־פִּיו׃

<small>his mouth – he open   not   and like mute   I hear   not   like deaf man   and I</small>

14. But I am like a deaf man who does not hear; I am like a dumb man who does not open his mouth.

וָאֱהִי כְּאִישׁ אֲשֶׁר לֹא־שֹׁמֵעַ וְאֵין בְּפִיו תּוֹכָחוֹת׃

<small>rebukes   in his mouth   and isn't   hears – not   who   like man   and I was</small>

15. Thus I was like a man who does not hear, and in whose mouth there are no rebukes.

כִּי־לְךָ יְהוָה הוֹחָלְתִּי אַתָּה תַעֲנֶה אֲדֹנָי אֱלֹהָי׃

<small>my Elohim   Adoni   you will answer   you   I hoped   ihvh   to you - like</small>

16. For in you, O Lord, I hope; you will answer, O Lord my God.

כִּי־אָמַרְתִּי פֶּן־יִשְׂמְחוּ־לִי בְּמוֹט רַגְלִי עָלַי הִגְדִּילוּ׃

<small>they magnify themselves   upon me   my foot   in slipping   to me – they be glad – lest   I said - like</small>

17. For I said, Lest they should rejoice over me; when my foot slips, they magnify themselves against me.

כִּי־אֲנִי לְצֶלַע נָכוֹן וּמַכְאוֹבִי נֶגְדִּי תָמִיד׃

<small>continually   before me   and my pain   prepared   to limp   I - like</small>

18. For I am ready to fall, and my pain is continually before me.

כִּי־עֲוֹנִי אַגִּיד אֶדְאַג מֵחַטָּאתִי׃

<small>from my sin   I anxious   I declare   my iniquity - like</small>

19. For I will declare my iniquity; I will be sorry for my sin.

וְאֹיְבַי חַיִּים עָצֵמוּ וְרַבּוּ שֹׂנְאַי שָׁקֶר׃

<small>lie   my haters   and multiplied   strong   life   and my enemies</small>

20. But my living enemies are strong; and those who hate me wrongfully are many.

וּמְשַׁלְּמֵי רָעָה תַּחַת טוֹבָה יִשְׂטְנוּנִי
and from my peace   evil   instead   good   oppose me

תַּחַת רְדוֹפִי [רָדְפִי] ־טוֹב׃
instead   I pursue   good -

21. (K) Those who render me evil for good are my adversaries because I follow after good.

אַל־תַּעַזְבֵנִי יְהֹוָה אֱלֹהַי אַל־תִּרְחַק מִמֶּנִּי׃
forsake me – don't   ihvh   my Elohim   be far – don't   from me

22. Do not forsake me, O Lord! O my God, do not be far from me!

חוּשָׁה לְעֶזְרָתִי אֲדֹנָי תְּשׁוּעָתִי׃
haste   to my help   Adoni   my salvation

23. Make haste to help me, O Lord my salvation!

PSALM 39

ספר תהילים פרק לט

לַמְנַצֵּחַ לִידִיתוּן [לִידוּתוּן] מִזְמוֹר לְדָוִד׃

to David — Psalm — to Juduthun — to one directing

1. (K) To the chief Musician, to Jeduthun, A Psalm of David.

אָמַרְתִּי אֶשְׁמְרָה דְרָכַי מֵחֲטוֹא בִלְשׁוֹנִי אֶשְׁמְרָה

I will heed — in my tongue — from sin — my ways — I will heed — I said

לְפִי מַחְסוֹם בְּעֹד רָשָׁע לְנֶגְדִּי׃

to before me — wicked — in still — muzzle — my mouth

2. I said, I will take heed to my ways, so that I should not sin with my tongue; I will muzzle my mouth, while the wicked man is before me.

נֶאֱלַמְתִּי דוּמִיָּה הֶחֱשֵׁיתִי מִטּוֹב וּכְאֵבִי נֶעְכָּר׃

he increased — and my pain — from good — the held my peace — silent — I was mute

3. I was dumb with silence, I held my peace, had no comfort, and my pain was stirred up.

חַם־לִבִּי בְּקִרְבִּי בַּהֲגִיגִי תִבְעַר־אֵשׁ דִּבַּרְתִּי בִלְשׁוֹנִי׃

in my tongue — I spoke — fire – it burned — in my meditation — in my inside — my heart - hot

4. My heart was hot within me; while I was musing the fire burned; then I spoke with my tongue,

הוֹדִיעֵנִי יְהוָה קִצִּי וּמִדַּת יָמַי

my days — and measure — my end — ihvh — let me know

מֶה־הִיא אֵדְעָה מֶה־חָדֵל אָנִי׃

I — fleeting - what — I know — it - what

5. Lord, let me know my end, and the measure of my days, what it is; that I may know how frail I am.

הִנֵּה טְפָחוֹת נָתַתָּה יָמַי וְחֶלְדִּי כְאַיִן נֶגְדֶּךָ

before you — like isn't — and my span — my days — you gave — hand breaths — here

אַךְ־כָּל־הֶבֶל כָּל־אָדָם נִצָּב סֶלָה׃

Sela — he stationed — Adam - all — vanity – all - then

6. Behold, you have made my days like handbreadths; and my age is nothing before you; truly every man at his best state is altogether vanity. Selah.

אַךְ־בְּצֶלֶם יִתְהַלֶּךְ־אִישׁ אַךְ־הֶבֶל יֶהֱמָיוּן יִצְבֹּר

he heaps up — they bustle about — vanity – then — man – he walks — in image - then

וְלֹא־יֵדַע מִי־אֹסְפָם׃

one gathering them – who — he knows - and not

7. Surely every man walks in a vain show; surely they are disquieted in vain; he heaps up riches, and does not know who shall gather them.

וְעַתָּה מַה־קִּוִּיתִי אֲדֹנָי תּוֹחַלְתִּי לְךָ הִיא:

it   to you   you my hope   Adoni   I wait - what   and now

8. And now, Lord, for what do I wait? My hope is in you.

מִכָּל־פְּשָׁעַי הַצִּילֵנִי חֶרְפַּת נָבָל אַל־תְּשִׂימֵנִי:

you make me - don't   food   scorn   save me   my transgression – from all

9. Save me from all my transgressions; do not make me the scorn of the villain.

נֶאֱלַמְתִּי לֹא אֶפְתַּח־פִּי כִּי אַתָּה עָשִׂיתָ:

did   you   like   my mouth – opened   not   I mute

10. I am dumb, I do not open my mouth; because it is you who did it.

הָסֵר מֵעָלַי נִגְעֶךָ מִתִּגְרַת יָדְךָ אֲנִי כָלִיתִי:

I consumed   I   your hand   from blow   your scourge   from upon me   remove

11. Remove your stroke away from me; I am consumed by the blow of your hand.

בְּתוֹכָחוֹת עַל־עָוֹן יִסַּרְתָּ אִישׁ

man   you discipline   iniquity – upon   in rebukes

וַתֶּמֶס כָּעָשׁ חֲמוּדוֹ אַךְ הֶבֶל כָּל־אָדָם סֶלָה:

Sela   Adam – all   vanity   then   his coveting   like moth   and it consume away

12. When you, with rebukes, chastise man for iniquity, you make his beauty consume
away like a moth; surely every man is vanity. Selah.

שִׁמְעָה־תְפִלָּתִי יְהֹוָה וְשַׁוְעָתִי

and my cry   ihvh   my prayer - hear

הַאֲזִינָה אֶל־דִּמְעָתִי אַל־תֶּחֱרַשׁ

you be silent – don't   my tear – unto   the give ear

כִּי גֵר אָנֹכִי עִמָּךְ תּוֹשָׁב כְּכָל־אֲבוֹתָי:

my fathers – like all   dweller   with you   I am   stranger   like

13. Hear my prayer, O Lord, and give ear to my cry; do not keep silence at my tears; for
I am a stranger with you, and a sojourner, like all my fathers were.

הָשַׁע מִמֶּנִּי וְאַבְלִיגָה בְּטֶרֶם אֵלֵךְ וְאֵינֶנִּי:

and I isn't   I go   before   and I smile   from me   the look away

14. Look away from me, that I may recover brightness, before I depart and be no more.

PSALM 40

ספר תהילים פרק מ

לַמְנַצֵּחַ   לְדָוִד   מִזְמֽוֹר׃

Psalm   to David   to him that is over

1. To the chief Musician, A Psalm of David.

קַוֹּה   קִוִּיתִי   יְהוָה   וַיֵּט   אֵלַי   וַיִּשְׁמַע   שַׁוְעָתִֽי׃

my cry   and he heard   unto me   and he inclined   ihvh   I expected   expect

2. I waited patiently for the Lord; and he inclined to me, and heard my cry.

וַיַּעֲלֵנִי   מִבּוֹר   שָׁאוֹן   מִטִּיט   הַיָּוֵן

the mire   from clay   gruesome   from pit   and he brought me up

וַיָּקֶם   עַל־סֶלַע   רַגְלַי   כּוֹנֵן   אֲשֻׁרָֽי׃

my progress   he established   my feet   crag - upon   and he raising

3. And he drew me up from the gruesome pit, out of the miry clay, and set my feet upon a rock, and made my footsteps secure.

וַיִּתֵּן   בְּפִי   שִׁיר   חָדָשׁ   תְּהִלָּה   לֵאלֹהֵינוּ

to our Elohim   prayer   new   song   in my mouth   and he gave

יִרְאוּ   רַבִּים   וְיִירָאוּ   וְיִבְטְחוּ   בַּיהוָֽה׃

in ihvh   and they trust   and they will fear   many   and they will see

4. And he has put a new song in my mouth, praise to our God; many shall see it, and fear, and shall trust in the Lord.

אַשְׁרֵי   הַגֶּבֶר   אֲשֶׁר־שָׂם   יְהוָה   מִבְטַחוֹ

from h s trust   ihvh   has placed - which   the gentleman   happy

וְלֹא־פָנָה   אֶל־רְהָבִים   וְשָׂטֵי   כָזָב׃

lie   and swerving   proud - unto   face - and not

5. Happy is the man who makes the Lord his trust, and does not turn to the proud, nor to those who go astray after lies.

רַבּוֹת   עָשִׂיתָ   אַתָּה   יְהוָה   אֱלֹהַי   נִפְלְאֹתֶיךָ

your mystical   my Elohim   ihvh   you   done   many

וּמַחְשְׁבֹתֶיךָ   אֵלֵינוּ   אֵין   עֲרֹךְ   אֵלֶיךָ

unto you   set order   nothing   unto us   and your thoughts

אַגִּידָה   וַאֲדַבֵּרָה   עָצְמוּ   מִסַּפֵּֽר׃

from numbered   they are standing close   and I will speak   I will tell

6. Many, O Lord my God, are your wonderful works which you have done, and your thoughts which are toward us; none can compare with you; if I would declare and tell of them, they would be more than can be numbered.

זֶבַח   וּמִנְחָה   לֹא־חָפַצְתָּ   אָזְנַיִם   כָּרִיתָ

you dug   ears   you delighted - not   and offering   sacrifice

לִי   עוֹלָה   וַחֲטָאָה   לֹא   שָׁאָלְתָּ׃

you asked   not   and sin   burnt offering   to me

7. You do not desire sacrifice and offering; you have dug open my ears; you have not required burnt offering and sin offering.

אָז   אָמַרְתִּי   הִנֵּה־בָאתִי   בִּמְגִלַּת־סֵפֶר   כָּתוּב   עָלָי׃

unto me   written   written book - in scroll   I come - here   I said   then

8. Then I said, behold, I come; in the scroll of the book it is written about me,

לַעֲשׂוֹת   רְצוֹנְךָ   אֱלֹהַי   חָפָצְתִּי   וְתוֹרָתְךָ   בְּתוֹךְ   מֵעָי׃

my bowels   in midst   and your law   I delighted   my Elohim   your pleasure   to do

9. I delight to do your will, O my God; your Torah is in my heart.

בִּשַּׂרְתִּי   צֶדֶק   בְּקָהָל   רָב   הִנֵּה   שְׂפָתַי

my lips   here   many   in congregation   righteousness   I preached

לֹא   אֶכְלָא   יְהוָה   אַתָּה   יָדָעְתָּ׃

you know   you   ihvh   I withhold   not

10. I have preached righteousness in the great congregation; behold, I did not refrain my lips, O Lord, you know.

צִדְקָתְךָ   לֹא־כִסִּיתִי   בְּתוֹךְ   לִבִּי

my heart   midst   I have hid - not   your righteousness

אֱמוּנָתְךָ   וּתְשׁוּעָתְךָ   אָמַרְתִּי   לֹא־כִחַדְתִּי

I have concealed - not   I have said   and your salvation   your faithfulness

חַסְדְּךָ   וַאֲמִתְּךָ   לְקָהָל   רָב׃

many   to congregation   and your truth   your kindness

11. I did not hide your righteousness in my heart; I have declared your faithfulness and your salvation; I have not concealed your loving kindness and your truth from the great congregation.

אַתָּה   יְהוָה   לֹא־תִכְלָא   רַחֲמֶיךָ   מִמֶּנִּי

from me   your compassion   you withhold - not   ihvh   you

חַסְדְּךָ   וַאֲמִתְּךָ   תָּמִיד   יִצְּרוּנִי׃

it preserves me   continually   and your truth   your mercy

12. Do not withhold, O Lord, your compassion from me; let your loving kindness and your truth continually preserve me.

כִּי   אָפְפוּ   עָלַי   רָעוֹת   עַד־אֵין   מִסְפָּר

numbered   nothing - till   evils   upon me   encompassed   like

הִשִּׂיגוּנִי   עֲוֹנֹתַי   וְלֹא־יָכֹלְתִּי   לִרְאוֹת

to see   I able - and not   my inequities   overtaken me

עָצְמוּ   מִשַּׂעֲרוֹת   רֹאשִׁי   וְלִבִּי   עֲזָבָנִי׃

forsaken me   and my heart   my head   from hairs   they many

13. For innumerable evils have surrounded me; my iniquities have overtaken me, so that

I am not able to see; they are more than the hairs of my head; therefore my heart fails me.

רְצֵה־יְהֹוָה לְהַצִּילֵנִי יְהֹוָה לְעֶזְרָתִי חוּשָׁה׃

haste · to my help · ihvh · to deliver me · ihvh - be pleased

14. Be pleased, O Lord, to save me; O Lord, make haste to help me.

יֵבֹשׁוּ וְיַחְפְּרוּ יַחַד מְבַקְשֵׁי נַפְשִׁי לִסְפּוֹתָהּ

to sweep up it · my soul · from seekers · together · and they abashed · they ashamed

יִסֹּגוּ אָחוֹר וְיִכָּלְמוּ חֲפֵצֵי רָעָתִי׃

my evil travails · delighters · and put to shame · backwards · it turned

15. Let those who seek after my soul to destroy it be altogether ashamed and confounded; let those who wish me evil be turned back and put to shame.

יָשֹׁמּוּ עַל־עֵקֶב בָּשְׁתָּם הָאֹמְרִים לִי הֶאָח הֶאָח׃

aha · aha · to me · the saying ones · their shame · consequence - upon · they desolate

16. Let those who say to me Aha, aha, be appalled, because of their shame.

יָשִׂישׂוּ וְיִשְׂמְחוּ בְּךָ כָּל־מְבַקְשֶׁיךָ

your enquirer's - all · in you · and they glad · they joyful

יֹאמְרוּ תָמִיד יִגְדַּל יְהֹוָה אֹהֲבֵי תְּשׁוּעָתֶךָ׃

your salvation · lovers · ihvh · magnified · continually · they say

17. Let all those who seek you rejoice and be glad in you; let those who love your salvation say continually, The Lord be magnified.

וַאֲנִי עָנִי וְאֶבְיוֹן אֲדֹנָי יַחֲשָׁב לִי עֶזְרָתִי

my help · to me · he thought · Adoni · and needed · poor · and I

וּמְפַלְטִי אַתָּה אֱלֹהַי אַל־תְּאַחַר׃

you delay - don't · my Elohim · you · and my deliverer

18. But I am poor and needy; yet the Lord takes thought for me; you are my help and my savior; delay not, O my God.

PSALM 41

ספר תהילים פרק מא

לַמְנַצֵּחַ מִזְמוֹר לְדָוִד:

to David   Psalm   to one directing

1. To the chief Musician, A Psalm of David.

אַשְׁרֵי מַשְׂכִּיל אֶל־דָּל בְּיוֹם רָעָה יְמַלְּטֵהוּ יְהֹוָה:

ihvh   he will deliver   evil   in day   weak - unto   contemplator   praiseworthy

2. Happy is he who considers the poor; the Lord will save in the day of evil.

יְהֹוָה יִשְׁמְרֵהוּ וִיחַיֵּהוּ יְאֻשַּׁר [וְאֻשַּׁר] בָּאָרֶץ

in earth   and happy   and he enliven you   he will preserve you   ihvh

וְאַל־תִּתְּנֵהוּ בְּנֶפֶשׁ אֹיְבָיו:

his enemies   in soul   you will give him – and don't

3. (K) The Lord will preserve him, and keep him alive; he is called happy on earth; and
you will not deliver him to the will of his enemies.

יְהֹוָה יִסְעָדֶנּוּ עַל־עֶרֶשׂ דְּוָי כָּל־מִשְׁכָּבוֹ הָפַכְתָּ בְחָלְיוֹ:

in his illness   you restore   his bed – all   sickness   couch – upon   he sustains you   ihvh

4. The Lord will strengthen him on his sick bed; whenever he is prostrate you will heal
all his illnesses.

אֲנִי־אָמַרְתִּי יְהֹוָה חָנֵּנִי רְפָאָה נַפְשִׁי כִּי־חָטָאתִי לָךְ:

to you   I sinned – like   my soul   heal   grant me   ihvh   I said - I

5. I said, Lord, be merciful to me; heal my soul; for I have sinned against you.

אוֹיְבַי יֹאמְרוּ רַע לִי מָתַי יָמוּת וְאָבַד שְׁמוֹ:

his name   and perish   he will die   when   to me   bad   they say   my enemies

6. My enemies speak evil of me, When shall he die, and his name perish?

וְאִם־בָּא לִרְאוֹת שָׁוְא יְדַבֵּר

he speaks   vanity   to see   come – and if

לִבּוֹ יִקְבָּץ־אָוֶן לוֹ יֵצֵא לַחוּץ יְדַבֵּר:

he speaks   to outside   goes out   to him   inequity – he gathers   his heart

7. And if one comes to see me, he speaks vanity; his heart gathers iniquity to itself;
when he goes out, he tells it.

יַחַד עָלַי יִתְלַחֲשׁוּ כָּל־שֹׂנְאָי עָלַי יַחְשְׁבוּ רָעָה לִי:

to me   evil   they devise   upon me   haters of me – all   they whisper   upon me   together

8. All who hate me whisper together against me; against me they plot my harm.

דְּבַר־בְּלִיַּעַל יָצוּק בּוֹ וַאֲשֶׁר שָׁכַב לֹא־יוֹסִיף לָקוּם:

to rise   again - not   he lies   and which   in it   it cleaves   in disease - speaking

9. They say, An evil disease cleaves fast to him, and from where he lies he shall rise up
no more.

גַּם אִישׁ־שְׁלוֹמִי אֲשֶׁר־בָּטַחְתִּי בוֹ

also   my peaceful – man   which – I trusted   in him

אוֹכֵל לַחְמִי הִגְדִּיל עָלַי עָקֵב:

eater   my bread   magnified   upon me   heel

10. Even my own close friend, in whom I trusted, who ate of my bread, has lifted up his heel against me.

וְאַתָּה יְהוָה חָנֵּנִי וַהֲקִימֵנִי וַאֲשַׁלְּמָה לָהֶם:

and you   ihvh   grant me   and the raise me up   and towards I pay   to them

11. But you, O Lord, be gracious to me, and raise me up, that I may pay them back.

בְּזֹאת יָדַעְתִּי כִּי־חָפַצְתָּ בִּי כִּי לֹא־יָרִיעַ אֹיְבִי עָלָי:

in this   I know   like – you favor   in me   like   not – he triumph   my enemy   upon me

12. By this I know that you favor me, because my enemy does not triumph over me.

וַאֲנִי בְּתֻמִּי תָּמַכְתָּ בִּי וַתַּצִּיבֵנִי לְפָנֶיךָ לְעוֹלָם:

and I   in my integrity   you supported   in me   you erected   before you   forever

13. And as for me, you uphold me in my integrity, and you set me before your face for ever.

בָּרוּךְ יְהוָה אֱלֹהֵי יִשְׂרָאֵל

blessed   ihvh   my Elohohim   Israel

מֵהָעוֹלָם וְעַד הָעוֹלָם אָמֵן וְאָמֵן:

from the forever   and till   the forever   amen   and amen

14. Blessed be the Lord God of Israel from everlasting, and to everlasting. Amen, and Amen.

PSALM 42

ספר תהילים פרק מב

לַמְנַצֵּחַ   מַשְׂכִּיל   לִבְנֵי־קֹרַח:

Korah - to sons   Maskil   to him that is over

1. To the chief Musician, A Maskil, for the sons of Korah.

כְּאַיָּל   תַּעֲרֹג   עַל־אֲפִיקֵי־מָיִם

water – brooks – upon   you pant   like the hart

כֵּן נַפְשִׁי תַעֲרֹג אֵלֶיךָ אֱלֹהִים:

Elohim   unto you   you pant   my soul   thus

2. As the hart longs for water streams, so does my soul long for you, O God.

צָמְאָה נַפְשִׁי לֵאלֹהִים לְאֵל חָי

living   to El   to Elohim   my soul   thirsts

מָתַי אָבוֹא וְאֵרָאֶה פְּנֵי אֱלֹהִים:

Elohim   face   and I appear   I come   when

3. My soul thirsts for God, for the living God; when shall I come and appear before God?

הָיְתָה־לִּי דִמְעָתִי לֶחֶם יוֹמָם וָלָיְלָה

and night   by day   bread   my tear   to me - was

בֶּאֱמֹר אֵלַי כָּל־הַיּוֹם אַיֵּה אֱלֹהֶיךָ:

your Elohim   where   the day – all   unto me   in saying

4. My tears have been my bread day and night, while they continually say to me, Where is your God?

אֵלֶּה אֶזְכְּרָה וְאֶשְׁפְּכָה עָלַי נַפְשִׁי

my soul   upon me   and I pour out   I remember   these

כִּי אֶעֱבֹר בַּסָּךְ   אֶדַּדֵּם   עַד־בֵּית אֱלֹהִים

Elohim   house – till   I wander with them   in multitude   I pass   like

בְּקוֹל־רִנָּה וְתוֹדָה הָמוֹן חוֹגֵג:

pilgrimage   multitude   and thanks   joy shouting - in voice

5. When I remember these things, I pour out my soul; how I went with the multitude, leading them in procession to the house of God, with the voice of joy and praise, a crowd keeping the festival.

מַה־תִּשְׁתּוֹחֲחִי נַפְשִׁי וַתֶּהֱמִי עָלָי

upon me   and disquieted   my soul   you **bowed** - why

הוֹחִילִי לֵאלֹהִים כִּי־עוֹד אוֹדֶנּוּ יְשׁוּעוֹת פָּנָיו:

his face   salvation   I give thanks   still – like   to Elohim   hope

6. Why are you cast down, O my soul? And why are you disquieted within me? Hope in God; for I shall again praise him for the help of his countenance.

אֱלֹהַי עָלַי נַפְשִׁי תִּשְׁתּוֹחָחִ
my Elohim | upon me | my soul | you be bowed down

עַל־כֵּן אֶזְכָּרְךָ מֵאֶרֶץ יַרְדֵּן וְחֶרְמוֹנִים מֵהַר מִצְעָר:
thus - upon | I remember | from land | Jordan | and Hermon ones | from Mountain | Mizar

7. O my God, my soul is cast down within me, because I remember you from the land of the Jordan, and the Hermon, from Mount Mizar.

תְּהוֹם אֶל־תְּהוֹם קוֹרֵא לְקוֹל צִנּוֹרֶיךָ
deep | deep – unto | caller | to voice | your conduits

כָּל־מִשְׁבָּרֶיךָ וְגַלֶּיךָ עָלַי עָבָרוּ:
your waves - all | and your billows | upon me | they passed

8. Deep calls to deep at the noise of your cataracts; all your waves and your billows have gone over me.

יוֹמָם יְצַוֶּה יְהֹוָה חַסְדּוֹ
by day | will command | ihvh | kindness

וּבַלַּיְלָה שִׁירֹה [שִׁירוֹ] עִמִּי תְּפִלָּה לְאֵל חַיָּי:
and in night | his song | with me | prayer | to El | my life

9. By day the Lord will command his loving kindness, and in the night his song shall be with me, a prayer to the God of my life.

אוֹמְרָה לְאֵל סַלְעִי
I say | to El | my crag

לָמָה שְׁכַחְתָּנִי לָמָּה־קֹדֵר אֵלֵךְ בְּלַחַץ אוֹיֵב:
why | you forgot me | mourning – why | I go | in oppression | enemy

10. I will say to God my rock, Why have you forgotten me? Why do I go mourning because of the oppression of the enemy?

בְּרֶצַח בְּעַצְמוֹתַי חֵרְפוּנִי צוֹרְרָי
in deadly wound | in my bones | they reproached me | my adversaries

בְּאָמְרָם אֵלַי כָּל־הַיּוֹם אַיֵּה אֱלֹהֶיךָ:
in their saying | unto me | the day – all | where | your Elohim

11. Like a deadly wound in my bones, my enemies taunt me; while they say daily to me, Where is your God?

מַה־תִּשְׁתּוֹחֲחִי נַפְשִׁי וּמַה־תֶּהֱמִי עָלָי
what - you bowed down | my soul | what – you disquieted | upon me

הוֹחִילִי לֵאלֹהִים כִּי־עוֹד אוֹדֶנּוּ יְשׁוּעֹת פָּנַי וֵאלֹהָי׃

and my Elohim   my face   salvations   I thank him   still – like   to Elohim   hope

12. Why are you cast down, O my soul? And why are you disquieted within me? Hope in God; for I shall again praise him, who is the health of my countenance, and my God.

PSALM 43

ספר תהילים פרק מג

שָׁפְטֵנִי אֱלֹהִים וְרִיבָה רִיבִי   מִגּוֹי לֹא־חָסִיד

pious – not   from nations   my cause   and plead   Elohim   judge me

מֵאִישׁ־מִרְמָה וְעַוְלָה תְפַלְּטֵנִי׃

deliver me   and iniquity   deceit - from man

1. Judge me, O God, and plead my cause against an ungodly nation; O save me from the deceitful and unjust man.

כִּי־אַתָּה אֱלֹהֵי מָעוּזִּי

my strength   my Elohim   you - like

לָמָה זְנַחְתָּנִי לָמָה־קֹדֵר אֶתְהַלֵּךְ בְּלַחַץ אוֹיֵב׃

enemy   in oppression   I walk   gloom - why   abandon me   why

2. For you are the God of my strength; why do you cast me off? Why do I go mourning because of the oppression of the enemy?

שְׁלַח־אוֹרְךָ וַאֲמִתְּךָ הֵמָּה יַנְחוּנִי

lead me   they are   and your truth   your light - send

יְבִיאוּנִי אֶל־הַר־קָדְשְׁךָ   וְאֶל־מִשְׁכְּנוֹתֶיךָ׃

your dwelling place - and unto   your holiness - mountain – unto   they bring me

3. O send out your light and your truth; let them lead me; let them bring me to your holy mountain, and to your dwelling places.

וְאָבוֹאָה אֶל־מִזְבַּח אֱלֹהִים אֶל־אֵל שִׂמְחַת גִּילִי

my joy   happiness   El – unto   Elohim   altar – unto   and I will come

וְאוֹדְךָ בְכִנּוֹר אֱלֹהִים אֱלֹהָי׃

my Elohim   Elohim   in harp   and I praise

4. Then I will go to the altar of God, to God my great joy; and I will praise you with the lyre, O God my God.

מַה־תִּשְׁתּוֹחֲחִי נַפְשִׁי וּמַה־תֶּהֱמִי עָלַי הוֹחִילִי לֵאלֹהִים

to Elohim   hope   upon me   disturbed - and what   my soul   you bow down - what

כִּי־עוֹד אוֹדֶנּוּ   יְשׁוּעֹת פָּנַי וֵאלֹהָי׃

and my Elohim   my face   salvations   I will thank him   yet - like

5. Why are you cast down, O my soul? And why are you disquieted within me? Hope in God; for I shall again praise him, who is the health of my countenance, and my God.

PSALM 44

ספר תהילים פרק מד

לַמְנַצֵּחַ לִבְנֵי־קֹרַח מַשְׂכִּיל:

Maskil   Korah - to sons   to chief Musician

1. To the chief Musician for the sons of Korah, A Maskil.

אֱלֹהִים בְּאָזְנֵינוּ שָׁמַעְנוּ אֲבוֹתֵינוּ סִפְּרוּ־לָנוּ

to us - declared   our fathers   we heard   in our ears   Elohim

פֹּעַל־פָּעַלְתָּ בִימֵיהֶם בִּימֵי קֶדֶם:

old   in days   in their days   you did - deed

2. We have heard with our ears, O God; our fathers have told us, what deeds you performed in their days, in the times of old;

אַתָּה יָדְךָ גּוֹיִם הוֹרַשְׁתָּ וַתִּטָּעֵם תָּרַע לְאֻמִּים וַתְּשַׁלְּחֵם:

and you spread them   to peoples   you did evil   and you planted them   you drove out   nations   your hand   you

3. How you drove out the nations with your hand, but planted them; how you afflicted the people, and cast them out.

כִּי לֹא בְחַרְבָּם יָרְשׁוּ־אָרֶץ

land – they inherited   in their sword   not   like

וּזְרוֹעָם לֹא־הוֹשִׁיעָה לָּמוֹ

to them   saved - not   and their arm

כִּי־יְמִינְךָ וּזְרוֹעֲךָ וְאוֹר פָּנֶיךָ כִּי רְצִיתָם:

favored them   like   your face   and light   and your arm   your hand – like

4. For they did not get the land in possession by their own sword, nor did their own arm save them; but your right hand, and your arm, and the light of your countenance, because you did favorably accept them.

אַתָּה־הוּא מַלְכִּי אֱלֹהִים צַוֵּה יְשׁוּעוֹת יַעֲקֹב:

Jacob   salvations   command   Elohim   my king   he – you

5. You are my King, O God; command deliverance for Jacob.

בְּךָ צָרֵינוּ נְנַגֵּחַ בְּשִׁמְךָ נָבוּס קָמֵינוּ:

our arisers   we will tread down   in your name   we will push down   our adversaries   in

6. Through you we will push down our enemies; through your name we will trample down those who rise up against us.

כִּי לֹא בְקַשְׁתִּי אֶבְטָח וְחַרְבִּי לֹא תוֹשִׁיעֵנִי:

will save me   not   and my sword   I will trust   in my bow   not   like

7. For I will not trust in my bow, nor shall my sword save me.

כִּי הוֹשַׁעְתָּנוּ מִצָּרֵינוּ וּמְשַׂנְאֵינוּ הֱבִישׁוֹת:

you put to shame   and from our haters   from our adversaries   you saved us   like

8. But you have saved us from our enemies, and have put to shame those who hate us.

בֵּאלֹהִים הִלַּלְנוּ כָל־הַיּוֹם וְשִׁמְךָ לְעוֹלָם נוֹדֶה סֶלָה׃

Sela we give thanks foreve‾ and your name the day – all we boasted in Elohim

9. In God we have gloried all the day long, and we praise your name for ever. Selah.

אַף־זָנַחְתָּ וַתַּכְלִימֵנוּ וְלֹא־תֵצֵא בְּצִבְאוֹתֵינוּ׃

in our hosts you go out – and not and put us to shame you cast off- then

10. But you have cast off, and put us to shame; and you do not go forth with our armies.

תְּשִׁיבֵנוּ אָחוֹר מִנִּי־צָר וּמְשַׂנְאֵינוּ שָׁסוּ לָמוֹ׃

to themselves they rob anc those who hate us adversary – from backward you return us

11. You make us turn back from the enemy; and those who hate us take plunder for themselves.

תִּתְּנֵנוּ כְּצֹאן מַאֲכָל וּבַגּוֹיִם זֵרִיתָנוּ׃

you scattered us and in nations from food like sheep you gave us

12. You have given us like sheep to be eaten; and have scattered us among the nations.

תִּמְכֹּר עַמְּךָ בְלֹא־הוֹן וְלֹא־רִבִּיתָ בִּמְחִירֵיהֶם׃

in their prices you increased – and not wealth – in not your people you sell

13. You sell your people for nothing, and you do not ask for a high price.

תְּשִׂימֵנוּ חֶרְפָּה לִשְׁכֵנֵינוּ לַעַג וָקֶלֶס לִסְבִיבוֹתֵינוּ׃

to our surrounders and derision to mocking to our neighbors reproach you make us

14. You make us a taunt to our neighbors, a scorn and a derision to those who are around us.

תְּשִׂימֵנוּ מָשָׁל בַּגּוֹיִם מְנוֹד־רֹאשׁ בַּלְאֻמִּים׃

in to nations head – shaking in nations proverb you make us

15. You make us a byword among the nations, a shaking of the head among the people.

כָּל־הַיּוֹם כְּלִמָּתִי נֶגְדִּי וּבֹשֶׁת פָּנַי כִּסָּתְנִי׃

covered me my face and in shame before me my dishonor the day - all

16. My confusion is before me all day, and the shame of my face has covered me,

מִקּוֹל מְחָרֵף וּמְגַדֵּף מִפְּנֵי אוֹיֵב וּמִתְנַקֵּם׃

and avenger enemy presence and blasphemer reproacher from voice

17. Because of the voice of him who taunts and blasphemes; because of the enemy and avenger.

כָּל־זֹאת בָּאַתְנוּ וְלֹא שְׁכַחֲנוּךָ וְלֹא־שִׁקַּרְנוּ בִּבְרִיתֶךָ׃

in your covenant we false – anc not we forgotten you and not come to us this - all

18. All this has come upon us; yet we have not forgotten you, nor have we been false to your covenant.

לֹא־נָסוֹג אָחוֹר לִבֵּנוּ וַתֵּט אֲשֻׁרֵינוּ מִנִּי אָרְחֶךָ׃

your path from our steps I declined our heart backward turned - not

19. Our heart is not turned back, nor have our steps departed from your way;

כִּי דִכִּיתָנוּ בִּמְקוֹם תַּנִּים וַתְּכַס עָלֵינוּ בְּצַלְמָוֶת:

<small>a deadly shade   upon us   and covered   jackals   in place   you crushed us   like</small>

20. Though you have crushed us in the place of jackals, and covered us with the shadow of death.

אִם־שָׁכַחְנוּ שֵׁם אֱלֹהֵינוּ וַנִּפְרֹשׁ כַּפֵּינוּ לְאֵל זָר:

<small>strange   to El   our palms   and we spread   our Elohim   name   we had forgotten - if</small>

21. If we had forgotten the name of our God, or stretched out our hands to a strange god;

הֲלֹא אֱלֹהִים יַחֲקָר־זֹאת כִּי הוּא יֹדֵעַ תַּעֲלֻמוֹת לֵב:

<small>heart   secrets   knowing   he   like   this - search   Elohim   the not</small>

22. Would not God search this out? For he knows the secrets of the heart.

כִּי־עָלֶיךָ הֹרַגְנוּ כָל־הַיּוֹם נֶחְשַׁבְנוּ כְּצֹאן טִבְחָה:

<small>slaughter   like sheep   we accounted   the day – all   we killed   upon you - like</small>

23. But for your sake we are killed all the day long; we are accounted as sheep for the slaughter.

עוּרָה לָמָּה תִישַׁן אֲדֹנָי הָקִיצָה אַל־תִּזְנַח לָנֶצַח:

<small>to victory   cut off - don't   the awake   Adoni   you sleep   why   awake</small>

24. Awake, why do you sleep, O Lord? Arise, do not cast us off for ever.

לָמָּה פָנֶיךָ תַסְתִּיר תִּשְׁכַּח עָנְיֵנוּ וְלַחֲצֵנוּ:

<small>and our oppression   our affliction   you forget   you hide   your face   why</small>

25. Why do you hide your face, and forget our affliction and our oppression?

כִּי שָׁחָה לֶעָפָר נַפְשֵׁנוּ דָּבְקָה לָאָרֶץ בִּטְנֵנוּ:

<small>our belly   to earth   cleaved   our soul   to dust   bowed   like</small>

26. For our soul is bowed down to the dust; our belly cleaves to the earth.

קוּמָה עֶזְרָתָה לָּנוּ וּפְדֵנוּ לְמַעַן חַסְדֶּךָ:

<small>your kindness   to end   and redeem us   to us   help   arise</small>

27. Arise for our help, and redeem us for the sake of your loving kindness.

PSALM 45

ספר תהילים פרק מה

לַמְנַצֵּחַ עַל־שֹׁשַׁנִּים לִבְנֵי־קֹרַח מַשְׂכִּיל שִׁיר יְדִידֹת׃

to him that is over | lillies – upon | Korah - to sons | contemplative poem | song | loves

1 To the chief Musician upon Shoshannim, for the sons of Korah, Maschil, A Song of loves.

רָחַשׁ לִבִּי דָּבָר טוֹב אֹמֵר אָנִי מַעֲשַׂי לְמֶלֶךְ

exuberant | my heart | speech | good | say | I | my works | to king

לְשׁוֹנִי עֵט סוֹפֵר מָהִיר׃

my tongue | pen | scribe | swift

My heart is inditing a good matter: I speak of the things which I have made touching the king: my tongue *is* the pen of a ready writer.

יָפְיָפִיתָ מִבְּנֵי אָדָם הוּצַק חֵן בְּשְׂפְתוֹתֶיךָ

you handsome | from sons | Adam | poured | grace | in your lips

עַל־כֵּן בֵּרַכְךָ אֱלֹהִים לְעוֹלָם׃

thus – upon | blessed you | Elohim | to forever

2 Thou art fairer than the children of men: grace is poured into thy lips: therefore God hath blessed thee for ever.

חֲגוֹר חַרְבְּךָ עַל־יָרֵךְ גִּבּוֹר הוֹדְךָ וַהֲדָרֶךָ׃

gird | your sword | your thigh - upon | mighty | your glory | and your majesty

3 Gird thy sword upon *thy* thigh, O *most* mighty, with thy glory and thy majesty.

וַהֲדָרְךָ צְלַח רְכַב עַל־דְּבַר־אֱמֶת וְעַנְוָה־צֶדֶק

and your majesty | prosper | ride | truth - speech – upon | righteousness - and humility

וְתוֹרְךָ נוֹרָאוֹת יְמִינֶךָ׃

and your Torah | awesome ones | your right hand

4 And in thy majesty ride prosperously because of truth and meekness *and* righteousness; and thy right hand shall teach thee terrible things.

חִצֶּיךָ שְׁנוּנִים עַמִּים תַּחְתֶּיךָ יִפְּלוּ בְּלֵב אוֹיְבֵי הַמֶּלֶךְ׃

your arrows | sharp ones | peoples | under you | they fall | in heart | enemies | the king

5 Thine arrows *are* sharp in the heart of the king's enemies; *whereby* the people fall under thee.

כִּסְאֲךָ אֱלֹהִים עוֹלָם וָעֶד שֵׁבֶט מִישֹׁר שֵׁבֶט מַלְכוּתֶךָ׃

your throne | Elohim | forever | and time | rod | integrity | rod | your kingdom

6 Thy throne, O God, *is* for ever and ever: the sceptre of thy kingdom *is* a right sceptre.

אָהַבְתָּ צֶּדֶק וַתִּשְׂנָא רֶשַׁע עַל־כֵּן מְשָׁחֲךָ אֱלֹהִים אֱלֹהֶיךָ

you love | righteousness | and you hate | wickedness | thus - upon | anointed you | Elohim | your Elohim

שֶׁמֶן שָׂשׂוֹן מֵחֲבֵרֶיךָ:

from your friends   rejoicing   oil

7 Thou lovest righteousness, and hatest wickedness: therefore God, thy God, hath anointed thee with the oil of gladness above thy fellows.

מֹר וַאֲהָלוֹת קְצִיעוֹת כָּל־בִּגְדֹתֶיךָ מִן־הֵיכְלֵי שֵׁן

ivory   palaces - among   your garments – all   cassias   and aloes   myrrh

מִנִּי שִׂמְּחוּךָ:

gladdened you   from those

8 All thy garments *smell* of myrrh, and aloes, *and* cassia, out of the ivory palaces, whereby they have made thee glad.

בְּנוֹת מְלָכִים בְּיִקְּרוֹתֶיךָ נִצְּבָה שֵׁגַל לִימִינְךָ בְּכֶתֶם אוֹפִיר:

Ophir   in fine gold   to your right hand   consort   stands erect   in your precious   kings   daughters

9 Kings' daughters *were* among thy honourable women: upon thy right hand did stand the queen in gold of Ophir.

שִׁמְעִי־בַת וּרְאִי וְהַטִּי אָזְנֵךְ וְשִׁכְחִי עַמֵּךְ וּבֵית אָבִיךְ:

your father   and house   your people   and forget   your ear   and incline   and see   daughter – hear

10 Hearken, O daughter, and consider, and incline thine ear; forget also thine own people, and thy father's house;

וְיִתְאָו הַמֶּלֶךְ יָפְיֵךְ כִּי הוּא אֲדֹנַיִךְ וְהִשְׁתַּחֲוִי־לוֹ:

to him - and bow down   your Adonai   he   like   your beauty   the king   and he desires

11 So shall the king greatly desire thy beauty: for he *is* thy Lord; and worship thou him.

וּבַת־צֹר בְּמִנְחָה פָּנַיִךְ יְחַלּוּ עֲשִׁירֵי עָם:

people   richest   they sought   your face   in offering   Tyre - and daughter

12 And the daughter of Tyre *shall be there* with a gift; *even* the rich among the people shall entreat thy favour.

כָּל־כְּבוּדָּה בַת־מֶלֶךְ פְּנִימָה מִמִּשְׁבְּצוֹת זָהָב לְבוּשָׁהּ:

her clothing   gold   from settings   towards inside   king - daughter   honor – all

13 The king's daughter *is* all glorious within: her clothing *is* of wrought gold.

לִרְקָמוֹת תּוּבַל לַמֶּלֶךְ בְּתוּלוֹת אַחֲרֶיהָ רֵעוֹתֶיהָ מוּבָאוֹת לָךְ:

to you   will be brought   her neighbors   after her   virgins   to king   it fetched   to embroideries

14 She shall be brought unto the king in raiment of needlework: the virgins her companions that follow her shall be brought unto thee.

תּוּבַלְנָה בִּשְׂמָחֹת וָגִיל תְּבֹאֶינָה בְּהֵיכַל מֶלֶךְ:

king   in palace   they enter   and joy   in happiness   they enter

15 With gladness and rejoicing shall they be brought: they shall enter into the king's palace.

תַּחַת אֲבֹתֶיךָ יִהְיוּ בָנֶיךָ תְּשִׁיתֵמוֹ לְשָׂרִים בְּכָל־הָאָרֶץ:

the earth - in all   to princes   you set them   your sons   will be   your fathers   under

16 Instead of thy fathers shall be thy children, whom thou mayest make princes in all

the earth.

עַמִּים   עַל־כֵּן   וָדֹר   בְּכָל־דֹּר   שִׁמְךָ   אַזְכִּירָה
peoples thus - upon and generation generation - in all your name I remembered

וָעֶד: לְעֹלָם   יְהוֹדֻךָ
and again to forever give you thanks

17 I will make thy name to be remembered in all generations: therefore shall the people praise thee for ever and ever.

PSALM 46

לַמְנַצֵּחַ　לִבְנֵי־קֹרַח　עַל־עֲלָמוֹת　שִׁיר:

song　Allamoth - upon　Korah – sons　to him that is over

1. To the chief Musician for the sons of Korah, A Song according to Alamoth.

אֱלֹהִים　לָנוּ　מַחֲסֶה　וָעֹז　עֶזְרָה　בְצָרוֹת　נִמְצָא　מְאֹד:

very　being found　in distress　help　and strength　refuge　to us　Elohim

2. God is our refuge and strength, a very present help in trouble.

עַל־כֵּן　לֹא־נִירָא　בְּהָמִיר　אָרֶץ　וּבְמוֹט　הָרִים　בְּלֵב　יַמִּים:

seas　in heart　mountains　and in slip　earth　in changing　we will fear – not　thus - upon

3. Therefore we will not fear, though the earth should change, and though the mountains be carried into the midst of the sea;

יֶהֱמוּ　יֶחְמְרוּ　מֵימָיו　יִרְעֲשׁוּ　הָרִים　בְּגַאֲוָתוֹ　סֶלָה:

Sela　in its pride　mountains　they tremble　from its waters　they foam　they roar

4. Tough its waters roar and are troubled, though the mountains shake with their swelling. Selah.

נָהָר　פְּלָגָיו　יְשַׂמְּחוּ　עִיר־אֱלֹהִים　קְדֹשׁ　מִשְׁכְּנֵי　עֶלְיוֹן:

most high　dwelling　holy　Elohim – city　they happy　its channels　river

5. There is a river, whose streams make glad the city of God, the holiest dwelling place of the most High.

אֱלֹהִים　בְּקִרְבָּהּ　בַּל־תִּמּוֹט　יַעְזְרֶהָ　אֱלֹהִים　לִפְנוֹת　בֹּקֶר:

morning　to faces　Elohim　will help her　she will be moved – in not　in its midst　Elohim

6. God is in the midst of her; she shall not be moved; God shall help her before morning.

הָמוּ　גוֹיִם　מָטוּ　מַמְלָכוֹת　נָתַן　בְּקוֹלוֹ　תָּמוּג　אָרֶץ:

earth　it melts　in his voice　gave　from kingdoms　totter　nations　rage

7. Nations rage, kingdoms totter; he utters his voice, the earth melts.

יְהוָה　צְבָאוֹת　עִמָּנוּ　מִשְׂגָּב־לָנוּ　אֱלֹהֵי　יַעֲקֹב　סֶלָה:

Sela　Jacob　my Elohim　to us – stronghold　with us　legions　ihvh

8. The Lord of hosts is with us; the God of Jacob is our refuge. Selah.

לְכוּ־חֲזוּ　מִפְעֲלוֹת　יְהוָה　אֲשֶׁר־שָׂם　שַׁמּוֹת　בָּאָרֶץ:

in earth　desolations　set – which　ihvh　from works　behold - go

9. Come, behold the works of the Lord, the desolations that he has made in the earth.

מַשְׁבִּית　מִלְחָמוֹת　עַד־קְצֵה　הָאָרֶץ　קֶשֶׁת　יְשַׁבֵּר

he breaks　bow　the earth　end - till　wars　from ceases

וְקִצֵּץ　חֲנִית　עֲגָלוֹת　יִשְׂרֹף　בָּאֵשׁ:

in fire　he burns　chariots　spear　and cuts

10. He makes wars cease to the end of the earth; he breaks the bow, and shatters the spear; he burns the chariot in the fire.

הַרְפּוּ   וּדְעוּ   כִּי־אָנֹכִי   אֱלֹהִים
Elohim   I am – like   and you know   you be still

אָרוּם   בַּגּוֹיִם   אָרוּם   בָּאָרֶץ:
in earth   I will be exalted   in nations   I will be exalted

11. Be still, and know that I am God; I will be exalted among the nations, I will be exalted in the earth.

יְהוָה   צְבָאוֹת   עִמָּנוּ   מִשְׂגָּב־לָנוּ   אֱלֹהֵי   יַעֲקֹב   סֶלָה:
Sela   Jacob   my Elohim   to us – refuge   with us   legions   ihvh

12. The Lord of hosts is with us; the God of Jacob is our refuge. Selah.

PSALM 47

ספר תהילים פרק מז

לַמְנַצֵּחַ לִבְנֵי־קֹרַח מִזְמוֹר׃
to him that is over   Korach - to sons   psalm

1. To the chief Musician, A Psalm for the sons of Korah.

כָּל־הָעַמִּים תִּקְעוּ־כָף הָרִיעוּ לֵאלֹהִים בְּקוֹל רִנָּה׃
the peoples - all   palm – clap you   the shout   to Elohim   in voice   joy shouting

2. O clap your hands, all you peoples; shout to God with the voice of triumph.

כִּי־יְהוָה עֶלְיוֹן נוֹרָא מֶלֶךְ גָּדוֹל עַל־כָּל־הָאָרֶץ׃
ihvh - like   most high   feared   king   great   the earth – all – upon

3. For the Lord most high is awesome; he is a great King over all the earth.

יַדְבֵּר עַמִּים תַּחְתֵּינוּ וּלְאֻמִּים תַּחַת רַגְלֵינוּ׃
he speaks   peoples   under us   and to peoples   under   our feet

4. He subdues peoples under us, and nations under our feet.

יִבְחַר־לָנוּ אֶת־נַחֲלָתֵנוּ אֶת גְּאוֹן יַעֲקֹב אֲשֶׁר־אָהֵב סֶלָה׃
to us – he chooses   our inheritance - that   that   pride   Jacob   he loved – which   Sela

5. He chooses our inheritance for us, the pride of Jacob whom he loves. Selah.

עָלָה אֱלֹהִים בִּתְרוּעָה יְהוָה בְּקוֹל שׁוֹפָר׃
ascend   Elohim   in alarm sound   ihvh   in voice   Shofar

6. God has gone up with a shout, the Lord with the sound of a shofar.

זַמְּרוּ אֱלֹהִים זַמֵּרוּ זַמְּרוּ לְמַלְכֵּנוּ זַמֵּרוּ׃
you sing psalms   Elohim   you sing psalms   you sing psalms   to our king   you sing psalms

7. Sing praises to God, sing praises; sing praises to our King, sing praises.

כִּי מֶלֶךְ כָּל־הָאָרֶץ אֱלֹהִים זַמְּרוּ מַשְׂכִּיל׃
like   king   the earth – all   Elohim   you sing psalms   enlightened

8. For God is the King of all the earth; sing a Maskil psalm.

מָלַךְ אֱלֹהִים עַל־גּוֹיִם אֱלֹהִים יָשַׁב עַל־כִּסֵּא קָדְשׁוֹ׃
reigns   Elohim   nations - upon   Elohim   sits   throne - upon   his holiness

9. God reigns over the nations; God sits on the throne of his holiness.

נְדִיבֵי עַמִּים נֶאֱסָפוּ עַם אֱלֹהֵי אַבְרָהָם
princes   peoples   gathered together   people   Elohim   Abraham

כִּי לֵאלֹהִים מָגִנֵּי־אֶרֶץ מְאֹד נַעֲלָה׃
like   to Elohim   earth – my shield   very   he exalted

10. The nobles of the peoples are gathered together, the people of the God of
Abraham; for the shields of the earth belong to God; he is greatly exalted.

PSALM 48

ספר תהילים פרק מח

שִׁיר מִזְמֹור לִבְנֵי־קֹרַח:

Korah - to sons   psalm   Song

1. A Song and Psalm for the sons of Korah.

גָּדֹול יְהֹוָה וּמְהֻלָּל מְאֹד בְּעִיר אֱלֹהֵינוּ הַר־קָדְשֹׁו:

his holiness - mount our Elohim in city very and from praised ihvh great

2. Great is the Lord, and highly to be praised in the city of our God. The mountain of his holiness,

יְפֵה נֹוף מְשֹׂושׂ כָּל־הָאָרֶץ הַר־צִיֹּון

Zion – mount earth – all elations undulating beautiful

יַרְכְּתֵי צָפֹון קִרְיַת מֶלֶךְ רָב:

much king city north sides

3. Beautiful for situation, the joy of the whole earth, is Mount Zion, on the sides of the north, the city of the great King.

אֱלֹהִים בְּאַרְמְנֹותֶיהָ נֹודַע לְמִשְׂגָּב:

to refuge known in her palaces Elohim

4. God is known in her palaces for a refuge.

כִּי־הִנֵּה הַמְּלָכִים נֹועֲדוּ עָבְרוּ יַחְדָּו:

together they passed by they combined the kings here - like

5. For, behold, the kings were assembled, they came on together.

הֵמָּה רָאוּ כֵּן תָּמָהוּ נִבְהֲלוּ נֶחְפָּזוּ:

they away they troubled they marveled thus they saw they are

6. As soon as they saw it, they were astounded; they were frightened; they fled away.

רְעָדָה אֲחָזָתַם שָׁם חִיל כַּיֹּולֵדָה:

like woman begetting convulsions there took hold them trembling

7. Fear took hold of them there, and pain, like a woman in labor.

בְּרוּחַ קָדִים תְּשַׁבֵּר אֳנִיֹּות תַּרְשִׁישׁ:

Tarshish ships you broke east in wind

8. You break the ships of Tarshish with an east wind.

כַּאֲשֶׁר שָׁמַעְנוּ כֵּן רָאִינוּ בְּעִיר יְהֹוָה צְבָאֹות בְּעִיר אֱלֹהֵינוּ

our Elohim in city legions ihvh in city we saw thus we heard when

אֱלֹהִים יְכֹונְנֶהָ עַד־עֹולָם סֶלָה:

Selah forever – till will establish it Elohim

9. As we have heard, so have we seen in the city of the Lord of hosts, in the city of our God; God will establish it for ever. Selah.

דִּמִּינוּ אֱלֹהִים חַסְדֶּךָ בְּקֶרֶב הֵיכָלֶךָ:

| your temple | in near | your kindness | Elohim | we likenessed |

10. We have thought of your loving kindness, O God, in the midst of your temple.

כְּשִׁמְךָ אֱלֹהִים כֵּן תְּהִלָּתְךָ עַל־קַצְוֵי־אֶרֶץ

| earth – far ends - upon | your prayers | thus | Elohim | like your name |

צֶדֶק מָלְאָה יְמִינֶךָ:

| your right hand | fills | righteous |

11. According to your name, O God, so is your praise to the ends of the earth; your right hand is full of righteousness.

יִשְׂמַח הַר־צִיּוֹן תָּגֵלְנָה בְּנוֹת יְהוּדָה לְמַעַן מִשְׁפָּטֶיךָ:

| your judgments | to end | Judah | daughters | you rejoice | Zion – mount | be happy |

12. Let Mount Zion rejoice, let the daughters of Judah be glad, because of your judgments.

סֹבּוּ צִיּוֹן וְהַקִּיפוּהָ סִפְרוּ מִגְדָּלֶיהָ:

| her towers | you surround | and enclose her | Zion | you walk around |

13. Walk about Zion, and go around her; count her towers.

שִׁיתוּ לִבְּכֶם לְחֵילָה פַּסְּגוּ אַרְמְנוֹתֶיהָ

| her palaces | you survey | to her rampart | your heart | you set |

לְמַעַן תְּסַפְּרוּ לְדוֹר אַחֲרוֹן:

| following | to generation | you story | to end |

14. Mark well her bulwarks, consider her palaces; that you may tell it to the following generation,

כִּי זֶה אֱלֹהִים אֱלֹהֵינוּ עוֹלָם וָעֵד הוּא יְנַהֲגֵנוּ עַל־מוּת:

| death – upon | he will guide us | he | and time | forever | our Elohim | Elohim | this | like |

15. That this is God, our God for ever and ever; he will be our guide till death.

PSALM 49

ספר תהילים פרק מט

לַמְנַצֵּחַ לִבְנֵי־קֹרַח מִזְמוֹר:

Psalm — Korak - to sons — to mnatsak

1. To the chief Musician, A Psalm for the sons of Korah.

שִׁמְעוּ־זֹאת כָּל־הָעַמִּים הַאֲזִינוּ כָּל־יֹשְׁבֵי חָלֶד:

transient — dwellers - all — the you give ear — the peoples - all — this - you hear

2. Hear this all you peoples; give ear, all you inhabitants of the world;

גַּם־בְּנֵי אָדָם גַּם־בְּנֵי־אִישׁ יַחַד עָשִׁיר וְאֶבְיוֹן:

and needy — rich — together — man - sons - also — Adam — sons - also

3. Both low and high, rich and poor, together.

פִּי יְדַבֵּר חָכְמוֹת וְהָגוּת לִבִּי תְבוּנוֹת:

will be understanding — my heart — and meditation — wisdom — it will speak — my mouth

4. My mouth shall speak of wisdom; and the meditation of my heart shall be understanding.

אַטֶּה לְמָשָׁל אָזְנִי אֶפְתַּח בְּכִנּוֹר חִידָתִי:

my riddle — in lyre — I will open — my ear — to parable — I will incline

5. I will incline my ear to a parable; I will open my riddle to the lyre.

לָמָּה אִירָא בִּימֵי רָע עֲוֹן עֲקֵבַי יְסוּבֵּנִי:

surrounds me — my foes — inequity — evil — in days — I fear — why

6. Why should I fear in the days of evil, when the iniquity of my persecutors surrounds me?

הַבֹּטְחִים עַל־חֵילָם וּבְרֹב עָשְׁרָם יִתְהַלָּלוּ:

they boast — riches — and in much — their wealth - upon — the confiding ones

7. Those who trust in their wealth, and boast themselves in the multitude of their riches;

אָח לֹא־פָדֹה יִפְדֶּה אִישׁ לֹא־יִתֵּן לֵאלֹהִים כָּפְרוֹ:

his ransom — to Elohim — he gives - not — man — will redeem — redeeming - not — brother

8. None of them can by any means ransom his brother, nor give to God a price for him;

וְיֵקַר פִּדְיוֹן נַפְשָׁם וְחָדַל לְעוֹלָם:

to forever — and forebears — their soul — redemption — and costly

9. For the ransom of their soul is costly, and it ceases for ever;

וִיחִי־עוֹד לָנֶצַח לֹא יִרְאֶה הַשָּׁחַת:

the pit — he see — not — to victory — again - and he lives

10. That he might still live for ever, and not see the pit.

כִּי יִרְאֶה חֲכָמִים יָמוּתוּ

they die — wise ones — he sees — like

יַחַד כְּסִיל וָבַעַר יֹאבֵדוּ וְעָזְבוּ לַאֲחֵרִים חֵילָם:

their wealth   to other ones   and leave   they perish   and brutish   fool   together

11. For when he sees that wise men die, that the fool and the stupid alike perish, and leave their wealth to others,

קִרְבָּם בָּתֵּימוֹ לְעוֹלָם מִשְׁכְּנֹתָם לְדֹר וָדֹר

and generation   to generation   their dwelling   to forever   their houses   their closeness

קָרְאוּ בִשְׁמוֹתָם עֲלֵי אֲדָמוֹת:

their soils   over   in their own names   they call

12. Their inward thought is that their houses shall continue for ever, and their dwelling places to all generations; they call their lands after their own names.

וְאָדָם בִּיקָר בַּל־יָלִין נִמְשַׁל כַּבְּהֵמוֹת נִדְמוּ:

they perish   like beasts   he comparable   he abides - in not   in honor   and Adam

13. Nevertheless man does not abide in honor; he is like the beasts that perish.

זֶה דַרְכָּם כֵּסֶל לָמוֹ וְאַחֲרֵיהֶם בְּפִיהֶם יִרְצוּ סֶלָה:

Sela   they pleased   in their mouth   and after them   to them   folly   their way   this

14. This is their way in their folly; yet their posterity approve their sayings. Selah.

כַּצֹּאן לִשְׁאוֹל שַׁתּוּ מָוֶת יִרְעֵם

he shepherds   death   they set   to Sheol   like sheep

וַיִּרְדּוּ בָם יְשָׁרִים לַבֹּקֶר וְצִירָם [וְצוּרָם]

and their form   to morning   upright ones   in them   and they descend

לְבַלּוֹת שְׁאוֹל מִזְּבֻל לוֹ:

to it   from residence   Sheol   to decay

15. (K) Like sheep they are appointed to Sheol; death shall be their shepherd;and the upright shall have dominion over them in the morning; and their form shall waste away in Sheol, leaving behind their dwelling.

אַךְ־אֱלֹהִים יִפְדֶּה נַפְשִׁי מִיַּד־שְׁאוֹל כִּי יִקָּחֵנִי סֶלָה:

Sela   he will take me   like   Sheol - from hand   my soul   will redeem   Elohim - then

16. But God will redeem my soul from the power of Sheol; for he shall receive me. Selah.

אַל־תִּירָא כִּי־יַעֲשִׁר אִישׁ כִּי־יִרְבֶּה כְּבוֹד בֵּיתוֹ:

his house   glory   he increase - like   man   he be enriched - like   fear - don't

17. Do not be afraid when one is made rich, when the glory of his house is increased;

כִּי לֹא בְמוֹתוֹ יִקַּח הַכֹּל לֹא־יֵרֵד אַחֲרָיו כְּבוֹדוֹ:

his glory   his after   he will descend - not   the all   he will take   in his dying   not   like

18. For when he dies he shall carry nothing away; his glory shall not go down after him.

כִּי־נַפְשׁוֹ בְּחַיָּיו יְבָרֵךְ וְיוֹדֻךָ כִּי־תֵיטִיב לָךְ:

to yourself   you do good - like   and they will praise you   he blesses   in his life   his soul - like

19. Though while he lives he blesses his soul; and though men will praise you when you

do well for yourself.

תָּבוֹא עַד־דּוֹר אֲבוֹתָיו עַד־נֵצַח לֹא יִרְאוּ־אוֹר:

light - they will see   not   victory - till   his fathers   generation - till   he will go

20. He shall go to the generation of his fathers; they shall never see light.

אָדָם בִּיקָר וְלֹא יָבִין נִמְשַׁל כַּבְּהֵמוֹת נִדְמוּ:

they perish   like beasts   comparable   he understands   and not   in precious   Adam

21. Man who is in honor, and does not understands, is like the beasts that perish.

PSALM 50

ספר תהילים פרק נ

מִזְמוֹר לְאָסָף
    to Asaph   Psalm

אֵל אֱלֹהִים יְהוָה
   ihvh   Elohim   El

דִּבֶּר וַיִּקְרָא־אָרֶץ מִמִּזְרַח־שֶׁמֶשׁ עַד־מְבֹאוֹ:
it's setting - till   sun – from rising   earth – and he called   spoke

1. A Psalm of Asaph. The mighty God, the Lord, speaks and summons the earth from the rising of the sun to its setting.

מִצִּיּוֹן מִכְלַל־יֹפִי אֱלֹהִים הוֹפִיעַ:
    shines   Elohim   beauty – from protection   from Zion

2. Out of Zion, the perfection of beauty, God shines forth.

יָבֹא אֱלֹהֵינוּ וְאַל־יֶחֱרַשׁ אֵשׁ־לְפָנָיו תֹּאכֵל
  it eats   before him – fire   he silent – and don't   our Elohim   he come

וּסְבִיבָיו נִשְׂעֲרָה מְאֹד:
    very   tempestuous   and around him

3. Our God comes, and does not keep silence; a fire devours before him, and there is a mighty tempest around him.

יִקְרָא אֶל־הַשָּׁמַיִם מֵעָל וְאֶל־הָאָרֶץ לָדִין עַמּוֹ:
his people   to judge   the earth - and unto   above   the heavens - unto   he calls

4. He calls to the heavens from above, and to the earth, that he may judge his people.

אִסְפוּ־לִי חֲסִידָי כֹּרְתֵי בְרִיתִי עֲלֵי־זָבַח:
sacrifice - upon   my covenant   cutter one   my pious   to me - they gather

5. Gather my pious ones together to me; those who have made a covenant with me by sacrifice.

וַיַּגִּידוּ שָׁמַיִם צִדְקוֹ כִּי־אֱלֹהִים שֹׁפֵט הוּא סֶלָה:
  Sela   he   judger   Elohim – like   his righteousness   heaven   and they declared

6. And the heavens shall declare his righteousness; for God is judge himself. Selah.

שִׁמְעָה עַמִּי וַאֲדַבֵּרָה יִשְׂרָאֵל וְאָעִידָה בָּךְ אֱלֹהִים
   Elohim   in you and I will testify   Israel   and I will speak   my people   hear

אֱלֹהֶיךָ אָנֹכִי:
   I am   your Elohim

7. Hear, O my people, and I will speak; O Israel, and I will testify against you; I am God, your God.

לֹא עַל־זְבָחֶיךָ אוֹכִיחֶךָ וְעוֹלֹתֶיךָ לְנֶגְדִּי תָמִיד:
continually   to before me   and your burnt offering   I will rebuke you   your sacrifices - upon   not

8. I will not reprove you for your sacrifices, and your burnt offerings are continually before me.

לֹא־אֶקַּח מִבֵּיתְךָ פָר מִמִּכְלְאֹתֶיךָ עַתּוּדִים׃

he goats	from your folds	bull	from your house	I will take - not

9. I will accept no bull from your house, nor male goats from your folds.

כִּי־לִי כָל־חַיְתוֹ־יָעַר בְּהֵמוֹת בְּהַרְרֵי־אָלֶף׃

thousand - in mountains	beasts	forest – it's life – all	to me - like

10. For every beast of the forest is mine, and the cattle upon a thousand mountains.

יָדַעְתִּי כָּל־עוֹף הָרִים וְזִיז שָׂדַי עִמָּדִי׃

with me	field	and mamals	mountains	fowl – all	I know

11. I know all the birds of the mountains; and the wild beasts of the field are mine.

אִם־אֶרְעַב לֹא־אֹמַר לָךְ כִּי־לִי תֵבֵל וּמְלֹאָהּ׃

and its fullness	world	to me	like	to you	I say - not	I hungry - if

12. If I were hungry, I would not tell you; for the world is mine, and all that fills it.

הַאוֹכַל בְּשַׂר אַבִּירִים וְדַם עַתּוּדִים אֶשְׁתֶּה׃

I drink	he goats	and blood	bulls	flesh	the eating

13. Do I eat the flesh of bulls, or drink the blood of goats?

זְבַח לֵאלֹהִים תּוֹדָה וְשַׁלֵּם לְעֶלְיוֹן נְדָרֶיךָ׃

your vows	to most high	and pay	thanks	to Elohim	sacrifice

14. Offer to God thanksgiving; and pay your vows to the most High;

וּקְרָאֵנִי בְּיוֹם צָרָה אֲחַלֶּצְךָ וּתְכַבְּדֵנִי׃

and you will glorify me	I will deliver you	trouble	in day	and call me

15. And call upon me in the day of trouble; I will save you, and you shall glorify me.

וְלָרָשָׁע אָמַר אֱלֹהִים מַה־לְּךָ לְסַפֵּר חֻקָּי׃

my statute	to declare	to you- what	Elohim	said	and wicked

וַתִּשָּׂא בְרִיתִי עֲלֵי־פִיךָ׃

my mouth - upon	my covenant	and you lift

16. But to the wicked man God says, What right have to you to declare my statutes, or to take my covenant in your mouth?

וְאַתָּה שָׂנֵאתָ מוּסָר וַתַּשְׁלֵךְ דְּבָרַי אַחֲרֶיךָ׃

behind you	my words	and you cast	instruction	hate	and you

17. For you hate instruction, and cast my words behind you.

אִם־רָאִיתָ גַנָּב וַתִּרֶץ עִמּוֹ וְעִם מְנָאֲפִים חֶלְקֶךָ׃

your portion	adulterers	and with	with him	and you pleased	thief	you see - if

18. If you see a thief, you consort with him, and you keep company with adulterers.

פִּיךָ שָׁלַחְתָּ בְרָעָה וּלְשׁוֹנְךָ תַּצְמִיד מִרְמָה׃

deceit	pairing	and your tongue	in evil	casts	your mouth

19. You give your mouth free rein for evil, and your tongue frames deceit.

תֵּשֵׁב בְּאָחִיךָ   תְדַבֵּר   בְּבֶן־אִמְּךָ   תִּתֶּן־דֹּפִי׃

scandal – you give   your mothers – in son   you speak   in your brother   you sit

20. You sit and speak against your brother; you slander the son of your own mother.

אֵלֶּה עָשִׂיתָ וְהֶחֱרַשְׁתִּי דְּמִיתָ הֱיוֹת אֶהְיֶה כָמוֹךָ

like you   I will be   being   you thought   and I was silent   you done   these

אוֹכִיחֲךָ   וְאֶעֶרְכָה לְעֵינֶיךָ׃

to your eyes   and I set in order   I will rebuke you

21. You have done these things, and I have kept silence; you thought that I was one like yourself; but I will rebuke you and set the matter before your eyes.

בִּינוּ־נָא זֹאת שֹׁכְחֵי אֱלוֹהַּ פֶּן־אֶטְרֹף וְאֵין מַצִּיל׃

rescuer   and isn't   I will tear pieces- lest   Elohim   forgeters   this   now - consider

22. Now consider this, you who forget God, lest I tear you in pieces, and there be none to save.

זֹבֵחַ תּוֹדָה יְכַבְּדָנְנִי וְשָׂם דֶּרֶךְ אַרְאֶנּוּ בְּיֵשַׁע אֱלֹהִים׃

Elohim   in salvation   I will look   way   and sets   glorifies me   thanksgiving   sacrifices

23. Whoever offers praise glorifies me; and to him who orders his way aright I will show the salvation of God.

PSALM 51

ספר תהילים פרק נא

לַמְנַצֵּחַ מִזְמוֹר לְדָוִד:

to David　psalm　to chief Musician

1. To the chief Musician, A Psalm of David,

בְּבוֹא־אֵלָיו נָתָן הַנָּבִיא כַּאֲשֶׁר־בָּא אֶל־בַּת־שָׁבַע:

Sheba – Bat – unto　came - when　the profit　Nathan　to him – in going

2. When Nathan the prophet came to him, after he had gone in to Bathsheba.

חׇנֵּנִי אֱלֹהִים כְּחַסְדֶּךָ כְּרֹב רַחֲמֶיךָ מְחֵה פְשָׁעָי:

my transgressions　blot out　your mercies　like much　like your kindness　Elohim　be gracious to me

3. Be gracious to me, O God, according to your loving kindness; according to the multitude of your mercies blot out my transgressions.

הַרְבֵּה [הֶרֶב] כַּבְּסֵנִי מֵעֲוֹנִי וּמֵחַטָּאתִי טַהֲרֵנִי:

cleanse me　and from my sin　from my iniquity　wash me　the much

4. (K) Wash me thoroughly from my iniquity, and cleanse me from my sin.

כִּי־פְשָׁעַי אֲנִי אֵדָע וְחַטָּאתִי נֶגְדִּי תָמִיד:

continually　before me　and my sin　know　I　my transgressions - like

5. For I acknowledge my transgressions; and my sin is always before me.

לְךָ לְבַדְּךָ חָטָאתִי וְהָרַע בְּעֵינֶיךָ

in your eyes　and the evil　I sinned　you alone　to you

עָשִׂיתִי לְמַעַן־תִּצְדַּק בְּדׇבְרֶךָ תִּזְכֶּה בְשָׁפְטֶךָ:

in your judging　you clear　in your speaking　you be justified - to end　I did

6. Against you, you alone, have I sinned, and done this evil in your sight; so that you are justified in your sentence, and clear in your judgment.

הֵן־בְּעָווֹן חוֹלָלְתִּי וּבְחֵטְא יֶחֱמַתְנִי אִמִּי:

my mother　conceived me　and in sin　I travailed　in inequity - here

7. Behold, I was shaped in iniquity, and in sin my mother conceived me.

הֵן־אֱמֶת חָפַצְתָּ בַטֻּחוֹת וּבְסָתֻם חׇכְמָה תוֹדִיעֵנִי:

you make me know　wisdom　and in secret place　in inward parts　your delighted in　truth - here

8. Behold, you desire truth in the inward parts; therefore teach me wisdom in the inmost heart.

תְּחַטְּאֵנִי בְאֵזוֹב וְאֶטְהָר תְּכַבְּסֵנִי וּמִשֶּׁלֶג אַלְבִּין:

I will be white　and from snow　you wash me　and I will be clean　in hyssop　you purge me

9. Purge me with hyssop, and I shall be clean; wash me, and I shall be whiter than snow.

תַּשְׁמִיעֵנִי שָׂשׂוֹן וְשִׂמְחָה תָּגֵלְנָה עֲצָמוֹת דִּכִּיתָ:

you crushed　bones　you rejoice　and happiness　rejoicing　you make me hear

10. Let me hear joy and gladness; that the bones which you have broken may rejoice.

הַסְתֵּר פָּנֶיךָ מֵחֲטָאָי וְכָל־עֲוֹנֹתַי מְחֵה:

blot out   my inequities - and all   from my sins   your face   hide

11. Hide your face from my sins, and blot out all my iniquities.

לֵב טָהוֹר בְּרָא־לִי אֱלֹהִים וְרוּחַ נָכוֹן חַדֵּשׁ בְּקִרְבִּי:

in my insides   renew   correct   and spirit   Elohim   to me – create   pure   heart

12. Create in me a clean heart, O God; and renew a constant spirit inside me.

אַל־תַּשְׁלִיכֵנִי מִלְּפָנֶיךָ וְרוּחַ קָדְשְׁךָ אַל־תִּקַּח מִמֶּנִּי:

from me   you take – don't   your holiness   and spirit   from your presence   you cast out me - don't

13. Do not cast me away from your presence; and do not take your holy spirit from me.

הָשִׁיבָה לִּי שְׂשׂוֹן יִשְׁעֶךָ וְרוּחַ נְדִיבָה תִסְמְכֵנִי:

you support me   willing   and spirit   your salvation   joy   to me   the restore

14. Restore to me the joy of your salvation; and uphold me with a willing spirit.

אֲלַמְּדָה פֹשְׁעִים דְּרָכֶיךָ וְחַטָּאִים אֵלֶיךָ יָשׁוּבוּ:

they will return   unto you   and sinners   your ways   transgressor ones   I will teach

15. Then I will teach transgressors your ways; and sinners shall return to you.

הַצִּילֵנִי מִדָּמִים אֱלֹהִים אֱלֹהֵי תְּשׁוּעָתִי

you my salvation   my Elohim   Elohim   from blood ones   deliver me

תְּרַנֵּן לְשׁוֹנִי צִדְקָתֶךָ:

your righteousness   my tongue   will joy shout

16. Save me from bloodguiltiness, O God, you God of my salvation; and my tongue shall sing aloud of your righteousness.

אֲדֹנָי שְׂפָתַי תִּפְתָּח וּפִי יַגִּיד תְּהִלָּתֶךָ:

your praise   it will tell   and my mouth   you open   my lips   Adonai

17. O Lord, open you my lips; and my mouth shall declare your praise.

כִּי לֹא־תַחְפֹּץ זֶבַח וְאֶתֵּנָה עוֹלָה לֹא תִרְצֶה:

you pleased   not   burnt offering   and I give it   sacrifice   delight – not   like

18. For you do not desire sacrifice; or else would I give it; you do not delight in burnt offering.

זִבְחֵי אֱלֹהִים רוּחַ נִשְׁבָּרָה

broken   spirit   Elohim   sacrifices

לֵב־נִשְׁבָּר וְנִדְכֶּה אֱלֹהִים לֹא תִבְזֶה:

you will despise   not   Elohim   and crushed   broken – heart

19. The sacrifices of God are a broken spirit; a broken and contrite heart, O God, you will not despise.

הֵיטִיבָה בִרְצוֹנְךָ אֶת־צִיּוֹן תִּבְנֶה חוֹמוֹת יְרוּשָׁלָםִ:

Jerusalem   walls   you build   Zion – that   in your favor   the good

20. Do good in your good will to Zion; build the walls of Jerusalem.

אָז תַּחְפֹּץ זִבְחֵי־צֶדֶק עוֹלָה וְכָלִיל
and whole burnt offering · burnt offering · righteous - sacrifices · you will delight · then

אָז יַעֲלוּ עַל־מִזְבַּחֲךָ פָרִים:
bulls · your altar – upon · they will offer up · then

21. Then shall you be pleased with the sacrifices of righteousness, with burnt offering and whole burnt offering; then shall they offer bulls upon your altar.

PSALM 52

ספר תהילים פרק נב

לַמְנַצֵּחַ   מַשְׂכִּיל   לְדָוִד:
to David   maskil   to him that is over

1. To the chief Musician, A Maskil of David.

בְּבוֹא דּוֹאֵג הָאֲדֹמִי וַיַּגֵּד לְשָׁאוּל
to Saul   and he told   the Edomite   Doeg   in coming

וַיֹּאמֶר לוֹ בָּא דָוִד אֶל־בֵּית אֲחִימֶלֶךְ:
Ahimelech   house – unto   David   come   to him   and he said

2. When Doeg the Edomite came and told Saul, and said to him, David has come to the house of Ahimelech.

מַה־תִּתְהַלֵּל בְּרָעָה הַגִּבּוֹר חֶסֶד אֵל כָּל־הַיּוֹם:
the day – all   El   kindness   the mighty man   in evil   you boast - what

3. Why do you boast of evil, O mighty man? The love of God lasts for all time.

הַוּוֹת תַּחְשֹׁב לְשׁוֹנֶךָ כְּתַעַר מְלֻטָּשׁ עֹשֵׂה רְמִיָּה:
deciet   doing   sharpened   like razor   to your tongue   you devised   destruction

4. Your tongue devises mischiefs; like a sharp razor, working deceitfully.

אָהַבְתָּ רָּע מִטּוֹב שֶׁקֶר מִדַּבֵּר צֶדֶק סֶלָה:
Sela   righteousness   from speaking   lie   from good   evil   you loved

5. You love evil more than good; and lying rather than speaking righteousness. Selah.

אָהַבְתָּ כָל־דִּבְרֵי־בָלַע לְשׁוֹן מִרְמָה:
deciet   tongue   devouring – speaking – all   you loved

6. You love all devouring words, O you deceitful tongue.

גַּם־אֵל יִתָּצְךָ לָנֶצַח יַחְתְּךָ וְיִסָּחֲךָ מֵאֹהֶל
from tent   and he will pluck you   he will seize   to victory   will shatter you   El - also

וְשֵׁרֶשְׁךָ מֵאֶרֶץ חַיִּים סֶלָה:
Sela   living   from earth   and will uproot you

7. God shall likewise destroy you for ever, he shall take you away, and pluck you out of your dwelling place, and root you out of the land of the living. Selah.

וְיִרְאוּ צַדִּיקִים וְיִירָאוּ וְעָלָיו יִשְׂחָקוּ:
they will laugh   and upon him   and they will fear   righteous ones   and they will see

8. And the righteous shall see, and fear, and shall laugh at him;

הִנֵּה הַגֶּבֶר לֹא־יָשִׂים אֱלֹהִים מָעוּזּוֹ
stronghold   Elohim   will set - not   the gentleman   here

וַיִּבְטַח בְּרֹב עָשְׁרוֹ יָעֹז בְּהַוָּתוֹ:
in his destruction   he strengthened him   his riches   in much   and he trusted

9. Behold, this is the man who did not make God his strength; but trusted in the

abundance of his riches, and strengthened himself in his wickedness.

וַאֲנִי כְּזַיִת רַעֲנָן בְּבֵית אֱלֹהִים בָּטַחְתִּי בְחֶסֶד

| in mercy | I trusted | Elohim | in house | flourishing | like olive | and I |

אֱלֹהִים עוֹלָם וָעֶד:

| and time | forever | Elohim |

10. But I am like a green olive tree in the house of God; I trust in the love of God for ever and ever.

אוֹדְךָ לְעוֹלָם כִּי עָשִׂיתָ וַאֲקַוֶּה שִׁמְךָ

| your name | and I will wait | you did | like | to forever | I will thank you |

כִי־טוֹב נֶגֶד חֲסִידֶיךָ:

| your devout | before | good – like |

11. I will give you thanks for ever, because you have done it; and I will wait on your name, for it is good, before your pious ones.

PSALM 53

ספר תהילים פרק נג

לַמְנַצֵּחַ   עַל־מָחֲלַת   מַשְׂכִּיל לְדָוִד:
to chief Musician   Mahalath - upon   maskil   to David

1. To the chief Musician according to Mahalath, A Maskil of David.

אָמַר נָבָל בְּלִבּוֹ אֵין אֱלֹהִים
said   fool   in his heart   isn't   Elohim

הִשְׁחִיתוּ וְהִתְעִיבוּ עָוֶל אֵין עֹשֵׂה־טוֹב:
they corrupt   and they abominable   inequity   isn't   good – doer

2. The fool has said in his heart, There is no God. They are corrupt, and have done abominable iniquity; there is none that does good.

אֱלֹהִים מִשָּׁמַיִם הִשְׁקִיף עַל־בְּנֵי אָדָם
Elohim   from heavens   looked down   sons – upon   Adam

לִרְאוֹת הֲיֵשׁ מַשְׂכִּיל דֹּרֵשׁ אֶת־אֱלֹהִים:
to see   the there is   intellect   seeker   Elohim – that

3. God looked down from heaven upon the children of men, to see if there were any who understand, who seek God.

כֻּלּוֹ סָג יַחְדָּו נֶאֱלָחוּ אֵין עֹשֵׂה־טוֹב אֵין גַּם אֶחָד:
everyone   dross   together   they depraved   isn't   good – doer   isn't   also   one

4. They have all fallen away; they have all become filthy; there is no one who does good, not even one.

הֲלֹא יָדְעוּ פֹּעֲלֵי אָוֶן אֹכְלֵי עַמִּי אָכְלוּ לֶחֶם
the not   they know   workers   inequity   eating   my people   they ate   bread

אֱלֹהִים לֹא קָרָאוּ:
Elohim   not   they call

5. Have the evil doers no knowledge, who eat up my people as they eat bread? Do they not call upon God?

שָׁם פָּחֲדוּ־פַחַד לֹא־הָיָה פָחַד
there   dread - they dread   was – not   dread

כִּי־אֱלֹהִים פִּזַּר עַצְמוֹת חֹנָךְ הֱבִשֹׁתָה כִּי־אֱלֹהִים מְאָסָם:
Elohim - like   scatters   bones   camper   to shame   Elohim – like   despised them

6. There were they in great fear, where no fear was; for God has scattered the bones of him who encamps against you; you have put them to shame, because God has rejected them.

מִי־יִתֵּן מִצִּיּוֹן יְשׁוּעוֹת יִשְׂרָאֵל בְּשׁוּב
gives - who   from Zion   salvations   Israel   in returning

אֱלֹהִים שְׁבוּת עַמּוֹ   יָגֵל יַעֲקֹב יִשְׂמַח יִשְׂרָאֵל׃

     Israel   will be happy   Jacob   rejoice   his people   captivity   Elohim

7. Oh that the salvation of Israel would come out of Zion! When God brings back the exile of his people, Jacob shall rejoice, and Israel shall be glad.

PSALM 54

ספר תהילים פרק נד

לַמְנַצֵּחַ   בִּנְגִינֹת   מַשְׂכִּיל לְדָוִד:

to David   Maskil   in Neigot   to chief musician

1. To the chief Musician for stringed instruments, A Maskil of David,

בְּבוֹא הַזִּיפִים וַיֹּאמְרוּ לְשָׁאוּל הֲלֹא־דָוִד מִסְתַּתֵּר עִמָּנוּ:

with us   from hiding   David – the not   to Saul   and they said   the Ziphites   in came

2. When the Ziphites came and said to Saul, Does not David hide himself with us?

אֱלֹהִים בְּשִׁמְךָ הוֹשִׁיעֵנִי וּבִגְבוּרָתְךָ תְדִינֵנִי:

you judge me   and in your might   save me   in your name   Elohim

3. Save me, O God, by your name, and judge me by your strength.

אֱלֹהִים שְׁמַע תְּפִלָּתִי הַאֲזִינָה לְאִמְרֵי־פִי:

my mouth - to words   the ear   my prayer   hear   Elohim

4. Hear my prayer, O God; give ear to the words of my mouth.

כִּי זָרִים קָמוּ עָלַי וְעָרִיצִים בִּקְשׁוּ נַפְשִׁי

my soul   they sought   and oppressor ones   upon me   they arose   strangers   like

לֹא שָׂמוּ אֱלֹהִים לְנֶגְדָּם סֶלָה:

Sela   to before them   Elohim   they set   not

5. For strangers have risen up against me, and oppressors seek after my soul; they have not set God before them. Selah.

הִנֵּה אֱלֹהִים עֹזֵר לִי אֲדֹנָי בְּסֹמְכֵי נַפְשִׁי:

my soul   in supporting   Adoni   to me   helper   Elohim   here

6. Behold, God is my helper; the Lord is with those who uphold my soul.

יָשׁוּב [יָשִׁיב] הָרַע לְשֹׁרְרִי בַּאֲמִתְּךָ הַצְמִיתֵם:

the efface them   in your truth   to lying in wait ones   the evil   he returns

7. (K) He rewards evil to my enemies. O, cut them off in your truth!

בִּנְדָבָה אֶזְבְּחָה־לָּךְ אוֹדֶה שִׁמְךָ יְהוָה כִּי־טוֹב:

good – like   ihvh   your name   I will thank   to you - I will sacrifice   in free will offering.

8. I will sacrifice a free will offering to you; I will praise your name, O Lord; for it is good.

כִּי מִכָּל־צָרָה הִצִּילָנִי וּבְאֹיְבַי רָאֲתָה עֵינִי:

my eye   has seen   and in my enemies   he delivered me   distress from all   like

9. For he has saved me from every trouble; and my eye has gazed upon my enemies.

Psalm 55

ספר תהילים פרק נה

לַמְנַצֵּחַ בִּנְגִינֹת מַשְׂכִּיל לְדָוִד׃

to David   Maskil   in Neginath   to chief Musician

1. To the chief Musician for stringed instruments, A Maskil of David.

הַאֲזִינָה אֱלֹהִים תְּפִלָּתִי וְאַל־תִּתְעַלַּם מִתְּחִנָּתִי׃

from my supplication   hide yourself and don't   my prayer   Elohim   the give ear

2. Give ear to my prayer, O God; and do not hide yourself from my supplication.

הַקְשִׁיבָה לִּי וַעֲנֵנִי אָרִיד בְּשִׂיחִי וְאָהִימָה׃

and I moan   in my complaint   I restless   and answer me   to me   the attend

3. Attend to me, and answer me; I so in my complaint, and moan,

מִקּוֹל אוֹיֵב מִפְּנֵי עָקַת רָשָׁע כִּי־יָמִיטוּ עָלַי

upon me   they cast   like   wicked   pressure   in front   enemy   from voice

אָוֶן וּבְאַף יִשְׂטְמוּנִי׃

they hate me   and in anger   iniquity

4. Because of the voice of the enemy, because of the oppression of the wicked; for they cast iniquity upon me, and in wrath they hate me.

לִבִּי יָחִיל בְּקִרְבִּי וְאֵימוֹת מָוֶת נָפְלוּ עָלָי׃

upon me   it fallen   death   and terrors   in my midst   anguish   my heart

5. My heart inside me is in anguish; and the terrors of death have fallen upon me.

יִרְאָה וָרַעַד יָבֹא בִי וַתְּכַסֵּנִי פַּלָּצוּת׃

horrors   and covered me   in me   it came   and trembling   fear

6. Fearfulness and trembling have come upon me, and horror has overwhelmed me.

וָאֹמַר מִי־יִתֶּן־לִּי אֵבֶר כַּיּוֹנָה אָעוּפָה וְאֶשְׁכֹּנָה׃

and roost   I fly away   like dove   wings   to me - it give - who   and I said

7. And I said, Oh that I had wings like a dove! For then I would fly away, and be at rest.

הִנֵּה אַרְחִיק נְדֹד אָלִין בַּמִּדְבָּר סֶלָה׃

Sela   the wilderness   I lodge   fleeting   I put far   here

8. Behold, then I would wander far off, and remain in the wilderness. Selah.

אָחִישָׁה מִפְלָט לִי מֵרוּחַ סֹעָה מִסָּעַר׃

from tempest   storming   from spirit   to me   escape   I hasten

9. I would hasten to find a refuge from the windy storm and the tempest.

בַּלַּע אֲדֹנָי פַּלַּג לְשׁוֹנָם כִּי־רָאִיתִי חָמָס וְרִיב בָּעִיר׃

in city   and strife   violence   I saw - like   their tongues   divide   Adonai   swallow up

10. Destroy, O Lord, and divide their tongues; for I have seen violence and strife in the city.

יוֹמָם וָלַיְלָה יְסוֹבְבֻהָ עַל־חוֹמֹתֶיהָ וְאָוֶן וְעָמָל בְּקִרְבָּהּ:

in its midst   and mischief   and iniquity   its walls - upon   they surround it   and night   by day

11. Day and night they go about it upon its walls; and mischief and trouble are in its midst.

הַוּוֹת בְּקִרְבָּהּ וְלֹא־יָמִישׁ מֵרְחֹבָהּ תֹּךְ וּמִרְמָה:

and deceit   oppression   from its streets   depart – and not   in its midst   destructions

12. Wickedness is in its midst; oppression and deceit do not depart from her streets.

כִּי לֹא־אוֹיֵב יְחָרְפֵנִי וְאֶשָּׂא לֹא־מְשַׂנְאִי עָלַי הִגְדִּיל

magnified   upon me   hating me – not   and I bear   he taunt me   enemy – not   like

וְאֶסָּתֵר מִמֶּנּוּ:

from him   and I will hide myself

13. For it was not an enemy who taunted me; then I could have borne it; nor was it one who hated me who magnified himself against me; then I could hide from him,

וְאַתָּה אֱנוֹשׁ כְּעֶרְכִּי אַלּוּפִי וּמְיֻדָּעִי:

and my close friend   my associate   like my rank   man   and you

14. But it was you, a man my equal, my companion, my close friend.

אֲשֶׁר יַחְדָּו נַמְתִּיק סוֹד בְּבֵית אֱלֹהִים נְהַלֵּךְ בְּרָגֶשׁ:

in throng   we walked   Elohim   in house   foundation   we sweeten   together   which

15. We took sweet counsel together, and walked to the house of God in company.

יַשִּׁימָוֶת [יַשִּׁיא מָוֶת] עָלֵימוֹ יֵרְדוּ שְׁאוֹל

Shoel   they descend   upon them   spread death

חַיִּים כִּי־רָעוֹת בִּמְגוּרָם בְּקִרְבָּם:

in their midst   in their sojourning   evil ones - like   living

16. (K) Let death spread its oblivion upon them, and let them go down alive into Sheol; for wickedness is in their dwellings, and among them.

אֲנִי אֶל־אֱלֹהִים אֶקְרָא וַיהֹוָה יוֹשִׁיעֵנִי:

he will save me   and ihvh   I will call   Elohim - unto   I

17. As for me, I will call upon God; and the Lord shall save me.

עֶרֶב וָבֹקֶר וְצָהֳרַיִם אָשִׂיחָה וְאֶהֱמֶה וַיִּשְׁמַע קוֹלִי:

my voice   and he heard   and I moan   I meditate   and noon   and morning   evening

18. Evening, and morning, and at noon, I pray, and cry aloud; and he hears my voice.

פָּדָה בְשָׁלוֹם נַפְשִׁי מִקְּרָב־לִי כִּי־בְרַבִּים הָיוּ עִמָּדִי:

with me   they were   in many - like   to me – from battle   my soul   in peace   he redeemed

19. He has saved my soul in peace from the battle that was against me; for there were many who strove against me.

יִשְׁמַע אֵל וְיַעֲנֵם וְיֹשֵׁב קֶדֶם סֶלָה אֲשֶׁר אֵין חֲלִיפוֹת

changes   isn't   which   Sela   of old   and he dwells   and he answers them   El   he will hear

לָמוֹ וְלֹא יָרְאוּ אֱלֹהִים׃

Elohim   they fear   and not   to them

20. God, who is enthroned from old, shall hear, and afflict them. Selah. Because they do not change, and do not fear God.

שָׁלַח יָדָיו בִּשְׁלֹמָיו חִלֵּל בְּרִיתוֹ׃

his covenant   he profaned   in his peace   his hands   he sent

21. He has put forth his hands against those who are at peace with him; he has broken his covenant.

חָלְקוּ מַחְמָאֹת פִּיו וּקֲרָב־לִבּוֹ רַכּוּ דְבָרָיו מִשֶּׁמֶן

from oil   his speakings   it soft   his heart – and battle   his mouth   from butter   they smooth

וְהֵמָּה פְתִחוֹת׃

drawn swords   and they were

22. The words of his mouth were smoother than butter, but war was in his heart; his words were softer than oil, yet they were drawn swords.

הַשְׁלֵךְ עַל־יְהֹוָה יְהָבְךָ וְהוּא יְכַלְכְּלֶךָ

will sustain you   and he   it your lot   ihvh - upon   cast

לֹא־יִתֵּן לְעוֹלָם מוֹט לַצַּדִּיק׃

to righteous   moving   to forever   he will give - not

23. Cast your burden upon the Lord, and he shall sustain you; he shall never let the righteous be moved.

וְאַתָּה אֱלֹהִים תּוֹרִדֵם לִבְאֵר שַׁחַת אַנְשֵׁי

men   grave   to pit   will bring down   Elohim   and you

דָמִים וּמִרְמָה לֹא־יֶחֱצוּ יְמֵיהֶם וַאֲנִי אֶבְטַח־בָּךְ׃

in you - I will trust   and I   their days   will it half - not   and deceit   bloods

24. But you, O God, shall bring them down into the pit of destruction; bloody and deceitful men shall not live out half their days; but I will trust in you.

PSALM 56

ספר תהילים פרק נו

לַמְנַצֵּחַ   עַל־יוֹנַת   אֵלֶם   רְחֹקִים

far ones   mute   dove – upon   to Chief Musician

לְדָוִד   מִכְתָּם   בֶּאֱחֹז   אֹתוֹ   פְלִשְׁתִּים   בְּגַת:

in Gath   Philistiness   to him   in seized   Miktam   to David

1. To the chief Musician, according to Jonat-helem-rechokim, A Miktam of David, when the Philistines seized him in Gath.

חָנֵּנִי   אֱלֹהִים   כִּי־שְׁאָפַנִי   אֱנוֹשׁ   כָּל־הַיּוֹם   לֹחֵם   יִלְחָצֵנִי:

will press me   fighter   the day - all   man   has panted – like   Elohim   be gracious to me

2. Be gracious to me, O God, for men long to swallow me up; all day long the warrior oppresses me.

שָׁאֲפוּ   שׁוֹרְרַי   כָּל־הַיּוֹם   כִּי־רַבִּים   לֹחֲמִים   לִי   מָרוֹם:

height   to me   fighter ones   many - like   the day – all   my watchers   panted for me

3. My enemies daily long to swallow me up; for they are many who fight against me, O you most High.

יוֹם   אִירָא   אֲנִי   אֵלֶיךָ   אֶבְטָח:

will trust   upon you   I   I afraid   day

4. When I am afraid, I will trust in you,

בֵּאלֹהִים   אֲהַלֵּל   דְּבָרוֹ   בֵּאלֹהִים   בָּטַחְתִּי

I trust   in Elohim   his speak   I will praise   in Elohim

לֹא   אִירָא   מַה־יַּעֲשֶׂה   בָשָׂר   לִי:

to me   flesh   it will do - what   I will fear   not

5. In God, whose word I praise, in God I have put my trust; I will not fear. What can flesh do to me?

כָּל־הַיּוֹם   דְּבָרַי   יְעַצֵּבוּ   עָלַי   כָּל־מַחְשְׁבֹתָם   לָרָע:

to evil   their thoughts – all   upon me   they will wrest   my speaking   the day - all

6. Every day they wrest my words; all their thoughts are against me for evil.

יָגוּרוּ   יִצְפִּינוּ [יִצְפּוֹנוּ]   הֵמָּה

they   they will hide   they gather together

עֲקֵבַי   יִשְׁמֹרוּ   כַּאֲשֶׁר   קִוּוּ   נַפְשִׁי:

my soul   they wait   when   they heed   my steps

7. (K) They gather themselves together, they hide themselves, they mark my steps, as they wait for my soul.

עַל־אָוֶן   פַּלֶּט־לָמוֹ   בְּאַף   עַמִּים   הוֹרֵד   אֱלֹהִים:

Elohim   cast down   peoples   in anger   to them – delivered   inequity - upon

8. Shall they escape by iniquity? In your anger cast down the peoples, O God.

נְדִי　　סָפַרְתָּה אַתָּה שִׂימָה דִמְעָתִי בְנֹאדֶךָ
my wandering　you counted　you　you put　my tears　in your bottle

הֲלֹא בְּסִפְרָתֶךָ:
the not　in your book

9. You have kept count of my wanderings; put my tears into your bottle. Are they not in your book?

אָז יָשׁוּבוּ אוֹיְבַי אָחוֹר בְּיוֹם אֶקְרָא
then　they will return　my enemies　backwards　in day　I call

זֶה־יָדַעְתִּי כִּי־אֱלֹהִים לִי:
I know - this　Elohim – like　to me

10. When I cry to you, then shall my enemies turn back; this I know, because God is for me.

בֵּאלֹהִים אֲהַלֵּל דָּבָר בַּיהוָֹה אֲהַלֵּל דָּבָר:
in Elohim　I praise　speech　in ihvh　I praise　speech

11. In God, whose word I praise; in the Lord, whose word I praise,

בֵּאלֹהִים בָּטַחְתִּי לֹא אִירָא מַה־יַּעֲשֶׂה אָדָם לִי:
in Elohim　my trust　not　I will fear　he will do - what　Adam　to me

12. In God have I put my trust; I will not be afraid. What man can do to me?

עָלַי אֱלֹהִים נְדָרֶיךָ אֲשַׁלֵּם תּוֹדֹת לָךְ:
upon me　Elohim　your vows　I will pay　thank offerings　to you

13. Your vows are upon me, O God, I will render thank offerings to you.

כִּי הִצַּלְתָּ נַפְשִׁי מִמָּוֶת הֲלֹא רַגְלַי
like　you delivered　my soul　from death　the not　my feet

מִדֶּחִי לְהִתְהַלֵּךְ לִפְנֵי אֱלֹהִים בְּאוֹר הַחַיִּים:
from expulsion　to cause walk　before　Elohim　in light　the life

14. For you have saved my soul from death, indeed my feet from falling, that I may walk before God in the light of the living.

PSALM 57

ספר תהילים פרק נז

לַמְנַצֵּחַ אַל־תַּשְׁחֵת לְדָוִד מִכְתָּם

to him that is over   don't   you destroy   to David   Michtam

בְּבָרְחוֹ מִפְּנֵי־שָׁאוּל בַּמְּעָרָה:

in his fleeing   Saul - from face   in cave

1. To the chief Musician, Altaschith, A Miktam of David, when he fled from Saul in the cave.

חָנֵּנִי אֱלֹהִים חָנֵּנִי כִּי בְךָ חָסָיָה נַפְשִׁי

my soul   takes refuge   in you   like   be gracious to me   Elohim   be gracious to me

וּבְצֵל־כְּנָפֶיךָ אֶחְסֶה עַד יַעֲבֹר הַוּוֹת:

destructions   it passes   till   I will take refuge   your wings – and in shadow

2. Be gracious to me, O God, be gracious to me, for my soul trusts in you; and in the shadow of your wings I will take refuge, until calamities have passed over.

אֶקְרָא לֵאלֹהִים עֶלְיוֹן לָאֵל גֹּמֵר עָלָי:

upon me   performs   to El   most high   to Elohim   I will call

3. I will cry to God most high; to God who performs all things for me.

יִשְׁלַח מִשָּׁמַיִם וְיוֹשִׁיעֵנִי חֵרֵף שֹׁאֲפִי סֶלָה

Sela   my gasping   reproaches   and he will save me   from heavens   he will send

יִשְׁלַח אֱלֹהִים חַסְדּוֹ וַאֲמִתּוֹ:

and his truth   his kindness   Elohim   he will send

4. He shall send from heaven, and save me; he scorns him who would swallow me up. Selah. God shall send forth his loving kindness and his truth.

נַפְשִׁי בְּתוֹךְ לְבָאִם אֶשְׁכְּבָה לֹהֲטִים

to flames   I lie down   loins   in midst   my soul

בְּנֵי־אָדָם שִׁנֵּיהֶם חֲנִית וְחִצִּים וּלְשׁוֹנָם חֶרֶב חַדָּה:

sharp   sword   and their tongue   and arrows   spear   their teeth   Adam - sons

5. My soul is among lions; and I lie down among those who are set on fire, the sons of men, whose teeth are spears and arrows, and their tongue a sharp sword.

רוּמָה עַל־הַשָּׁמַיִם אֱלֹהִים עַל כָּל־הָאָרֶץ כְּבוֹדֶךָ:

your glory   the earth - all   upon   Elohim   the heaven – upon   be exhaulted

6. Be exalted, O God, above the heavens; let your glory be above all the earth.

רֶשֶׁת הֵכִינוּ לִפְעָמַי כָּפַף נַפְשִׁי

my soul   bowed down   to my steps   they prepared   net

כָּרוּ לְפָנַי שִׁיחָה נָפְלוּ בְתוֹכָה סֶלָה:

Sela   in midst   they fallen   pit   before me   they dug

7. They have prepared a net for my steps; my soul is bowed down; they dug a pit before

me, and into its midst they have fallen themselves. Selah.

נָכוֹן לִבִּי אֱלֹהִים נָכוֹן לִבִּי אָשִׁירָה וַאֲזַמֵּרָה׃

| I will sing psalms | I will sing | my heart | correct | Elohim | my heart | correct |

8. My heart is constant, O God, my heart is constant; I will sing and give praise.

עוּרָה כְבוֹדִי עוּרָה הַנֵּבֶל וְכִנּוֹר אָעִירָה שָּׁחַר׃

| dawn | I will awake | and harp | the lyre | awake | my glory | awake |

9. Awake up, O my glory! Awake, O lyre and harp! I will awake the dawn!

אוֹדְךָ בָעַמִּים אֲדֹנָי אֲזַמֶּרְךָ בַּל־אֻמִּים׃

| dawn – into | I will sing psalms | Adoni | in peoples | I will give thanks |

10. I will praise you, O Lord, among the peoples; I will sing to you among the nations.

כִּי־גָדֹל עַד־שָׁמַיִם חַסְדֶּךָ וְעַד־שְׁחָקִים אֲמִתֶּךָ׃

| your truth | sk es – and till | your kindness | heavens – till | great - like |

11. For your loving kindness is great to the heavens, and your truth to the clouds.

רוּמָה עַל־שָׁמַיִם אֱלֹהִים עַל כָּל־הָאָרֶץ כְּבוֹדֶךָ׃

| your glory | the earth – all | upon | Elohim | heavens – upon | be exhaulted |

12. Be exalted, O God, above the heavens; let your glory be above all the earth.

PSALM 58

ספר תהילים פרק נח

לַמְנַצֵּחַ אַל־תַּשְׁחֵת לְדָוִד מִכְתָּם:

Miktam   to David   destroy - don't   to Chief Musician

1. To the chief Musician, Altaschith, A Miktam of David.

הַאֻמְנָם אֵלֶם צֶדֶק תְּדַבֵּרוּן מֵישָׁרִים תִּשְׁפְּטוּ בְּנֵי אָדָם:

Adam   sons   you will judge   fairness's   you will speak   righteous   indeed   the true decree

2. Do you indeed decree what is right? Do you judge uprightly, O you sons of men?

אַף־בְּלֵב עוֹלֹת תִּפְעָלוּן בָּאָרֶץ חֲמַס יְדֵיכֶם תְּפַלֵּסוּן:

you deal out   your hands   violence   in earth   you will work   inequities   in heart - then

3. But in your hearts you work wickedness; your hands deal out violence on the earth.

זֹרוּ רְשָׁעִים מֵרָחֶם תָּעוּ מִבֶּטֶן דֹּבְרֵי כָזָב:

falsehood   speaking   from belly   they error   from womb   wicked ones   astray

4. The wicked go astray from the womb; they err from birth speaking lies.

חֲמַת־לָמוֹ כִּדְמוּת חֲמַת־נָחָשׁ כְּמוֹ־פֶתֶן חֵרֵשׁ יַאְטֵם אָזְנוֹ:

its ears   cobra   deaf   viper - like   serpent - poison   like likeness   to them - poison

5. Their poison is like the poison of a serpent; they are like the deaf adder that stops its ear;

אֲשֶׁר לֹא־יִשְׁמַע לְקוֹל מְלַחֲשִׁים חוֹבֵר חֲבָרִים מְחֻכָּם:

being wise   friends   charmer   whispering ones   to voice   he hear – not   which

6. Which will not listen to the voice of charmers, or of the cunning enchanter.

אֱלֹהִים הֲרָס־שִׁנֵּימוֹ בְּפִימוֹ מַלְתְּעוֹת כְּפִירִים נְתֹץ יְהוָה:

ihvh   tear out   young lions   molars   in his mouth   their teeth - break   Elohim

7. Break their teeth, O God, in their mouth; break out the fangs of the young lions, O Lord.

יִמָּאֲסוּ כְמוֹ־מַיִם יִתְהַלְּכוּ־לָמוֹ

to them - they will flows   waters – like   they will melt

יִדְרֹךְ חִצָּו [חִצָּיו] כְּמוֹ יִתְמֹלָלוּ:

they snipped off   like   his arrows   he bend

8. Let them melt away like waters which run continually; when he aims his arrows, let them be as if cut in pieces.

כְּמוֹ שַׁבְּלוּל תֶּמֶס יַהֲלֹךְ נֵפֶל אֵשֶׁת בַּל־חָזוּ שָׁמֶשׁ:

the sun   beholds – not   woman   still birth   it goes   melt   snail   like

9. Like the slimy track of a snail which disappears; like the untimely births of a woman that do not see the sun.

בְּטֶרֶם יָבִינוּ סִירֹתֵיכֶם אָטָד כְּמוֹ־חַי כְּמוֹ־חָרוֹן יִשְׂעָרֶנּוּ:

stormily   vigor – like   life – like   thorn   your pots   they perceive   before

10. Before your pots can feel the thorns, he shall sweep them away as with a whirlwind, both the green and the burning.

יִשְׂמַח צַדִּיק כִּי־חָזָה נָקָם פְּעָמָיו יִרְחַץ בְּדַם הָרָשָׁע׃

the wicked   in blood   he will wash   his steps   vengeance   beheld – like   righteous   be happy

11. The righteous shall rejoice when he sees the vengeance; he shall wash his feet in the blood of the wicked.

וְיֹאמַר אָדָם אַךְ־פְּרִי לַצַּדִּיק אַךְ יֵשׁ־אֱלֹהִים שֹׁפְטִים בָּאָרֶץ׃

in earth   judging ones   Elohim – there is   surely   to righteous   fruit – surely   Adam   and he say

12. So that a man shall say, Truly there is a reward for the righteous; truly there is a God who judges on earth.

PSALM 59

לַמְנַצֵּחַ אַל־תַּשְׁחֵת לְדָוִד מִכְתָּם
<small>Miktam to David you destroy – don't to him that is over</small>

בִּשְׁלֹחַ שָׁאוּל וַיִּשְׁמְרוּ אֶת־הַבַּיִת לַהֲמִיתוֹ:
<small>to the his kill the house – that and they heeded Saul in sending</small>

1. To the chief Musician, Altaschith, A Miktam of David; when Saul sent,

הַצִּילֵנִי מֵאֹיְבַי אֱלֹהָי מִמִּתְקוֹמְמַי תְּשַׂגְּבֵנִי:
<small>you set me on high from rising against me my Elohim from my enemies deliver me</small>

2. **and they watched the house to kill him**. Save me from my enemies, O my God; defend me from those who rise up against me.

הַצִּילֵנִי מִפֹּעֲלֵי אָוֶן וּמֵאַנְשֵׁי דָמִים הוֹשִׁיעֵנִי:
<small>save me bloods and from men iniquity from doers deliver me</small>

3. Save me from the evil doers, and save me from bloody men.

כִּי הִנֵּה אָרְבוּ לְנַפְשִׁי יָגוּרוּ עָלַי עַזִּים
<small>strong ones upon me they gather to my soul they lie in wait here like</small>

לֹא־פִשְׁעִי וְלֹא־חַטָּאתִי יְהוָֹה:
<small>ihvh my sin - and not my transgression – not</small>

4. For, behold, they lie in wait for my soul; fierce men are gathered against me; not for my transgression, nor for my sin, O Lord.

בְּלִי־עָוֹן יְרוּצוּן וְיִכּוֹנָנוּ עוּרָה לִקְרָאתִי וּרְאֵה:
<small>and see to meet me **awake** and they prepare they run iniquity – without</small>

5. They run and prepare themselves for no fault of mine; awake to help me, and behold.

וְאַתָּה יְהוָֹה־אֱלֹהִים צְבָאוֹת אֱלֹהֵי יִשְׂרָאֵל
<small>Israel my Elohim hosts Elohim – ihvh and you</small>

הָקִיצָה לִפְקֹד כָּל־הַגּוֹיִם אַל־תָּחֹן כָּל־בֹּגְדֵי אָוֶן סֶלָה:
<small>Sela iniquity treacherous – all you be gracious – don't the nations - all to visit awake</small>

6. You therefore, O Lord God of hosts, the God of Israel, awake to punish all the nations; do not be merciful to any wicked traitors. Selah.

יָשׁוּבוּ לָעֶרֶב יֶהֱמוּ כַכָּלֶב וִיסוֹבְבוּ עִיר:
<small>city and they go round like dog they snare to evening they return</small>

7. They return at evening; they howl like dogs, and go prowling around the city.

הִנֵּה יַבִּיעוּן בְּפִיהֶם חֲרָבוֹת בְּשִׂפְתוֹתֵיהֶם כִּי מִי שֹׁמֵעַ:
<small>hearer who like in their lips swords in their mouths they utter here</small>

8. Behold, they belch out with their mouth; swords are in their lips; for Who hears?, say they.

וְאַתָּה יְהוָה תִּשְׂחַק־לָמוֹ תִּלְעַג לְכָל־גּוֹיִם:

nations – to al   you will mock   to them - you will laugh   ihvh   and you

9. But you, O Lord, shall laugh at them; you shall have all the nations in derision.

עֻזּוֹ   אֵלֶיךָ אֶשְׁמֹרָה כִּי אֱלֹהִים מִשְׂגַּבִּי:

my high fortress   Elohim   like   I will heed   unto you   his strength

10. O my strength, upon you I will wait! For God is my fortress.

אֱלֹהֵי חַסְדּוֹ [חַסְדִּי] יְקַדְּמֵנִי אֱלֹהִים יַרְאֵנִי בְשֹׁרְרָי:

in my adversaries   he sees me   Elohim   he meets me   my kindness   my Elohim

11. (K) God who loves me shall come to meet me; God shall let me gaze upon my enemies.

אַל־תַּהַרְגֵם פֶּן־יִשְׁכְּחוּ עַמִּי הֲנִיעֵמוֹ בְחֵילְךָ

in your might   the his scatter   my people   they forget - lest   slay them – don't

וְהוֹרִידֵמוֹ מָגִנֵּנוּ אֲדֹנָי:

Adonai   our shield   and his bringing them

12. Do not slay them, lest my people forget; scatter them by your power; and bring them down, O Lord our shield.

חַטַּאת פִּימוֹ דְּבַר־שְׂפָתֵימוֹ וְיִלָּכְדוּ בִגְאוֹנָם

in their pride   and they be caught   their lips – speech   their mouth   sin

וּמֵאָלָה וּמִכַּחַשׁ יְסַפֵּרוּ:

they story   and from arrogance   and from cursing

13. For the sin of their mouth and the words of their lips let them be taken in their arrogance; and for cursing and lying which they speak.

כַּלֵּה בְחֵמָה כַּלֵּה וְאֵינֵמוֹ

and isn't them   consume   in wrath   consume

וְיֵדְעוּ   כִּי־אֱלֹהִים מֹשֵׁל בְּיַעֲקֹב לְאַפְסֵי הָאָרֶץ סֶלָה:

Sela   the earth   to far ends   in Jacob   ruler   Elohim – like   and you make known

14. Consume them in wrath, consume them, till they are no more; and let them know that God rules in Jacob to the ends of the earth. Selah.

וְיָשׁוּבוּ לָעֶרֶב יֶהֱמוּ כַכָּלֶב וִיסוֹבְבוּ עִיר:

city   and they go round   like dog   they howl   to evening   and they return

15. And at evening let them return; and let them howl like a dog, and go prowling around the city.

הֵמָּה יְנוּעוּן [יְנִיעוּן] לֶאֱכֹל אִם־לֹא יִשְׂבְּעוּ וַיָּלִינוּ:

and they spend night   they satisfied   not – if   to eat   they wonder   they

16. (K) Let them wander up and down for food, and growl if they do not get their fill.

וַאֲנִי אָשִׁיר עֻזֶּךָ וַאֲרַנֵּן לַבֹּקֶר חַסְדֶּךָ

your mercy   to morning   and will I joy shout   your strength   I will sing   and I

כִּי־הָיִיתָ　　מִשְׂגָּב　לִי　וּמָנוֹס　בְּיוֹם　צַר־לִי׃

<small>to me – trouble　in day　and refuge　to me　stronghold　you have been – like</small>

17. But I will sing of your power; indeed, I will sing aloud of your loving kindness in the morning; for you have been my fortress and my refuge in the day of my trouble.

עֻזִּי　אֵלֶיךָ　אֲזַמֵּרָה　כִּי־אֱלֹהִים　מִשְׂגַּבִּי　אֱלֹהֵי　חַסְדִּי׃

<small>my kindness　my Elohim　my fortress　Elohim – like　I will sing psalms　unto you　my strength</small>

18. To you, O my strength, I will sing; for God is my fortress, and the God who loves me.

PSALM 60

ספר תהילים פרק ס

לַמְנַצֵּחַ   עַל־שׁוּשַׁן   עֵדוּת   מִכְתָּם   לְדָוִד   לְלַמֵּד:

to teach | to David | Miktam | testimony | lilly - upon | to him that is over

1. To the chief Musician, according to Shushan-Eduth, A Miktam of David, to teach;

בְּהַצּוֹתוֹ   אֶת   אֲרַם   נַהֲרַיִם   וְאֶת־אֲרַם   צוֹבָה

Zobah | Syria - and that | two rivers | Syria | that | in his striving

וַיָּשָׁב   יוֹאָב   וַיַּךְ   אֶת־אֱדוֹם   בְּגֵיא־מֶלַח   שְׁנֵים   עָשָׂר   אָלֶף:

thousand | - twelve - | salt - in valley | Edom - that | and smote | Joab | and returned

2. When he strove with Aram-Naharaim and with Aram-Zobah, when Joab returned, and struck twelve thousand of Edom in the Valley of Salt.

אֱלֹהִים   זְנַחְתָּנוּ   פְרַצְתָּנוּ   אָנַפְתָּ   תְּשׁוֹבֵב   לָנוּ:

to us | you restore | you were angry | broken down us | casted us off | Elohim

3. O God, you have cast us off, you have scattered us, you have been angry; O turn yourself to us again.

הִרְעַשְׁתָּה   אֶרֶץ   פְּצַמְתָּהּ   רְפָה   שְׁבָרֶיהָ   כִי־מָטָה:

totters - like | its branches | heal | have cleft it | earth | cause to tremble

4. You have made the earth tremble; you have broken it; heal its breaches; for it totters.

הִרְאִיתָה   עַמְּךָ   קָשָׁה   הִשְׁקִיתָנוּ   יַיִן   תַּרְעֵלָה:

reeling | wine | you made us drink | hard thing | your people | you shown

5. You have shown your people hard things; you have made us drink the wine of staggering.

נָתַתָּה   לִּירֵאֶיךָ   נֵּס   לְהִתְנוֹסֵס   מִפְּנֵי   קֹשֶׁט   סֶלָה:

Sela | verity | before | to display | banner | to your fearers | you given

6. You have given a banner to those who fear you, that it may be displayed because of the truth. Selah.

לְמַעַן   יֵחָלְצוּן   יְדִידֶיךָ   הוֹשִׁיעָה   יְמִינְךָ   וַעֲנֵנוּ [וַעֲנֵנִי]:

and answer me | your right hand | save | your beloved | they delivered | to end

7. (K) That your beloved ones may be saved; save with your right hand, and answer me.

אֱלֹהִים   דִּבֶּר   בְּקָדְשׁוֹ

in his holiness | spoken | Elohim

אֶעְלֹזָה   אֲחַלְּקָה   שְׁכֶם   וְעֵמֶק   סֻכּוֹת   אֲמַדֵּד:

I measure | Succoth | and valley | Shechem | I divide | I will exult

8. God has spoken in his holiness; I will rejoice, I will divide Shechem, and measure out the Valley of Succoth.

לִי   גִלְעָד   וְלִי   מְנַשֶּׁה   וְאֶפְרַיִם   מָעוֹז   רֹאשִׁי   יְהוּדָה   מְחֹקְקִי:

my lawmaker | Judah | my head | stronghold | and Ephraim | Mannasseh | and to me | Gilead | to me

9. Gilead is mine, and Manasseh is mine; Ephraim also is the strength of my head; Judah is my scepter;

מוֹאָב סִיר רַחְצִי עַל־אֱדוֹם אַשְׁלִיךְ נַעֲלִי

| Moab | pot | my washing | Edom - upon | I will cast | my shoe |

עָלַי פְּלֶשֶׁת הִתְרוֹעָעִי׃

| upon me | Phillista | I shout |

10. Moab is my washbasin; over Edom I will cast my shoe; over Philistia I shout in triumph.

מִי יֹבִלֵנִי עִיר מָצוֹר מִי נָחַנִי עַד־אֱדוֹם׃

| who | he will bring | city | siege | who | will lead me | Edom - till |

11. Who will bring me to the fortified city? Who will lead me to Edom?

הֲלֹא־אַתָּה אֱלֹהִים זְנַחְתָּנוּ וְלֹא־תֵצֵא אֱלֹהִים בְּצִבְאוֹתֵינוּ׃

| the not | you - | Elohim | casted us off | and not - you go out | Elohim | in our hosts |

12. Have you not rejected us, O God, so that you do not go forth with our armies?

הָבָה־לָּנוּ עֶזְרָת מִצָּר וְשָׁוְא תְּשׁוּעַת אָדָם׃

| in it the - to us | help | from adversary | and vanity | salvation | Adam |

13. Give us help against the enemy; for vain is the help of man.

בֵּאלֹהִים נַעֲשֶׂה־חָיִל וְהוּא יָבוּס צָרֵינוּ׃

| in Elohim | we will do - might | and he | will tread down | our adversaries |

14. Through God we shall do bravely; for he it is who shall trample down our enemies.

PSALM 61

ספר תהילים פרק סא

לַמְנַצֵּחַ   עַל־נְגִינַת לְדָוִד׃

<small>to David   Negimoth - upon   to Chief Musician</small>

1. To the chief Musician, for stringed instruments, A Psalm of David.

שִׁמְעָה אֱלֹהִים רִנָּתִי הַקְשִׁיבָה תְּפִלָּתִי׃

<small>my prayer   the attend   my outcry   Elohim   hear</small>

2. Hear my cry, O God; attend to my prayer.

מִקְצֵה הָאָרֶץ אֵלֶיךָ אֶקְרָא בַּעֲטֹף לִבִּי

<small>my heart   in fainting   I call   unto you   the earth   from end</small>

בְּצוּר־יָרוּם מִמֶּנִּי תַנְחֵנִי׃

<small>lead me   from me   it high - in rock</small>

3. From the end of the earth I will cry to you, when my heart is faint; lead me to the rock that is too high for me.

כִּי־הָיִיתָ מַחְסֶה לִי מִגְדַּל־עֹז מִפְּנֵי אוֹיֵב׃

<small>enemy   from me   strength - tower   to me   refuge   you have been - like</small>

4. For you have been a shelter for me, and a strong tower against the enemy.

אָגוּרָה בְאָהָלְךָ עוֹלָמִים אֶחֱסֶה בְסֵתֶר כְּנָפֶיךָ סֶּלָה׃

<small>Sela   your wings   in shelter   I take refuge   forevers   in your tent   I sojourn</small>

5. I will abide in your tent for ever; I will trust in the shelter of your wings. Selah.

כִּי־אַתָּה אֱלֹהִים שָׁמַעְתָּ לִנְדָרָי נָתַתָּ יְרֻשַּׁת יִרְאֵי שְׁמֶךָ׃

<small>your name   fearing ones   inheritance   you gave   my vows   you heard   Elohim   you- like</small>

6. For you, O God, have heard my vows; you have given me the heritage of those who fear your name.

יָמִים עַל־יְמֵי־מֶלֶךְ תּוֹסִיף שְׁנוֹתָיו כְּמוֹ־דֹר וָדֹר׃

<small>and generation   generation – like   his years   you add   king- days-upon   days</small>

7. Prolong the king's life; may his years be as many generations.

יֵשֵׁב עוֹלָם לִפְנֵי אֱלֹהִים חֶסֶד וֶאֱמֶת מַן יִנְצְרֻהוּ׃

<small>they preserve him   appoint   and truth   kindness   Elohim   before   forever   he sits</small>

8. May he be enthroned before God for ever; O appoint love and truth, that they may preserve him.

כֵּן אֲזַמְּרָה שִׁמְךָ לָעַד לְשַׁלְּמִי נְדָרַי יוֹם יוֹם׃

<small>day   day   my vows   to my pay   to time   your name   I will sing psalms   thus</small>

9. So I will sing praise to your name for ever, as I daily perform my vows.

PSALM 62

ספר תהילים פרק סב

לַמְנַצֵּחַ　עַל־יְדוּתוּן　מִזְמוֹר　לְדָוִד:
to David　psalm　Jeduthun - upon　to chief Musician

1. To the chief Musician, to Jeduthun, A Psalm of David.

אַךְ　אֶל־אֱלֹהִים　דּוּמִיָּה　נַפְשִׁי　מִמֶּנּוּ　יְשׁוּעָתִי:
my salvation　from him　my soul　silence　Elohim - unto　only

2. My soul waits in silence only for God; from him comes my salvation.

אַךְ־הוּא　צוּרִי　וִישׁוּעָתִי　מִשְׂגַּבִּי　לֹא־אֶמּוֹט　רַבָּה:
much　I will be moved – not　my high place　and my salvation　my rock　he - only

3. He alone is my rock and my salvation; he is my fortress; I shall not be greatly moved.

עַד־אָנָה　תְּהוֹתְתוּ　עַל־אִישׁ　תְּרָצְּחוּ
you seek murder　man - upon　you will rush　when - till

כֻּלְּכֶם　כְּקִיר　נָטוּי　גָּדֵר　הַדְּחוּיָה:
the tottering　fence　leaning　like wall　all of you

4. How long will you seek to overwhelm a man? You will be, all of you, demolished like a leaning wall, or a tottering fence.

אַךְ　מִשְּׂאֵתוֹ　יָעֲצוּ　לְהַדִּיחַ　יִרְצוּ
they be pleased　to drive out　they consulted　from his dignity　surely

כָּזָב　בְּפִיו　יְבָרֵכוּ　וּבְקִרְבָּם　יְקַלְלוּ־סֶלָה:
Sela – they curse　and in their inward part　they bless　in his mouths　lies

5. They even plot to cast him down from his majesty; they delight in lies; they bless with their mouth, but they curse inwardly. Selah.

אַךְ　לֵאלֹהִים　דּוֹמִּי　נַפְשִׁי　כִּי־מִמֶּנּוּ　תִּקְוָתִי:
my hope　from him - like　my soul　silent　to Elohim　only

6. My soul waits only for God in silence; for my hope is from him.

אַךְ־הוּא　צוּרִי　וִישׁוּעָתִי　מִשְׂגַּבִּי　לֹא　אֶמּוֹט:
I moved　not　my high place　and my salvation　my rock　he - only

7. He alone is my rock and my salvation; he is my refuge; I shall not be moved.

עַל־אֱלֹהִים　יִשְׁעִי　וּכְבוֹדִי　צוּר־עֻזִּי　מַחְסִי　בֵּאלֹהִים:
in Elohim　my refuge　my strength – rock　and my glory　my salvation　Elohim - upon

8. In God is my salvation and my glory; the rock of my strength and my refuge is in God.

בִּטְחוּ　בוֹ　בְכָל־עֵת　עָם　שִׁפְכוּ
pour out　people　time - in all　in him　be confident

לְפָנָיו　לְבַבְכֶם　אֱלֹהִים　מַחֲסֶה־לָנוּ　סֶלָה:
Sela　to us - refuge　Elohim　your heart　before him

9. Trust in him at all times; you people, pour out your heart before him; God is a refuge for us. Selah.

אַךְ הֶבֶל בְּנֵי־אָדָם כָּזָב בְּנֵי אִישׁ בְּמֹאזְנַיִם לַעֲלוֹת
<small>to ascend   in scales   man   sons   lie   Adam – sons   vanity   surely</small>

הֵמָּה מֵהֶבֶל יָחַד׃
<small>together   from vanity   they</small>

10. Surely men of low estate are but a breath, and men of high estate are a lie; to be laid in the scales, they are altogether lighter than a breath.

אַל־תִּבְטְחוּ בְעֹשֶׁק וּבְגָזֵל אַל־תֶּהְבָּלוּ חַיִל
<small>power   you be vain – don't   and in robbery   in oppression   you confide – don't</small>

כִּי יָנוּב אַל־תָּשִׁיתוּ לֵב׃
<small>heart   you act - don't   it increases   like</small>

11. Do not trust in oppression, and become not vain in robbery; if riches increase, do not set your heart upon them.

אַחַת דִּבֶּר אֱלֹהִים שְׁתַּיִם־זוּ שָׁמָעְתִּי כִּי עֹז לֵאלֹהִים׃
<small>to Elohim   strength   like   I heard   those - two   Elohim   spoken   once</small>

12. God has spoken once; twice have I heard this; that power belongs to God.

וּלְךָ־אֲדֹנָי חָסֶד כִּי־אַתָּה תְשַׁלֵּם לְאִישׁ כְּמַעֲשֵׂהוּ׃
<small>like to his work   to man   you will pay   you – like   kindness   Adoni – and to you</small>

13. And to you, O Lord, belongs loving kindness; for you render to every man according to his work.

Psalm 63

ספר תהילים פרק סג

מִזְמוֹר לְדָוִד בִּהְיוֹתוֹ בְּמִדְבַּר יְהוּדָה:

Judah — in wilderness — in his being — to David — psalm

1. A Psalm of David, when he was in the wilderness of Judah.

אֱלֹהִים אֵלִי אַתָּה אֲשַׁחֲרֶךָּ צָמְאָה לְךָ נַפְשִׁי

my soul — to you — thirsts — I seek you — you — my El — Elohim

כָּמַהּ לְךָ בְשָׂרִי בְּאֶרֶץ־צִיָּה וְעָיֵף בְּלִי־מָיִם:

water – without — and weary — dry - in land — my flesh — to you — longs

2. O God, you are my God; I seek you; my soul thirsts for you, my flesh longs for you in a dry and thirsty land, where no water is,

כֵּן בַּקֹּדֶשׁ חֲזִיתִיךָ לִרְאוֹת עֻזְּךָ וּכְבוֹדֶךָ:

and your glory — your strength — to seeings — I beheld you — in holy place — thus

3. To see your power and your glory, as I have seen you in the sanctuary.

כִּי־טוֹב חַסְדְּךָ מֵחַיִּים שְׂפָתַי יְשַׁבְּחוּנְךָ:

they will praise you — my lips — from life — your mercy — good - like

4. Because your loving kindness is better than life, my lips shall praise you.

כֵּן אֲבָרֶכְךָ בְחַיָּי בְּשִׁמְךָ אֶשָּׂא כַפָּי:

my palms — I will lift up — in your name — in my life — I will bless you — thus

5. Thus I will bless you while I live; I will lift up my hands in your name.

כְּמוֹ חֵלֶב וָדֶשֶׁן תִּשְׂבַּע נַפְשִׁי וְשִׂפְתֵי רְנָנוֹת יְהַלֶּל־פִּי:

my mouth - it praises — shouting joy — and my lips — my soul — it will satisfy — and fatness — fat — like

6. My soul shall be satisfied as with marrow and fatness; and my mouth shall praise you with joyful lips;

אִם־זְכַרְתִּיךָ עַל־יְצוּעָי בְּאַשְׁמֻרוֹת אֶהְגֶּה־בָּךְ:

in you - I meditate — in watches of night — my couch – upon — I remember you - if

7. When upon my bed I remember you, and meditate on you in the watches of the night.

כִּי־הָיִיתָ עֶזְרָתָה לִּי וּבְצֵל כְּנָפֶיךָ אֲרַנֵּן:

I will rejoice — your wings — and in shadow — to me — help — you were - like

8. Because you have been my help, therefore in the shadow of your wings I will rejoice.

דָּבְקָה נַפְשִׁי אַחֲרֶיךָ בִּי תָּמְכָה יְמִינֶךָ:

your right hand — supported — in me — after you — my soul — clings

9. My soul clings to you; your right hand upholds me.

וְהֵמָּה לְשׁוֹאָה יְבַקְשׁוּ נַפְשִׁי יָבֹאוּ בְּתַחְתִּיּוֹת הָאָרֶץ:

the earth — in lowest of parts — they will come — my soul — they seek — to destruction — and they

10. But those who seek my soul, to destroy it, shall go into the lower parts of the earth.

יַגִּירֻהוּ   עַל־יְדֵי־חָרֶב   מְנָת   שֻׁעָלִים   יִהְיוּ׃

they will be | foxes | portion | sword - hands - upon | they will deliver him

11. They shall be given over to the sword; they shall be a prey for foxes.

וְהַמֶּלֶךְ   יִשְׂמַח   בֵּאלֹהִים   יִתְהַלֵּל   כָּל־הַנִּשְׁבָּע   בּוֹ

in him | the swearing - all | he will be glorified | in Elohim | he will be happy | and the king

כִּי   יִסָּכֵר   פִּי   דוֹבְרֵי־שָׁקֶר׃

lie - speakers | mouth | will be stopped | like

12. But the king shall rejoice in God; every one who swears by him shall glory; but the mouth of those who speak lies shall be stopped.

PSALM 64

ספר תהילים פרק סד

לַמְנַצֵּחַ מִזְמוֹר לְדָוִד:
to David   psalm   to him that is over

1. To the chief Musician, A Psalm of David.

שְׁמַע אֱלֹהִים קוֹלִי בְשִׂיחִי מִפַּחַד אוֹיֵב תִּצֹּר חַיָּי:
my life   you preserve   enemy   from fear   in my complaint   my voice   Elohim   hear

2. Hear my voice, O God, in my prayer; preserve my life from fear of the enemy.

תַּסְתִּירֵנִי מִסּוֹד מְרֵעִים מֵרִגְשַׁת פֹּעֲלֵי אָוֶן:
iniquity   workers   from throng   from wicked ones   from counsel   you hide me

3. Hide me from the secret counsel of the wicked; from the tumult of the evil doers;

אֲשֶׁר שָׁנְנוּ כַחֶרֶב לְשׁוֹנָם דָּרְכוּ חִצָּם דָּבָר מָר:
bitter   speech   their arrows   stretched   their tongue   like sword   sharpened   which

4. Who whet their tongue like a sword, and aim bitter words like arrows.

לִירוֹת בַּמִּסְתָּרִים תָּם פִּתְאֹם יֹרֻהוּ וְלֹא יִירָאוּ:
they will fear   and not   they shoot   suddenly   perfect   in ambush   to shoot

5. To shoot from ambush at the blameless; suddenly they shoot at him, without fear.

יְחַזְּקוּ־לָמוֹ דָּבָר רָע יְסַפְּרוּ לִטְמוֹן מוֹקְשִׁים
traps   to hide   they story   evil   speech   to themselves - they encourage

אָמְרוּ מִי יִרְאֶה־לָּמוֹ:
to them – will see   who   they say

6. They encourage one another in an evil matter; they talk of laying snares secretly; they say, Who shall see them?

יַחְפְּשׂוּ עוֹלֹת תַּמְנוּ חֵפֶשׂ מְחֻפָּשׂ
diligent search   scheme   we completed   iniquities   they search out

וְקֶרֶב אִישׁ וְלֵב עָמֹק:
deep   and heart   man   and inward part

7. They search out iniquities; they accomplish a diligent search; both the inward thought of man, and the heart, is deep.

וַיֹּרֵם אֱלֹהִים חֵץ פִּתְאוֹם הָיוּ מַכּוֹתָם:
their wounds   it will be   suddenly   arrow   Elohim   and shoots them

8. But God shoots his arrows at them; suddenly they shall be wounded.

וַיַּכְשִׁילוּהוּ עָלֵימוֹ לְשׁוֹנָם יִתְנוֹדְדוּ כָּל־רֹאֵה בָם:
in them   seeing - all   they strike   their tongue   upon them   and they make it to stumble

9. So they make their own tongue a stumbling to themselves; all who see them shall shake their head.

וַיִּירְאוּ   כָּל־אָדָם וַיַּגִּידוּ פֹּעַל אֱלֹהִים וּמַעֲשֵׂהוּ הִשְׂכִּילוּ׃

they comprehend   and his works   Eloh m   work   and they told   Adam – all   and they will fear

10. And all men shall fear, and shall declare the work of God; for they shall wisely consider of his doing.

יִשְׂמַח צַדִּיק בַּיהוָה וְחָסָה   בוֹ וְיִתְהַלְלוּ כָּל־יִשְׁרֵי־לֵב׃

heart – upright- all   and will praise   in him   and take refuge   in ihvh   righteous   be happy

11. The righteous man shall be glad in the Lord, and shall trust in him; and all the upright in heart shall glory.

PSALM 65

ספר תהילים פרק סה

לַמְנַצֵּחַ מִזְמוֹר לְדָוִד שִׁיר:

song   to David   psalm   to chief Musician

1. To the chief Musician, A Psalm and Song of David.

לְךָ דֻמִיָּה תְהִלָּה אֱלֹהִים בְּצִיּוֹן וּלְךָ יְשֻׁלַּם־נֶדֶר:

vow - he be paid   and to you   in Zion   Elohim   praise   silence   and to you

2. Praise awaits you, O God, in Zion; and to you shall the vow be performed.

שֹׁמֵעַ תְּפִלָּה עָדֶיךָ כָּל־בָּשָׂר יָבֹאוּ:

they come   flesh - all   to you   prayer   hear

3. O you who hear prayer, to you shall all flesh come.

דִּבְרֵי עֲוֹנֹת גָּבְרוּ מֶנִּי פְּשָׁעֵינוּ אַתָּה תְכַפְּרֵם:

you will purge them   you   our transgressions   from me   they were mighty   iniquities   speakings

4. Iniquities prevail against me; as for our transgressions, you shall purge them away.

אַשְׁרֵי תִּבְחַר וּתְקָרֵב יִשְׁכֹּן חֲצֵרֶיךָ

your courts   he dwells   and you bring near   you choose   happy

נִשְׂבְּעָה בְּטוּב בֵּיתֶךָ קְדֹשׁ הֵיכָלֶךָ:

your temple   holy   your house   in good   we will be satisfied

5. Happy is the man whom you choose, and bring near, that he may dwell in your courts; we shall be satisfied with the goodness of your house, of your holy temple.

נוֹרָאוֹת בְּצֶדֶק תַּעֲנֵנוּ אֱלֹהֵי

my Elohim   you will answer us   in righteousness   awesome ones

יִשְׁעֵנוּ מִבְטָח כָּל־קַצְוֵי־אֶרֶץ וְיָם רְחֹקִים:

far ones   and sea   earth – ends- all   confidence   our salvation

6. By awesome things in righteousness will you answer us, O God of our salvation; you are the confidence of all the ends of the earth, and of the farthest sea;

מֵכִין הָרִים בְּכֹחוֹ נֶאְזָר בִּגְבוּרָה:

in power   girded   in his strength   mountains   established

7. Who by his strength has established the mountains; being girded with power;

מַשְׁבִּיחַ שְׁאוֹן יַמִּים שְׁאוֹן גַּלֵּיהֶם וַהֲמוֹן לְאֻמִּים:

to peoples   and tumult   their billows   roaring   seas   roaring   from sitting

8. Who stills the noise of the seas, the roaring of their waves, and the tumult of the peoples.

וַיִּירְאוּ יֹשְׁבֵי קְצָוֹת מֵאוֹתֹתֶיךָ

from your signs   uppermost parts   inhabitants   and they afraid

מוֹצָאֵי־בֹקֶר וָעֶרֶב תַּרְנִין:

you joy shout   and evening   morning – going forth

9. And those who dwell in the uttermost parts are afraid of your signs; you make the outgoings of the morning and evening to rejoice.

פְּקַדְתָּ הָאָרֶץ וַתְּשֹׁקְקֶהָ רַבַּת

abundantly   and you watered   the earth   you visit

תְּעַשְׁרֶנָּה פֶּלֶג אֱלֹהִים מָלֵא מָיִם

water   full   Elohim   river   you enriched it

תָּכִין דְּגָנָם כִּי־כֵן תְּכִינֶהָ:

you prepare her   thus – like   their corn   you prepare

10. You visit the earth, and water it; you greatly enrich it with the river of God, which is full of water; you preparest them corn, when you hast so provided for it.

תְּלָמֶיהָ רַוֵּה נַחֵת גְּדוּדֶיהָ בִּרְבִיבִים תְּמֹגְגֶנָּה צִמְחָהּ תְּבָרֵךְ:

you bless   its sprouting   you soften   in showers   her ridges   leveling   soak   her furrows

11. You water her furrows abundantly; you settle her ridges; you make it soft with showers; you bless its growth.

עִטַּרְתָּ שְׁנַת טוֹבָתֶךָ וּמַעְגָּלֶיךָ יִרְעֲפוּן דָּשֶׁן:

fatness   they drop   and your tracks   your goodness   year   you crowned

12. You crown the year with your goodness; and your paths drop fatness.

יִרְעֲפוּ נְאוֹת מִדְבָּר וְגִיל גְּבָעוֹת תַּחְגֹּרְנָה:

gi-ded   hills   and joy   wilderness   pastures   they drop on

13. The pastures of the wilderness drip; and the hills rejoice on every side.

לָבְשׁוּ כָרִים הַצֹּאן וַעֲמָקִים יַעַטְפוּ־בָר

corn – cover over   and the valleys   the sheep   meadows   you clothed

יִתְרוֹעֲעוּ אַף־יָשִׁירוּ:

they sing – thus   they shout

14. The meadows are clothed with flocks; the valleys also are covered over with grain; they shout for joy, they also sing.

PSALM 66

לַמְנַצֵּחַ　שִׁיר　מִזְמוֹר　הָרִיעוּ　לֵאלֹהִים　כָּל־הָאָרֶץ:

to him that is over　song　psalm　you shout　to Elohim　the earth - all

1. To the chief Musician, A Song, a Psalm. Make a joyful noise to God, all the earth;

זַמְּרוּ　כְבוֹד־שְׁמוֹ　שִׂימוּ　כָבוֹד　תְּהִלָּתוֹ:

you sing psalms　his name - glory　you set　glory　his praise

2. Sing to the honor of his name; make his praise glorious.

אִמְרוּ　לֵאלֹהִים　מַה־נּוֹרָא　מַעֲשֶׂיךָ

you say　to Elohim　awesome – how　your works

בְּרֹב　עֻזְּךָ　יְכַחֲשׁוּ־לְךָ　אֹיְבֶיךָ:

in much　your strength　to you – they cringe　your enemies

3. Say to God, How awesome are your works! Through the greatness of your power shall your enemies cringe before you.

כָּל־הָאָרֶץ　יִשְׁתַּחֲווּ　לְךָ　וִיזַמְּרוּ־לָךְ

the earth - all　will bow down　to you　to you – and they will sing psalm

יְזַמְּרוּ　שִׁמְךָ　סֶלָה:

they will sing psalms　your name　Sela

4. All the earth shall worship you, and shall sing to you; they shall sing to your name. Selah.

לְכוּ　וּרְאוּ　מִפְעֲלוֹת　אֱלֹהִים　נוֹרָא　עֲלִילָה　עַל־בְּנֵי　אָדָם:

you go　and you see　from works　Elohim　awesome　rising　deeds　upon - sons　Adam

5. Come and see the works of God; he is awesome in his doing toward the children of men.

הָפַךְ　יָם　לְיַבָּשָׁה　בַּנָּהָר　יַעַבְרוּ　בְרָגֶל　שָׁם　נִשְׂמְחָה־בּוֹ:

turned　sea　to dry land　in river　they pass　in foot　there　in him – we be glad

6. He turned the sea into dry land; they passed through the river on foot; there did we rejoice in him.

מֹשֵׁל　בִּגְבוּרָתוֹ　עוֹלָם　עֵינָיו　בַּגּוֹיִם　תִּצְפֶּינָה

ruler　in his might　forever　his eyes　in nations　behold

הַסּוֹרְרִים　אַל־יָרִימוּ　[יָרוּמוּ]　לָמוֹ　סֶלָה:

the revolters　you be exulted - don't　you be exulted - don't　to themselves　Sela

7. (K) He rules by his power for ever; his eyes behold the nations; let not the rebellious exalt themselves. Selah.

בָּרְכוּ　עַמִּים　אֱלֹהֵינוּ　וְהַשְׁמִיעוּ　קוֹל　תְּהִלָּתוֹ:

bless　peoples　our Elohim　and the you hear　voice　his praise

8. O bless our God, you peoples, and let the voice of his praise be heard;

הַשָּׂם נַפְשֵׁנוּ בַּחַיִּים וְלֹא־נָתַן לַמּוֹט רַגְלֵנוּ׃

our feet   to wavering   given – and no   in life   our souls   the set

9. Who has kept our soul among the living, and does not let our feet be moved.

כִּי־בְחַנְתָּנוּ אֱלֹהִים צְרַפְתָּנוּ כִּצְרָף־כָּסֶף׃

silver - like the refining   you refined us   Elohim   you proved us - like

10. For you, O God, have tested us; you have tried us, as silver is refined.

הֲבֵאתָנוּ בַמְּצוּדָה שַׂמְתָּ מוּעָקָה בְמָתְנֵינוּ׃

in our loins   pressure   you laid   in net   the brought us

11. You have brought us into the net; you laid affliction upon our loins.

הִרְכַּבְתָּ אֱנוֹשׁ לְרֹאשֵׁנוּ בָּאנוּ־בָאֵשׁ וּבַמַּיִם

and in water   in fire - we came   to our heads   man   you caused to ride

וַתּוֹצִיאֵנוּ לָרְוָיָה׃

to overflowing   and you brought out us

12. You have caused men to ride over our heads; we went through fire and through water; but you brought us out into abundance .

אָבוֹא בֵיתְךָ בְעוֹלוֹת אֲשַׁלֵּם לְךָ נְדָרָי׃

my vows   to you   I will pay them   in burnt offerings   your house   I come

13. I will go into your house with burnt offerings; I will pay you my vows,

אֲשֶׁר־פָּצוּ שְׂפָתָי וְדִבֶּר־פִּי בַּצַּר־לִי׃

to me - in distress   my mouth – and spoke   my lips   opened - which

14. Which my lips have uttered, and my mouth has spoken, when I was in trouble.

עֹלוֹת מֵחִים אַעֲלֶה־לָּךְ

to you – I will offer up   fat animals   burnt offerings

עִם־קְטֹרֶת אֵילִים אֶעֱשֶׂה בָקָר עִם־עַתּוּדִים סֶלָה׃

Sela   goats - with   cattle   I will make   rams   incense - with

15. I will offer to you burnt sacrifices of fatlings, with the smoke of rams; I will offer bulls with goats. Selah.

לְכוּ שִׁמְעוּ וַאֲסַפְּרָה כָּל־יִרְאֵי אֱלֹהִים אֲשֶׁר עָשָׂה לְנַפְשִׁי׃

to my soul   he did   which   Elohim   fearers – all   and I will declare   you hear   you go

16. Come and hear, all you who fear God, and I will declare what he has done for my soul.

אֵלָיו פִּי־קָרָאתִי וְרוֹמַם תַּחַת לְשׁוֹנִי׃

my tongue   under   and high praise   I called - my mouth   unto him

17. I cried to him with my mouth, and he was extolled with my tongue.

אָוֶן אִם־רָאִיתִי בְלִבִּי לֹא יִשְׁמַע אֲדֹנָי׃

Adoni   he hear   not   in my heart   I saw – if   iniquity

18. If I had looked on iniquity in my heart, the Lord would not have heard;

אָכֵן שָׁמַע אֱלֹהִים הִקְשִׁיב בְּקוֹל תְּפִלָּתִי:

my prayer   in voice   he attended   Elohim   heard   rightly

19. But truly God has heard me; he has attended to the voice of my prayer.

בָּרוּךְ אֱלֹהִים אֲשֶׁר לֹא־הֵסִיר תְּפִלָּתִי וְחַסְדּוֹ מֵאִתִּי:

from me   and his kindness   my prayer   has turned away – not   which   Elohim   blessed

20. Blessed be God, who has not rejected my prayer, nor removed his loving kindness from me.

PSALM 67

ספר תהילים פרק סז

לַמְנַצֵּחַ   בִּנְגִינֹת   מִזְמוֹר שִׁיר:

song   psalm   in Neginoth   to him that is over

To the chief Musician for stringed instruments, A Psalm Song.

אֱלֹהִים יְחָנֵּנוּ   וִיבָרְכֵנוּ   יָאֵר   פָּנָיו אִתָּנוּ סֶלָה:

Sela   tc us   his face   he shines   and he bless us   he gracious to us   Elohim

2. God be gracious to us, and bless us; and let his face shine upon us. Selah.

לָדַעַת בָּאָרֶץ   דַּרְכֶּךָ   בְּכָל־גּוֹיִם יְשׁוּעָתֶךָ:

your salvation   nations - in all   your way   in earth   to know

3. That your way may be known on earth, your salvation among all nations.

יוֹדוּךָ   עַמִּים   אֱלֹהִים יוֹדוּךָ   עַמִּים כֻּלָּם:

all them   peoples   you thank   Elohim   peoples   you acclaim

4. Let the peoples praise you, O God; let all the peoples praise you.

יִשְׂמְחוּ   וִירַנְּנוּ   לְאֻמִּים כִּי־תִשְׁפֹּט   עַמִּים מִישׁוֹר

fairly   peoples   you will judge - like   to peoples   and they shout joy   they happy

וּלְאֻמִּים בָּאָרֶץ   תַּנְחֵם   סֶלָה:

Sela   you lead them   in earth   and to peoples

5. O let the nations be glad and sing for joy; for you shall judge the peoples righteously,
and govern the nations on earth. Selah

יוֹדוּךָ   עַמִּים   אֱלֹהִים יוֹדוּךָ   עַמִּים כֻּלָּם:

all them   peoples   you thank   Elohim   peoples   you thank

6. Let the peoples praise you, O God; let all the peoples praise you.

אֶרֶץ   נָתְנָה יְבוּלָהּ יְבָרְכֵנוּ אֱלֹהִים אֱלֹהֵינוּ:

our Elohim   Elohim   he will bless us   its produce   has given   earth

7. The earth has yielded her produce; and God, our own God, shall bless us.

יְבָרְכֵנוּ אֱלֹהִים   וְיִירְאוּ   אֹתוֹ כָּל־אַפְסֵי־אָרֶץ:

earth – far encs – all   to him   and they will fear   Elohim   he will bless us

8. God shall bless us; let all the ends of the earth fear him.

PSALM 68

ספר תהילים פרק סח

לַמְנַצֵּחַ לְדָוִד מִזְמוֹר שִׁיר:

song   psalm   to David   to him that is over

1. To the chief Musician, A Psalm Song of David.

יָקוּם אֱלֹהִים יָפוּצוּ אוֹיְבָיו וְיָנוּסוּ מְשַׂנְאָיו מִפָּנָיו:

from before him   his haters   and they flee   his enemies   they be scattered   Elohim   he arise

2. Let God arise, let his enemies be scattered; let those who hate him flee before him.

כְּהִנְדֹּף עָשָׁן תִּנְדֹּף כְּהִמֵּס דּוֹנַג מִפְּנֵי־אֵשׁ

fire – before   wax   like melting   you drive away   smoke   like the driving away

יֹאבְדוּ רְשָׁעִים מִפְּנֵי אֱלֹהִים:

Elohim   before   wicked ones   they perish

3. As smoke is driven away, so drive them away; as wax melts before the fire, so let the wicked perish at the presence of God.

וְצַדִּיקִים יִשְׂמְחוּ יַעַלְצוּ לִפְנֵי אֱלֹהִים וְיָשִׂישׂוּ בְשִׂמְחָה:

in happiness   and they joyful   Elohim   before   they exult   they happy   and righteous ones

4. But let the righteous be glad; let them rejoice before God; let them joyfully exult.

שִׁירוּ לֵאלֹהִים זַמְּרוּ שְׁמוֹ סֹלּוּ לָרֹכֵב בָּעֲרָבוֹת

in clouds   to rider   you extol   his name   you sing psalms   to Elohim   you sing

בְּיָהּ שְׁמוֹ וְעִלְזוּ לְפָנָיו:

before him   and exult   his name   in Yah

5. Sing to God, sing praises to his name; extol him who rides on the clouds; his name is the Lord, rejoice before him.

אֲבִי יְתוֹמִים וְדַיַּן אַלְמָנוֹת אֱלֹהִים בִּמְעוֹן קָדְשׁוֹ:

his holy   in habitation   Elohim   widows   and judge   orphan   fathers

6. A father to the orphans, and a judge to the widows, is God in his holy habitation.

אֱלֹהִים מוֹשִׁיב יְחִידִים בַּיְתָה

home   solitary ones   dweller   Elohim

מוֹצִיא אֲסִירִים בַּכּוֹשָׁרוֹת אַךְ־סוֹרְרִים שָׁכְנוּ צְחִיחָה:

parched land   dwell   revolted ones – only   in prosperities   prisoners   bringing out

7. God gives the lonely ones a home to dwell in; he leads out the prisoners to prosperity; but the rebellious dwell in a parched land.

אֱלֹהִים בְּצֵאתְךָ לִפְנֵי עַמֶּךָ בְּצַעְדְּךָ בִישִׁימוֹן סֶלָה:

Sela   in desolation   in your marching   your people   before   in your going out   Elohim

8. O God, when you went forth before your people, when you marched through the wilderness; Selah;

אֶרֶץ רָעָשָׁה אַף־שָׁמַיִם נָטְפוּ מִפְּנֵי
from before   dropped   heavens – surely   quaked   earth

אֱלֹהִים זֶה סִינַי מִפְּנֵי אֱלֹהִים אֱלֹהֵי יִשְׂרָאֵל׃
Israel   my Elohim   Elohim   presence   Sinai   this   Elohim

9. The earth shook, the heavens dropped at the presence of God; even Sinai itself was moved at the presence of God, the God of Israel.

גֶּשֶׁם נְדָבוֹת תָּנִיף אֱלֹהִים נַחֲלָתְךָ וְנִלְאָה אַתָּה כוֹנַנְתָּהּ׃
established   you   and it wearied   your inheritance   Elohim   you shed   bountifulness   shower

10. You, O God, sent a plentiful rain, to strengthen your inheritance, when it languished.

חַיָּתְךָ יָשְׁבוּ־בָהּ תָּכִין בְּטוֹבָתְךָ לֶעָנִי אֱלֹהִים׃
Elohim   to poor   in goodness   you prepared   in it – dwelt   your clan

11. Your flock found a dwelling in it; you, O God, have prepared of your goodness for the poor.

אֲדֹנָי יִתֶּן־אֹמֶר הַמְבַשְּׂרוֹת צָבָא רָב׃
great   host   the bearing of tidings   word – he gives   Adoni

12. The Lord gives the word; great is the company of those who bear the tidings.

מַלְכֵי צְבָאוֹת יִדֹּדוּן יִדֹּדוּן וּנְוַת בַּיִת תְּחַלֵּק שָׁלָל׃
spoils   she apportions   house   and homestead   they flee   they flee   hosts   kings

13. Kings of armies flee, they flee; and she who dwells in the house divides the booty.

אִם־תִּשְׁכְּבוּן בֵּין שְׁפַתָּיִם כַּנְפֵי יוֹנָה נֶחְפָּה בַכֶּסֶף
in silver   covered   dove   wings   hearth stones   between   you will lie down - with

וְאֶבְרוֹתֶיהָ בִּירַקְרַק חָרוּץ׃
fine gold   in yellow light   and her pinions

14. Though you lie among the sheep folds you shall shine like the wings of a dove covered with silver, and her pinions with yellow gold.

בְּפָרֵשׂ שַׁדַּי מְלָכִים בָּהּ תַּשְׁלֵג בְּצַלְמוֹן׃
in Zalmon   it snow   in it   kings   Shadi   in scattered

15. When the Almighty scattered kings in it, snow fell in Zalmon.

הַר־אֱלֹהִים הַר־בָּשָׁן הַר־גַּבְנֻנִּים הַר־בָּשָׁן׃
Bashan - mountain   peaks – mountain   Bashan – mountain   Elohim -mountain

16. O mighty mountain! O Mountain of Bashan! O many peaked mountain! O Mountain of Bashan!

לָמָּה תְּרַצְּדוּן הָרִים גַּבְנֻנִּים הָהָר חָמַד אֱלֹהִים לְשִׁבְתּוֹ
to inhabit   Elohim   covets   the mountain   peaks   mountains   you look enviously   why

אַף־יְהוָה יִשְׁכֹּן לָנֶצַח׃
to victory   he will dwell   ihvh - yes

17. Why do look with envy, O many peaked mountain, at the mountain which God desired for his abode? Truly the Lord will dwell there forever.

רֶכֶב אֱלֹהִים רִבֹּתַיִם אַלְפֵי שִׁנְאָן אֲדֹנָי בָם סִינַי בַּקֹּדֶשׁ:

| in holy place | Sinai | in them | Adoni | repetition | thousands | ten thousands | Elohim | chariots |

18. The chariots of God are twice ten thousand, thousands upon thousands; the Lord is among them, as in Sinai, in the holy place.

עָלִיתָ לַמָּרוֹם שָׁבִיתָ שֶּׁבִי לָקַחְתָּ מַתָּנוֹת בָּאָדָם

| in Adam | gifts | you captive | you led | captive | to height | you gone up |

וְאַף סוֹרְרִים לִשְׁכֹּן יָהּ אֱלֹהִים:

| Elohim | Yah | to dwell | revolted ones | and yeah |

19. You have ascended on high, you have led captivity captive; you have received gifts from men; from the rebellious also, that the Lord God might dwell among them.

בָּרוּךְ אֲדֹנָי יוֹם יוֹם יַעֲמָס־לָנוּ הָאֵל יְשׁוּעָתֵנוּ סֶלָה:

| Sela | our salvation | the El | to us – he beareth | day | day | Adoni | blessed |

20. Blessed be the Lord, who daily bears our burden, the God of our salvation. Selah.

הָאֵל לָנוּ אֵל לְמוֹשָׁעוֹת וְלֵיהוִה אֲדֹנָי לַמָּוֶת תּוֹצָאוֹת:

| escapes | to death | Adoni | and to ihvh | to salvations | El | to us | the El |

21. He who is our God is the God of salvation; and to God the Lord belong the issues of death.

אַךְ־אֱלֹהִים יִמְחַץ רֹאשׁ אֹיְבָיו קָדְקֹד

| scalp | his enemies | head | he will wound | Elohim - yeah |

שֵׂעָר מִתְהַלֵּךְ בַּאֲשָׁמָיו:

| in his guilt | walking | hair |

22. But God will strike the head of his enemies, and the hairy scalp of him who still goes on in his trespasses.

אָמַר אֲדֹנָי מִבָּשָׁן אָשִׁיב אָשִׁיב מִמְּצֻלוֹת יָם:

| Sela | from depths | I will bring | I will bring | from Bashan | Adoni | said |

23. The Lord said, I will bring them back from Bashan, I will bring them back from the depths of the sea;

לְמַעַן תִּמְחַץ רַגְלְךָ בְּדָם לְשׁוֹן כְּלָבֶיךָ מֵאֹיְבִים מִנֵּהוּ:

| its portion | from your enemies | your dogs | tongue | in blood | your foot | you stir | to end |

24. That your foot may be dipped in the blood of your enemies, and the tongue of your dogs may have their portion from the enemy.

רָאוּ הֲלִיכוֹתֶיךָ אֱלֹהִים הֲלִיכוֹת אֵלִי מַלְכִּי בַקֹּדֶשׁ:

| in holy place | my king | my El | the goings | Elohim | your goings | they saw |

25. They have seen your processions, O God; the processions of my God, my King, in the sanctuary.

קִדְּמוּ שָׁרִים אַחַר נֹגְנִים בְּתוֹךְ עֲלָמוֹת תּוֹפֵפוֹת:

| playing tambourines | damsels | in midst | instrument players | afterwards | singers | went before |

26. The singers went before, the players on instruments followed after; among them were the young women beating tambourines.

בְּמַקְהֵלוֹת בָּרְכוּ אֱלֹהִים יְהֹוָה מִמְּקוֹר יִשְׂרָאֵל׃

<small>Israel   from fountain   ihvh   Elohim   bless you   in congregation</small>

27. Bless God in the congregations, the Lord, from the fountain of Israel.

שָׁם בִּנְיָמִן צָעִיר רֹדֵם שָׂרֵי יְהוּדָה רִגְמָתָם שָׂרֵי

<small>princes   their throng   Judah   prince   ruling them   little   Benjamin   there</small>

זְבֻלוּן שָׂרֵי נַפְתָּלִי׃

<small>Naphtali   princes   Zebulun</small>

28. There is Benjamin, the youngest, leading them, the princes of Judah and their council, the princes of Zebulun, and the princes of Naphtali.

צִוָּה אֱלֹהֶיךָ עֻזֶּךָ עוּזָּה אֱלֹהִים זוּ פָּעַלְתָּ לָּנוּ׃

<small>to us   you works   that   Elohim   strengthen   your strength   your Elohim   commanded</small>

29. Your God has commanded your strength; strengthen, O God, that which you have done for us.

מֵהֵיכָלֶךָ עַל־יְרוּשָׁלָ͏ִם לְךָ יוֹבִילוּ מְלָכִים שָׁי׃

<small>presents   kings   will bring   to you   Jerusalem – upon   from your temple</small>

30. Because of your temple at Jerusalem kings bring presents to you.

גְּעַר חַיַּת קָנֶה עֲדַת אַבִּירִים בְּעֶגְלֵי עַמִּים מִתְרַפֵּס

<small>humbling   himself   nations   claves   bulls troop   reeds   beasts   rebuke</small>

בְּרַצֵּי־כָסֶף בִּזַּר עַמִּים קְרָבוֹת יֶחְפָּצוּ׃

<small>they delight   in battles   peoples   he scattered   silver - in pieces</small>

31. Rebuke the beast of the reed grass, the herd of bulls, with the calves of the peoples, who seek to ingratiate themselves with pieces of silver; scatter the peoples who delight in war.

יֶאֱתָיוּ חַשְׁמַנִּים מִנִּי מִצְרָיִם כּוּשׁ תָּרִיץ יָדָיו לֵאלֹהִים׃

<small>to Elohim   his hands   will run   Cush   Egypt   from   magnates   will come</small>

32. Princes shall come from Egypt; Kush shall soon stretch out her hands to God.

מַמְלְכוֹת הָאָרֶץ שִׁירוּ לֵאלֹהִים זַמְּרוּ אֲדֹנָי סֶלָה׃

<small>Sela   Adoni   you sing psalm   to Elohim   you sing   the earth   from kingdoms</small>

33. Sing to God, you kingdoms of the earth; O sing praises to the Lord; Selah;

לָרֹכֵב בִּשְׁמֵי שְׁמֵי־קֶדֶם הֵן יִתֵּן בְּקוֹלוֹ קוֹל עֹז׃

<small>strength   voice   in his voice   he give - thus   old – heavens   in heavens   to rider</small>

34. To him who rides upon the heavens of heavens, which are of old; behold, he sends out his voice, a mighty voice.

תְּנוּ עֹז לֵאלֹהִים עַל־יִשְׂרָאֵל גַּאֲוָתוֹ וְעֻזּוֹ בַּשְּׁחָקִים׃

<small>in skies   and his strength   his excellency   Israel - upon   to Elohim   strength   give you</small>

35. Ascribe strength to God; his majesty is over Israel, and his strength is in the clouds.

נוֹרָא אֱלֹהִים מִמִּקְדָּשֶׁיךָ

<small>from your sanctuaries   Elohim   terrible</small>

אֵל יִשְׂרָאֵל הוּא נֹתֵן עֹז וְתַעֲצֻמוֹת לָעָם בָּרוּךְ אֱלֹהִים:

Elohim   blessed   to people   and powers   strength   giving   he   Israel   El

36. O God, you are awesome from your holy places; the God of Israel is he who gives strength and power to his people. Blessed be God.

PSALM 69

ספר תהילים פרק סט

לַמְנַצֵּחַ עַל־שֹׁשַׁנִּים לְדָוִד:

to David   lilies – upon   to chief Musician

1. To the chief Musician, according to Shoshannim, A Psalm of David.

הוֹשִׁיעֵנִי אֱלֹהִים כִּי בָאוּ מַיִם עַד־נָפֶשׁ:

soul - till   waters   they came   like   Elohim   save me

2. Save me, O God; for the waters have come up to my soul.

טָבַעְתִּי בִּיוֵן מְצוּלָה וְאֵין מָעֳמָד בָּאתִי בְמַעֲמַקֵּי־מַיִם

waters - in deep places   I came   standing   and isn't   swamp   in mire   I sink

וְשִׁבֹּלֶת שְׁטָפָתְנִי:

overflowed me   and flood

3. I sink in deep mire, where there is no standing; I have come into deep waters, and the flood sweeps over me.

יָגַעְתִּי בְקָרְאִי נִחַר גְּרוֹנִי כָּלוּ עֵינַי מְיַחֵל לֵאלֹהָי:

to my Elohim   from hoping   my eyes   failed   my throat   burned   in my calling   I am weary

4. I am weary of my crying; my throat is parched; my eyes fail while I wait for my God.

רַבּוּ מִשַּׂעֲרוֹת רֹאשִׁי שֹׂנְאַי חִנָּם עָצְמוּ

has powerful   causelessly   my haters   my head   from hairs   they much

מַצְמִיתַי אֹיְבַי שֶׁקֶר אֲשֶׁר לֹא־גָזַלְתִּי אָז אָשִׁיב:

I restored   then   took by spoil - not   which   falsehood   my enemies   my effacer ones

5. Those who hate me without cause are more than the hairs of my head; those who would destroy me, who are my enemies wrongfully, are mighty. What I did not steal, must I restore?

אֱלֹהִים אַתָּה יָדַעְתָּ לְאִוַּלְתִּי וְאַשְׁמוֹתַי מִמְּךָ לֹא־נִכְחָדוּ:

have concealed - not   from you   and my trespasses   to my foolishness   know   you   Elohim

6. O God, you know my folly; and my sins are not hidden from you.

אַל־יֵבֹשׁוּ בִי קֹוֶיךָ אֲדֹנָי יְהוִה צְבָאוֹת

hosts   ihvh   Adoni   waiters on you   in me   you ashamed - not

אַל־יִכָּלְמוּ בִי מְבַקְשֶׁיךָ אֱלֹהֵי יִשְׂרָאֵל:

israel   my Elohim   from seekers   in me   let be – don't

7. Let not those who wait on you, O Lord God of hosts, be ashamed for my sake; let not those who seek you be ashamed for my sake, O God of Israel.

כִּי־עָלֶיךָ נָשָׂאתִי חֶרְפָּה כִּסְּתָה כְלִמָּה פָנָי:

my face   dishonor   it covered   reproach   I lifted   upon you - like

8. Because for your sake I have suffered insult; shame has covered my face.

מוּזָר הָיִיתִי לְאֶחָי וְנָכְרִי לִבְנֵי אִמִּי׃

stranger	I was	to my brother	and alien	to sons	my mother

9. I have become a stranger to my brothers, and an alien to my mother's children.

כִּי־קִנְאַת בֵּיתְךָ אֲכָלָתְנִי וְחֶרְפּוֹת חוֹרְפֶיךָ נָפְלוּ עָלָי׃

jealously - like	your house	has eaten me	and reproaches	your reproachers	fell	upon me

10. For zeal for your house has consumed me; and the taunts of those who taunted you have fallen upon me.

וָאֶבְכֶּה בַצּוֹם נַפְשִׁי וַתְּהִי לַחֲרָפוֹת לִי׃

and I wept	in fasting	my soul	and it was	to reproaches	to me

11. When I wept, and chastened my soul with fasting, that became a reproach to me.

וָאֶתְּנָה לְבוּשִׁי שָׂק וָאֱהִי לָהֶם לְמָשָׁל׃

and I made	my clothing	sackcloth	and I was	to them	to proverb

12. I made sackcloth my clothing; and I became a proverb to them.

יָשִׂיחוּ בִי יֹשְׁבֵי שָׁעַר וּנְגִינוֹת שׁוֹתֵי שֵׁכָר׃

they curse	in me	sitters	gate	and songs	drinkers	strong drink

13. Those who sit in the gate speak against me; and I am the song of the drunkards.

וַאֲנִי תְפִלָּתִי־לְךָ יְהוָה עֵת רָצוֹן אֱלֹהִים בְּרָב־חַסְדֶּךָ

and I	my prayer – to you	ihvh	season	pleasing	Elohim	in much – your kindness

עֲנֵנִי בֶּאֱמֶת יִשְׁעֶךָ׃

answer me	in truth	your salvation

14. But as for me, let my prayer be to you, O Lord, in an acceptable time; O God, in the greatness of your loving kindness answer me, in the truth of your salvation.

הַצִּילֵנִי מִטִּיט וְאַל־אֶטְבָּעָה אִנָּצְלָה

deliver me	from mine	let sink – and not	I be delivered

מִשֹּׂנְאַי וּמִמַּעֲמַקֵּי־מָיִם׃

from my haters	waters - and from deep places

15. Rescue me from the mire, and do not let me sink; let me be saved from those who hate me, and from the deep waters.

אַל־תִּשְׁטְפֵנִי שִׁבֹּלֶת מַיִם וְאַל־תִּבְלָעֵנִי מְצוּלָה

let overflow me - not	flood	waters	let swallow me – and not	gulf

וְאַל־תֶּאְטַר עָלַי בְּאֵר פִּיהָ׃

let shout – and that	upon me	pit	it's mouth

16. Do not let the flood of water sweep over me, or the deep swallow me up, or the pit shut her mouth over me.

עֲנֵנִי יְהוָה כִּי־טוֹב חַסְדֶּךָ כְּרֹב רַחֲמֶיךָ פְּנֵה אֵלָי׃

answer me	ihvh	good – like	your kindness	like much	your tender	turn you	unto me

17. Answer me, O Lord; for your loving kindness is good; turn to me according to the multitude of your mercies.

וְאַל־תַּסְתֵּר פָּנֶיךָ מֵעַבְדֶּךָ כִּי־צַר־לִי מַהֵר עֲנֵנִי:

answer me   seedily   to me - distress – like   from your servant   your face   hide - and don't

18. And do not hide your face from your servant; for I am in trouble; answer me quickly.

קָרְבָה אֶל־נַפְשִׁי גְאָלָהּ לְמַעַן אֹיְבַי פְּדֵנִי:

redeem me   my enemies   to end   redeem it   my soul - unto   draw near

19. Draw near to my soul, and redeem it; ransom me because of my enemies.

אַתָּה יָדַעְתָּ חֶרְפָּתִי וּבָשְׁתִּי וּכְלִמָּתִי נֶגְדְּךָ כָּל־צוֹרְרָי:

my adversaries – all   before you   and my dishonor   and my shame   my reproach   known   you

20. You know my reproach, and my shame, and my dishonor; my adversaries are all before you.

חֶרְפָּה שָׁבְרָה לִבִּי וָאָנוּשָׁה

and I was weak   my heart   broken   reproach

וָאֲקַוֶּה לָנוּד וָאַיִן וְלַמְנַחֲמִים וְלֹא מָצָאתִי:

I found   and not   and to comforters   and isn't   to condole   and I expected

21. Insults have broken my heart; and I am in despair; and I looked for some to take pity, but there was none; and for comforters, but I found none.

וַיִּתְּנוּ בְּבָרוּתִי רֹאשׁ וְלִצְמָאִי יַשְׁקוּנִי חֹמֶץ:

vinegar   they make me drink   and to my thirst   poison   in my meal   and they gave

22. And they gave me poison in my food; and for my thirst they gave me vinegar to drink.

יְהִי שֻׁלְחָנָם לִפְנֵיהֶם לְפָח וְלִשְׁלוֹמִים לְמוֹקֵשׁ:

to trap   and to peace ones   to snare   before them   their table   it be

23. Let their table become a snare before them; and when they are at peace, let it be a trap.

תֶּחְשַׁכְנָה עֵינֵיהֶם מֵרְאוֹת וּמָתְנֵיהֶם תָּמִיד הַמְעַד:

the tottering   always   and their loins   from seeings   their eyes   it be dark

24. Let their eyes be darkened, that they see not; and make their loins shake continually.

שְׁפָךְ־עֲלֵיהֶם זַעְמֶךָ וַחֲרוֹן אַפְּךָ יַשִּׂיגֵם:

it overtake them   your anger   and wrath   your indignation   upon them – pour out

25. Pour out your indignation upon them, and let your wrathful anger take hold of them.

תְּהִי־טִירָתָם נְשַׁמָּה בְּאָהֳלֵיהֶם אַל־יְהִי יֹשֵׁב:

dwellers   it be – don't   in their tents   desolate   their encampment – it be

26. Let their habitation be desolate; and let none dwell in their tents.

כִּי־אַתָּה אֲשֶׁר־הִכִּיתָ רָדָפוּ וְאֶל־מַכְאוֹב חֲלָלֶיךָ יְסַפֵּרוּ:

they declare   your wounded   pain – and unto   they pursued   you smitten - which   you - like

27. For they persecute him whom you have struck; and they tell of the grief of those whom you have wounded.

תְּנָה־עָוֹן עַל־עֲוֺנָם וְאַל־יָבֹאוּ בְּצִדְקָתֶךָ׃

in your righteousness   they come - and not   their iniquity – upon   iniquity - put

28. Add iniquity to their iniquity; and let them not be admitted into your righteousness.

יִמָּחוּ מִסֵּפֶר חַיִּים וְעִם צַדִּיקִים אַל־יִכָּתֵבוּ׃

they be written – don't   righteous ones   and with   life   from book   they be blotted

29. Let them be blotted out of the book of the living, and not be written with the righteous.

וַאֲנִי עָנִי וְכוֹאֵב יְשׁוּעָתְךָ אֱלֹהִים תְּשַׂגְּבֵנִי׃

you set me on high   Elohim   your salvation   and pained   poor   and I

30. But I am afflicted and in pain; let your salvation, O God, set me on high.

אֲהַלְלָה שֵׁם־אֱלֹהִים בְּשִׁיר וַאֲגַדְּלֶנּוּ בְתוֹדָה׃

in thanksgiving   and I magnify him   in song   Elohim – name   I praise

31. I will praise the name of God with a song, and I will magnify him with thanksgiving.

וְתִיטַב לַיהֹוָה מִשּׁוֹר פָּר מַקְרִן מַפְרִיס׃

hoofed   horned   bull   more ox   to ihvh   and it be good

32. And it shall please the Lord better than an ox or a bull that has horns and hoofs.

רָאוּ עֲנָוִים יִשְׂמָחוּ דֹּרְשֵׁי אֱלֹהִים וִיחִי לְבַבְכֶם׃

your heart   and live   Elohim   seekers   they happy   humble   you will see

33. The humble shall see this, and be glad; and let your hearts revive, you who seek God.

כִּי־שֹׁמֵעַ אֶל־אֶבְיוֹנִים יְהֹוָה וְאֶת־אֲסִירָיו לֹא בָזָה׃

he despised   not   his prisoners - and that   ihvh   needy ones – unto   hearing - like

34. For the Lord hears the poor, and does not despise his prisoners.

יְהַלְלוּהוּ שָׁמַיִם וָאָרֶץ יַמִּים וְכָל־רֹמֵשׂ בָּם׃

in them   moving – and all   seas   and earth   heavens   they praise him

35. Let the heaven and earth praise him, the seas, and every thing that moves in it.

כִּי אֱלֹהִים יוֹשִׁיעַ צִיּוֹן

Zion   he will save   Elohim   like

וְיִבְנֶה עָרֵי יְהוּדָה וְיָשְׁבוּ שָׁם וִירֵשׁוּהָ׃

to inherit it   there   and they dwell   Judah   cities   and he will build

36. For God will save Zion, and will rebuild the cities of Judah; that they may dwell there, and have it in possession.

וְזֶרַע עֲבָדָיו יִנְחָלוּהָ וְאֹהֲבֵי שְׁמוֹ יִשְׁכְּנוּ־בָהּ׃

in it - will dwell   his name   and lovers   they will inherit it   his servants   and seed

37. And the seed of his servants shall inherit it; and those who love his name shall dwell in it.

Psalm 70

ספר תהילים פרק ע

לַמְנַצֵּחַ לְדָוִד לְהַזְכִּיר׃
to chief Musician · to David · to bring remembrance

1. To the chief Musician, A Psalm of David, to bring to remembrance.

אֱלֹהִים לְהַצִּילֵנִי יְהוָה לְעֶזְרָתִי חוּשָׁה׃
Elohim · to deliver me · ihvh · to my help · haste

2. Make haste, O God, to save me; make haste to help me, O Lord.

יֵבֹשׁוּ וְיַחְפְּרוּ מְבַקְשֵׁי נַפְשִׁי
they ashamed · and they abashed · seekers · my soul

יִסֹּגוּ אָחוֹר וְיִכָּלְמוּ חֲפֵצֵי רָעָתִי׃
they turned away · backwards · and they confounded · my delighting · my bad

3. Let those who seek after my soul be ashamed and confounded; let those who desire
my harm be turned backward, and put to confusion.

יָשׁוּבוּ עַל־עֵקֶב בָּשְׁתָּם הָאֹמְרִים הֶאָח הֶאָח׃
they returned · upon - consequence · their shame · the saying ones · aha · aha

4. Let those who say Aha, aha, be turned back, because of their shame;

יָשִׂישׂוּ וְיִשְׂמְחוּ בְּךָ כָּל־מְבַקְשֶׁיךָ
they joyful · and they happy · in you · all - your seekers

וְיֹאמְרוּ תָמִיד יִגְדַּל אֱלֹהִים אֹהֲבֵי יְשׁוּעָתֶךָ׃
and they say · always · he great · Elohim · lovers · your salvation

5. Let all those who seek you rejoice and be glad in you; and let those who love your
salvation say continually, Let God be magnified.

וַאֲנִי עָנִי וְאֶבְיוֹן אֱלֹהִים חוּשָׁה־לִּי עֶזְרִי
and I · poor · and needed · Elohim · to me – hasten · my help

וּמְפַלְטִי אַתָּה יְהוָה אַל־תְּאַחַר׃
and my deliverer · you · ihvh · delay - don't

6. But I am poor and needy; make haste to me, O God; you are my help and my savior;
O Lord, delay not.

PSALM 71

ספר תהילים פרק עא

בְּךָ־יְהוָֹה חָסִיתִי אַל־אֵבוֹשָׁה לְעוֹלָם׃

<small>forever   I ashamed – don't   I sought refuge   ihvh – in you</small>

1. In you, O Lord, I take refuge; let me never be put to confusion.

בְּצִדְקָתְךָ תַּצִּילֵנִי וּתְפַלְּטֵנִי הַטֵּה־אֵלַי אָזְנְךָ וְהוֹשִׁיעֵנִי׃

<small>and save me   your ear   unto me - incline   and you escape me   deliver me   in your righteousness</small>

2. Save me in your righteousness, and cause me to escape; incline your ear to me, and save me.

הֱיֵה לִי לְצוּר מָעוֹן לָבוֹא תָּמִיד צִוִּיתָ

<small>you commanded   always   to come   habitation   to rock   to me   it be</small>

לְהוֹשִׁיעֵנִי כִּי־סַלְעִי וּמְצוּדָתִי אָתָּה׃

<small>you   and my fortress   my crag – like   to save me</small>

3. Be my strong habitation, to which I may continually resort, which you have appointed to save me; for you are my rock and my fortress.

אֱלֹהַי פַּלְּטֵנִי מִיַּד רָשָׁע מִכַּף מְעַוֵּל וְחוֹמֵץ׃

<small>and sour man   unjust   from palm   wicked   from hand   escape me   my Elohim</small>

4. Save me, O my God, from the hand of the wicked, from the hand of the unrighteous and cruel man.

כִּי־אַתָּה תִקְוָתִי אֲדֹנָי יְהוִֹה מִבְטַחִי מִנְּעוּרָי׃

<small>from my youth   my confidence   ihvh   Adoni   my expectation   you - like</small>

5. For you are my hope, O Lord God; you are my trust from my youth.

עָלֶיךָ נִסְמַכְתִּי מִבֶּטֶן מִמְּעֵי אִמִּי אַתָּה גוֹזִי

<small>my benefactor   you   my mother   from bowels   from womb   I have rested   upon you</small>

בְּךָ תְהִלָּתִי תָמִיד׃

<small>always   my praise   in you</small>

6. By you have I been sustained from the womb; you are he who took me from my mother's bowels; my praise is continually of you.

כְּמוֹפֵת הָיִיתִי לְרַבִּים וְאַתָּה מַחֲסִי־עֹז׃

<small>strength - my refuge   and you   to many   I was   like wonderer</small>

7. I am a wonder to many; but you are my strong refuge.

יִמָּלֵא פִי תְּהִלָּתֶךָ כָּל־הַיּוֹם תִּפְאַרְתֶּךָ׃

<small>your honor   the day - all   your praise   my mouth   be filled with</small>

8. Let my mouth be filled with your praise and with your honor all the day.

אַל־תַּשְׁלִיכֵנִי לְעֵת זִקְנָה כִּכְלוֹת כֹּחִי אַל־תַּעַזְבֵנִי׃

<small>forsake me – don't   my vigor   to ending   old age   to season   cast me away - not</small>

9. Cast me not off in the time of old age; forsake me not when my strength fails.

כִּי־אָמְרוּ אוֹיְבַי לִי וְשֹׁמְרֵי נַפְשִׁי נוֹעֲצוּ יַחְדָּו׃

together | they consult | my soul | and watchers | to me | my enemies | have said - like

10. For my enemies speak against me; and those who watch for my soul consult together,

לֵאמֹר אֱלֹהִים עֲזָבוֹ רִדְפוּ וְתִפְשֹׂוּהוּ כִּי אֵין מַצִּיל׃

deliverer | isn't | ike | and you seize him | you pursue | his forsaken | Elohim | to saying

11. Saying, God has forsaken him; pursue and seize him; for there is none to save him.

אֱלֹהִים אַל־תִּרְחַק מִמֶּנִּי אֱלֹהַי לְעֶזְרָתִי חִישָׁה [חוּשָׁה]׃

hasten | to my help | my Elohim | from me | you be far - don't | Elohim

12. (K) O God, do not be far from me, O my God, make haste to help me.

יֵבֹשׁוּ יִכְלוּ שֹׂטְנֵי נַפְשִׁי יַעֲטוּ חֶרְפָּה וּכְלִמָּה

and dishonor | reproach | they be covered | my soul | adversaries | they be consumed | they be shamed

מְבַקְשֵׁי רָעָתִי׃

evil for me | those who seek

13. Let those who are adversaries to my soul be put to shame and consumed; let those who seek my hurt be covered with reproach and dishonor.

וַאֲנִי תָּמִיד אֲיַחֵל וְהוֹסַפְתִּי עַל־כָּל־תְּהִלָּתֶךָ׃

your praise – all – upon | and I will add | I will hope | always | and I

14. But I will hope continually, and will yet praise you more and more.

פִּי יְסַפֵּר צִדְקָתֶךָ כָּל־הַיּוֹם תְּשׁוּעָתֶךָ

your salvation | the day – all | your righteousness | will declare | my mouth

כִּי לֹא יָדַעְתִּי סְפֹרוֹת׃

numbers | I known | not | like

15. My mouth shall declare your righteousness and your salvation all day; for their numbers is past my knowledge.

אָבוֹא בִּגְבֻרוֹת אֲדֹנָי יְהוִֹה אַזְכִּיר צִדְקָתְךָ לְבַדֶּךָ׃

yours alone | your righteousness | I will mention | ihvh | Adoni | in mightiness | I will come

16. I will come to celebrate the mighty acts of the Lord God; I will mention your righteousness, yours alone.

אֱלֹהִים לִמַּדְתַּנִי מִנְּעוּרָי וְעַד־הֵנָּה אַגִּיד נִפְלְאוֹתֶיךָ׃

your wondrous works | I tell | this – and till | from my youth | you taught me | Elohim

17. O God, you have taught me from my youth; and I still declare your wondrous deeds.

וְגַם עַד־זִקְנָה וְשֵׂיבָה אֱלֹהִים אַל־תַּעַזְבֵנִי

forsake me – don't | Elohim | and gray hairs | old age – till | and also

עַד־אַגִּיד זְרוֹעֲךָ לְדוֹר לְכָל־יָבוֹא גְּבוּרָתֶךָ׃

your might | will come – to all | to generation | your arm | I tell – till

18. And also now when I am old and grey haired, O God, do not forsake me; till I proclaim your might to this generation, and your power to every one who is to come.

וְצִדְקָתְךָ֤ אֱלֹהִים֙ עַד־מָר֔וֹם

heights – till   Elohim   and your righteousness

אֲשֶׁר־עָשִׂ֥יתָ גְדֹל֑וֹת אֱלֹהִ֖ים מִ֣י כָמֽוֹךָ׃

like you   who   Elohim   great things   have done – which

19. Your righteousness also, O God, reaches the high heavens; you have done great things; O God, who is like you!

אֲשֶׁ֤ר הִרְאִיתַ֨נוּ [הִרְאִיתַ֨נִי] צָר֥וֹת רַבּ֗וֹת וְרָע֑וֹת תָּשׁ֥וּב

you return   and evils   many   distresses   have made me see   which

תְּחַיֵּ֫ינוּ [תְּחַיֵּ֫ינִי] וּֽמִתְּהֹמ֥וֹת הָ֝אָ֗רֶץ תָּשׁ֥וּב תַּעֲלֵֽנִי׃

you bring me up   you return   the earth   and from depths   you return

20. (K) You, who have shown me many and grievous troubles, restore me back to life, and bring me back from the depths of the earth.

תֶּ֤רֶב גְּֽדֻלָּתִ֗י וְתִסֹּ֥ב תְּֽנַחֲמֵֽנִי׃

you comfort me   and you turn   my greatness   you increase

21. Increase my greatness, and comfort me on every side.

גַּם־אֲנִ֤י ׀ אוֹדְךָ֣ בִכְלִי־נֶ֘בֶל֮

lyre – instrument   give you thanks   I – also

אֲמִתְּךָ֥ אֱלֹהָ֑י אֲזַמְּרָ֣ה לְךָ֣ בְכִנּ֑וֹר קְד֝֗וֹשׁ יִשְׂרָאֵֽל׃

Israel   holy   in harp   to you   I sing psalms   my Elohim   your truth

22. I also will praise you with the harp, speaking of your truth, O my God; to you I will sing with the lyre, O you Holy One of Israel.

תְּרַנֵּ֣נָּה שְׂ֭פָתַי כִּ֣י אֲזַמְּרָה־לָּ֑ךְ וְ֝נַפְשִׁ֗י אֲשֶׁ֣ר פָּדִֽיתָ׃

you redeemed   which   and my soul   to you - I sing psalms   like   my lips   you shout for joy

23. My lips shall greatly rejoice when I sing to you; and my soul, which you have redeemed.

גַּם־לְשׁוֹנִ֗י כָּל־הַ֭יּוֹם תֶּהְגֶּ֣ה צִדְקָתֶ֑ךָ

your righteousness   declare   the day – all   my tongue - also

כִּי־בֹ֥שׁוּ כִֽי־חָ֝פְר֗וּ מְבַקְשֵׁ֥י רָעָתִֽי׃

evil to me   those who seek   confounded - like   ashamed – like

24. My tongue also shall declare your righteousness all the day long; for those who seek my harm are confounded, they are brought to shame.

PSALM 72

סֵפֶר תְּהִילִים פֶּרֶק עב

לִשְׁלֹמֹה אֱלֹהִים מִשְׁפָּטֶיךָ לְמֶלֶךְ תֵּן וְצִדְקָתְךָ לְבֶן־מֶלֶךְ׃

king - to son	and your righteousness	give	to king	your judgments	Elohim	to Solomon

1. A Psalm for Solomon. Give the king your judgments, O God, and your righteousness to the king's son.

יָדִין עַמְּךָ בְצֶדֶק וַעֲנִיֶּיךָ בְמִשְׁפָּט׃

in judgment	and your poor	in righteousness	your people	he judge

2. That he may judge your people with righteousness, and your poor with judgment.

יִשְׂאוּ הָרִים שָׁלוֹם לָעָם וּגְבָעוֹת בִּצְדָקָה׃

in righteousness	and hills	to people	peace	the mountains	lift

3. Let the mountains bring peace to the people, and the hills, by righteousness.

יִשְׁפֹּט עֲנִיֵּי־עָם יוֹשִׁיעַ לִבְנֵי אֶבְיוֹן וִידַכֵּא עוֹשֵׁק׃

oppressor	and he crush	needy	to sons	he save	people – poor	he judge

4. May he judge the poor of the people, may he save the children of the needy, and may he break in pieces the oppressor.

יִירָאוּךָ עִם־שָׁמֶשׁ וְלִפְנֵי יָרֵחַ דּוֹר דּוֹרִים׃

generations	generation	moon	and before	sun – with	they will fear you

5. May they fear you as long as the sun and moon endure, throughout all generations.

יֵרֵד כְּמָטָר עַל־גֵּז כִּרְבִיבִים זַרְזִיף אָרֶץ׃

earth	pouring rain	like showers	cut grass - upon	like rain	he descends

6. May he come down like rain that falls on the mown grass; like showers that water the earth.

יִפְרַח־בְּיָמָיו צַדִּיק וְרֹב שָׁלוֹם עַד־בְּלִי יָרֵחַ׃

moon	without – until	peace	and much	righteous	in his days - he flourish

7. Let the righteous flourish in his days; and let there be abundance of peace till the moon is no more.

וְיֵרְדְּ מִיָּם עַד־יָם וּמִנָּהָר עַד־אַפְסֵי־אָרֶץ׃

earth - ends – until	and from river	sea – until	from sea	and he descends

8. May he have dominion also from sea to sea, and from the river to the ends of the earth.

לְפָנָיו יִכְרְעוּ צִיִּים וְאֹיְבָיו עָפָר יְלַחֵכוּ׃

they lick	dust	and his enemies	wilderness dwellers	they bow down	before him

9. Let those who dwell in the wilderness bow down before him; and let his enemies lick the dust.

מַלְכֵי תַרְשִׁישׁ וְאִיִּים מִנְחָה יָשִׁיבוּ

will bring	offering	and sea coasts	Tarshish	kings

מַלְכֵי שְׁבָא וּסְבָא אֶשְׁכָּר יַקְרִיבוּ:

they bring near   levy   and Seba   Sheba   kings

10. May the kings of Tarshish and of the islands bring presents; may the kings of Sheba and Seba offer gifts.

וְיִשְׁתַּחֲווּ־לוֹ כָל־מְלָכִים כָּל־גּוֹיִם יַעַבְדוּהוּ:

they serve him   nations – all   kings – all   to him - and they bow down

11. And may all kings fall down before him; may all nations serve him.

כִּי־יַצִּיל אֶבְיוֹן מְשַׁוֵּעַ וְעָנִי וְאֵין־עֹזֵר לוֹ:

to him   helper - and isn't   and poor   from cries   needy   he will deliver - like

12. For he shall save the needy when he calls; the poor also, and him who has no helper.

יָחֹס עַל־דַּל וְאֶבְיוֹן וְנַפְשׁוֹת אֶבְיוֹנִים יוֹשִׁיעַ:

he will save   needy ones   and souls   and needy   poor – upon   he have pity

13. He will spare the poor and needy, and will save the souls of the needy.

מִתּוֹךְ וּמֵחָמָס יִגְאַל נַפְשָׁם וְיֵיקַר דָּמָם בְּעֵינָיו:

in his eyes   their blood   and will be precious   their souls   he will redeem   and from violence   from fraud

14. He shall redeem their soul from deceit and violence; and precious shall their blood be in his sight.

וִיחִי וְיִתֶּן־לוֹ מִזְּהַב

from gold   to him - and will give   and he live

שְׁבָא וְיִתְפַּלֵּל בַּעֲדוֹ תָמִיד כָּל־הַיּוֹם יְבָרֲכֶנְהוּ:

he blesses him   the day – all   continually   in his account   and he pray   Sheba

15. Long may he live, and may the gold of Sheba be given to him; may prayer be made for him continually; and may he daily be blessed.

יְהִי פִסַּת־בַּר בָּאָרֶץ בְּרֹאשׁ הָרִים יִרְעַשׁ כַּלְּבָנוֹן פִּרְיוֹ

its fruit   like Lebanon   will shake   mountains   in head   in earth   corn – abundance   there be

וְיָצִיצוּ מֵעִיר כְּעֵשֶׂב הָאָרֶץ:

the earth   like grass   from city   and they will flourish

16. May there be abundance of grain in the land, may it wave on the tops of the mountains; may its fruit be like Lebanon; and may the men of the city flourish like grass of the earth.

יְהִי שְׁמוֹ לְעוֹלָם לִפְנֵי שֶׁמֶשׁ יָנִין [יִנּוֹן] שְׁמוֹ

his name   it propagate   sun   before   to forever   his name   it be

וְיִתְבָּרְכוּ בוֹ כָּל־גּוֹיִם יְאַשְּׁרוּהוּ:

they happy him   nations – all   in him   and they bless you

17. (K) May his name endure for ever; may his name be continued as long as the sun; may men be blessed in him; may all nations call him happy.

בָּרוּךְ יְהוָה אֱלֹהִים אֱלֹהֵי יִשְׂרָאֵל עֹשֵׂה נִפְלָאוֹת לְבַדּוֹ:

alone   mysticals   does   Israel   my Elohim   Elohim   ihvh   blessed

18. Blessed be the Lord God, the God of Israel, who alone does wondrous things.

וּבָרוּךְ שֵׁם כְּבוֹדוֹ לְעוֹלָם

and blessed name his glory to forever

וְיִמָּלֵא כְבוֹדוֹ אֶת־כָּל־הָאָרֶץ אָמֵן וְאָמֵן׃

and it be filled his glory that – all – the earth amen and amen

19. And blessed be his glorious name for ever; and let the whole earth be filled with his glory; Amen, and Amen.

כָּלּוּ תְפִלּוֹת דָּוִד בֶּן־יִשָׁי׃

it ended prayers David son – Jesse

20. The prayers of David the son of Jesse are ended.

PSALM 73

ספר תהילים פרק עג

מִזְמוֹר לְאָסָף אַךְ טוֹב לְיִשְׂרָאֵל אֱלֹהִים לְבָרֵי לֵבָב:

heart   to pure   Elohim   to Israel   good   surely   to Asaph   psalm

1. A Psalm of Asaph. Truly God is good to Israel, to those who are of a clean heart.

וַאֲנִי כִּמְעַט נָטוּי [נָטָיוּ] רַגְלָי כְּאַיִן שֻׁפְּכָה [שֻׁפְּכוּ] אֲשֻׁרָי:

my progress   poured out   like isn't   my feet   turned aside   like little   and I

2. (K) But as for me, my feet were almost gone; my steps had well near slipped.

כִּי־קִנֵּאתִי בַּהוֹלְלִים שְׁלוֹם רְשָׁעִים אֶרְאֶה:

I saw   wicked ones   peace   in boasting ones   I was envious - like

3. For I was envious of the arrogant, when I saw the prosperity of the wicked.

כִּי אֵין חַרְצֻבּוֹת לְמוֹתָם וּבָרִיא אוּלָם:

their physique   and plump   to their death   hindrances   isn't   like

4. For there are no pangs in their death; their body is firm.

בַּעֲמַל אֱנוֹשׁ אֵינֵמוֹ וְעִם־אָדָם לֹא יְנֻגָּעוּ:

they plagued   not   Adam – and with   them not   man   in travail

5. They are not in trouble like other men; nor are they plagued like other men.

לָכֵן עֲנָקַתְמוֹ גַאֲוָה יַעֲטָף־שִׁית חָמָס לָמוֹ:

to them   violence   robe – he covers   pride   his necklace   to thus

6. Therefore arrogance is their necklace; violence covers them like a garment.

יָצָא מֵחֵלֶב עֵינֵמוֹ עָבְרוּ מַשְׂכִּיּוֹת לֵבָב:

heart   from fancies   they overflow   their eyes   fatness   it gone out

7. Their eyes stand out with fatness; they have more than heart could wish.

יָמִיקוּ וִידַבְּרוּ בְרָע עֹשֶׁק מִמָּרוֹם יְדַבֵּרוּ:

they speak   from on high   oppression   in evil   and they speak   they scoff

8. They scoff, and speak wickedly; concerning oppression they speak loftily.

שַׁתּוּ בַשָּׁמַיִם פִּיהֶם וּלְשׁוֹנָם תִּהֲלַךְ בָּאָרֶץ:

in earth   it goes   and their tongue   their mouth   in heavens   they set

9. They set their mouth against the heavens, and their tongue struts through the earth.

לָכֵן יָשִׁיב [יָשׁוּב] עַמּוֹ הֲלֹם וּמֵי מָלֵא יִמָּצוּ לָמוֹ:

to them   they wrung out   full   and waters   hither   his people   it returns   to thus

10. (K) Therefore his people return here; and abundant waters are drained out by them.

וְאָמְרוּ אֵיכָה יָדַע־אֵל וְיֵשׁ דֵּעָה בְעֶלְיוֹן:

in most high   knowledge   and there is   El– know   how   and they said

11. And they say, How does God know? And is there knowledge in the most High?

הִנֵּה־אֵלֶּה רְשָׁעִים וְשַׁלְוֵי עוֹלָם הִשְׂגּוּ־חָיִל:

power - increased   [the] age   and prosperous   wicked ones   these - here

12. Behold, these are the wicked, who prosper in the world; they increase in riches.

אַךְ־רִיק   זִכִּיתִי לְבָבִי וָאֶרְחַץ בְּנִקָּיוֹן כַּפָּי׃

my hands in innocency and washed my heart I cleansed vanity - surely

13. Truly I have cleansed my heart in vain, and washed my hands in innocency.

וָאֱהִי נָגוּעַ כָּל־הַיּוֹם וְתוֹכַחְתִּי לַבְּקָרִים׃

to mornings and my rebuking the day – all smitten and I was

14. For all the day long have I been stricken, and chastened every morning.

אִם־אָמַרְתִּי אֲסַפְּרָה כְמוֹ הִנֵּה דוֹר בָּנֶיךָ בָגָדְתִּי׃

I betrayed your sons generation here like thus I will declare I said - if

15. If I say, I will speak thus; behold, I should offend against the generation of your children.

וָאֲחַשְּׁבָה לָדַעַת זֹאת עָמָל הִיא [הוּא] בְעֵינָי׃

in my enemy it grievousness this to know and I thought

16. When I pondered how I might understand this, it was too wearisome for me;

עַד־אָבוֹא אֶל־מִקְדְּשֵׁי־אֵל אָבִינָה לְאַחֲרִיתָם׃

to their end I understood El – sanctuary - unto I come - till

17. Until I went into the sanctuary of God; then I understood their end.

אַךְ בַּחֲלָקוֹת תָּשִׁית לָמוֹ הִפַּלְתָּם לְמַשּׁוּאוֹת׃

to deceptions caused them fall to them you set in slippery places surely

18. Surely you set them in slippery places; you cast them down into ruin.

אֵיךְ הָיוּ לְשַׁמָּה כְרָגַע סָפוּ תַמּוּ מִן־בַּלָּהוֹת׃

terrors - between they ended they completed like moment to desolation they were how

19. How are they brought into desolation in a moment, utterly consumed with terrors!

כַּחֲלוֹם מֵהָקִיץ אֲדֹנָי בָּעִיר צַלְמָם תִּבְזֶה׃

you will plunder their image in rouse Adoni from awakening like a dream

20. As a dream when one awakes; so, O Lord, when you awake, you shall despise their image.

כִּי־יִתְחַמֵּץ לְבָבִי וְכִלְיוֹתַי אֶשְׁתּוֹנָן׃

I vacillated and my kidneys my heart he soured - like

21. When my heart was grieved, and I was pricked in my insides.

וַאֲנִי־בַעַר וְלֹא אֵדָע בְּהֵמוֹת הָיִיתִי עִמָּךְ׃

with you I was beast I know and not brutish - and I

22. I was foolish and ignorant; I was like a beast before you.

וַאֲנִי תָמִיד עִמָּךְ אָחַזְתָּ בְּיַד־יְמִינִי׃

my right – in hand you hold with you continually and I

23. Nevertheless I am continually with you; you hold my right hand.

בַּעֲצָתְךָ תַנְחֵנִי וְאַחַר כָּבוֹד תִּקָּחֵנִי׃

you take me glory and after you will lead me in your counsel

24. You shall guide me with your counsel, and afterwards receive me to glory.

מִי־לִי בַשָּׁמָיִם וְעִמְּךָ לֹא־חָפַצְתִּי בָאָרֶץ׃

in earth   I delighted not   and with you   in heavens   to me - who

25. Whom have I in heaven but you? And there is none on earth that I desire beside you.

כָּלָה שְׁאֵרִי וּלְבָבִי צוּר־לְבָבִי וְחֶלְקִי אֱלֹהִים לְעוֹלָם׃

to forever   Elohim   and my portion   my heart – rock   and my heart   my flesh   consumed

26. My flesh and my heart fail; but God is the strength of my heart, and my portion for ever.

כִּי־הִנֵּה רְחֵקֶיךָ יֹאבֵדוּ הִצְמַתָּה כָּל־זוֹנֶה מִמֶּךָּ׃

from you   whoring - all   you cut off   you will perish   far from you   here - like

27. For, behold, those who are far from you shall perish; you have destroyed all those who go astray from you.

וַאֲנִי קִרֲבַת אֱלֹהִים לִי־טוֹב

good – to me   Elohim   drawing near   and I

שַׁתִּי בַּאדֹנָי יְהוִֹה מַחְסִי לְסַפֵּר כָּל־מַלְאֲכוֹתֶיךָ׃

your works - all   to declare   my refuge   ihvh   in Adoni   I have set

28. But for me it is good to be near God; I have made the Lord God my refuge, that I may declare all your works.

PSALM 74

מַשְׂכִּיל לְאָסָף לָמָה אֱלֹהִים זָנַחְתָּ לָנֶצַח

forever cast off Elohim why to Asaph contemplative

יֶעְשַׁן אַפְּךָ בְּצֹאן מַרְעִיתֶךָ:

your pasture in sheep your anger smoke

1. A Maskil of Asaph. O God, why have you cast us off for ever? Why does your anger smoke against the sheep of your pasture?

זְכֹר עֲדָתְךָ קָנִיתָ קֶּדֶם גָּאַלְתָּ שֵׁבֶט

rod you redeemed of old you passed your congregation remember

נַחֲלָתֶךָ הַר־צִיּוֹן זֶה שָׁכַנְתָּ בּוֹ:

in it you dwelt this Zion - mountain your inheritance

2. Remember your congregation, which you have purchased of old; the tribe of your inheritance, which you have redeemed; this Mount Zion, where you have dwelt.

הָרִימָה פְּעָמֶיךָ לְמַשֻּׁאוֹת נֶצַח כָּל־הֵרַע אוֹיֵב בַּקֹּדֶשׁ:

in holy place enemy done evil - all victory to ruins your steps lift up

3. Lift up your feet to the perpetual desolations; the enemy has destroyed everything in the sanctuary.

שָׁאֲגוּ צֹרְרֶיךָ בְּקֶרֶב מוֹעֲדֶךָ שָׂמוּ אוֹתֹתָם אֹתוֹת:

signs their signs they set your meeting place in midst your adversaries have reared

4. Your enemies roar in the midst of your congregations; they set up their own signs for signs.

יִוָּדַע כְּמֵבִיא לְמָעְלָה בִּסֲבָךְ־עֵץ קַרְדֻּמּוֹת:

axes wood – in thicket to inward like wielding known

5. They are known as swingers of axes in the thick forest.

וְעַתְּ [וְעַתָּה] פִּתּוּחֶיהָ יָּחַד בְּכַשִּׁיל וְכֵילַפֹּת יַהֲלֹמוּן:

they strike down and hammers in hatchet together its carvings and now

6. But now they break down its carved work altogether with axes and hammers.

שִׁלְחוּ בָאֵשׁ מִקְדָּשֶׁךָ לָאָרֶץ חִלְּלוּ מִשְׁכַּן־שְׁמֶךָ:

your name - tabernacle they profaned to earth your sanctuary in fire they sent

7. They have burned with fire your sanctuary, they have defiled the dwelling place of your name.

אָמְרוּ בְלִבָּם נִינָם יָּחַד שָׂרְפוּ כָל־מוֹעֲדֵי־אֵל בָּאָרֶץ:

in earth El – meeting places - all they burned together we oppress them in their hearts they said

8. They said in their hearts, Let us destroy them together; they have burned up all the meeting places of God in the land.

אֹתֹתֵינוּ לֹא־רָאִינוּ אֵין־עוֹד נָבִיא וְלֹא־אִתָּנוּ יֹדֵעַ עַד־מָה:

| our signs | not - we seen | isn't - again | prophet | and not - with us | knower | till - what |

9. We do not see our signs; there is no prophet any longer; nor is there among us any who knows how long.

עַד־מָתַי אֱלֹהִים יְחָרֵף צָר יְנָאֵץ אוֹיֵב שִׁמְךָ לָנֶצַח:

| till - when | Elohim | he reproach | adversary | he despise | enemy | your name | to victory |

10. O God, how long shall the adversary taunt? Shall the enemy blaspheme your name for ever?

לָמָּה תָשִׁיב יָדְךָ וִימִינֶךָ מִקֶּרֶב חוֹקְךָ [חֵיקְךָ] כַלֵּה:

| why | you return | your hand | and your right hand | from midst | your bosom | consume |

11. (K) Why do you withdraw your hand, your right hand? Take it out of your bosom!

וֵאלֹהִים מַלְכִּי מִקֶּדֶם פֹּעֵל יְשׁוּעוֹת בְּקֶרֶב הָאָרֶץ:

| and Elohim | my king | from old | working | salvations | in midst | the earth |

12. For God is my King of old, working salvation in the midst of the earth.

אַתָּה פוֹרַרְתָּ בְעָזְּךָ יָם שִׁבַּרְתָּ רָאשֵׁי תַנִּינִים עַל־הַמָּיִם:

| you | divided | in your strength | sea | you broke | heads | monsters | upon - the waters |

13. You parted the sea by your strength; you broke the heads of the crocodiles in the waters.

אַתָּה רִצַּצְתָּ רָאשֵׁי לִוְיָתָן

| you | broken | heads | Leviathan |

תִּתְּנֶנּוּ מַאֲכָל לְעָם לְצִיִּים:

| you give it | food | to people | to wilderness ones |

14. You crushed the heads of Leviathan, and gave him for food to the people inhabiting the wilderness.

אַתָּה בָקַעְתָּ מַעְיָן וָנָחַל אַתָּה

| you | in cleave | spring | and stream | you |

הוֹבַשְׁתָּ נַהֲרוֹת אֵיתָן:

| dried up | rivers | perennial |

15. You cleaved open springs and brooks; you dried up ever flowing streams.

לְךָ יוֹם אַף־לְךָ לָיְלָה אַתָּה

| to you | day | to you - surely | night | you |

הֲכִינוֹתָ מָאוֹר וָשָׁמֶשׁ:

| the you prepared | from light | and sun |

16. The day is yours, the night also is yours; you have prepared the light and the sun.

אַתָּה הִצַּבְתָּ כָּל־גְּבוּלוֹת אָרֶץ קַיִץ

| you | made to stand | borders - all | earth | summer |

וָחֹרֶף אַתָּה יְצַרְתָּם:

| and winter | you | formed them |

17. You have set all the borders of the earth; you have made summer and winter.

זְכָר־זֹאת אוֹיֵב חֵרֵף יְהֹוָה וְעַם־נָבָל נִאֲצוּ שְׁמֶךָ׃
<small>your name   despised   fooish - and people   ihvh   reproached   enemy   this - remember</small>

18. Remember this, how the enemy has insulted, O Lord, and how a base people have blasphemed your name.

אַל־תִּתֵּן לְחַיַּת נֶפֶשׁ תּוֹרֶךָ   חַיַּת
<small>animals   your turtle dove   soul   to animals   give – don't</small>

עֲנִיֶּיךָ אַל־תִּשְׁכַּח לָנֶצַח׃
<small>to victory   you forget – don't   your poor</small>

19. O do not deliver the soul of your dove to the wild beasts; do not forget the congregation of your poor for ever.

הַבֵּט־לַבְּרִית כִּי־מָלְאוּ מַחֲשַׁכֵּי־אֶרֶץ נְאוֹת חָמָס׃
<small>violence   pastures   earth – dark places   it full - like   to covenant - look</small>

20. Look upon the covenant; for the dark places of the earth are full of the habitations of cruelty.

אַל־יָשֹׁב דַּךְ נִכְלָם עָנִי וְאֶבְיוֹן יְהַלְלוּ שְׁמֶךָ׃
<small>your name   they praise   and needy   poor   their shame   oppressed   it return - don't</small>

21. O let not the oppressed return ashamed; let the poor and needy praise your name.

קוּמָה אֱלֹהִים רִיבָה רִיבֶךָ
<small>your cause   plead   Elohim   arise</small>

זְכֹר   חֶרְפָּתְךָ מִנִּי־נָבָל כָּל־הַיּוֹם׃
<small>the day – all   fool – from me   your reproach   remember</small>

22. Arise, O God, plead your own cause; remember how the villain insults you daily.

אַל־תִּשְׁכַּח קוֹל צֹרְרֶיךָ שְׁאוֹן קָמֶיךָ עֹלֶה תָמִיד׃
<small>always   going up   risers against you   sound   your adversaries   voice   forget – don't</small>

23. Do not forget the voice of your enemies; the tumult of those who rise up against you increases continually.

PSALM 75

ספר תהילים פרק עה

לַמְנַצֵּחַ   אַל־תַּשְׁחֵת מִזְמוֹר לְאָסָף שִׁיר:

to Chief Musician   you destroy – don't   psalm   to Asaph   song

1. To the chief Musician, Altaschith, A Psalm Song of Asaph.

הוֹדִינוּ לְּךָ אֱלֹהִים הוֹדִינוּ וְקָרוֹב שְׁמֶךָ סִפְּרוּ נִפְלְאוֹתֶיךָ:

we thank   to you   Elohim   we thank   and near   your name   they declared   your mysticals

2. To you, O God, we give thanks, to you we give thanks; men declare your wondrous works.

כִּי־אֶקַּח מוֹעֵד אֲנִי מֵישָׁרִים אֶשְׁפֹּט:

I take – like   appointed time   I   fairness   I will judge

3. Surely at the set time which I appoint I will judge with equity.

נְמוֹגִים־אֶרֶץ וְכָל־יֹשְׁבֶיהָ אָנֹכִי תִכַּנְתִּי עַמּוּדֶיהָ סֶלָה:

earth – dissolved ones   its inhabitants – and all   I   it established   its pillars   Sela

4. When the earth and all its inhabitants are dissolved, I bear up its pillars. Selah.

אָמַרְתִּי לַהוֹלְלִים אַל־תָּהֹלּוּ וְלָרְשָׁעִים אַל־תָּרִימוּ קָרֶן:

I said   to boastful ones   you boast – don't   and to wicked ones   you lift up – don't   horn

5. I said to the boastful, Do not boast; and to the wicked, Do not lift up your horn;

אַל־תָּרִימוּ לַמָּרוֹם קַרְנְכֶם תְּדַבְּרוּ בְצַוָּאר עָתָק:

you lift up – don't   to high place   your horn   you speak it   in neck   insolent

6. Lift not up your horn on high; speak not with an insolent neck.

כִּי לֹא מִמּוֹצָא וּמִמַּעֲרָב וְלֹא מִמִּדְבַּר הָרִים:

like   not   from coming forth   and from west   and not   from wilderness   mountains

7. For judgment comes not from the east, nor from the west, nor from the mountains of the desert.

כִּי־אֱלֹהִים שֹׁפֵט זֶה יַשְׁפִּיל וְזֶה יָרִים:

Elohim – like   judger   this   he lowers   and this   he raises

8. But God is the judge; he puts down one, and sets up another.

כִּי כוֹס בְּיַד־יְהוָה וְיַיִן חָמַר מָלֵא מֶסֶךְ

like   glass   ihvh – in hand   and wine   thick   full   mature

וַיַּגֵּר מִזֶּה אַךְ־שְׁמָרֶיהָ יִמְצוּ יִשְׁתּוּ כֹּל רִשְׁעֵי־אָרֶץ:

and it spills   from this   it heeds – surely   they squeeze   they drink   all   earth – wicked

9. For in the hand of the Lord there is a cup, with foaming wine; it is well mixed; and he pours from it; but the wicked of the earth shall drink and drain it to the dregs.

וַאֲנִי אַגִּיד לְעֹלָם אֲזַמְּרָה לֵאלֹהֵי יַעֲקֹב:

and I   I will tell   to ever   I will sing psalms   to my Elohim   Jacob

10. But I will declare for ever; I will sing praises to the God of Jacob.

וְכָל־קַרְנֵי רְשָׁעִים אֲגַדֵּעַ תְּרוֹמַמְנָה קַרְנוֹת צַדִּיק׃

| horns - and all | wicked ones | I will cut off | it will be exalted | horns | righteous |

11. And all the horns of the wicked will I cut off; but the horns of the righteous shall be exalted.

PSALM 76

ספר תהילים פרק עו

לַמְנַצֵּחַ בִּנְגִינֹת מִזְמוֹר לְאָסָף שִׁיר:

song	to Asaph	Psalm	in Neginoth	to chief Musician

1. To the chief Musician for stringed instruments, A Psalm Song of Asaph.

נוֹדָע בִּיהוּדָה אֱלֹהִים בְּיִשְׂרָאֵל גָּדוֹל שְׁמוֹ:

his name	great	in Israel	Elohim	in Judah	know

2. In Judah is God known; his name is great in Israel.

וַיְהִי בְשָׁלֵם סֻכּוֹ וּמְעוֹנָתוֹ בְצִיּוֹן:

in Zion	and his dwelling place	his pavilion	in Salem	and was

3. And in Salem is his tabernacle, and his dwelling place is in Zion.

שָׁמָּה שִׁבַּר רִשְׁפֵי־קָשֶׁת מָגֵן וְחֶרֶב וּמִלְחָמָה סֶלָה:

Sela	and war	and sword	shield	arrows – fiery darts	he broke	there

4. There he broke the flashing arrows, the shield, and the sword, and the battle. Selah.

נָאוֹר אַתָּה אַדִּיר מֵהַרְרֵי־טָרֶף:

prey - from mountains	excellent	you	illuminated

5. You are more glorious and excellent than the mountains of prey.

אֶשְׁתּוֹלְלוּ אַבִּירֵי לֵב נָמוּ שְׁנָתָם

their sleep	they slumber	heart	sturdy ones	unreasonable

וְלֹא־מָצְאוּ כָל־אַנְשֵׁי־חַיִל יְדֵיהֶם:

their hands	force - men – all	they found - and not

6. The stouthearted are bereft of reason, they have slept their sleep; and none of the men of might have found their hands.

מִגַּעֲרָתְךָ אֱלֹהֵי יַעֲקֹב נִרְדָּם וְרֶכֶב וָסוּס:

and horse	and chariot	stunned	Jacob	my Elohim	from your rebuke

7. At your rebuke, O God of Jacob, he is put to sleep, together with chariot and horse.

אַתָּה נוֹרָא אַתָּה וּמִי־יַעֲמֹד לְפָנֶיךָ מֵאָז אַפֶּךָ:

your anger	from when	to your face	will stand - and who	you	awesome	you

8. You, awesome are you! And who can stand in your sight when once your anger is aroused?

מִשָּׁמַיִם הִשְׁמַעְתָּ דִּין אֶרֶץ יָרְאָה וְשָׁקָטָה:

and was still	feared	earth	judgment	you heard	from heavens

9. You caused judgment to be heard from heaven; the earth feared, and was still,

בְּקוּם־לַמִּשְׁפָּט אֱלֹהִים לְהוֹשִׁיעַ כָּל־עַנְוֵי־אֶרֶץ סֶלָה:

Sela	earth - humble – all	to save	Elohim	to judgment – in rising

10. When God arose to judgment, to save all the humble of the earth. Selah.

כִּי־חֲמַת אָדָם תּוֹדֶךָ שְׁאֵרִית חֵמֹת תַּחְגֹּר

you will gird   wraths   remainder   will thank   Adam   rage - like

11. Surely the wrath of man shall praise you; you will gird yourself with the remainder
of wrath.

נִדְרוּ וְשַׁלְּמוּ לַיהֹוָה אֱלֹהֵיכֶם

their Elohim   to ihvh   and pay them   you vow

כָּל־סְבִיבָיו יֹבִילוּ שַׁי לַמּוֹרָא׃

to awesome one   presents   they bring   around him – all

12. Make a vow, and pay to the Lord your God; let all who are around him bring
presents to him who is to be feared.

יִבְצֹר רוּחַ נְגִידִים נוֹרָא לְמַלְכֵי־אָרֶץ׃

earth - to kings   awesome   princes   spirit   he will cut off

13. He shall cut off the spirit of princes; he is awesome to the kings of the earth.

Psalm 77

ספר תהילים פרק עז

לַמְנַצֵּחַ   עַל־יְדִיתוּן [יְדוּתוּן] לְאָסָף מִזְמוֹר:

psalm   to Asaph   Jeduthun   – upon   to Chief Musician

1. (K) To the chief Musician, to Jeduthun, A Psalm of Asaph.

קוֹלִי אֶל־אֱלֹהִים וְאֶצְעָקָה קוֹלִי אֶל־אֱלֹהִים וְהַאֲזִין אֵלָי:

unto me   and the give ear   Elohim – unto   my voice   and I cry   Elohim – unto   my voice

2. I cry aloud to God, aloud to God, that he may hear me.

בְּיוֹם צָרָתִי אֲדֹנָי דָּרָשְׁתִּי יָדִי לַיְלָה נִגְּרָה

stretched out   night   my hand   I sought   Adoni   my trouble   in day

וְלֹא תָפוּג מֵאֲנָה הִנָּחֵם נַפְשִׁי:

my soul   comfort   refused   was numb   and not

3. In the day of my trouble I seek the Lord; my hand is stretched out in the night, and does not rest; my soul refuses to be comforted.

אֶזְכְּרָה אֱלֹהִים וְאֶהֱמָיָה אָשִׂיחָה וְתִתְעַטֵּף רוּחִי   סֶלָה:

Sela   my spirit   and it faint   I meditate   and I clamoring   Elohim   I remember

4. I remember God, and I moan; I meditate and my spirit faints. Selah.

אָחַזְתָּ שְׁמֻרוֹת עֵינָי נִפְעַמְתִּי וְלֹא אֲדַבֵּר:

I speak   and not   I am troubled   my eyes   lids   you took hold

5. You hold my eyelids from closing; I am so troubled that I cannot speak.

חִשַּׁבְתִּי יָמִים מִקֶּדֶם שְׁנוֹת עוֹלָמִים:

ancient times   years   from old   the days   I thought

6. I consider the days of old, the years of ancient times.

אֶזְכְּרָה נְגִינָתִי בַּלַּיְלָה עִם־לְבָבִי אָשִׂיחָה וַיְחַפֵּשׂ רוּחִי:

my spirit   and searched   I meditate   my heart – with   in night   my melody   I remember

7. I remember my melody in the night; I talk with my heart; and my spirit searches.

הַלְעוֹלָמִים יִזְנַח אֲדֹנָי וְלֹא־יֹסִיף לִרְצוֹת עוֹד:

again   to be pleased   he add – and not   Adoni   he cast off   the to forevers

8. Will the Lord cast off for ever? And will he be favorable no more?

הֶאָפֵס לָנֶצַח חַסְדּוֹ גָּמַר אֹמֶר לְדֹר   וָדֹר:

and generation   to generation   sayer   comes to an end   his kindness   to victory   has failed

9. Has his loving kindness ceased for ever? Does his promise fail for evermore?

הֲשָׁכַח חַנּוֹת אֵל אִם־קָפַץ בְּאַף רַחֲמָיו סֶלָה:

Sela   his mercies   in anger   has stopped – if   El   gracious   the forgotten

10. Has God forgotten to be gracious? Has he in anger shut up his tender mercies? Selah.

וָאֹמַר חַלּוֹתִי הִיא שְׁנוֹת יְמִין עֶלְיוֹן׃

most high   right hand   years   she   my sickness   and I said

11. And I said, It is my sickness that the right hand of the Most High has changed.

אֶזְכִּיר [אֶזְכּוֹר] מַעַלְלֵי־יָהּ כִּי־אֶזְכְּרָה מִקֶּדֶם פִּלְאֶךָ׃

your wonder   from old   I remember – like   Yah - actions   I will remember

12. (K) I will remember the works of the Lord; surely I will remember your wonders of old.

וְהָגִיתִי בְכָל־פָּעֳלֶךָ וּבַעֲלִילוֹתֶיךָ אָשִׂיחָה׃

I meditate   and in your deeds   your works – in all   and I muse

13. And I will meditate on all your work, and muse on your deeds.

אֱלֹהִים בַּקֹּדֶשׁ דַּרְכֶּךָ מִי־אֵל גָּדוֹל כֵּאלֹהִים׃

like Elohim   great   El – who   your way   in holy place   Elohim

14. Your way, O God, is holy. Who is so great a God as our God?

אַתָּה הָאֵל עֹשֵׂה פֶלֶא הוֹדַעְתָּ בָעַמִּים עֻזֶּךָ׃

your strength   in people   you make known   wonder   doing   the El   you

15. You are the God that does wonders; you have declared your strength among the people.

גָּאַלְתָּ בִּזְרוֹעַ עַמֶּךָ בְּנֵי־יַעֲקֹב וְיוֹסֵף סֶלָה׃

Sela   and Joseph   Jacob – son   your people   in arm   you redeemed

16. With your arm you have redeemed your people, the sons of Jacob and Joseph. Selah.

רָאוּךָ מַּיִם אֱלֹהִים רָאוּךָ מַּיִם

waters   saw you   Elohim   waters   saw you

יָחִילוּ אַף יִרְגְּזוּ תְּהֹמוֹת׃

depths   they troubled   then   they travailed

17. The waters saw you, O God, the waters saw you; they were afraid; the depths also trembled.

זֹרְמוּ מַיִם עָבוֹת קוֹל נָתְנוּ שְׁחָקִים

skies   they gave   voice   clouds   water   poured out it

אַף־חֲצָצֶיךָ יִתְהַלָּכוּ׃

they go forth   your arrows - then

18. The clouds poured out water; the skies sent out a sound; your arrows flashed on every side.

קוֹל רַעַמְךָ בַּגַּלְגַּל הֵאִירוּ בְרָקִים תֵּבֵל

inhabited world   in lightnings   lightened   in whirlwind   your thunder   voice

רָגְזָה וַתִּרְעַשׁ הָאָרֶץ׃

the earth   and trembled   troubled

19. The voice of your thunder was in the whirlwind; the lightnings lightened the world; the earth trembled and shook.

בַּיָּם דַּרְכֶּךָ וּשְׁבִילֶיךָ [וּשְׁבִילְךָ] בְּמַיִם רַבִּים

great   in waters   and your path   your way   in sea

וְעִקְּבוֹתֶיךָ לֹא נֹדָעוּ:

they known   not   and your footsteps

20. (K) Your way was through the sea, and your path through the great waters; and your footsteps were not known.

נָחִיתָ כַצֹּאן עַמֶּךָ בְּיַד־מֹשֶׁה וְאַהֲרֹן:

and Aaron   Moses – in hand   your people   sheep   you led

21. You led your people like a flock by the hand of Moses and Aaron.

PSALM 78

ספר תהילים פרק עח

מַשְׂכִּיל לְאָסָף הַאֲזִינָה עַמִּי תּוֹרָתִי
m▾Torah　my people　the towards ear　to Asaph　Maskil

הַטּוּ אָזְנְכֶם לְאִמְרֵי־פִי:
my mouth - to words　your ear　you incline

1. A Maskil of Asaph. Give ear, O my people, to my Torah; incline your ears to the words of my mouth.

אֶפְתְּחָה בְמָשָׁל פִּי אַבִּיעָה חִידוֹת מִנִּי־קֶדֶם:
aforetime – concerning　riddles　I utter　my mouth　in parable　I open

2. I will open my mouth in a parable; I will utter riddles concerning ancient times.

אֲשֶׁר שָׁמַעְנוּ וַנֵּדָעֵם וַאֲבוֹתֵינוּ סִפְּרוּ־לָנוּ:
to us – they tell　and our fathers　and we know　we heard　which

3. Of that which we have heard and known, and our fathers have told us.

לֹא נְכַחֵד מִבְּנֵיהֶם לְדוֹר אַחֲרוֹן מְסַפְּרִים תְּהִלּוֹת יְהֹוָה
ihvh　prayers　declaring ones　following　to generation　from their sons　we suppress　not

וֶעֱזוּזוֹ וְנִפְלְאוֹתָיו אֲשֶׁר עָשָׂה:
he did　which　and his mystical works　and his strength

4. We will not hide them from their children, but tell to the latter generation the praises of the Lord, and his strength, and his wonderful works that he has done.

וַיָּקֶם עֵדוּת בְּיַעֲקֹב וְתוֹרָה שָׂב בְּיִשְׂרָאֵל אֲשֶׁר־צִוָּה
he commanded – which　in Israel　he set　and Torah　in Jacob　testimony　and he established

אֶת־אֲבוֹתֵינוּ לְהוֹדִיעָם לִבְנֵיהֶם:
to their sons　to make known them　our fathers - that

5. For he established a testimony in Jacob, and appointed a Torah in Israel, which he commanded our fathers, that they should make them known to their children;

לְמַעַן יֵדְעוּ דוֹר אַחֲרוֹן בָּנִים יִוָּלֵדוּ יָקֻמוּ וִיסַפְּרוּ לִבְנֵיהֶם:
to their sons　and tell　they arise　they born　sons　following　generation　you know　to end

6. That the generation to come might know them, the children who should be born; who should arise and tell them to their children.

וְיָשִׂימוּ בֵאלֹהִים כִּסְלָם וְלֹא יִשְׁכְּחוּ מַעַלְלֵי־אֵל
El – actions　they forget　and not　their confidence　in Elohim　and they set

וּמִצְוֹתָיו יִנְצֹרוּ:
they preserve　and his commandments

7. That they might set their hope in God, and not forget the works of God, but keep his commandments;

וְלֹא יִהְיוּ כַּאֲבוֹתָם דּוֹר סוֹרֵר וּמֹרֶה דּוֹר לֹא־הֵכִין לִבּוֹ

his heart   established – not   generation   and rebellious   stubborn   generation   like their fathers   they be   and not

וְלֹא־נֶאֶמְנָה אֶת־אֵל רוּחוֹ:

his spirit   El – that   faithful – and not

8. And that they should not be like their fathers, a stubborn and rebellious generation; a generation whose heart was not constant, and whose spirit was not faithful to God.

בְּנֵי־אֶפְרַיִם נוֹשְׁקֵי רוֹמֵי־קָשֶׁת הָפְכוּ בְּיוֹם קְרָב:

battle   in day   they turned back   bow – casting   armed   Ephram - sons

9. The children of Ephraim, being armed, and carrying bows, turned back in the day of battle.

לֹא שָׁמְרוּ בְּרִית אֱלֹהִים וּבְתוֹרָתוֹ מֵאֲנוּ לָלֶכֶת:

to walk   they refused   and in his law   Elohim   covenant   they heeded   not

10. They did not keep the covenant of God, and refused to walk according to his Torah.

וַיִּשְׁכְּחוּ עֲלִילוֹתָיו וְנִפְלְאוֹתָיו אֲשֶׁר הֶרְאָם:

he showed them   which   his mystical works   his activities   and they forgot

11. And forgot his works, and his wonders that he had shown them.

נֶגֶד אֲבוֹתָם עָשָׂה פֶלֶא בְּאֶרֶץ מִצְרַיִם שְׂדֵה־צֹעַן:

Zoan – field   Egypt   in land   wondrous   he did   their fathers   before

12. He did marvelous things in the sight of their fathers, in the land of Egypt, in the field of Zoan.

בָּקַע יָם וַיַּעֲבִירֵם וַיַּצֶּב־מַיִם כְּמוֹ־נֵד:

heap – like   waters – and he stood   and passed them   sea   he cleft

13. He parted the sea, and caused them to pass through; and he made the waters stand like a heap.

וַיַּנְחֵם בֶּעָנָן יוֹמָם וְכָל־הַלַּיְלָה בְּאוֹר אֵשׁ:

fire   in light   the night – and all   by day   in cloud   and he led them

14. And in the daytime he led them with a cloud, and all the night with a light of fire.

יְבַקַּע צֻרִים בַּמִּדְבָּר וַיַּשְׁקְ כִּתְהֹמוֹת רַבָּה:

much   like depths   and he gave drink   in wilderness   rocks   he split

15. He split rocks in the wilderness, and gave them drink as from the deep.

וַיּוֹצִא נוֹזְלִים מִסָּלַע וַיּוֹרֶד כַּנְּהָרוֹת מָיִם:

waters   like rivers   and it descended   from craig   flowing waters   and he brought out

16. He made streams come from the rock, and caused waters to run down like rivers.

וַיּוֹסִיפוּ עוֹד לַחֲטֹא־לוֹ לַמְרוֹת עֶלְיוֹן בַּצִּיָּה:

in arid place   most high   to rebel   to him – to sin   yet   and they added

17. And they sinned yet more against him, rebelling against the most High in the wilderness.

וַיְנַסּוּ־אֵל בִּלְבָבָם לִשְׁאָל־אֹכֶל לְנַפְשָׁם׃

to their soul   food – to ask   in their hearts   El – and they probed

18. And they tempted God in their heart by asking food for their craving.

וַיְדַבְּרוּ בֵּאלֹהִים אָמְרוּ הֲיוּכַל אֵל לַעֲרֹךְ שֻׁלְחָן בַּמִּדְבָּר׃

in wilderness   table   to set [table]   El   the be able   they said   in Elohim   and they spoke

19. And they spoke against God; they said, Can God spread a table in the wilderness?

הֵן הִכָּה־צוּר וַיָּזוּבוּ מַיִם

waters   and they gushed out   rock – he smote   thus

וּנְחָלִים יִשְׁטֹפוּ הֲגַם־לֶחֶם יוּכַל־תֵּת אִם־יָכִין שְׁאֵר לְעַמּוֹ׃

to his people   meat   he provide – with   give – he able   bread – the also   they overflowed   and streams

20. Behold, he struck the rock, so that the waters gushed out, and the streams overflowed; can he give bread also? Can he provide meat for his people?

לָכֵן שָׁמַע יְהֹוָה וַיִּתְעַבָּר וְאֵשׁ נִשְּׂקָה בְיַעֲקֹב

in Jacob   kindled   and fire   and he wroth   ihvh   heard   therefore

וְגַם־אַף עָלָה בְיִשְׂרָאֵל׃

in Israel   went up   anger and also

21. Therefore the Lord heard this, and was angry; so a fire was kindled against Jacob, and anger also came up against Israel.

כִּי לֹא הֶאֱמִינוּ בֵּאלֹהִים וְלֹא בָטְחוּ בִּישׁוּעָתוֹ׃

in his salvation   they trusted   and not   in Elohim   they believed   not   like

22. Because they did not believe in God, and did not trust in his salvation.

וַיְצַו שְׁחָקִים מִמָּעַל וְדַלְתֵי שָׁמַיִם פָּתָח׃

opened   heavens   and doors   from above   skys   and he commanded

23. Though he had commanded the clouds from above, and opened the doors of heaven,

וַיַּמְטֵר עֲלֵיהֶם מָן לֶאֱכֹל וּדְגַן שָׁמַיִם נָתַן לָמוֹ׃

to them   he gave   heavens   and corn   to eat   manna   upon them   and he rained down

24. And rained down manna upon them to eat, and had given them of the grain of heaven.

לֶחֶם אַבִּירִים אָכַל אִישׁ צֵידָה שָׁלַח לָהֶם לָשֹׂבַע׃

to full satisfaction   to them   he sent   provision   man   ate   mighty ones   bread

25. Man ate the bread of angels; he sent them food in abundance.

יַסַּע קָדִים בַּשָּׁמָיִם וַיְנַהֵג בְּעֻזּוֹ תֵימָן׃

south wind   in his strength   and he driving   in heavens   east   he stormed

26. He caused an east wind to blow in the sky; and by his power he brought on the south wind.

וַיַּמְטֵר עֲלֵיהֶם כֶּעָפָר שְׁאֵר וּכְחוֹל יַמִּים עוֹף כָּנָף׃

wing   fowl   seas   and like sand   meat   like dust   upon them   and he rained down

27. And he rained meat upon them like dust, and feathered birds like the sand of the sea;

וַיַּפֵּל   בְּקֶרֶב   מַחֲנֵהוּ   סָבִיב   לְמִשְׁכְּנֹתָיו:
and he let fall   in midst   his camp   around   to his tabernacle

28. And he let it fall in the midst of their camp, around their habitations.

וַיֹּאכְלוּ   וַיִּשְׂבְּעוּ   מְאֹד   וְתַאֲוָתָם   יָבִא   לָהֶם:
and they ate   and they satisfied   very   and their desire   he bring   to them

29. So they ate, and were well filled; for he gave them their own desire;

לֹא־זָרוּ   מִתַּאֲוָתָם   עוֹד   אָכְלָם   בְּפִיהֶם:
they estranged - not   from their yearning   yet   their food   in their mouth

30. They were not yet sated with their lust. But while their food was still in their mouths,

וְאַף   אֱלֹהִים   עָלָה   בָהֶם
and anger   Elohim   went up   in them

וַיַּהֲרֹג   בְּמִשְׁמַנֵּיהֶם   וּבַחוּרֵי   יִשְׂרָאֵל   הִכְרִיעַ:
and he slew   in their fat ones   and young men   Israel   he struck down

31. The wrath of God came upon them, and slew the fattest of them, and struck down the young men of Israel.

בְּכָל־זֹאת   חָטְאוּ־עוֹד   וְלֹא   הֶאֱמִינוּ   בְּנִפְלְאוֹתָיו:
this – in all   yet – they sinned   and not   they believed   in his mystical works

32. For all this they still sinned, and did not believe in his wondrous works.

וַיְכַל־בַּהֶבֶל   יְמֵיהֶם   וּשְׁנוֹתָם   בַּבֶּהָלָה:
in vanity – and he finished   their days   and their years   in panic

33. Therefore he ended their days with emptiness, and their years with trouble.

אִם־הֲרָגָם   וּדְרָשׁוּהוּ   וְשָׁבוּ   וְשִׁחֲרוּ־אֵל:
he slew them - with   and sought him   and turned   El – and sought earnestly

34. When he slew them, then they sought him; and they returned and earnestly sought God.

וַיִּזְכְּרוּ   כִּי־אֱלֹהִים   צוּרָם   וְאֵל   עֶלְיוֹן   גֹּאֲלָם:
they remembered   Elohim- like   their rock   and El   most high   their redeemer

35. And they remembered that God was their rock, and the high God their redeemer.

וַיְפַתּוּהוּ   בְּפִיהֶם   וּבִלְשׁוֹנָם   יְכַזְּבוּ־לוֹ:
and they enticed him   in their mouth   and in their tongue   to him - they lied

36. Nevertheless they flattered him with their mouth, and they lied to him with their tongues.

וְלִבָּם   לֹא־נָכוֹן   עִמּוֹ   וְלֹא   נֶאֶמְנוּ   בִּבְרִיתוֹ:
and their hearts   firm – not   with him   and not   they faithful   in his covenant

37. For their heart was not constant with him, nor were they faithful in his covenant.

וְהוּא רַחוּם יְכַפֵּר עָוֹן וְלֹא יַשְׁחִית

<small>he destroy   and not   inequity   he purge   merciful   and he</small>

וְהִרְבָּה לְהָשִׁיב אַפּוֹ וְלֹא־יָעִיר כָּל־חֲמָתוֹ:

<small>his wrath – all   he arouse – and not   his anger   to the return   and he multiplied</small>

38. But he, being full of compassion, forgave their iniquity, and did not destroy them;
often he turned away his anger, and did not stir up all his wrath.

וַיִּזְכֹּר כִּי־בָשָׂר הֵמָּה רוּחַ הוֹלֵךְ וְלֹא יָשׁוּב:

<small>it return   and not   going   spirit   they were   flesh – like   and he remembered</small>

39. For he remembered that they were but flesh; a wind that passes away, and does not
come again.

כַּמָּה יַמְרוּהוּ בַמִּדְבָּר יַעֲצִיבוּהוּ בִּישִׁימוֹן:

<small>in desolation   they grieved him   in wilderness   they rebel   how much</small>

40. How often they rebelled against him in the wilderness, and grieved him in the desert!

וַיָּשׁוּבוּ וַיְנַסּוּ אֵל וּקְדוֹשׁ יִשְׂרָאֵל הִתְווּ:

<small>they set mark   Israel   and holy   El   and they probed   and they returned</small>

41. And they turned back and tempted God, and pained the Holy One of Israel.

לֹא־זָכְרוּ אֶת־יָדוֹ יוֹם אֲשֶׁר־פָּדָם מִנִּי־צָר:

<small>adversary – from   he redeemed – which   day   his hand – that   they remembered - not</small>

42. They did not remember his hand, nor the day when he saved them from the enemy.

אֲשֶׁר־שָׂם בְּמִצְרַיִם אֹתוֹתָיו וּמוֹפְתָיו בִּשְׂדֵה־צֹעַן:

<small>Zoan – in field   and his wonders   his signs   in Egypt   set - which</small>

43. How he had done his signs in Egypt, and his wonders in the field of Zoan;

וַיַּהֲפֹךְ לְדָם יְאֹרֵיהֶם וְנֹזְלֵיהֶם בַּל־יִשְׁתָּיוּן:

<small>they drink – in not   and their running waters   their rivers   to blood   and he turned</small>

44. And had turned their rivers into blood; so that they could not drink of their streams.

יְשַׁלַּח בָּהֶם עָרֹב וַיֹּאכְלֵם וּצְפַרְדֵּעַ וַתַּשְׁחִיתֵם:

<small>and it destroy them   and frogs   and they eat   swarms of flies   in them   he send</small>

45. He sent swarms of gnats among them, which devoured them; and frogs, which
destroyed them.

וַיִּתֵּן לֶחָסִיל יְבוּלָם וִיגִיעָם לָאַרְבֶּה:

<small>to locust   and their effort   their produce   to caterpillar   and he gave</small>

46. He gave also their crops to the caterpillar, and the fruit of their labor to the locust.

יַהֲרֹג בַּבָּרָד גַּפְנָם וְשִׁקְמוֹתָם בַּחֲנָמַל:

<small>in frost   and their sycamores   their vines   in the hail   he killed</small>

47. He destroyed their vines with hail, and their sycamore trees with frost.

וַיַּסְגֵּר לַבָּרָד בְּעִירָם וּמִקְנֵיהֶם לָרְשָׁפִים:

<small>to thunder bolts   and their cattle   their flocks   to hail   and he gave over</small>

48. He gave over their cattle also to the hail, and their flocks to hot thunderbolts.

יְשַׁלַּח־בָּם   חֲרוֹן אַפּוֹ עֶבְרָה וָזַעַם

and indignation   rage   his anger   heat   to them – he will send

וְצָרָה   מִשְׁלַחַת מַלְאֲכֵי רָעִים׃

evil ones   angels   from sending   and trouble

49. He cast upon them the fierceness of his anger, wrath, and indignation, and trouble, by sending evil angels among them.

יְפַלֵּס   נָתִיב לְאַפּוֹ

to his anger   track   he pondered

לֹא־חָשַׂךְ   מִמָּוֶת נַפְשָׁם וְחַיָּתָם לַדֶּבֶר   הִסְגִּיר׃

he surrendered   to pestilence   and their life   their souls   from death   he held back – not

50. He made a path for his anger; he spared not their soul from death, but gave their life over to the pestilence;

וַיַּךְ   כָּל־בְּכוֹר בְּמִצְרָיִם רֵאשִׁית אוֹנִים בְּאָהֳלֵי־חָם׃

Ham – tents   beings   first   in Egypt   first born – all   and he smote

51. And struck all the firstborn in Egypt; the first of their strength in the tents of Ham;

וַיַּסַּע   כַּצֹּאן עַמּוֹ וַיְנַהֲגֵם כָּעֵדֶר בַּמִּדְבָּר׃

in wilderness   like flock   and he directed them   his people   like sheep   and he went forth

52. But made his own people to go forth like sheep, and guided them in the wilderness like a flock.

וַיַּנְחֵם   לָבֶטַח וְלֹא פָחָדוּ וְאֶת־אוֹיְבֵיהֶם כִּסָּה הַיָּם׃

the sea   covered   their enemies – and that   they feared   and not   to safety   and he led them

53. And he led them on safely, so that they did not fear; but the sea overwhelmed their enemies.

וַיְבִיאֵם   אֶל־גְּבוּל קָדְשׁוֹ הַר־זֶה קָנְתָה יְמִינוֹ׃

his right hand   possessed   this – mountain   his holy place   border – unto   and he brought them

54. And he brought them to his holy border, to the mountain which his right hand had won.

וַיְגָרֶשׁ   מִפְּנֵיהֶם גּוֹיִם וַיַּפִּילֵם בְּחֶבֶל נַחֲלָה

inheritance   in a line   and allotted them   nations   from before them   and he drove out

וַיַּשְׁכֵּן   בְּאָהֳלֵיהֶם שִׁבְטֵי יִשְׂרָאֵל׃

Israel   tribes   in their tents   and he dwell

55. He cast out nations before them, and apportioned to them an inheritance by line, and made the tribes of Israel dwell in their tents.

וַיְנַסּוּ   וַיַּמְרוּ אֶת־אֱלֹהִים עֶלְיוֹן וְעֵדוֹתָיו לֹא שָׁמָרוּ׃

they heeded   not   and his testimonies   most high   Elohim – that   and rebelled   and they probed

56. Yet they tempted and rebelled against the most high God, and did not keep his testimonies;

וַיִּסֹּגוּ וַיִּבְגְּדוּ כַּאֲבוֹתָם נֶהְפְּכוּ כְּקֶשֶׁת רְמִיָּה:

<small>deceit   like bow   they turned aside   like their fathers   and they betrayed   they turned back</small>

57. But turned back, and dealt unfaithfully like their fathers; they were turned aside like a deceitful bow.

וַיַּכְעִיסוּהוּ בְּבָמוֹתָם וּבִפְסִילֵיהֶם יַקְנִיאוּהוּ:

<small>they made him jealous   and in their graven images   in their high places   and they made him angry</small>

58. For they provoked him to anger with their high places, and moved him to jealousy with their carved idols.

שָׁמַע אֱלֹהִים וַיִּתְעַבָּר וַיִּמְאַס מְאֹד בְּיִשְׂרָאֵל:

<small>in Israel   greatly   and he rejected   and he wroth   Elohim   heard</small>

59. When God heard this, he was angry, and greatly loathed Israel;

וַיִּטֹּשׁ מִשְׁכַּן שִׁלוֹ אֹהֶל שִׁכֵּן בָּאָדָם:

<small>in Adam   pitched   tent   Shiloh   tabernacle   and he left</small>

60. So that he forsook the tabernacle of Shiloh, the tent where he made his dwelling among men;

וַיִּתֵּן לַשְּׁבִי עֻזּוֹ וְתִפְאַרְתּוֹ בְיַד־צָר:

<small>adversary – in hand   and his glory   his strength   to captivity   and he gave</small>

61. And delivered his strength into captivity, and his glory into the enemy's hand.

וַיַּסְגֵּר לַחֶרֶב עַמּוֹ וּבְנַחֲלָתוֹ הִתְעַבָּר:

<small>he enraged   and in his inheritance   his people   to sword   and he gave over</small>

62. He gave his people over also to the sword; and was angry with his inheritance.

בַּחוּרָיו אָכְלָה־אֵשׁ וּבְתוּלֹתָיו לֹא הוּלָּלוּ:

<small>they praised   not   and his virgins   fire – ate   their young men</small>

63. The fire consumed their young men; and their virgins had no marriage songs.

כֹּהֲנָיו בַּחֶרֶב נָפָלוּ וְאַלְמְנֹתָיו לֹא תִבְכֶּינָה:

<small>it weep   not   and their widows   they fell   in the sword   his priests</small>

64. Their priests fell by the sword; and their widows made no lamentation.

וַיִּקַץ כְּיָשֵׁן אֲדֹנָי כְּגִבּוֹר מִתְרוֹנֵן מִיָּיִן:

<small>from wine   shouting for joy   like mighty   Adoni   like sleeping   and awoke</small>

65. Then the Lord awoke as from sleep, and like a mighty man who shouts because of wine.

וַיַּךְ־צָרָיו אָחוֹר חֶרְפַּת עוֹלָם נָתַן לָמוֹ:

<small>to them   he gave   ever   reproach   backward   his adversaries – and he smote</small>

66. And he struck his enemies backward; he put upon them an everlasting reproach.

וַיִּמְאַס בְּאֹהֶל יוֹסֵף וּבְשֵׁבֶט אֶפְרַיִם לֹא בָחָר:

<small>he chose   not   Ephraim   and in tribe   Joseph   in tent   and he rejected</small>

67. And he rejected the tent of Joseph, and chose not the tribe of Ephraim;

וַיִּבְחַר אֶת־שֵׁבֶט יְהוּדָה אֶת־הַר צִיּוֹן אֲשֶׁר אָהֵב׃

| he loved | which | Zion | mountain – that | Judah | tribe – that | and he chose |

68. But chose the tribe of Judah, the Mount Zion which he loved.

וַיִּבֶן כְּמוֹ־רָמִים מִקְדָּשׁוֹ כְּאֶרֶץ יְסָדָהּ לְעוֹלָם׃

| forever | he founded | like earth | his sanctuary | exalted places – like | and he built |

69. And he built his sanctuary like the high heavens, like the earth which he has established for ever.

וַיִּבְחַר בְּדָוִד עַבְדּוֹ וַיִּקָּחֵהוּ מִמִּכְלְאֹת צֹאן׃

| sheep | from folds | and he took him | his servant | in David | and he chose |

70. And he chose David his servant, and took him from the sheepfolds;

מֵאַחַר עָלוֹת הֱבִיאוֹ לִרְעוֹת בְּיַעֲקֹב עַמּוֹ

| his people | in Jacob | to shepherd | brought him | ewes | from after |

וּבְיִשְׂרָאֵל נַחֲלָתוֹ׃

| his inheritance | and in Israel |

71. From following the ewes that had young he brought him to be the shepherd of Jacob his people, and Israel his inheritance.

וַיִּרְעֵם כְּתֹם לְבָבוֹ וּבִתְבוּנוֹת כַּפָּיו יַנְחֵם׃

| he lead them | his palms | and in understanding | his heart | like integrity | and he tended them |

72. So he tended them according to the integrity of his heart; and guided them with skilful hand.

Psalm 79

ספר תהילים פרק עט

מִזְמוֹר לְאָסָף
to Ashaph   psalm

אֱלֹהִים בָּאוּ גוֹיִם בְּנַחֲלָתֶךָ טִמְּאוּ אֶת־הֵיכַל קָדְשֶׁךָ
your holiness   temple – that   they have defiled   in their inheritance   nations   he come   Elohim

שָׂמוּ אֶת־יְרוּשָׁלַ͏ִם לְעִיִּים׃
to heaps   Jerusalem – that   they set

1. A Psalm of Asaph. O God, nations have come into your inheritance; your holy temple have they defiled; they have laid Jerusalem on heaps.

נָתְנוּ אֶת־נִבְלַת עֲבָדֶיךָ מַאֲכָל
food   your servants   dead body – that   they gave

לְעוֹף הַשָּׁמָיִם בְּשַׂר חֲסִידֶיךָ לְחַיְתוֹ־אָרֶץ׃
earth - to his beasts   your pious   flesh   the heavens   to fowl

2. The dead bodies of your servants have they given to be food to the birds of the sky, the flesh of your pious ones to the beasts of the earth.

שָׁפְכוּ דָמָם כַּמַּיִם סְבִיבוֹת יְרוּשָׁלַ͏ִם וְאֵין קוֹבֵר׃
buryer   and isn't   Jerusalem   around   like water   their blood   they poured

3. Their blood have they shed like water around Jerusalem; and there was none to bury them.

הָיִינוּ חֶרְפָּה לִשְׁכֵנֵינוּ לַעַג וָקֶלֶס לִסְבִיבוֹתֵינוּ׃
to those around us   and scoffing   mocking   to our neighbors   [a] reproach   we were

4. We have become a taunt to our neighbors, a scorn and derision to those who are around us.

עַד־מָה יְהֹוָה תֶּאֱנַף לָנֶצַח תִּבְעַר כְּמוֹ־אֵשׁ קִנְאָתֶךָ׃
your jealousy   fire – like   you will burn   to victory   be angry   ihvh   what - till

5. How long, Lord? Will you be angry for ever? Shall your jealousy burn like fire?

שְׁפֹךְ חֲמָתְךָ אֶל־הַגּוֹיִם אֲשֶׁר לֹא־יְדָעוּךָ
have known you - not   which   the nations – unto   your wrath   pour

וְעַל מַמְלָכוֹת אֲשֶׁר בְּשִׁמְךָ לֹא קָרָאוּ׃
called you   not   in your name   which   kingdoms   and upon

6. Pour out your wrath on the nations that have not known you, and on the kingdoms that have not called upon your name.

כִּי־אָכַל אֶת־יַעֲקֹב וְאֶת־נָוֵהוּ הֵשַׁמּוּ׃
they desolated   his habitation – and that   Jacob - that   eaten - like

7. For they have devoured Jacob, and laid waste his dwelling place.

אַל־תִּזְכָּר־לָנוּ עֲוֹנֹת
inequities   to us – you remember - don't

רִאשֹׁנִים מַהֵר יְקַדְּמוּנוּ רַחֲמֶיךָ כִּי דַלּוֹנוּ מְאֹד:
very   we impoverished   like   your tender mercies   they meet us   speedily   first ones

8. O do not remember against us our former iniquities; let your tender mercies speedily come to meet us; for we are brought very low.

עָזְרֵנוּ אֱלֹהֵי יִשְׁעֵנוּ עַל־דְּבַר כְּבוֹד־שְׁמֶךָ
your name - glory   matter – upon   our salvation   my Elohim   help us

וְהַצִּילֵנוּ וְכַפֵּר עַל־חַטֹּאתֵינוּ לְמַעַן שְׁמֶךָ:
your name   to end   our sins - upon   and purge   and deliver us

9. Help us, O God of our salvation, for the glory of your name; and save us, and forgive our sins, for your name's sake.

לָמָּה יֹאמְרוּ הַגּוֹיִם אַיֵּה אֱלֹהֵיהֶם
their Elohim   where   the nations   they say   why

יִוָּדַע בַּגֹּיִם [בַּגּוֹיִם] לְעֵינֵינוּ נִקְמַת דַּם־עֲבָדֶיךָ הַשָּׁפוּךְ:
the shed   your servant – blood   vengeance   to our eyes   in nations   he be known

10. (K) Why should the nations say, Where is their God? let the revenging of the blood of your servants which is shed be made manifest among the nations, and before our eyes.

תָּבוֹא לְפָנֶיךָ
before you   it come

אֶנְקַת אָסִיר כְּגֹדֶל זְרוֹעֲךָ הוֹתֵר בְּנֵי תְמוּתָה:
death   sons   preserve you   your power   like greater   prisoner   sighing

11. Let the groans of the prisoner come before you; according to the greatness of your power preserve those who are appointed to die;

וְהָשֵׁב לִשְׁכֵנֵינוּ שִׁבְעָתַיִם אֶל־חֵיקָם חֶרְפָּתָם
their insult   their bosom – unto   seven ones   to our neighbors   and the return

אֲשֶׁר חֵרְפוּךָ אֲדֹנָי:
Adoni   they disgraced you   which

12. And render to our neighbors sevenfold into their bosom their insult, with which they have insulted you, O Lord.

וַאֲנַחְנוּ עַמְּךָ וְצֹאן מַרְעִיתֶךָ נוֹדֶה לְּךָ לְעוֹלָם
to ever   to you   we give thanks   your pasture   and sheep   your people   and we

לְדֹר וָדֹר נְסַפֵּר תְּהִלָּתֶךָ:
your praise   we will declare   and generation   to generation

13. So we your people and sheep of your pasture will give you thanks for ever; we will tell your praise to all generations.

PSALM 80

ספר תהילים פרק פ

לַמְנַצֵּחַ אֶל־שֹׁשַׁנִּים עֵדוּת לְאָסָף מִזְמוֹר:

to chief Musician · lilies – unto · testimony · to Asaph · psalm

1. To the chief Musician, according to Shoshannim, a Testimony, A Psalm of Asaph.

רֹעֵה יִשְׂרָאֵל הַאֲזִינָה נֹהֵג כַּצֹּאן יוֹסֵף

shepherd · Israel · the ear · director · like sheep · Joseph

יֹשֵׁב הַכְּרוּבִים הוֹפִיעָה:

dwells · the cherubim · shine forth

2. Give ear, O Shepherd of Israel, you who lead Joseph like a flock; you who are enthroned upon the cherubim, shine forth,

לִפְנֵי אֶפְרַיִם וּבִנְיָמִן וּמְנַשֶּׁה עוֹרְרָה אֶת־גְּבוּרָתֶךָ

before · Ephraim · and Benjamin · and Manasseh · arouse · that – your mighty

וּלְכָה לִישֻׁעָתָה לָּנוּ:

and come · to salvation · to us

3. Before Ephraim, and Benjamin, and Manasseh. Stir up your strength, and come and save us.

אֱלֹהִים הֲשִׁיבֵנוּ וְהָאֵר פָּנֶיךָ וְנִוָּשֵׁעָה:

Elohim · the restore us · and the shine · your face · and we will be saved

4. Restore, O God, and let your face shine; and we shall be saved.

יְהוָֹה אֱלֹהִים צְבָאוֹת עַד־מָתַי עָשַׁנְתָּ בִּתְפִלַּת עַמֶּךָ:

ihvh · Elohim · hosts · when – till · you smoked · in prayer · your people

5. O Lord God of hosts, how long will you be angry against the prayer of your people?

הֶאֱכַלְתָּם לֶחֶם דִּמְעָה וַתַּשְׁקֵמוֹ בִּדְמָעוֹת שָׁלִישׁ:

the ate them · bread · tears · and you made them drink · in tears · three times

6. You feed them with the bread of tears; and gives them tears to drink in great measure.

תְּשִׂימֵנוּ מָדוֹן לִשְׁכֵנֵינוּ וְאֹיְבֵינוּ יִלְעֲגוּ־לָמוֹ:

you made us · strife · to our neighbors · and our enemies · they deride – to themselves

7. You make us a strife to our neighbors; and our enemies laugh among themselves.

אֱלֹהִים צְבָאוֹת הֲשִׁיבֵנוּ וְהָאֵר פָּנֶיךָ וְנִוָּשֵׁעָה:

Elohim · hosts · the restorer · and to shine · your face · and we will be saved

8. Restore us, O God of hosts, and let your face shine; and we shall be saved.

גֶּפֶן מִמִּצְרַיִם תַּסִּיעַ תְּגָרֵשׁ גּוֹיִם וַתִּטָּעֶהָ:

vine · from Egypt · you cause journey · you driven out · nations · and you planted it

9. You have brought a vine from Egypt; you have cast out the nations, and planted it.

פִּנִּיתָ לְפָנֶיהָ וַתַּשְׁרֵשׁ שָׁרָשֶׁיהָ וַתְּמַלֵּא־אָרֶץ:

land   and you filled   its roots   and you rooted   before it   you cleared

10. You cleared a space for it, and you caused it to take deep root, and it filled the land.

כָּסוּ הָרִים צִלָּהּ וַעֲנָפֶיהָ אַרְזֵי־אֵל:

El – cedars   and its boughs   shadow   mountains   you covered

11. The mountains were covered with its shade, and the mighty cedars with its boughs.

תְּשַׁלַּח קְצִירֶהָ עַד־יָם וְאֶל־נָהָר יוֹנְקוֹתֶיהָ:

its shoots   river - and unto   day – till   its branches   it sent

12. She sent out her boughs to the sea, and her branches to the river.

לָמָּה פָּרַצְתָּ גְדֵרֶיהָ וְאָרוּהָ כָּל־עֹבְרֵי דָרֶךְ:

way   passing ones – all   and picked   fences   you broken down   why

13. Why have you then broken down her hedges, so that all those who pass by the way pluck her fruit?

יְכַרְסְמֶנָּה חֲזִיר מִיָּעַר וְזִיז שָׂדַי יִרְעֶנָּה:

he devours it   field   and wild beast   from forest   boar   he will tear it

14. The boar from the wood destroys it, and the wild beast of the field devours it.

אֱלֹהִים צְבָאוֹת שׁוּב־נָא הַבֵּט מִשָּׁמַיִם וּרְאֵה וּפְקֹד גֶּפֶן זֹאת:

this   vine   and visit   and see   from heavens   look   now – return   legions   Elohim

15. Return, we beseech you, O God of hosts; look down from heaven, and behold, and have regard for this vine;

וְכַנָּה אֲשֶׁר־נָטְעָה יְמִינֶךָ וְעַל־בֵּן אִמַּצְתָּה לָּךְ:

to you   you strengthened   son – and upon   your right hand   planted – which   and stock

16. And the vineyard which your right hand has planted, and the branch that you made strong for yourself.

שְׂרֻפָה בָאֵשׁ כְּסוּחָה מִגַּעֲרַת פָּנֶיךָ יֹאבֵדוּ:

they perish   your face   from rebuke   cut down   in fire   burned

17. It is burned with fire, it is cut down; they perish at the rebuke of your countenance.

תְּהִי־יָדְךָ עַל־אִישׁ יְמִינֶךָ עַל־בֶּן־אָדָם אִמַּצְתָּ לָּךְ:

to you   you strengthened   Adam – son – upon   your right hand   fire – upon   your hand – let be

18. Let your hand be upon the man of your right hand, upon the son of a man whom you made strong for yourself.

וְלֹא־נָסוֹג מִמֶּךָּ תְּחַיֵּנוּ וּבְשִׁמְךָ נִקְרָא:

we will call   and in your name   you keep us alive   from you   we will go back - and not

19. Then we will never turn back from you; revive us, and we will call upon your name.

יְהוָה אֱלֹהִים צְבָאוֹת הֲשִׁיבֵנוּ הָאֵר פָּנֶיךָ וְנִוָּשֵׁעָה:

and we will be saved   your face   the shine   the restore us   legions   Elohim   ihvh

20. Restore us, O Lord God of hosts, let your face shine; and we shall be saved.

PSALM 81

ספר תהילים פרק פא

לַמְנַצֵּחַ עַל־הַגִּתִּית לְאָסָף׃

to Asaph   the Gittit – upon   to chief Musician

1. To the chief Musician, according to Gittit, A Psalm of Asaph.

הַרְנִינוּ לֵאלֹהִים עוּזֵּנוּ הָרִיעוּ לֵאלֹהֵי יַעֲקֹב׃

Jacob   to Elohim   you shout joy   our strength   to Elohim   the shout joy

2. Sing aloud to God our strength; make a joyful noise to the God of Jacob.

שְׂאוּ־זִמְרָה וּתְנוּ־תֹף כִּנּוֹר נָעִים עִם־נָבֶל׃

lyre - with   pleasant ones   harp   timbrel - and you give   psalm song - you lift

3. Raise a song, and beat the tambourine, the sweet lyre with the harp.

תִּקְעוּ בַחֹדֶשׁ שׁוֹפָר בַּכֵּסֶה לְיוֹם חַגֵּנוּ׃

our festival   to day   in full moon   shofar   in new moon   you blow

4. Blow a shofar at the new moon, at the full moon on our feast day.

כִּי חֹק לְיִשְׂרָאֵל הוּא מִשְׁפָּט לֵאלֹהֵי יַעֲקֹב׃

Jacob   to Elohim   judgment   it   to Israel   statute   like

5. For this is a statute for Israel, an ordinance of the God of Jacob.

עֵדוּת בִּיהוֹסֵף שָׂמוֹ בְּצֵאתוֹ עַל־אֶרֶץ מִצְרָיִם

Egypt   earth – upon   in his going out   placed him   in Joseph   testimony

שְׂפַת לֹא־יָדַעְתִּי אֶשְׁמָע׃

I heard   my knowing – not   language

6. This he ordained in Joseph for a testimony, when he went out through the land of Egypt. I heard the language of one whom I had not known,

הֲסִירוֹתִי מִסֵּבֶל שִׁכְמוֹ כַּפָּיו מִדּוּד תַּעֲבֹרְנָה׃

it passed away   from basket   his palms   his shoulder   from burdens   I removed

7. Saying, I removed his shoulder from the burden; his hands are freed from the basket.

בַּצָּרָה קָרָאתָ וָאֲחַלְּצֶךָּ אֶעֶנְךָ בְּסֵתֶר רַעַם

thunder   in hiding place   I answered you   and I delivered you   you called   in trouble

אֶבְחָנְךָ עַל־מֵי מְרִיבָה סֶלָה׃

Sela   Meribah (strife)   waters – upon   I tested you

8. You called in trouble, and I saved you; I answered you in the secret place of thunder; I tested you at the waters of Meribah. Selah.

שְׁמַע עַמִּי וְאָעִידָה בָּךְ יִשְׂרָאֵל אִם־תִּשְׁמַע־לִי׃

to me - you will hear – if   Israel   in you   and I will testify   my people   hear

9. Hear, O my people, and I will warn you, O Israel, if you will listen to me:

לֹא־יִהְיֶה בְךָ אֵל זָר וְלֹא תִשְׁתַּחֲוֶה לְאֵל נֵכָר׃

alien   to El   you will bow down   and not   strange   El   in you   it will be - not

10. There shall be no strange god among you; nor shall you worship any foreign god.

אָנֹכִי יְהוָה אֱלֹהֶיךָ הַמַּעַלְךָ מֵאֶרֶץ מִצְרָיִם

Egypt   from land   the elevated you   your Elohim   ihvh   I am

הַרְחֶב־פִּיךָ וַאֲמַלְאֵהוּ׃

and I will fill it   your mouth - the wide

11. I am the Lord your God, who brought you out of the land of Egypt; open your mouth wide, and I will fill it.

וְלֹא־שָׁמַע עַמִּי לְקוֹלִי וְיִשְׂרָאֵל לֹא־אָבָה לִי׃

to me   willing – not   and Israel   to my voice   my people   hear - and not

12. But my people would not listen to my voice; and Israel would have none of me.

וָאֲשַׁלְּחֵהוּ בִּשְׁרִירוּת לִבָּם יֵלְכוּ בְּמוֹעֲצוֹתֵיהֶם׃

in their own counsels   they walked   their heart   in obstinacies   and I sent them

13. So I gave them over to their stubborn hearts, and they walked in their own counsels.

לוּ עַמִּי שֹׁמֵעַ לִי יִשְׂרָאֵל בִּדְרָכַי יְהַלֵּכוּ׃

they walk   in my way   Israel   to me   hearers   my people   to you

14. Oh that my people would listen to me, and that Israel would walk in my ways!

כִּמְעַט אוֹיְבֵיהֶם אַכְנִיעַ וְעַל־צָרֵיהֶם אָשִׁיב יָדִי׃

my hand   I will return   their adversaries - and upon   I subdue   their enemies   like little

15. I should soon subdue their enemies, and turn my hand against their adversaries.

מְשַׂנְאֵי יְהוָה יְכַחֲשׁוּ־לוֹ וִיהִי עִתָּם לְעוֹלָם׃

to forever   their season   and will be   to him - will cringe   ihvh   from haters

16. Let the haters of the Lord cringe before him, and their punishment should last for ever.

וַיַּאֲכִילֵהוּ מֵחֵלֶב חִטָּה וּמִצּוּר דְּבַשׁ אַשְׂבִּיעֶךָ׃

I satisfy you   honey   and from rock   wheat   from fat   and they feed him

17. And he would feed him with the finest of the wheat; and I would satisfy you with honey from the rock.

PSALM 82

ספר תהילים פרק פב

מִזְמוֹר לְאָסָף
Psalm — to Asaph

אֱלֹהִים נִצָּב בַּעֲדַת־אֵל בְּקֶרֶב אֱלֹהִים יִשְׁפֹּט:
Elohim — stands — El - in congregation — in near — E ohim — he judges

1. A Psalm of Asaph. God stands in the congregation of God; he judges among the judges.

עַד־מָתַי תִּשְׁפְּטוּ־עָוֶל וּפְנֵי רְשָׁעִים תִּשְׂאוּ־סֶלָה:
when - till — inequity - will he judge it — and face — wicked ones — you will uplift — Sela

2. How long will you judge unjustly, and accept the persons of the wicked? Selah.

שִׁפְטוּ־דַל וְיָתוֹם עָנִי וָרָשׁ הַצְדִּיקוּ:
feeble - judge — poor and orphan — and destitute — the righting

3. Do justice to the poor and the orphan; vindicate the afflicted and needy.

פַּלְּטוּ־דַל וְאֶבְיוֹן מִיַּד רְשָׁעִים הַצִּילוּ:
feeble - deliver — and needy — from hand — wicked ones — deliver

4. Save the poor and needy; rescue them from the hand of the wicked.

לֹא יָדְעוּ וְלֹא יָבִינוּ בַּחֲשֵׁכָה יִתְהַלָּכוּ
not — they know — and not — they understand — in darkness — they walk

יִמּוֹטוּ כָּל־מוֹסְדֵי אָרֶץ:
they collapse — foundations - all — earth

5. They do not know, nor will they understand; they walk in darkness; all the foundations of the earth are shaken.

אֲנִי אָמַרְתִּי אֱלֹהִים אַתֶּם וּבְנֵי עֶלְיוֹן כֻּלְּכֶם:
I — I said — Elohim — you — and sons — most high — all them

6. I have said, You are angels; and all of you are sons of the most High.

אָכֵן כְּאָדָם תְּמוּתוּן וּכְאַחַד הַשָּׂרִים תִּפֹּלוּ:
surely — like Adam — you will die — and like one — the princes — you fall it

7. Nevertheless, you shall die like men, and fall like any prince.

קוּמָה אֱלֹהִים שָׁפְטָה הָאָרֶץ כִּי־אַתָּה תִנְחַל בְּכָל־הַגּוֹיִם:
arise — Elohim — judge — the earth — you - like — you will allot — the nations - in all

8. Arise, O God, judge the earth; for to you shall all nations belong.

Psalm 83

ספר תהילים פרק פג

שִׁיר מִזְמוֹר לְאָסָף׃

to Asaph   pslm   song

1. A Song Psalm of Asaph.

אֱלֹהִים אַל־דֳּמִי־לָךְ אַל־תֶּחֱרַשׁ וְאַל־תִּשְׁקֹט אֵל׃

El   you be quiet – and don't   you be silent – don't   to you - silence – don't   Elohim

2. Do not keep silent, O God; do not hold your peace and be still, O God.

כִּי־הִנֵּה אוֹיְבֶיךָ יֶהֱמָיוּן וּמְשַׂנְאֶיךָ נָשְׂאוּ רֹאשׁ׃

head   they lifted   and from your haters   they disquieted   your enemies   here - like

3. For, behold, your enemies make a tumult; and those who hate you have lifted up the head.

עַל־עַמְּךָ יַעֲרִימוּ סוֹד וְיִתְיָעֲצוּ עַל־צְפוּנֶיךָ׃

your hidden ones – upon   and they consult   foundation   they devise   your people - upon

4. They have taken crafty counsel against your people, and consulted against your hidden ones.

אָמְרוּ לְכוּ וְנַכְחִידֵם מִגּוֹי

from nations   and we will cut off them   you go   they said

וְלֹא־יִזָּכֵר שֵׁם־יִשְׂרָאֵל עוֹד׃

again   Israel – name   it remembered – and not

5. They have said, Come, and let us cut them off from being a nation; that the name of Israel may no longer be remembered.

כִּי נוֹעֲצוּ לֵב יַחְדָּו עָלֶיךָ בְּרִית יִכְרֹתוּ׃

they are cutting   covenant   against you   together   heart   they consulted   like

6. For they conspire together with one accord; they make an alliance against you:

אָהֳלֵי אֱדוֹם וְיִשְׁמְעֵאלִים מוֹאָב וְהַגְרִים׃

and the Hagarite ones   Moab   and Ishamelite ones   Edom   tents

7. The tents of Edom, and the Ishmaelites; of Moab, and the Hagarites;

גְּבָל וְעַמּוֹן וַעֲמָלֵק פְּלֶשֶׁת עִם־יֹשְׁבֵי צוֹר׃

Tyre   inhabitants - with   Philistia   and Amalek   and Ammon   Gebal

8. Gebal, and Ammon, and Amalek; the Philistines with the inhabitants of Tyre;

גַּם־אַשּׁוּר נִלְוָה עִמָּם הָיוּ זְרוֹעַ לִבְנֵי־לוֹט סֶלָה׃

Sela   lot – to sons   arm   they were   with them   joined   Assyria - also

9. Assyria also has joined them; they are the strong arm of the children of Lot. Selah.

עֲשֵׂה־לָהֶם כְּמִדְיָן כְּסִיסְרָא כְיָבִין בְּנַחַל קִישׁוֹן׃

Kishon   in stream   like Jabin   like Sisera   like Midian   to them - do

10. Do to them as you did to the Midianites; as you did to Sisera, as you did to Jabin at

the brook of Kishon;

נִשְׁמְדוּ בְּעֵין־דֹּאר הָיוּ דֹמֶן לָאֲדָמָה:

they were destroyed	in eye – generation	they were	dung	to ground

11. Who perished at Ein-Dor; they became like dung on the earth.

שִׁיתֵמוֹ נְדִיבֵמוֹ כְּעֹרֵב וְכִזְאֵב וּכְזֶבַח

make them	their princes	like Oreb	and like Zeeb	and like Zebah

וּכְצַלְמֻנָּע כָּל־נְסִיכֵמוֹ:

and ike Zalmunna	their rulers – all

12. Make their nobles like Oreb, and like Zeeb; and all their princes like Zebah, and Zalmunna;

אֲשֶׁר אָמְרוּ נִירְשָׁה לָּנוּ אֵת נְאוֹת אֱלֹהִים:

which	you said	we inherit	to ourselves	that	habitation	Elohim

13. Who said, Let us take possession for ourselves of the pastures of God.

אֱלֹהַי שִׁיתֵמוֹ כַגַּלְגַּל כְּקַשׁ לִפְנֵי־רוּחַ:

my Elohim	he sets them	like circling	like stubble	wind - before

14. O my God, make them like whirling tumbleweed, like chaff before the wind.

כְּאֵשׁ תִּבְעַר־יָעַר וּכְלֶהָבָה תְּלַהֵט הָרִים:

like fire	forest – it burns	and like flame	it set on fire	mountains

15. As the fire burns a wood, and as the flame sets the mountains on fire;

כֵּן תִּרְדְּפֵם בְּסַעֲרֶךָ וּבְסוּפָתְךָ תְבַהֲלֵם:

thus	pursue them	in your tempest	and in your storm	you terrify them

16. So pursue them with your tempest, and terrify them with your storm.

מַלֵּא פְנֵיהֶם קָלוֹן וִיבַקְשׁוּ שִׁמְךָ יְהֹוָה:

fill	their faces	shame	and they seek	your name	ihvh

17. Fill their faces with shame; that they may seek your name, O Lord.

יֵבֹשׁוּ וְיִבָּהֲלוּ עֲדֵי־עַד וְיַחְפְּרוּ וְיֹאבֵדוּ:

they ashamed	and troubled	time – till	and they disgraced	and they perish

18. Let them be put to shame and dismayed for ever; and let them be put to shame, and perish,

וְיֵדְעוּ כִּי־אַתָּה שִׁמְךָ יְהֹוָה לְבַדֶּךָ עֶלְיוֹן עַל־כָּל־הָאָרֶץ:

and they know	you – like	your name	ihvh	yours alone	most high	upon – all – the earth

19. That men may know that you alone, whose name is the Lord, are the most high over all the earth.

Psalm 84

לַמְנַצֵּחַ עַל־הַגִּתִּית לִבְנֵי־קֹרַח מִזְמוֹר:

psalm   Korach – to sons   Gittit – upon   to chief Musician

1. To the chief Musician, according to Gittit, A Psalm for the sons of Korah.

מַה־יְּדִידוֹת מִשְׁכְּנוֹתֶיךָ יְהוָה צְבָאוֹת:

hosts   ihvh   your tabernacles   lover - what

2. How lovely are your dwelling places, O Lord of hosts!

נִכְסְפָה וְגַם־כָּלְתָה נַפְשִׁי לְחַצְרוֹת יְהוָה

ihvh   to courts   my soul   consumed - and also   yearns

לִבִּי וּבְשָׂרִי יְרַנְּנוּ אֶל־אֵל־חָי:

living   El – unto   they cry out   and my flesh   my heart

3. My soul longs, indeed it faints for the courts of the Lord; my heart and my flesh cry
out for the living God.

גַּם־צִפּוֹר מָצְאָה בַיִת וּדְרוֹר קֵן לָהּ אֲשֶׁר־שָׁתָה

she set – which   to her   nest   and [the]swallow   house   found   sparrow - also

אֶפְרֹחֶיהָ אֶת־מִזְבְּחוֹתֶיךָ יְהוָה צְבָאוֹת מַלְכִּי וֵאלֹהָי:

and my Elohim   my king   hosts   ihvh   your altars – that   her young ones

4. Even the sparrow has found a house, and the swallow a nest for herself, where she
may lay her young, at your altars, O Lord of hosts, my King, and my God.

אַשְׁרֵי יוֹשְׁבֵי בֵיתֶךָ עוֹד יְהַלְלוּךָ סֶּלָה:

Sela   they praise you   still   your house   dwellers   they are

5. Happy are those who dwell in your house, ever praising you. Selah.

אַשְׁרֵי אָדָם עוֹז לוֹ־בָךְ מְסִלּוֹת בִּלְבָבָם:

in their hearts   highways   in you – to him   strength   Adam   they are

6. Happy is the man whose strength is in you; in whose heart are the highways,

עֹבְרֵי בְּעֵמֶק הַבָּכָא מַעְיָן יְשִׁיתוּהוּ גַּם־בְּרָכוֹת יַעְטֶה מוֹרֶה:

early rain   it muffles   blessings – also   they set it   from spring   the Baca   in valley   passing

7. Which, passing through the valley of Baca, make it a place of springs; the early rain
also covers it with blessings.

יֵלְכוּ מֵחַיִל אֶל־חָיִל יֵרָאֶה אֶל־אֱלֹהִים בְּצִיּוֹן:

in Zion   Elohim – unto   he appears   power - unto   from power   they go

8. They go from strength to strength, every one of them appears before God in Zion.

יְהוָה אֱלֹהִים צְבָאוֹת שִׁמְעָה תְפִלָּתִי הַאֲזִינָה

give the ear   my prayer   hear   hosts   Elohim   ihvh

אֱלֹהֵי יַעֲקֹב סֶלָה:

Sela   Jacob   Elohim

9. O Lord God of hosts, hear my prayer; give ear, O God of Jacob. Selah.

מָגִנֵּנוּ רְאֵה אֱלֹהִים וְהַבֵּט פְּנֵי מְשִׁיחֶךָ:

anointed   face   and the look   Elohim   you see   our shield

10. Behold, O God our shield, and look upon the face of your anointed.

כִּי טוֹב־יוֹם בַּחֲצֵרֶיךָ מֵאָלֶף בָּחַרְתִּי

I have chosen   from one thousand   in the your courts   day – good   like

הִסְתּוֹפֵף בְּבֵית אֱלֹהַי מִדּוּר בְּאָהֳלֵי־רֶשַׁע:

wicked – in tent   from abiding   my Elohim   in house   be threshold

11. For a day in your courts is better than a thousand. I had rather be at the threshold in the house of my God, than dwell in the tents of the wicked.

כִּי שֶׁמֶשׁ וּמָגֵן יְהוָה אֱלֹהִים חֵן וְכָבוֹד יִתֵּן יְהוָה

ihvh   he give   and glory   grace   Elohim   ihvh   and shield   sun   like

לֹא־יִמְנַע טוֹב לַהֹלְכִים בְּתָמִים:

in perfectness   to walking ones   good   he will withhold - not

12. For the Lord God is a sun and shield; the Lord will give loving kindness and glory; no good thing will he withhold from those who walk uprightly.

יְהוָה צְבָאוֹת אַשְׁרֵי אָדָם בֹּטֵחַ בָּךְ:

in you   trusts   Adam   happy   legions   ihvh

13. O Lord of hosts, happy is the man who trusts in you.

PSALM 85

לַמְנַצֵּחַ לִבְנֵי־קֹרַח מִזְמוֹר׃
psalm   Korach - to sons   to chief Musician

1. To the chief Musician, A Psalm for the sons of Korah.

רָצִיתָ יְהֹוָה אַרְצֶךָ שַׁבְתָּ שְׁבוּת [שְׁבִית] יַעֲקֹב׃
Jacob   captivity   you returned   your land   ihvh   you favored

2. (K) Lord, you have been favorable to your land; you have brought back the captivity of Jacob.

נָשָׂאתָ עֲוֹן עַמֶּךָ כִּסִּיתָ כָל־חַטָּאתָם סֶלָה׃
Sela   their sins - all   you covered   your people   inequity   you lifted

3. You have forgiven the iniquity of your people, you have pardoned all their sin. Selah.

אָסַפְתָּ כָל־עֶבְרָתֶךָ הֱשִׁיבוֹתָ מֵחֲרוֹן אַפֶּךָ׃
your anger   from heat   you turned away   your rage - all   you gathered

4. You have withdrawn all your wrath; you have turned from the fierceness of your anger.

שׁוּבֵנוּ אֱלֹהֵי יִשְׁעֵנוּ וְהָפֵר כַּעַסְךָ עִמָּנוּ׃
with us   your anger   and ceased   our salvation   my Elohim   turn us

5. Restore us, O God of our salvation, and cease your anger toward us.

הַלְעוֹלָם תֶּאֱנַף־בָּנוּ תִּמְשֹׁךְ אַפְּךָ לְדֹר וָדֹר׃
and generation   to generation   your anger   you draw out   with us – will you be angry   the forever

6. Will you be angry with us for ever? Will you draw out your anger to all generations?

הֲלֹא־אַתָּה תָּשׁוּב תְּחַיֵּנוּ וְעַמְּךָ יִשְׂמְחוּ־בָךְ׃
in you - they be happy   and your people   you revive us   you return   you – the not

7. Will you not revive us again, that your people may rejoice in you?

הַרְאֵנוּ יְהֹוָה חַסְדֶּךָ וְיֶשְׁעֲךָ תִּתֶּן־לָנוּ׃
to us - you give   and your salvation   your kindness   ihvh   the see us

8. Show us your loving kindness, O Lord, and grant us your salvation.

אֶשְׁמְעָה מַה־יְדַבֵּר הָאֵל יְהֹוָה כִּי יְדַבֵּר שָׁלוֹם אֶל־עַמּוֹ
his people – unto   peace   he will speak   like   ihvh   the El   he will speak – what   I will hear

וְאֶל־חֲסִידָיו וְאַל־יָשׁוּבוּ לְכִסְלָה׃
to folly   they return – and not   his saints – and unto

9. I will hear what God the Lord will speak; for he will speak peace to his people, and to his pious ones; but let them not turn back to folly.

אַךְ קָרוֹב לִירֵאָיו יִשְׁעוֹ לִשְׁכֹּן כָּבוֹד בְּאַרְצֵנוּ׃
in our land   glory   to dwell   his salvation   to fearers of him   near   surely

10. Surely his salvation is near to those who fear him; that glory may dwell in our land.

חֶסֶד־וֶאֱמֶת נִפְגָּשׁוּ צֶדֶק וְשָׁלוֹם נָשָׁקוּ׃
they kissed   and peace   righteousness they meet   and truth - kindness

11. Loving kindness and truth meet together; righteousness and peace kiss each other.

אֱמֶת מֵאֶרֶץ תִּצְמָח וְצֶדֶק מִשָּׁמַיִם נִשְׁקָף׃
will look down from heavens and righteous it will spring from earth   truth

12. Truth shall spring from the earth; and righteousness shall look down from heaven.

גַּם־יְהֹוָה יִתֵּן הַטּוֹב וְאַרְצֵנוּ תִּתֵּן יְבוּלָהּ׃
its produce   will give and our land the good will give   ihvh - also

13. Also, the Lord shall give that which is good; and our land shall yield her produce.

צֶדֶק לְפָנָיו יְהַלֵּךְ וְיָשֵׂם לְדֶרֶךְ פְּעָמָיו׃
his footsteps   to way   and set   will walk before him   righteousness

14. Righteousness shall go before him; and walk in the way of his steps.

PSALM 86

ספר תהילים פרק פו

תְּפִלָּה לְדָוִד

to David   prayer

הַטֵּה יְהֹוָה אָזְנְךָ עֲנֵנִי כִּי־עָנִי וְאֶבְיוֹן אָנִי:

I   and needy   poor - like   answer me   your ear   ihvh   incline

1. A Prayer of David. Incline your ear, O Lord, answer me; for I am poor and needy.

שָׁמְרָה נַפְשִׁי כִּי־חָסִיד אָנִי הוֹשַׁע עַבְדְּךָ אַתָּה

you   your servant   save   I   kindness – like   my soul   heed

אֱלֹהַי הַבּוֹטֵחַ אֵלֶיךָ:

unto you   the trust   my Elohim

2. Preserve my soul; for I am pious; O my God, save your servant who trusts in you.

חָנֵּנִי אֲדֹנָי כִּי־אֵלֶיךָ אֶקְרָא כָּל־הַיּוֹם:

the day – all   I call   unto you – like   Adoni   be gracious

3. Be merciful to me, O Lord; for I cry to you daily.

שַׂמֵּחַ נֶפֶשׁ עַבְדֶּךָ כִּי אֵלֶיךָ אֲדֹנָי נַפְשִׁי אֶשָּׂא:

I lift up   my soul   Adoni   unto you   like   your servant   soul   gladden

4. Rejoice the soul of your servant; for to you, O Lord, I lift up my soul.

כִּי־אַתָּה אֲדֹנָי טוֹב וְסַלָּח וְרַב־חֶסֶד לְכָל־קֹרְאֶיךָ:

your callers - to all   kindness – and many   and pardoning   good   Adoni   you - like

5. For you, Lord, are good, and ready to forgive; and of bountiful love toward all those who call upon you.

הַאֲזִינָה יְהֹוָה תְּפִלָּתִי וְהַקְשִׁיבָה בְּקוֹל תַּחֲנוּנוֹתָי:

my supplications   in voice   and the attend   my prayer   ihvh   the give ear

6. Give ear, O Lord, to my prayer; and attend to the voice of my supplications.

בְּיוֹם צָרָתִי אֶקְרָאֶךָ כִּי תַעֲנֵנִי:

you answer me   like   I call you   my trouble   in day

7. On the day of my trouble I will call on you; for you will answer me.

אֵין־כָּמוֹךָ בָאֱלֹהִים אֲדֹנָי וְאֵין כְּמַעֲשֶׂיךָ:

like your works   and isn't   Adoni   in Elohim   like you – isn't

8. Among the gods there is none like you, O Lord; nor are there any works like yours.

כָּל־גּוֹיִם אֲשֶׁר עָשִׂיתָ יָבוֹאוּ וְיִשְׁתַּחֲווּ לְפָנֶיךָ אֲדֹנָי

Adoni   before you   and bow down   they come   you made   which   nations - all

וִיכַבְּדוּ לִשְׁמֶךָ:

and you name   and they glorify

9. All nations whom you have made shall come and worship before you, O Lord; and

shall glorify your name.

כִּי־גָדוֹל אַתָּה וְעֹשֵׂה נִפְלָאוֹת אַתָּה אֱלֹהִים לְבַדֶּךָ:

| you alone | Elohim | you | mysticals | and doing | you | great - like |

10. For you are great, and you do wondrous things; you alone are God.

הוֹרֵנִי יְהֹוָה דַּרְכֶּךָ אֲהַלֵּךְ בַּאֲמִתֶּךָ יַחֵד לְבָבִי לְיִרְאָה שְׁמֶךָ:

| your name | to fear | my heart | unite | in your truth | I walk | your way | ihvh | teach me |

11. Teach me your way, O Lord; I will walk in your truth; unite my heart to fear your name.

אוֹדְךָ אֲדֹנָי אֱלֹהַי בְּכָל־לְבָבִי וַאֲכַבְּדָה שִׁמְךָ לְעוֹלָם:

| to forever | your name | and I glorify | my heart – in all | my Elohim | Adoni | I thank you |

12. I will thank you, O Lord my God, with all my heart; and I will glorify your name for evermore.

כִּי־חַסְדְּךָ גָּדוֹל עָלָי וְהִצַּלְתָּ נַפְשִׁי מִשְּׁאוֹל תַּחְתִּיָּה:

| depths | from Sheol | my soul | and you delivered | upon me | big | your kindness - like |

13. For great is your loving kindness toward me; and you have saved my soul from the depths of Sheol.

אֱלֹהִים זֵדִים קָמוּ עָלַי וַעֲדַת עָרִיצִים

| ruthless ones | and congregation | upon me | they rose | proud ones | Elohim |

בִּקְשׁוּ נַפְשִׁי וְלֹא שָׂמוּךָ לְנֶגְדָּם:

| before them | they set you | and not | my soul | they sought |

14. O God, the arrogant have risen against me, and the assembly of violent men have sought after my soul; and have not set you before them.

וְאַתָּה אֲדֹנָי אֵל־רַחוּם וְחַנּוּן אֶרֶךְ אַפַּיִם וְרַב־חֶסֶד וֶאֱמֶת:

| and truth | kindness - and many | ange- | slow | and gracious | merciful – El | Adoni | and you |

15. But you, O Lord, are a God full of compassion, and gracious, long suffering, and bountiful in loving kindness and truth.

פְּנֵה אֵלַי וְחָנֵּנִי תְּנָה־עֻזְּךָ לְעַבְדֶּךָ

| to your servant | your strength - give | and be gracious | unto me | turn |

וְהוֹשִׁיעָה לְבֶן־אֲמָתֶךָ:

| your handmaid – to sons | and save |

16. O turn to me, and have mercy upon me; give your strength to your servant, and save the son of your maidservant.

עֲשֵׂה־עִמִּי אוֹת לְטוֹבָה וְיִרְאוּ שֹׂנְאַי וְיֵבֹשׁוּ

| and they ashamed | my hated | and they see | to good | sign | with me - make |

כִּי־אַתָּה יְהֹוָה עֲזַרְתַּנִי וְנִחַמְתָּנִי:

| and comforted me | helped me | ihvh | you – like |

17. Show me a sign for good; that they who hate me may see it, and be ashamed; because you, Lord, have helped me, and comforted me.

PSALM 87

ספר תהילים פרק פז

לִבְנֵי־קֹרַח מִזְמוֹר שִׁיר יְסוּדָתוֹ בְּהַרְרֵי־קֹדֶשׁ׃

holy – in mountains   his foundation   song   psalm   Korah – to sons

1. A Psalm Song for the sons of Korah. His foundation is in the holy mountains.

אֹהֵב יְהוָה שַׁעֲרֵי צִיּוֹן מִכֹּל מִשְׁכְּנוֹת יַעֲקֹב׃

Jacob   tabernacles   from all   Zion   gates   ihvh   love

2. The Lord loves the gates of Zion more than all the dwellings of Jacob.

נִכְבָּדוֹת מְדֻבָּר בָּךְ עִיר הָאֱלֹהִים סֶלָה׃

Sela   the Elohim   city   in you   spoken   glorious things

3. Glorious things are spoken of you, O city of God. Selah.

אַזְכִּיר רַהַב וּבָבֶל לְיֹדְעָי הִנֵּה פְלֶשֶׁת

Philista   here   to my knowers   and Babylon   Rahab   mention

וְצוֹר עִם־כּוּשׁ זֶה יֻלַּד־שָׁם׃

there – born   this   Cush – with   and Tyre

4. I will make mention of Rahab and Babylon to those who know me; behold Philistia, and Tyre, with Kush, saying, This man was born there.

וּלְצִיּוֹן יֵאָמַר אִישׁ וְאִישׁ יֻלַּד־בָּהּ וְהוּא יְכוֹנְנֶהָ עֶלְיוֹן׃

most high   establish her   and he   in her –born   and man   man   will be said   and to Zion

5. And of Zion it shall be said, This and that man was born in her; and the highest himself shall establish her.

יְהוָה יִסְפֹּר בִּכְתוֹב עַמִּים זֶה יֻלַּד־שָׁם סֶלָה׃

Sela   there - was born   this   peoples   in writing   he will count   ihvh

6. The Lord shall record, when he registers up the peoples, that this man was born there. Selah.

וְשָׁרִים כְּחֹלְלִים כָּל־מַעְיָנַי בָּךְ׃

in you   my springs – all   like dancers   and singers

7. And singers and dancers alike shall say; All my springs are in you.

PSALM 88

ספר תהילים פרק פח

שִׁיר מִזְמוֹר לִבְנֵי קֹרַח לַמְנַצֵּחַ עַל־מַחֲלַת

Mahalath – upon   to chief Musician   Korah   to sons   psalm   song

לְעַנּוֹת מַשְׂכִּיל לְהֵימָן הָאֶזְרָחִי:

the Ezrahite   to Heman   contemplation   Leannoth

1. A Song Psalm for the sons of Korah, to the chief Musician, according to Mahalath Leannoth, A Maskil of Heman the Ezrahite.

יְהֹוָה אֱלֹהֵי יְשׁוּעָתִי יוֹם צָעַקְתִּי בַלַּיְלָה נֶגְדֶּךָ:

before you   in night   I cried   day   my salvation   Elohei   ihvh

2. O Lord God of my salvation, I have cried day and night before you;

תָּבוֹא לְפָנֶיךָ תְּפִלָּתִי הַטֵּה־אָזְנְךָ לְרִנָּתִי:

to my joy cry   your ear – incline   my prayer   before you   you come

3. Let my prayer come before you; incline your ear to my cry;

כִּי־שָׂבְעָה בְרָעוֹת נַפְשִׁי וְחַיַּי לִשְׁאוֹל הִגִּיעוּ:

it draws near   to Sheol   and my life   my soul   in evils   filled - like

4. For my soul is full of troubles; and my life draws near to Sheol.

נֶחְשַׁבְתִּי עִם־יוֹרְדֵי בוֹר הָיִיתִי כְּגֶבֶר אֵין־אֱיָל:

strength – isn't   like gentle man   I was   pit   descenders – with   I reckoned

5. I am counted with those who go down into the pit; I am like a man who has no strength,

בַּמֵּתִים חָפְשִׁי כְּמוֹ חֲלָלִים שֹׁכְבֵי קֶבֶר

grave   lie down ones   wounded ones   like   free   in dead ones

אֲשֶׁר לֹא זְכַרְתָּם עוֹד וְהֵמָּה מִיָּדְךָ נִגְזָרוּ:

they cut off   from your hand   and they still   remembered you   not   which

6. Free among the dead, like the slain who lie in the grave, whom you do not remember any more; and they are cut off from your hand.

שַׁתַּנִי בְּבוֹר תַּחְתִּיּוֹת בְּמַחֲשַׁכִּים בִּמְצֹלוֹת:

in depths   in dark places   lowest pit   in pit   you laid me

7. You have laid me in the lowest pit in darkness, in the deeps.

עָלַי סָמְכָה חֲמָתֶךָ וְכָל־מִשְׁבָּרֶיךָ עִנִּיתָ סֶּלָה:

Sela   you afflicted   your waves – and all   your wrath   bears down   upon me

8. Your wrath lies hard on me, and you have afflicted me with all your waves. Selah.

הִרְחַקְתָּ מְיֻדָּעַי מִמֶּנִּי

from me   my acquaintance   you put far

שַׁתַּנִי תוֹעֵבוֹת לָמוֹ כָּלֻא וְלֹא אֵצֵא:

I come out   and not   shut up   to them   abominations   you set me

9. You have put away my acquaintance far from me; you have made me an abomination to them; I am shut up, and I cannot come forth.

עֵינִי דָאֲבָה מִנִּי עֹנִי קְרָאתִיךָ יְהֹוָה

ihvh   I called you   my affliction   on account of   has pined   my eye

בְּכָל־יוֹם שִׁטַּחְתִּי אֵלֶיךָ כַפָּי:

my palm   unto you   I spread out   day – in all

10. My eye grows dim through affliction; Lord, I have called daily upon you, I have stretched out my hands to you.

הֲלַמֵּתִים תַּעֲשֶׂה־פֶּלֶא אִם־רְפָאִים יָקוּמוּ יוֹדוּךָ סֶּלָה:

Sela   they praise you   they arise   sick ones – with   wonder – you will do   the "to dead"

11. Will you work wonders to the dead? Shall the shades arise and praise you? Selah.

הַיְסֻפַּר בַּקֶּבֶר חַסְדֶּךָ אֱמוּנָתְךָ בָּאֲבַדּוֹן:

in destruction   your faithfulness   kindness   in grave   the declared

12. Shall your loving kindness be declared in the grave? Your faithfulness in Avaddon?

הֲיִוָּדַע בַּחֹשֶׁךְ פִּלְאֶךָ וְצִדְקָתְךָ בְּאֶרֶץ נְשִׁיָּה:

forgetfulness   in land   and your righteousness   your wonder   in darkness   the known

13. Shall your wonders be known in the dark? And your righteousness in the land of forgetfulness?

וַאֲנִי אֵלֶיךָ יְהֹוָה שִׁוַּעְתִּי וּבַבֹּקֶר תְּפִלָּתִי תְקַדְּמֶךָּ:

will meet you   my prayer   and in morning   I cried   ihvh   unto you   and I

14. But to you I have cried, O Lord; and in the morning shall my prayer attend you.

לָמָה יְהֹוָה תִּזְנַח נַפְשִׁי תַּסְתִּיר פָּנֶיךָ מִמֶּנִּי:

from me   your face   you hide   my soul   you cast   ihvh   why

15. Lord, why do you cast off my soul? Why do you hide your face from me?

עָנִי אֲנִי וְגֹוֵעַ מִנֹּעַר נָשָׂאתִי אֵמֶיךָ אָפוּנָה:

I distracted   your terrors   I borne   from youth   and close to death   I   poor

16. I am afflicted and close to death from my youth up; while I suffer your terrors I am distracted.

עָלַי עָבְרוּ חֲרוֹנֶיךָ בִּעוּתֶיךָ צִמְּתוּתֻנִי:

cut me off   your terrors   your wraths   it passed   upon me

17. Your fierce wrath goes over me; your terrors have cut me off.

סַבּוּנִי כַמַּיִם כָּל־הַיּוֹם הִקִּיפוּ עָלַי יָחַד:

together   upon me   they enclosed   the day – all   like waters   they surrounded me

18. They surround me daily like water; they close in upon me together.

הִרְחַקְתָּ מִמֶּנִּי אֹהֵב וָרֵעַ מְיֻדָּעַי מַחְשָׁךְ:

from darkness   my acquaintance   and neighbor   love   from me   you put far

19. Loving friend and companion have you put far from me, and my acquaintances are in darkness.

PSALM 89

ספר תהילים פרק פט

מַשְׂכִּיל   לְאֵיתָן   הָאֶזְרָחִי׃
a didactic poem   to Ethan   the Ezrahite

1. A Maskil of Ethan the Ezrahite.

חַסְדֵי   יְהוָֹה   עוֹלָם   אָשִׁירָה
kindness   ihvh   forever   I sing

לְדֹר   וָדֹר   אוֹדִיעַ   אֱמוּנָתְךָ   בְּפִי׃
in my mouth   your faithfulness   I will make known   and generation   to generation

2. I will sing of the constant love of the Lord for ever; with my mouth I will make known your faithfulness to all generations.

כִּי־אָמַרְתִּי   עוֹלָם   חֶסֶד   יִבָּנֶה   שָׁמַיִם   תָּכִן   אֱמוּנָתְךָ   בָהֶם׃
I said - like   forever   kindness   he built   heavens   you will establish   your faithfulness   in them

3. For I have said, The world is built by love; your faithfulness shall you establish in the very heavens.

כָּרַתִּי   בְרִית   לִבְחִירִי   נִשְׁבַּעְתִּי   לְדָוִד   עַבְדִּי׃
I contracted   covenant   to my chosen   I swore   to David   my servant

4. I have made a covenant with my chosen, I have sworn to David my servant,

עַד־עוֹלָם   אָכִין   זַרְעֶךָ   וּבָנִיתִי   לְדֹר־וָדוֹר   כִּסְאֲךָ   סֶלָה׃
for ever - till   I establish   your seed   and I build   to generation – and generation   your throne   Sela

5. Your seed I will establish for ever, and build up your throne to all generations. Selah.

וְיוֹדוּ   שָׁמַיִם   פִּלְאֲךָ   יְהוָֹה   אַף־אֱמוּנָתְךָ   בִּקְהַל   קְדֹשִׁים׃
and they thank   heavens   your wonders   ihvh   your faithfulness - yea   in congregation   saints

6. And the heavens shall praise your wonders, O Lord; your faithfulness also in the congregation of the holy ones.

כִּי   מִי   בַשַּׁחַק   יַעֲרֹךְ   לַיהוָֹה   יִדְמֶה   לַיהוָֹה   בִּבְנֵי   אֵלִים׃
like   who   in the sky   will set   to ihvh   he be like   to ihvh   in sons   Elohim

7. For who in the skies can be compared to the Lord? Who among the sons of the mighty can be likened to the Lord?

אֵל   נַעֲרָץ   בְּסוֹד־קְדֹשִׁים   רַבָּה   וְנוֹרָא   עַל־כָּל־סְבִיבָיו׃
El   to be feared   pious ones - in council   much   and awesome   upon – all – his surounders

8. God is greatly feared in the assembly of the holy ones, and held in reverence by all those who are around him.

יְהוָֹה   אֱלֹהֵי   צְבָאוֹת   מִי־כָמוֹךָ   חֲסִין   יָהּ
ihvh   my Elohim   hosts   like you – who   invincible   Ya

וֶאֱמוּנָתְךָ   סְבִיבוֹתֶיךָ׃
and your faithfulness   surrounds you

9. O Lord God of hosts, who is strong like you, O Lord? Or to your faithfulness around you?

אַתָּה מוֹשֵׁל בְּגֵאוּת הַיָּם בְּשׂוֹא גַלָּיו אַתָּה תְשַׁבְּחֵם:

| still them | you | its billows | in lifting up | the sea | in pride | ruler | you |

10. You rule the raging of the sea; when its waves arise, you still them.

אַתָּה דִכִּאתָ כֶחָלָל רָהַב בִּזְרוֹעַ עֻזְּךָ פִּזַּרְתָּ אוֹיְבֶיךָ:

| your enemies | you scattered | your strength | in arm | Rahab | wounded | crushed | you |

11. You have trampled down Rahab like carrion; you have scattered your enemies with your strong arm.

לְךָ שָׁמַיִם אַף־לְךָ אָרֶץ תֵּבֵל וּמְלֹאָהּ אַתָּה יְסַדְתָּם:

| founded them | you | and its fullness | world | earth | to you – then | heavens | to you |

12. The heavens are yours, the earth also is yours; you have founded the world and all that is in it.

צָפוֹן וְיָמִין אַתָּה בְרָאתָם תָּבוֹר וְחֶרְמוֹן בְּשִׁמְךָ יְרַנֵּנוּ:

| will joy shout | in your name | and Hermon | labor | created them | you | to right | north |

13. The north and the south you have created them; Tabor and Hermon shall rejoice in your name.

לְךָ זְרוֹעַ עִם־גְּבוּרָה תָּעֹז יָדְךָ תָּרוּם יְמִינֶךָ:

| your right hand | you exalted | your hand | you strong | might –with | arm | to you |

14. You have a mighty arm; strong is your hand, and high is your right hand.

צֶדֶק וּמִשְׁפָּט מְכוֹן כִּסְאֶךָ חֶסֶד וֶאֱמֶת יְקַדְּמוּ פָנֶיךָ:

| your face | they presence | and truth | kindness | your throne | place | and judgment | righteousness |

15. Righteousness and justice are the foundation of your throne; love and truth shall go before you.

אַשְׁרֵי הָעָם יוֹדְעֵי תְרוּעָה יְהוָה בְּאוֹר־פָּנֶיךָ יְהַלֵּכוּן:

| they will walk | your face - in light | ihvh | sounding | knows | the people | blessings |

16. Happy is the people who know the joyful sound; they shall walk, O Lord, in the light of your countenance.

בְּשִׁמְךָ יְגִילוּן כָּל־הַיּוֹם וּבְצִדְקָתְךָ יָרוּמוּ:

| they will exalt | and in your righteousness | the day – all | they will rejoice | in your name |

17. In your name shall they rejoice all the day; and in your righteousness shall they be exalted.

כִּי־תִפְאֶרֶת עֻזָּמוֹ אָתָּה וּבִרְצוֹנְךָ תָּרִים [תָּרוּם] קַרְנֵנוּ:

| our horn | will be exalted | and in your favor | you | their strength | glory - like |

18. (K) For you are the glory of their strength; and in your favor our horn shall be exalted.

כִּי לַיהוָה מָגִנֵּנוּ וְלִקְדוֹשׁ יִשְׂרָאֵל מַלְכֵּנוּ:

| our king | Israel | and to holy | our shield | to ihvh | like |

19. For our shield belongs to the Lord; and the Holy One of Israel is our king.

אָז דִּבַּרְתָּ־בְחָזוֹן לַחֲסִידֶיךָ
to your pious   in vision – you speak   then

וַתֹּאמֶר שִׁוִּיתִי עֵזֶר עַל־גִּבּוֹר הֲרִימוֹתִי בָחוּר מֵעָם:
from people chosen one I lfted up mighty one – upon help I set and you said

20. Then you spoke in a vision to your pious one, and said, I have laid help upon one who is mighty; I have exalted one chosen from the people.

מָצָאתִי דָּוִד עַבְדִּי בְּשֶׁמֶן קָדְשִׁי מְשַׁחְתִּיו:
I anointed him my holiness in oil my servant David I have found

21. I have found David my servant; with my holy oil have I anointed him,

אֲשֶׁר יָדִי תִּכּוֹן עִמּוֹ אַף־זְרוֹעִי תְאַמְּצֶנּוּ:
you will strengthen him my arm – thus with him you will establish hand which

22. With whom my hand shall be established; my arm also shall strengthen him.

לֹא־יַשִּׁא אוֹיֵב בּוֹ וּבֶן־עַוְלָה לֹא יְעַנֶּנּוּ:
he will afflict him not iniquity - and son in him enemy he will exact - not

23. The enemy shall not exact upon him; nor the son of wickedness afflict him.

וְכַתּוֹתִי מִפָּנָיו צָרָיו וּמְשַׂנְאָיו אֶגּוֹף:
I strike and from his haters his adversaries from before him and I will beat down

24. And I will beat down his enemies before his face, and strike down those who hate him.

וֶאֱמוּנָתִי וְחַסְדִּי עִמּוֹ וּבִשְׁמִי תָּרוּם קַרְנוֹ:
his horn you will exalt and in my name with him and my kindness and my faithfulness

25. But my faithfulness and my loving kindness shall be with him; and in my name shall his horn be exalted.

וְשַׂמְתִּי בַיָּם יָדוֹ וּבַנְּהָרוֹת יְמִינוֹ:
his right hand and in rivers his hand in sea and I will set

26. I will set his hand also on the sea, and his right hand on the rivers.

הוּא יִקְרָאֵנִי אָבִי אָתָּה אֵלִי וְצוּר יְשׁוּעָתִי:
my salvation and rock my El you my father he will call me he

27. He shall cry to me, You are my father, my God, and the rock of my salvation.

אַף־אָנִי בְּכוֹר אֶתְּנֵהוּ עֶלְיוֹן לְמַלְכֵי־אָרֶץ:
earth – to kings most high I give him first born I - then

28. Also I will make him my firstborn, higher than the kings of the earth.

לְעוֹלָם אֶשְׁמוֹר [אֶשְׁמָר]־לוֹ חַסְדִּי וּבְרִיתִי נֶאֱמֶנֶת לוֹ:
to him will steadfast and my covenant my kindness to him – I will heed to forever

29. (K) I will keep my truth with him for evermore, and my covenant shall stand fast with him.

וְשַׂמְתִּי לָעַד זַרְעוֹ וְכִסְאוֹ כִּימֵי שָׁמָיִם:
heavens like days and his throne his seed to time and I will set

30. His seed also I will make to endure for ever, and his throne like the days of heaven.

אִם־יַעַזְבוּ בָנָיו תּוֹרָתִי וּבְמִשְׁפָּטַי לֹא יֵלֵכוּן:

they walk   not   and in my judgments   my Torah   his sons   he forsake - if

31. If his children forsake my Torah, and do not walk in my judgments;

אִם־חֻקֹּתַי יְחַלֵּלוּ וּמִצְוֹתַי לֹא יִשְׁמֹרוּ:

they keep   not   and my commandments   they profane   my statutes - if

32. If they break my statutes, and do not keep my commandments;

וּפָקַדְתִּי בְשֵׁבֶט פִּשְׁעָם וּבִנְגָעִים עֲוֺנָם:

their inequity   with stripes   their transgression   in rod   and I will visit

33. Then I will punish their transgression with the rod, and their iniquity with strokes.

וְחַסְדִּי לֹא־אָפִיר מֵעִמּוֹ וְלֹא אֲשַׁקֵּר בֶּאֱמוּנָתִי:

in my faithfulness   I be false   and not   from with him   I void – not   and my kindness

34. Nevertheless my loving kindness I will not utterly take from him, nor suffer my faithfulness to fail.

לֹא־אֲחַלֵּל בְּרִיתִי וּמוֹצָא שְׂפָתַי לֹא אֲשַׁנֶּה:

I change   not   my lips   and gone out   my covenant   I will profane - not

35. My covenant I will not break, nor alter the word which was issued from my lips.

אַחַת נִשְׁבַּעְתִּי בְקָדְשִׁי אִם־לְדָוִד אֲכַזֵּב:

I lie   to David - if   in my holiness   I swore   you

36. Once have I sworn by my holiness that I will not lie to David.

זַרְעוֹ לְעוֹלָם יִהְיֶה וְכִסְאוֹ כַשֶּׁמֶשׁ נֶגְדִּי:

before me   like sun   and his throne   will be   forever   his seed

37. His seed shall endure for ever, and his throne like the sun before me.

כְּיָרֵחַ יִכּוֹן עוֹלָם וְעֵד בַּשַּׁחַק נֶאֱמָן סֶלָה:

Sela   steadfast   in sky   and time   forever   he established   like moon

38. It shall be established for ever like the moon, and like a faithful witness in heaven. Selah.

וְאַתָּה זָנַחְתָּ וַתִּמְאָס הִתְעַבַּרְתָּ עִם־מְשִׁיחֶךָ:

your anointed – with   you wroth   and rejected   you cast off   and you

39. But you have cast off and rejected, you have been angry with your anointed.

נֵאַרְתָּה בְּרִית עַבְדֶּךָ חִלַּלְתָּ לָאָרֶץ נִזְרוֹ:

his crown   to earth   you profaned   your servant   covenant   you renounced

40. You have renounced the covenant of your servant; you have profaned his crown to the ground.

פָּרַצְתָּ כָל־גְּדֵרֹתָיו שַׂמְתָּ מִבְצָרָיו מְחִתָּה:

ruin   his fortresses   you set   his fences - all   you broke down

41. You have broken down all his hedges; you have brought his fortresses to ruin.

שַׁסֻּהוּ כָּל־עֹבְרֵי דָרֶךְ הָיָה חֶרְפָּה לִשְׁכֵנָיו׃

| to his neighbors | reproach | he was | way | who pass by – all | spoiled him |

42. All who pass by the way plunder him; he is a taunt to his neighbors.

הֲרִימוֹתָ יְמִין צָרָיו הִשְׂמַחְתָּ כָּל־אוֹיְבָיו׃

| his enemies – all | cause rejoice | his adversaries | right hand | you lifted up |

43. You have exalted the right hand of his adversaries; you have made all his enemies rejoice.

אַף־תָּשִׁיב צוּר חַרְבּוֹ וְלֹא הֲקֵימֹתוֹ בַּמִּלְחָמָה׃

| in war | the his stand | and not | his sword | edge | you turned - then |

44. You have turned back the edge of his sword, and have not made him stand in the battle.

הִשְׁבַּתָּ מִטְּהָרוֹ וְכִסְאוֹ לָאָרֶץ מִגַּרְתָּה׃

| you cast down | to earth | and his throne | from his purity | you ceased |

45. You have made his brightness cease, and cast his throne down to the ground.

הִקְצַרְתָּ יְמֵי עֲלוּמָיו הֶעֱטִיתָ עָלָיו בּוּשָׁה סֶלָה׃

| Sela | shame | upon him | you wrapped | his youth | days | you shortened |

46. The days of his youth you have shortened; you have covered him with shame. Selah.

עַד־מָה יְהֹוָה תִּסָּתֵר לָנֶצַח תִּבְעַר כְּמוֹ־אֵשׁ חֲמָתֶךָ׃

| your wrath | fire – like | you consume | to victory | you hide | ihvh | when - until |

47. How long, Lord, will you hide yourself for ever? Shall your wrath burn like fire?

זְכָר־אֲנִי מֶה־חָלֶד עַל־מַה־שָּׁוְא בָּרָאתָ כָל־בְּנֵי־אָדָם׃

| Adam – sons – all | you created | vanity – what – upon | transient – what | I - remember |

48. Remember how short my time is; for what nothingness you have created all the sons of men!

מִי גֶבֶר יִחְיֶה וְלֹא יִרְאֶה־מָּוֶת

| death – he will see | and not | he lives | gentlemen | what |

יְמַלֵּט נַפְשׁוֹ מִיַּד־שְׁאוֹל סֶלָה׃

| Sela | Shoel - from hand | his soul | he will deliver |

49. Who is the man who lives, and shall not see death? Shall he save his soul from the power of Sheol? Selah.

אַיֵּה חֲסָדֶיךָ הָרִאשֹׁנִים אֲדֹנָי נִשְׁבַּעְתָּ לְדָוִד בֶּאֱמוּנָתֶךָ׃

| in your faithfulness | to David | you swore | Adonai | the former ones | your kindness | where |

50. Lord, where are your former oaths of loving kindness, which you swore to David in your faithfulness?

זְכֹר אֲדֹנָי חֶרְפַּת עֲבָדֶיךָ שְׂאֵתִי בְחֵיקִי כָּל־רַבִּים עַמִּים׃

| peoples | many ones – all | in my bosom | I carry | your servant | reproach | Adonai | remember |

51. Remember, Lord, the disgrace of your servants; how I carry in my bosom the insults of all the many peoples;

אֲשֶׁר חֵרְפוּ אוֹיְבֶיךָ יְהוָה אֲשֶׁר חֵרְפוּ עִקְּבוֹת מְשִׁיחֶךָ:
your anointed footsteps they reproached which ihvh your enemies they reproached which

52. With which your enemies have insulted, O Lord; with which they have insulted the footsteps of your anointed.

בָּרוּךְ יְהוָה לְעוֹלָם אָמֵן וְאָמֵן:
and amen amen to forever ihvh blessed

53. Blessed be the Lord for evermore. Amen, and Amen.

Psalm 90

ספר תהילים פרק צ

תְּפִלָּה לְמֹשֶׁה אִישׁ־הָאֱלֹהִים אֲדֹנָי

| Adoni | the Elohim - man | to Moses | prayer |

מָעוֹן   אַתָּה הָיִיתָ לָּנוּ   בְּדֹר   וָדֹר:

| and generation | in generation | to us | were | you | high dwelling place |

1 A Prayer of Moses the man of God. LORD, thou hast been our dwelling place in all generations.

בְּטֶרֶם הָרִים יֻלָּדוּ וַתְּחוֹלֵל אֶרֶץ וְתֵבֵל

| and inhabitants | earth | and you fashioned | they born | mountains | in before |

וּמֵעוֹלָם עַד־עוֹלָם אַתָּה אֵל:

| El | you | forever – until | and from forever |

2 Before the mountains were brought forth, or ever thou hadst formed the earth and the world, even from everlasting to everlasting, thou art God.

תָּשֵׁב אֱנוֹשׁ עַד־דַּכָּא וַתֹּאמֶר שׁוּבוּ בְנֵי־אָדָם:

| Adam – sons | you return | and you say | crushed – till | mortal man | return |

3 Thou turnest man to destruction; and sayest, Return, ye children of men.

כִּי אֶלֶף שָׁנִים בְּעֵינֶיךָ כְּיוֹם אֶתְמוֹל

| yesterday | like day | in your eyes | years | thousand | like |

כִּי יַעֲבֹר וְאַשְׁמוּרָה בַלָּיְלָה:

| in night | and [a] watch | it passes | like |

4 For a thousand years in thy sight are but as yesterday when it is past, and as a watch in the night.

זְרַמְתָּם שֵׁנָה יִהְיוּ בַּבֹּקֶר כֶּחָצִיר יַחֲלֹף:

| it sprouts | like short lived grass | in morning | they be | sleep | you storm them |

5 Thou carriest them away as with a flood; they are as a sleep: in the morning they are like grass which groweth up.

בַּבֹּקֶר יָצִיץ וְחָלָף לָעֶרֶב יְמוֹלֵל וְיָבֵשׁ:

| and it drysout | it cut down | to evening | and sprouts | it blossoms | in morning |

6 In the morning it flourisheth, and groweth up; in the evening it is cut down, and withereth.

כִּי־כָלִינוּ בְאַפֶּךָ וּבַחֲמָתְךָ נִבְהָלְנוּ:

| we troubled | and in your wrath | in your anger | we consumed – like |

7 For we are consumed by thine anger, and by thy wrath are we troubled.

שַׁתָּ [שַׁתָּה] עֲוֺנֹתֵינוּ לְנֶגְדֶּךָ עֲלֻמֵנוּ לִמְאוֹר פָּנֶיךָ:

| your face | to reflect | our immaturity | to before you | our inequities | you set |

8 Thou hast set our iniquities before thee, our secret sins in the light of thy

countenance.

כִּי כָל־יָמֵינוּ פָּנוּ בְעֶבְרָתֶךָ כִּלִּינוּ שָׁנֵינוּ כְמוֹ־הֶגֶה:

the tale – like   our years   we consumed   in your rage   turned   our days – all   like

9 For all our days are passed away in thy wrath: we spend our years as a tale that is told.

יְמֵי שְׁנוֹתֵינוּ בָהֶם שִׁבְעִים שָׁנָה וְאִם בִּגְבוּרֹת שְׁמוֹנִים שָׁנָה

years   eighty   in might   and if   years   seventy   in them   our years   days

וְרָהְבָּם עָמָל וָאָוֶן כִּי־גָז חִישׁ וַנָּעֻפָה:

and we fly away   swiftly   sheared off – like   and affliction   toil   and their pride

10 The days of our years are threescore years and ten; and if by reason of strength they be fourscore years, yet is their strength labour and sorrow; for it is soon cut off, and we fly away.

מִי־יוֹדֵעַ עֹז אַפֶּךָ וּכְיִרְאָתְךָ עֶבְרָתֶךָ:

your rage   and like your fear   your anger   strength   knows – who

11 Who knoweth the power of thine anger? even according to thy fear, so is thy wrath.

לִמְנוֹת יָמֵינוּ כֵּן הוֹדַע וְנָבִא לְבַב חָכְמָה:

wisdom   heart   and we come   make us know   thus   our days   to count

12 So teach us to number our days, that we may apply our hearts unto wisdom.

שׁוּבָה יְהוָה עַד־מָתָי וְהִנָּחֵם עַל־עֲבָדֶיךָ:

your servants - upon   and comfort   when – until   ihvh   return

13 Return, O LORD, how long? and let it repent thee concerning thy servants.

שַׂבְּעֵנוּ בַבֹּקֶר חַסְדֶּךָ וּנְרַנְּנָה וְנִשְׂמְחָה בְּכָל־יָמֵינוּ:

our days – in all   and we be happy   and we shout w/ joy   your mercy   in morning   satisfy us

14 O satisfy us early with thy mercy; that we may rejoice and be glad all our days.

שַׂמְּחֵנוּ כִּימוֹת עִנִּיתָנוּ שְׁנוֹת רָאִינוּ רָעָה:

evil   we saw   years   you afflicted us   like days   make happy us

15 Make us glad according to the days wherein thou hast afflicted us, and the years wherein we have seen evil.

יֵרָאֶה אֶל־עֲבָדֶיךָ פָעֳלֶךָ וַהֲדָרְךָ עַל־בְּנֵיהֶם:

their sons – upon   and your majesty   your works   your servants – unto   will see

16 Let thy work appear unto thy servants, and thy glory unto their children.

וִיהִי נֹעַם אֲדֹנָי אֱלֹהֵינוּ עָלֵינוּ

upon us   our Elohim   Adonai   pleasantness   and let

וּמַעֲשֵׂה יָדֵינוּ כּוֹנְנָה עָלֵינוּ

upon us   establish   our hands   and works

וּמַעֲשֵׂה יָדֵינוּ כּוֹנְנֵהוּ:

establish it   our hands   and works

17 And let the beauty of the LORD our God be upon us: and establish thou the work of our hands upon us; yea, the work of our hands establish thou it.

PSALM 91

ספר תהילים פרק צא

יֵשֵׁב בְּסֵתֶר עֶלְיוֹן בְּצֵל שַׁדַּי יִתְלוֹנָן׃

will lodge   Shadi   in shade   most high   secret place   he sits

1 He that dwelleth in the secret place of the most High shall abide under the shadow of the Almighty.

אֹמַר לַיהֹוָה מַחְסִי וּמְצוּדָתִי אֱלֹהַי אֶבְטַח־בּוֹ׃

in him – I trust   my Elohim   and my fortress   my refuge   to ihvh   I say

2 I will say of the LORD, *He is* my refuge and my fortress: my God; in him will I trust.

כִּי הוּא יַצִּילְךָ מִפַּח יָקוּשׁ מִדֶּבֶר הַוּוֹת׃

woes   from pestilence   trapper   from snare   will deliver you   he   like

3 Surely he shall deliver thee from the snare of the fowler, *and* from the noisome pestilence.

בְּאֶבְרָתוֹ יָסֶךְ לָךְ וְתַחַת כְּנָפָיו תֶּחְסֶה

you will be protected   his wings   and under   to you   he cover   in his feathers

צִנָּה וְסֹחֵרָה אֲמִתּוֹ׃

his truth   and buckler   shield

4 He shall cover thee with his feathers, and under his wings shalt thou trust: his truth *shall be thy* shield and buckler.

לֹא־תִירָא מִפַּחַד לָיְלָה מֵחֵץ יָעוּף יוֹמָם׃

by day   flying   from arrow   night   from terror   you fear – not

5 Thou shalt not be afraid for the terror by night; *nor* for the arrow *that* flieth by day;

מִדֶּבֶר בָּאֹפֶל יַהֲלֹךְ מִקֶּטֶב יָשׁוּד צָהֳרָיִם

noon   lays waste   from sting   he walks   in gloom   from pestilence

6 *Nor* for the pestilence *that* walketh in darkness; *nor* for the destruction *that* wasteth at noonday.

יִפֹּל מִצִּדְּךָ אֶלֶף וּרְבָבָה מִימִינֶךָ אֵלֶיךָ לֹא יִגָּשׁ׃

he near touch   not   unto you   from your right hand   and multitudes   thousand   from your side   he falls

7 A thousand shall fall at thy side, and ten thousand at thy right hand; *but* it shall not come nigh thee.

רַק בְּעֵינֶיךָ תַבִּיט וְשִׁלֻּמַת רְשָׁעִים תִּרְאֶה׃

you see   wicked ones   and reward   you behold   in your eyes   only

8 Only with thine eyes shalt thou behold and see the reward of the wicked.

כִּי־אַתָּה יְהֹוָה מַחְסִי עֶלְיוֹן שַׂמְתָּ מְעוֹנֶךָ׃

from your habitation   you set   most high place   my refuge   ihvh   you – like

9 Because thou hast made the LORD, *which is* my refuge, *even* the most High, thy habitation;

לֹא־תְאֻנֶּה אֵלֶיךָ רָעָה וְנֶגַע לֹא־יִקְרַב בְּאָהֳלֶךָ:

in your tent   it come near – not   and plague   evil   unto you   it befall – not

10 There shall no evil befall thee, neither shall any plague come nigh thy dwelling.

כִּי מַלְאָכָיו יְצַוֶּה־לָּךְ לִשְׁמָרְךָ בְּכָל־דְּרָכֶיךָ:

your ways – in all   to your heeding   to you – he charges   his angels   like

11 For he shall give his angels charge over thee, to keep thee in all thy ways.

עַל־כַּפַּיִם יִשָּׂאוּנְךָ פֶּן־תִּגֹּף בָּאֶבֶן רַגְלֶךָ:

your foot   in stone   you strike – lest   they bear you   their palms – upon

12 They shall bear thee up in *their* hands, lest thou dash thy foot against a stone.

עַל־שַׁחַל וָפֶתֶן תִּדְרֹךְ תִּרְמֹס כְּפִיר וְתַנִּין:

and big reptile   young lion   you trample   you tread   and viper   lion – upon

13 Thou shalt tread upon the lion and adder: the young lion and the dragon shalt thou trample under feet.

כִּי בִי חָשַׁק וַאֲפַלְּטֵהוּ אֲשַׂגְּבֵהוּ כִּי־יָדַע שְׁמִי:

my name   he knows – like   I elevate him   and I will deliver him   attached   in me   like

14 Because he hath set his love upon me, therefore will I deliver him: I will set him on high, because he hath known my name.

יִקְרָאֵנִי וְאֶעֱנֵהוּ עִמּוֹ אָנֹכִי בְצָרָה אֲחַלְּצֵהוּ וַאֲכַבְּדֵהוּ:

and I honor him   I will deliver him   in trouble   I am   with him   and I will answer him   he will call me

15 He shall call upon me, and I will answer him: I *will be* with him in trouble; I will deliver him, and honour him.

אֹרֶךְ יָמִים אַשְׂבִּיעֵהוּ וְאַרְאֵהוּ בִּישׁוּעָתִי:

in my salvation   and I show him   I will satisfy him   days   length

16 With long life will I satisfy him, and shew him my salvation.

Psalm 92

ספר תהילים פרק צב

מִזְמוֹר שִׁיר לְיוֹם הַשַּׁבָּת:
the Shabbat   to day   song   Psalm

1 A Psalm or Song for the sabbath day.

טוֹב לְהֹדוֹת לַיהוָֹה וּלְזַמֵּר לְשִׁמְךָ עֶלְיוֹן:
upon high to your name and to sing psalms to ihvh to thank good

It is a good thing to give thanks unto the LORD, and to sing praises unto thy name, O most High:

לְהַגִּיד בַּבֹּקֶר חַסְדֶּךָ וֶאֱמוּנָתְךָ בַּלֵּילוֹת:
in nights and your faithfulness your mercy in morning to the telling

2 To shew forth thy lovingkindness in the morning, and thy faithfulness every night,

עֲלֵי־עָשׂוֹר וַעֲלֵי־נָבֶל עֲלֵי הִגָּיוֹן בְּכִנּוֹר:
in harp chant upon my lyre - and upon my ten [string] - upon my

3 Upon an instrument of ten strings, and upon the psaltery; upon the harp with a solemn sound.

כִּי שִׂמַּחְתַּנִי יְהוָֹה בְּפָעֳלֶךָ בְּמַעֲשֵׂי יָדֶיךָ אֲרַנֵּן:
I joy shout your hands in deeds in your work ihvh you gladdened me like

4 For thou, LORD, hast made me glad through thy work: I will triumph in the works of thy hands.

מַה־גָּדְלוּ מַעֲשֶׂיךָ יְהוָֹה מְאֹד עָמְקוּ מַחְשְׁבֹתֶיךָ:
you thoughts t deep very ihvh your works great it – how

5 O LORD, how great are thy works! and thy thoughts are very deep.

אִישׁ בַּעַר לֹא יֵדָע וּכְסִיל לֹא־יָבִין אֶת־זֹאת:
this – that understand – not and fool know not brutish man

6 A brutish man knoweth not, neither doth a fool understand this.

בִּפְרֹחַ רְשָׁעִים כְּמוֹ עֵשֶׂב וַיָּצִיצוּ כָּל־פֹּעֲלֵי אָוֶן
iniquity they workers - all and they blossom grass like wicked ones in sprouting forth

לְהִשָּׁמְדָם עֲדֵי־עַד:
time – until to their destruction

7 When the wicked spring as the grass, and when all the workers of iniquity do flourish; it is that they shall be destroyed for ever:

וְאַתָּה מָרוֹם לְעֹלָם יְהוָֹה:
ihvh to forever highest and you

8 But thou, LORD, art most high for evermore.

כִּי הִנֵּה אֹיְבֶיךָ יְהוָֹה כִּי־הִנֵּה אֹיְבֶיךָ יֹאבֵדוּ
they perish your enemies here – like ihvh your enemies here like

יִתְפָּרְדוּ   כָּל־פֹּעֲלֵי   אָוֶן:

they scatter   those workers – all   iniquity

9 For, lo, thine enemies, O LORD, for, lo, thine enemies shall perish; all the workers of iniquity shall be scattered.

וַתָּרֶם   כִּרְאֵים   קַרְנִי   בַּלֹּתִי   בְּשֶׁמֶן   רַעֲנָן:

and you lifted   like wild ox   my horn   in anointed   in oil   fresh

10 But my horn shalt thou exalt like the horn of an unicorn: I shall be anointed with fresh oil.

וַתַּבֵּט   עֵינִי   בְּשׁוּרָי   בַּקָּמִים   עָלַי   מְרֵעִים   תִּשְׁמַעְנָה   אָזְנָי:

and looked   my eyes   in my watching foes   in rising ones   upon me   from bad ones   it hearing so   my ears

11 Mine eye also shall see my desire on mine enemies, and mine ears shall hear my desire of the wicked that rise up against me.

צַדִּיק   כַּתָּמָר   יִפְרָח   כְּאֶרֶז   בַּלְּבָנוֹן   יִשְׂגֶּה:

righteous   like palm tree   he flourishes   like cedar   in the Lebanon   he grows great

12 The righteous shall flourish like the palm tree: he shall grow like a cedar in Lebanon.

שְׁתוּלִים   בְּבֵית   יְהֹוָה   בְּחַצְרוֹת   אֱלֹהֵינוּ   יַפְרִיחוּ:

planted ones   in house   ihvh   in courtyard   our Elohim   they flourish

13 Those that be planted in the house of the LORD shall flourish in the courts of our God.

עוֹד   יְנוּבוּן   בְּשֵׂיבָה   דְּשֵׁנִים   וְרַעֲנַנִּים   יִהְיוּ:

still   they will be fruitful   in old age   fat ones   and fresh ones   they will be

14 They shall still bring forth fruit in old age; they shall be fat and flourishing;

לְהַגִּיד   כִּי־יָשָׁר   יְהֹוָה   צוּרִי   וְלֹא־עָלָתָה   [עַוְלָתָה]   בּוֹ:

to the declare   upright – like   ihvh   my rock cliff   inequity - and not   upright – like   in him

15 To shew that the LORD is upright: he is my rock, and there is no unrighteousness.

Psalm 93

ספר תהילים פרק צג

יְהוָה מָלָךְ גֵּאוּת לָבֵשׁ

is clothed   majesty   reigns   ihvh

לָבֵשׁ יְהוָה עֹז הִתְאַזָּר אַף־תִּכּוֹן תֵּבֵל בַּל־תִּמּוֹט:

be moved - in not   inhabited word   he established - then   girded   strength   ihvh   is clothed

1. The Lord reigns, he is clothed with majesty; the Lord is clothed with strength, with which he has girded himself; the world also is established, that it cannot be moved.

נָכוֹן כִּסְאֲךָ מֵאָז מֵעוֹלָם אָתָּה:

you   from forever   from old   your throne   established

2. Your throne is established of old; you are from everlasting.

נָשְׂאוּ נְהָרוֹת יְהוָה

ihvh   rivers   they lifted

נָשְׂאוּ נְהָרוֹת קוֹלָם יִשְׂאוּ נְהָרוֹת דָּכְיָם:

their roaring   rivers   they lift   their voices   rivers   they lifted

3. The floods have lifted up, O Lord, the floods have lifted up their voice; the floods lift up their roaring.

מִקֹּלוֹת מַיִם רַבִּים אַדִּירִים מִשְׁבְּרֵי־יָם אַדִּיר בַּמָּרוֹם יְהוָה:

ihvh   in heights   mighty   sea - from waves   mighty ones   many ones   water   from voices

4. The Lord on high is mightier than the noise of many waters, than the mighty waves of the sea.

עֵדֹתֶיךָ נֶאֶמְנוּ מְאֹד

again   they faithful   your testimonies

לְבֵיתְךָ נָאֲוָה־קֹדֶשׁ יְהוָה לְאֹרֶךְ יָמִים:

days   to length   ihvh   holy - attractive   to your house

5. Your testimonies are very sure; holiness becomes your house, O Lord, for length of days.

Psalm 94

ספר תהילים פרק צד

אֶל־נְקָמוֹת יְהֹוָה אֵל נְקָמוֹת הוֹפִיעַ׃

<small>shine forth   revenges   El   ihvh   revenges - El</small>

1. O Lord God, to whom vengeance belongs; O God, to whom vengeance belongs, shine forth.

הִנָּשֵׂא שֹׁפֵט הָאָרֶץ הָשֵׁב גְּמוּל עַל־גֵּאִים׃

<small>proud - upon   reward   the return   the earth   judge   lift up</small>

2. Lift up yourself, you judge of the earth; render to the arrogant their reward.

עַד־מָתַי רְשָׁעִים יְהֹוָה עַד־מָתַי רְשָׁעִים יַעֲלֹזוּ׃

<small>they will triumph   wicked ones   when - until   ihvh   wicked ones   when - until</small>

3. Lord, how long shall the wicked, how long shall the wicked triumph?

יַבִּיעוּ יְדַבְּרוּ עָתָק יִתְאַמְּרוּ כָּל־פֹּעֲלֵי אָוֶן׃

<small>inequity   doers - all   they will say   impertinance   they speak   they will utter</small>

4. How long shall they utter and speak hard things? And all the evil doers boast themselves?

עַמְּךָ יְהֹוָה יְדַכְּאוּ וְנַחֲלָתְךָ יְעַנּוּ׃

<small>they afflict   and your inheritance   they crush   ihvh   your people</small>

5. They crush your people, O Lord, and afflict your heritage.

אַלְמָנָה וְגֵר יַהֲרֹגוּ וִיתוֹמִים יְרַצֵּחוּ׃

<small>they murder   and the orphans ones   they slay   and stranger   widow</small>

6. They slay the widow and the stranger, and murder the orphan.

וַיֹּאמְרוּ לֹא יִרְאֶה־יָּהּ וְלֹא־יָבִין אֱלֹהֵי יַעֲקֹב׃

<small>Jacob   Elohim   will understand - and not   Ya - will see   not   and they say</small>

7. Yet they say, The Lord shall not see, nor shall the God of Jacob regard it.

בִּינוּ בֹּעֲרִים בָּעָם וּכְסִילִים מָתַי תַּשְׂכִּילוּ׃

<small>you will wise up   when   and fool ones   in people   brutish ones   you understand</small>

8. Understand, you stupid among the people; and you fools, when will you be wise?

הֲנֹטַע אֹזֶן הֲלֹא יִשְׁמָע אִם־יֹצֵר עַיִן הֲלֹא יַבִּיט׃

<small>he will behold   the not   eye   he formed - if   he will hear   the not   ear   the planter</small>

9. He who planted the ear, shall he not hear? He who formed the eye, shall he not see?

הֲיֹסֵר גּוֹיִם הֲלֹא יוֹכִיחַ הַמְלַמֵּד אָדָם דָּעַת׃

<small>knowledge   Adam   the teacher   he will rebuke   the not   nations   the chastiser</small>

10. He who chastises the nations, shall he not chastise? He who teaches man knowledge,

יְהֹוָה יֹדֵעַ מַחְשְׁבוֹת אָדָם כִּי הֵמָּה הָבֶל׃

<small>vanity   they are   like   Adam   thoughts   knows   ihvh</small>

11. The Lord, knows the thoughts of man, that they are vanity.

אַשְׁרֵי הַגֶּבֶר אֲשֶׁר־תְּיַסְּרֶנּוּ יָהּ וּמִתּוֹרָתְךָ תְלַמְּדֶנּוּ׃

<small>you teach us   and from you - Torah   Ya   you admonish - which   the gentleman   they are</small>

12. Happy is the man whom you chasten, O Lord, and whom you teach from your Torah;

לְהַשְׁקִיט לוֹ מִימֵי רָע עַד יִכָּרֶה לָרָשָׁע שָׁחַת׃

<small>pit   to wicked   he dug   till   bad   from day   to him   to the make still</small>

13. That you may give him rest from the days of adversity, until the pit is dug for the wicked.

כִּי לֹא־יִטֹּשׁ יְהֹוָה עַמּוֹ וְנַחֲלָתוֹ לֹא יַעֲזֹב׃

<small>he will forsake   not   and his inheritance   his people   ihvh   will cost off - not   like</small>

14. For the Lord will not cast off his people, nor will he forsake his inheritance.

כִּי־עַד־צֶדֶק יָשׁוּב מִשְׁפָּט וְאַחֲרָיו כָּל־יִשְׁרֵי־לֵב׃

<small>heart - upright - all   and his after   judgment   will return   righteousness - till - like</small>

15. But judgment shall return to righteousness; and all the upright in heart shall follow it.

מִי־יָקוּם לִי עִם־מְרֵעִים מִי־יִתְיַצֵּב לִי עִם־פֹּעֲלֵי אָוֶן׃

<small>inequity   doers - with   to me   will set himself - who   wicked deeds - with   to me   he will rise - who</small>

16. Who will rise up for me against the evil doers? Who will stand up for me against the evil doers?

לוּלֵי יְהֹוָה עֶזְרָתָה לִּי כִּמְעַט שָׁכְנָה דוּמָה נַפְשִׁי׃

<small>my soul   silence   dwelt   like little   to me   help   ihvh   unless</small>

17. Unless the Lord had been my help, my soul would soon had dwelt in silence.

אִם־אָמַרְתִּי מָטָה רַגְלִי חַסְדְּךָ יְהֹוָה יִסְעָדֵנִי׃

<small>he supported me   ihvh   your kindness   my foot   slips   I said - if</small>

18. When I said, My foot slips; your loving kindness, O Lord, held me up.

בְּרֹב שַׂרְעַפַּי בְּקִרְבִּי תַּנְחוּמֶיךָ יְשַׁעַשְׁעוּ נַפְשִׁי׃

<small>my soul   they delight   your comforts   in my midst   my cares   in much</small>

19. When the cares of my heart are many your comforts delight my soul.

הַיְחָבְרְךָ כִּסֵּא הַוּוֹת יֹצֵר עָמָל עֲלֵי־חֹק׃

<small>statute - upon   grievousness   forming   woes   seat   the your partner</small>

20. Shall the seat of iniquity, which frames mischief by law, have fellowship with you?

יָגוֹדּוּ עַל־נֶפֶשׁ צַדִּיק וְדָם נָקִי יַרְשִׁיעוּ׃

<small>they will condemn   innocent   and blood   righteous   lower soul - upon   they will gather together</small>

21. They gather themselves together against the soul of the righteous, and condemn the innocent blood.

וַיְהִי יְהֹוָה לִי לְמִשְׂגָּב וֵאלֹהַי לְצוּר מַחְסִי׃

<small>my refuge   to rock   and my Elohim   to fortress   to me   ihvh   and it was</small>

22. But the Lord has become my fortress; and my God, the rock of my refuge.

וַיָּשֶׁב　　עֲלֵיהֶם　אֶת־אוֹנָם　וּבְרָעָתָם　יַצְמִיתֵם

he will cut them off　　and in their evil　their violence - that　upon them　and he will return

יַצְמִיתֵם　　יְהֹוָה　אֱלֹהֵינוּ׃

Elohim　　ihvh　he will cut them off

23. And he shall bring upon them their own iniquity, and shall cut them off in their own wickedness; the Lord our God shall cut them off.

PSALM 95

ספר תהילים פרק צה

לְכוּ   נְרַנְּנָה   לַיהֹוָה   נָרִיעָה   לְצוּר   יִשְׁעֵנוּ׃

<small>our salvation   ▭ rock   we will shout   to ihvh   we will shout for joy   let's go</small>

1. O come, let us sing to the Lord; let us make a joyful noise to the rock of our salvation.

נְקַדְּמָה   פָנָיו   בְּתוֹדָה   בִּזְמִרוֹת   נָרִיעַ   לוֹ׃

<small>to him   we will shout   in singing psalms   in thanks   his face   we will greet</small>

2. Let us come before his presence with thanksgiving, and make a joyful noise to him with psalms.

כִּי   אֵל   גָּדוֹל   יְהֹוָה   וּמֶלֶךְ   גָּדוֹל   עַל־כָּל־אֱלֹהִים׃

<small>Elohim - all - upon   great   and king   ihvh   great   El   like</small>

3. For the Lord is a great God, and a great King above all gods.

אֲשֶׁר   בְּיָדוֹ   מֶחְקְרֵי־אָרֶץ   וְתוֹעֲפוֹת   הָרִים   לוֹ׃

<small>to him   the mountains   and summits   earth - from hidden mysteries   in his hand   which</small>

4. In his hand are the deep places of the earth; the heights of the mountains are also his.

אֲשֶׁר־לוֹ   הַיָּם   וְהוּא   עָשָׂהוּ   וְיַבֶּשֶׁת   יָדָיו   יָצָרוּ׃

<small>they formed   his hands   and dry land   made it   and he   the sea   to him – which</small>

5. The sea is his, and he made it; and his hands formed the dry land.

בֹּאוּ   נִשְׁתַּחֲוֶה   וְנִכְרָעָה   נִבְרְכָה   לִפְנֵי־יְהֹוָה   עֹשֵׂנוּ׃

<small>made us   ihvh - before   kneel   and bend   bow down   come</small>

6. O come, let us worship and bow down; let us kneel before the Lord our maker.

כִּי   הוּא   אֱלֹהֵינוּ   וַאֲנַחְנוּ   עַם   מַרְעִיתוֹ

<small>from his pasture   people   and we   our Elohim   he   like</small>

וְצֹאן   יָדוֹ   הַיּוֹם   אִם־בְּקֹלוֹ   תִשְׁמָעוּ׃

<small>you will hear   in his voice - if   the day   his hand   and sheep</small>

7. For he is our God; and we are the people of his pasture, and the sheep of his hand. Even today, if you will only listen to his voice!

אַל־תַּקְשׁוּ   לְבַבְכֶם   כִּמְרִיבָה   כְּיוֹם   מַסָּה   בַּמִּדְבָּר׃

<small>in desert   Massah   like day   like Merivah   your hearts   harden - don't</small>

8. Do not harden your hearts, like you did at Meribah, and like you did in the day of Massah in the wilderness;

אֲשֶׁר   נִסּוּנִי   אֲבוֹתֵיכֶם   בְּחָנוּנִי   גַּם־רָאוּ   פָעֳלִי׃

<small>my deed   they saw - also   tested me   your fathers   tried me   which</small>

9. When your fathers tempted me, and tested me, even though they had seen my deeds.

אַרְבָּעִים שָׁנָה אָקוּט בְּדוֹר

in generation   I loathed   years   forty

וָאֹמַר עַם תֹּעֵי לֵבָב הֵם וְהֵם לֹא־יָדְעוּ דְרָכָי:

my ways   they know - not   and them   them   heart   wandering   people   and I said

10. For forty years I loathed that generation, and said, They are a people who err in their heart, and they do not know my ways.

אֲשֶׁר־נִשְׁבַּעְתִּי בְאַפִּי אִם־יְבֹאוּן אֶל־מְנוּחָתִי:

my contentment - unto   they will come - if   in my anger   I swore - which

11. Therefore I swore in my wrath that they should not enter into my rest.

PSALM 96

ספר תהילים פרק צו

שִׁירוּ לַיהֹוָה שִׁיר חָדָשׁ שִׁירוּ לַיהֹוָה כָּל־הָאָרֶץ:

the earth - all | to ihvh | they sing | new | song | to ihvh | they sing

1. O sing to the Lord a new song; sing to the Lord, all the earth.

שִׁירוּ לַיהֹוָה בָּרְכוּ שְׁמוֹ בַּשְּׂרוּ מִיּוֹם־לְיוֹם יְשׁוּעָתוֹ:

his salvation | to day - from day | in announcing | his name | they bless | to ihvh | they sing

2. Sing to the Lord, bless his name; announce his salvation from day to day.

סַפְּרוּ בַגּוֹיִם כְּבוֹדוֹ בְּכָל־הָעַמִּים נִפְלְאוֹתָיו:

his mystical works | the peoples - in all | his glory | in nations | they declared

3. Declare his glory among the nations, his wonders among all the peoples.

כִּי גָדוֹל יְהֹוָה וּמְהֻלָּל מְאֹד נוֹרָא הוּא עַל־כָּל־אֱלֹהִים:

Elohim - all - upon | he | be feared | again | and from praised | ihvh | great | like

4. For the Lord is great, and greatly to be praised; he is to be feared above all gods.

כִּי כָּל־אֱלֹהֵי הָעַמִּים אֱלִילִים וַיהֹוָה שָׁמַיִם עָשָׂה:

made | heavens | and ihvh | worthless gods | the peoples | Elohim - all | like

5. For all the gods of the nations are idols; but the Lord made the heavens.

הוֹד־וְהָדָר לְפָנָיו עֹז וְתִפְאֶרֶת בְּמִקְדָּשׁוֹ:

in his sanctuary | and beauty | strength | before him | and majesty - glory

6. Honor and majesty are before him; strength and beauty are in his sanctuary.

הָבוּ לַיהֹוָה מִשְׁפְּחוֹת עַמִּים הָבוּ לַיהֹוָה כָּבוֹד וָעֹז:

and strength | glory | to ihvh | ascribe | peoples | families | to ihvh | ascribe

7. Ascribe to the Lord, O families of the people, ascribe to the Lord glory and strength.

הָבוּ לַיהֹוָה כְּבוֹד שְׁמוֹ שְׂאוּ־מִנְחָה וּבֹאוּ לְחַצְרוֹתָיו:

to his courts | and come | offering - bring | his name | honor | to ihvh | ascribe

8. Ascribe to the Lord the glory due to his name; bring an offering, and come into his courts.

הִשְׁתַּחֲווּ לַיהֹוָה בְּהַדְרַת־קֹדֶשׁ חִילוּ מִפָּנָיו כָּל־הָאָרֶץ:

the earth - all | from before him | you tremble | holy - in majesty | to ihvh | bow down

9. O worship the Lord in the beauty of holiness; tremble before him, all the earth.

אִמְרוּ בַגּוֹיִם יְהֹוָה מָלָךְ אַף־תִּכּוֹן תֵּבֵל בַּל־תִּמּוֹט

will move - in not | inhabited world | established – so | reigns | ihvh | in nations | you say

יָדִין עַמִּים בְּמֵישָׁרִים:

in fairness | peoples | and will judge

10. Say among the nations that the Lord reigns; the world also is established so that it shall not be moved; he shall judge the people with equity.

יִשְׂמְחוּ הַשָּׁמַיִם וְתָגֵל הָאָרֶץ יִרְעַם הַיָּם וּמְלֹאוֹ:

and its fullness   the sea   roar   the earth   and rejoice   the heavens   you be glad

11. Let the heavens rejoice, and let the earth be glad; let the sea roar, and all that is in it.

יַעֲלֹז שָׂדַי וְכָל־אֲשֶׁר־בּוֹ אָז יְרַנְּנוּ כָּל־עֲצֵי־יָעַר:

forests - trees - all   will shout for joy   then   in it - which - and all   field   exult

12. Let the field be joyful, and everything in it; then shall all the trees of the wood sing for joy.

לִפְנֵי יְהֹוָה כִּי בָא כִּי בָא לִשְׁפֹּט הָאָרֶץ

the earth   to judge   comes   like   comes   like   ihvh   before

יִשְׁפֹּט־תֵּבֵל בְּצֶדֶק וְעַמִּים בֶּאֱמוּנָתוֹ:

in his truth   and peoples   in righteousness   inhabited world - he will judge

13. Before the Lord; for he comes, for he comes to judge the earth; he shall judge the world with righteousness, and the peoples with his faithfulness.

PSALM 97

ספר תהילים פרק צז

יְהוָה מָלָךְ תָּגֵל הָאָרֶץ יִשְׂמְחוּ אִיִּים רַבִּים:

many · sea coasts · you be glad · the earth · rejoice · reigns · ihvh

1. The Lord reigns; let the earth rejoice; let the multitude of islands be glad.

עָנָן וַעֲרָפֶל סְבִיבָיו צֶדֶק וּמִשְׁפָּט מְכוֹן כִּסְאוֹ:

his throne · from place · and judgment · righteousness · around him · and darkness · cloud

2. Clouds and darkness are around him; righteousness and judgment are the foundation of his throne.

אֵשׁ לְפָנָיו תֵּלֵךְ וּתְלַהֵט סָבִיב צָרָיו:

his adversaries · around · and set on fire · goes · before him · fire

3. A fire goes before him, and burns up his enemies around.

הֵאִירוּ בְרָקָיו תֵּבֵל רָאֲתָה וַתָּחֵל הָאָרֶץ:

the earth · and trembles · sees · inhabited world · his lightenings · the lightened

4. His lightnings lighten the world; the earth sees, and trembles.

הָרִים כַּדּוֹנַג נָמַסּוּ מִלִּפְנֵי יְהוָה מִלִּפְנֵי אֲדוֹן כָּל־הָאָרֶץ:

the earth - all · Adon · from before · ihvh · from before · melted · like wax · the mountains

5. The mountains melt like wax at the presence of the Lord, at the presence of the Lord of the whole earth.

הִגִּידוּ הַשָּׁמַיִם צִדְקוֹ וְרָאוּ כָל־הָעַמִּים כְּבוֹדוֹ:

his glory · the peoples - all · and you see · his righteousness · the heavens · declare

6. The heavens declare his righteousness, and all the peoples see his glory.

יֵבֹשׁוּ כָּל־עֹבְדֵי פֶסֶל הַמִּתְהַלְלִים בָּאֱלִילִים

in worthless gods · the boasting ones · idol · serving - all · humiliated

הִשְׁתַּחֲווּ־לוֹ כָּל־אֱלֹהִים:

Elohim - all · to him - they bow down

7. Confounded are all those who serve carved idols, who boast themselves of idols; bow down before him, all you gods.

שָׁמְעָה וַתִּשְׂמַח צִיּוֹן וַתָּגֵלְנָה בְּנוֹת יְהוּדָה

Judah · in daughters · and exult · Zion · and he glad · I hear

לְמַעַן מִשְׁפָּטֶיךָ יְהוָה:

ihvh · your judgments · to end

8. Zion hears, and is glad, and the daughters of Judah rejoice because of your judgments, O Lord.

כִּי־אַתָּה יְהוָה עֶלְיוֹן עַל־כָּל־הָאָרֶץ

the earth - all - upon · most high · ihvh · you - like

מְאֹד נַעֲלֵיתָ עַל־כָּל־אֱלֹהִים:

Elohim - all - upon   exalted   again

9. For you, Lord, are high above all the earth; you are exalted far above all gods.

אֹהֲבֵי יְהוָה שִׂנְאוּ רָע שֹׁמֵר נַפְשׁוֹת חֲסִידָיו

his devoted   souls   heed evil you hate ihvh   lovers

מִיַּד רְשָׁעִים יַצִּילֵם:

he rescues them   wicked ones from hand

10. You who love the Lord, hate evil! He preserves the souls of his pious ones; he saves them from the hand of the wicked.

אוֹר זָרֻעַ לַצַּדִּיק וּלְיִשְׁרֵי־לֵב שִׂמְחָה:

gladness   heart - and to upright to righteous sown   light

11. Light is sown for the righteous, and gladness for the upright in heart.

שִׂמְחוּ צַדִּיקִים בַּיהוָה וְהוֹדוּ לְזֵכֶר קָדְשׁוֹ:

his holiness to memorial and they give thanks in ihvh righteous ones you happy

12. Rejoice in the Lord, you righteous; and give thanks to his holy name.

PSALM 98

ספר תהילים פרק צח

מִזְמוֹר שִׁירוּ לַיהֹוָה שִׁיר חָדָשׁ

new   song   to ihvh   you sing   psalm

כִּי־נִפְלָאוֹת עָשָׂה הוֹשִׁיעָה־לּוֹ יְמִינוֹ וּזְרוֹעַ קָדְשׁוֹ:

his holy   and his arm stretched   his right hand   to him – salvation   has done   mysticals - like

1. A Psalm. O sing to the Lord a new song; for he has done marvelous things; his right hand, and his holy arm, have gained him the victory.

הוֹדִיעַ יְהֹוָה יְשׁוּעָתוֹ לְעֵינֵי הַגּוֹיִם גִּלָּה צִדְקָתוֹ:

his righteousness revealed   the nations   to eyes   his salvation   ihvh   made known

2. The Lord has made known his salvation; he has revealed his righteousness to the eyes of the nations.

זָכַר חַסְדּוֹ וֶאֱמוּנָתוֹ לְבֵית יִשְׂרָאֵל

Israel   to house   and his truthfulness   his mercy   he remembered

רָאוּ כָל־אַפְסֵי־אָרֶץ אֵת יְשׁוּעַת אֱלֹהֵינוּ:

our Elohim   salvation   that   earth – ends - all   have seen

3. He has remembered his love and his truth toward the house of Israel; all the ends of the earth have seen the salvation of our God.

הָרִיעוּ לַיהֹוָה כָּל־הָאָרֶץ פִּצְחוּ וְרַנְּנוּ וְזַמֵּרוּ:

and you sing psalms   and shriek w/ joy   open mouth   the earth - all   to ihvh   the joyful sound

4. Make a joyful noise to the Lord, all the earth; make a loud noise, and rejoice, and sing praise.

זַמְּרוּ לַיהֹוָה בְּכִנּוֹר בְּכִנּוֹר וְקוֹל זִמְרָה:

psalm song   and voice   in lyre   in lyre   to ihvh   you sing psalms

5. Sing to the Lord with the lyre; with the lyre, and the voice of a psalm.

בַּחֲצֹצְרוֹת וְקוֹל שׁוֹפָר הָרִיעוּ לִפְנֵי הַמֶּלֶךְ יְהֹוָה:

ihvh   the king   before   you joy shout   shofar   and voice   in the trumpets

6. With trumpets and the sound of a shofar make a joyful noise before the Lord, the King.

יִרְעַם הַיָּם וּמְלֹאוֹ תֵּבֵל וְיֹשְׁבֵי בָהּ:

in it   and those dwell   inhabited world   and his filling   the sea   it roar

7. Let the sea roar, and all that fills it; the world, and those who dwell in it.

נְהָרוֹת יִמְחֲאוּ־כָף יַחַד הָרִים יְרַנֵּנוּ:

will shriek w/ joy   mountains   together   palms – they clap   rivers

8. Let the rivers clap their hands; let the mountains sing for joy together,

לִפְנֵי־יְהֹוָה כִּי בָא לִשְׁפֹּט הָאָרֶץ

the earth   to judge   comes   like   ihvh - before

יִשְׁפֹּט־תֵּבֵל   בְּצֶדֶק וְעַמִּים בְּמֵישָׁרִים׃

in from upright ones   and peoples   in righteous   inhabited world – he will judge

9. Before the Lord, for he comes to judge the earth; with righteousness shall he judge the world, and the peoples with equity.

Psalm 99

ספר תהילים פרק צט

יְהוָה מָלָךְ יִרְגְּזוּ עַמִּים יֹשֵׁב כְּרוּבִים תָּנוּט הָאָרֶץ:

the earth shake cherubim ones he sit peoples tremble reigns ihvh

1. The Lord reigns; let the peoples tremble; he sits between the kerubim; let the earth be moved.

יְהוָה בְּצִיּוֹן גָּדוֹל וְרָם הוּא עַל־כָּל־הָעַמִּים:

the peoples - all - above he and exulted great in Zion ihvh

2. The Lord is great in Zion; and he is high above all the peoples.

יוֹדוּ שִׁמְךָ גָּדוֹל וְנוֹרָא קָדוֹשׁ הוּא:

it holy and awesome great your name they thank

3. Let them praise your great and awesome name; for it is holy.

וְעֹז מֶלֶךְ מִשְׁפָּט אָהֵב אַתָּה כּוֹנַנְתָּ מֵישָׁרִים מִשְׁפָּט

judgment fair ones established you loved judgment king and power

וּצְדָקָה בְּיַעֲקֹב אַתָּה עָשִׂיתָ:

have done you in Jacob and righteousness

4. The might of the king who loves judgment! You establish equity, you execute judgment and righteousness in Jacob.

רוֹמְמוּ יְהוָה אֱלֹהֵינוּ וְהִשְׁתַּחֲווּ לַהֲדֹם רַגְלָיו

his feet to footstool and bow down our Elohim ihvh exalt

קָדוֹשׁ הוּא:

he holy

5. Exalt the Lord our God, and worship at his footstool; for he is holy.

מֹשֶׁה וְאַהֲרֹן בְּכֹהֲנָיו וּשְׁמוּאֵל בְּקֹרְאֵי שְׁמוֹ

his name in my calling and Samuel in his priests and Aaron Moses

קֹרִאים אֶל־יְהוָה וְהוּא יַעֲנֵם:

answered them and he ihvh - onto calling ones

6. Moses and Aaron were among his priests, and Samuel was among those who called upon his name; they called upon the Lord, and he answered them.

בְּעַמּוּד עָנָן יְדַבֵּר אֲלֵיהֶם שָׁמְרוּ עֵדֹתָיו וְחֹק נָתַן־לָמוֹ:

to them - he gave and statute his testimonies they heeded unto them he spoke cloud in pillar

7. He spoke to them in the cloudy pillar; they kept his testimonies, and the statute that he gave them.

יְהוָה אֱלֹהֵינוּ אַתָּה עֲנִיתָם אֵל

El answered them you our Elohim ihvh

נֹשֵׂא הָיִיתָ לָהֶם וְנֹקֵם עַל־עֲלִילוֹתָם:

their inequity - upon and avenging to them you were pardoning

8. You answered them, O Lord our God; you were a forgiving God to them, though you took vengeance for their wrong doings.

רוֹמְמוּ יְהוָה אֱלֹהֵינוּ וְהִשְׁתַּחֲווּ לְהַר   קָדְשׁוֹ

Exalt	ihvh	Elohim	and bow down	to mountain	his holiness

כִּי־קָדוֹשׁ יְהוָה אֱלֹהֵינוּ:

holy - like	ihvh	our Elohim

9. Exalt the Lord our God, and worship at his holy mountain; for the Lord, our God, is holy.

PSALM 100

ספר תהילים פרק ק

מִזְמוֹר לְתוֹדָה הָרִיעוּ לַיהֹוָה כָּל־הָאָרֶץ:

the earth - all   to ihvh   you joy shout   to thank   Psalm

1. A Psalm of thanksgiving. Make a joyful noise to the Lord, all the earth.

עִבְדוּ אֶת־יְהֹוָה בְּשִׂמְחָה בֹּאוּ לְפָנָיו בִּרְנָנָה:

in jubilation   to before him   you come   in happiness   ihvh - that   you serve

2. Serve the Lord with gladness; come before his presence with singing.

דְּעוּ כִּי יְהֹוָה הוּא אֱלֹהִים הוּא עָשָׂנוּ

made us   he   Elohim   he   ihvh   like   you know

וְלֹא [וְלוֹ] אֲנַחְנוּ עַמּוֹ וְצֹאן מַרְעִיתוֹ:

from his pasture   and sheep   his people   we   [and to us]   and not

3. (K) Know that the Lord is God; it is he who made us, and we belong to him; we are
his people, and the sheep of his pasture.

בֹּאוּ שְׁעָרָיו בְּתוֹדָה חֲצֵרֹתָיו בִּתְהִלָּה

in praise   his courts   in thanks   his gate   you come

הוֹדוּ לוֹ בָּרֲכוּ שְׁמוֹ:

his name   you bless   to him   you give thanks

4. Enter into his gates with thanksgiving, and into his courts with praise; be thankful to
him, and bless his name.

כִּי־טוֹב יְהֹוָה לְעוֹלָם חַסְדּוֹ וְעַד־דֹּר וָדֹר אֱמוּנָתוֹ:

his faithfulness   and generation   generation - and till   his mercy   to forever   ihvh   good - like

5. For the Lord is good; his loving kindness is everlasting; and his faithfulness endures
to all generations.

Psalm 101

ספר תהילים פרק קא

לְדָוִד מִזְמוֹר חֶסֶד־וּמִשְׁפָּט אָשִׁירָה לְךָ יְהֹוָה אֲזַמֵּרָה׃
<small>I will sing psalms   ihvh   to you   I will sing   and judgment - kindness   Psalm   to David</small>

1. A Psalm of David. I will sing of loving kindness and justice; to you, O Lord, I will sing.

אַשְׂכִּילָה בְּדֶרֶךְ תָּמִים מָתַי תָּבוֹא אֵלָי
<small>unto me   you come   when   perfect   in way   I act wisely</small>

אֶתְהַלֵּךְ בְּתָם־לְבָבִי בְּקֶרֶב בֵּיתִי׃
<small>my house   in close   my heart - in perfect   that walk</small>

2. I will celebrate with a Maskil psalm the way of integrity. O when will you come to me? I will walk inside my house with integrity of heart.

לֹא־אָשִׁית לְנֶגֶד עֵינַי דְּבַר־בְּלִיָּעַל עֲשֹׂה־סֵטִים שָׂנֵאתִי
<small>I hated   wayward ones - doings   wothless – matter   my eyes   to front   I set - not</small>

לֹא יִדְבַּק בִּי׃
<small>in me   it clings   not</small>

3. I will set no wicked thing before my eyes; I hate the work of those who turn aside; it shall not cleave to me.

לֵבָב עִקֵּשׁ יָסוּר מִמֶּנִּי רָע לֹא אֵדָע׃
<small>I will know   not   evil   from me   will depart   perverted   heart</small>

4. A perverse heart shall depart from me; I will know nothing of evil.

מְלוֹשְׁנִי [מְלָשְׁנִי] בַסֵּתֶר רֵעֵהוּ אוֹתוֹ
<small>to him   his neighbor   in secret   my slanderer</small>

אַצְמִית גְּבַהּ־עֵינַיִם וּרְחַב לֵבָב אֹתוֹ לֹא אוּכָל׃
<small>able   not   to him   heart   and expanded   eyes - proud   I will cut off</small>

5. (K) I will cut off whoever secretly slanders his neighbor; I will not endure the man who has a haughty look and an arrogant heart.

עֵינַי בְּנֶאֶמְנֵי־אֶרֶץ לָשֶׁבֶת עִמָּדִי
<small>with me   to sit   earth - in faithful   my eyes</small>

הֹלֵךְ בְּדֶרֶךְ תָּמִים הוּא יְשָׁרְתֵנִי׃
<small>he will minister me   he   perfect   in way   walker</small>

6. My eyes shall be upon the faithful of the land, that they may dwell with me; he who walks in the way of integrity, he shall serve me.

לֹא־יֵשֵׁב בְּקֶרֶב בֵּיתִי עֹשֵׂה רְמִיָּה דֹּבֵר שְׁקָרִים
<small>falsehoods   speaker   deceit   doer   my house   in close   he dwell - not</small>

לֹא־יִכּוֹן לְנֶגֶד עֵינָי׃
<small>my eyes   to before   he established – not</small>

7. He who works deceit shall not dwell in my house; he who tells lies shall not remain in my sight.

לַבְּקָרִים אַצְמִית כָּל־רִשְׁעֵי־אָרֶץ לְהַכְרִית מֵעִיר־יְהֹוָה

| ihvh – from city | to cut of | earth – wicked – all | I destroy | to mornings |

כָּל־פֹּעֲלֵי אָוֶן:

| inequity | workers - all |

8. Morning by morning I will destroy all the wicked of the land; that I may cut off all the evil doers from the city of the Lord.

PSALM 102

ספר תהילים פרק קב

תְּפִלָּה לְעָנִי כִי־יַעֲטֹף וְלִפְנֵי יְהֹוָה יִשְׁפֹּךְ שִׂיחוֹ:

his complaint   he pour out   ihvh   and before   he faint – like   to aflicted   prayer

1. A Prayer of the afflicted, when he faints, and pours out his complaint before the Lord.

יְהֹוָה שִׁמְעָה תְפִלָּתִי וְשַׁוְעָתִי אֵלֶיךָ תָבוֹא:

it comes   unto you   and my cry   my prayer   hear   ihvh

2. Hear my prayer, O Lord, and let my cry reach you.

אַל־תַּסְתֵּר פָּנֶיךָ מִמֶּנִּי בְּיוֹם צַר לִי

to me   distress   in day   from me   your face   hide - don't

הַטֵּה־אֵלַי אָזְנֶךָ בְּיוֹם אֶקְרָא מַהֵר עֲנֵנִי:

answer me   speedily   I call   in day   your ear   unto me – incline

3. Do not hide your face from me in the day when I am in trouble; incline your ear to me; answer me speedily in the day when I call.

כִּי־כָלוּ בְעָשָׁן יָמָי וְעַצְמוֹתַי כְּמוֹקֵד נִחָרוּ:

it burned   like hearth   and my bones   my days   in smoke   consumed - like

4. For my days pass away like smoke, and my bones burn like a furnace.

הוּכָּה־כָעֵשֶׂב וַיִּבַשׁ לִבִּי כִּי־שָׁכַחְתִּי מֵאֲכֹל לַחְמִי:

my bread   from eating   I forgot – like   my heart   and dried up   grass - struck

5. My heart is struck and withered like grass; so that I forget to eat my bread.

מִקּוֹל אַנְחָתִי דָּבְקָה עַצְמִי לִבְשָׂרִי:

to my flesh   my bone   cleaved   my groaning   from voice

6. Because of my loud groaning my bones cleave to my skin.

דָּמִיתִי לִקְאַת מִדְבָּר הָיִיתִי כְּכוֹס חֳרָבוֹת:

waste places   like owl   I've been   wildrness   to pelican   i seem

7. I am like an owl of the wilderness; I am like a night flier of the desert.

שָׁקַדְתִּי וָאֶהְיֶה כְּצִפּוֹר בּוֹדֵד עַל־גָּג:

roof - upon   lonely   like bird   and am   I watch

8. I watch; I am like a lonely bird on the roof top.

כָּל־הַיּוֹם חֵרְפוּנִי אוֹיְבָי מְהוֹלָלַי בִּי נִשְׁבָּעוּ:

they sworn   in me   from mad   my enemies   reproached me   the day - all

9. My enemies insult me all the day; and they who are mad against me are sworn against me.

כִּי אֵפֶר כַּלֶּחֶם אָכָלְתִּי וְשִׁקֻּוַי בִּבְכִי מָסָכְתִּי:

I mixed   in weeping   and my drink   I ate   like bread   ashes   like

10. For I have eaten ashes like bread, and mingled my drink with weeping,

מִפְּנֵי־זַעַמְךָ   וְקִצְפֶּךָ   כִּי   נְשָׂאתַנִי   וַתַּשְׁלִיכֵנִי׃

and cast me down | you lifted me | like | and your anger | your indignation – from face

11. Because of your indignation and your wrath; for you have lifted me up, and cast me down.

יָמַי   כְּצֵל   נָטוּי   וַאֲנִי   כָּעֵשֶׂב   אִיבָשׁ׃

dried up | like grass | and I | stretched out | like shadow | my days

12. My days are like an evening shadow; and I am withered like grass.

וְאַתָּה   יְהֹוָה   לְעוֹלָם   תֵּשֵׁב   וְזִכְרְךָ   לְדֹר   וָדֹר׃

and generation | to generation | and your memorial | you dwell | to forever | ihvh | and you

13. But you, O Lord, are enthroned for ever; and your name endures to all generations.

אַתָּה   תָקוּם   תְּרַחֵם   צִיּוֹן

Zion | you compassionate | you arise | you

כִּי   עֵת   לְחֶנְנָהּ   כִּי   בָא   מוֹעֵד׃

set time | come | like | to be gracious to her | season | like

14. You shall arise, and have mercy upon Zion; for it is time to favor her, the set time has come.

כִּי־רָצוּ   עֲבָדֶיךָ   אֶת־אֲבָנֶיהָ   וְאֶת־עֲפָרָהּ   יְחֹנֵנוּ׃

they be gracious | dust – and that | stones – that | your servants | pleased – like

15. For your servants hold her stones dear, and have pity on her dust.

וְיִירְאוּ   גוֹיִם   אֶת־שֵׁם   יְהֹוָה   וְכָל־מַלְכֵי   הָאָרֶץ   אֶת־כְּבוֹדֶךָ׃

your glory – that | the earth | kings – and all | ihvh | name – that | nations | and they will fear

16. So the nations shall fear the name of the Lord, and all the kings of the earth your glory.

כִּי־בָנָה   יְהֹוָה   צִיּוֹן   נִרְאָה   בִּכְבוֹדוֹ׃

in his glory | will appear | Zion | ihvh | build – like

17. For the Lord shall build up Zion, he shall appear in his glory.

פָּנָה   אֶל־תְּפִלַּת   הָעַרְעָר   וְלֹא־בָזָה   אֶת־תְּפִלָּתָם׃

their player – that | despised – and not | the destitute | prayer – unto | he faced

18. He will regard the prayer of the destitute, and not despise their prayer.

תִּכָּתֶב   זֹאת   לְדוֹר   אַחֲרוֹן   וְעַם   נִבְרָא   יְהַלֶּל־יָהּ׃

Ya – it praise | created | and people | afterwards | to generation | this | it will be written

19. This shall be written for the generation to come, so that a people yet unborn may praise the Lord.

כִּי־הִשְׁקִיף   מִמְּרוֹם   קָדְשׁוֹ   יְהֹוָה   מִשָּׁמַיִם   אֶל־אֶרֶץ   הִבִּיט׃

looked | earth – onto | from heavens | ihvh | his holy | from high | looked down – like

20. For he has looked down from the height of his sanctuary; from heaven the Lord looked at the earth,

לִשְׁמֹעַ אֶנְקַת אָסִיר לְפַתֵּחַ בְּנֵי תְמוּתָה׃

death   son   to loose   prisoner   sighing   to hear

21. To hear the groans of the prisoner; to set free those who are appointed to die;

לְסַפֵּר בְּצִיּוֹן שֵׁם יְהוָה וּתְהִלָּתוֹ בִּירוּשָׁלָם׃

in Jerusalem   and his prayers   ihvh   name   in Zion   to declare

22. That men may declare the name of the Lord in Zion, and his praise in Jerusalem,

בְּהִקָּבֵץ עַמִּים יַחְדָּו וּמַמְלָכוֹת לַעֲבֹד אֶת־יְהוָה׃

ihvh – that   to serve   and kingdoms   united   people   in being gathered

23. When the people are gathered together, and the kingdoms, to serve the Lord.

עִנָּה בַדֶּרֶךְ כֹּחוֹ [כֹּחִי] קִצַּר יָמָי׃

my days   he shortened   my strength   in way   he humbled

24. (K) He weakened my strength in the way; he shortened my days.

אֹמַר אֵלִי אַל־תַּעֲלֵנִי בַּחֲצִי יָמָי בְּדוֹר דּוֹרִים שְׁנוֹתֶיךָ׃

your years   generation ones   in generation   my days   in half   take me away - don't   my El   I say

25. I say, O my God, do not take me away in the midst of my days; you whose years endure throughout all generations.

לְפָנִים הָאָרֶץ יָסַדְתָּ וּמַעֲשֵׂה יָדֶיךָ שָׁמָיִם׃

heavens   your hands   and works   you founded   the earth   to faces

26. Of old you laid the foundation of the earth; and the heavens are the work of your hands.

הֵמָּה יֹאבֵדוּ וְאַתָּה תַעֲמֹד וְכֻלָּם

and all them   you stand   and you   they perish   they are

כַּבֶּגֶד יִבְלוּ כַּלְּבוּשׁ תַּחֲלִיפֵם וְיַחֲלֹפוּ׃

and they will be changed   it will change them   like clothing   they wax old   like garment

27. They shall perish, but you shall endure; all of them shall become old like a garment; like clothing you shall change them, and they will pass away;

וְאַתָּה־הוּא וּשְׁנוֹתֶיךָ לֹא יִתָּמּוּ׃

they end   not   and your years   he - and you

28. But you are the same, and your years shall have no end.

בְּנֵי־עֲבָדֶיךָ יִשְׁכּוֹנוּ וְזַרְעָם לְפָנֶיךָ יִכּוֹן׃

it established   before you   their seed   they dwell   your servants - sons

29. The children of your servants shall continue, and their seed shall be established before you.

PSALM 103

ספר תהילים פרק קג

לְדָוִד בָּרְכִי נַפְשִׁי אֶת־יְהֹוָה וְכָל־קְרָבַי אֶת־שֵׁם קָדְשׁוֹ׃

holiness   name – that   within me – and all   ihvh – that   my soul   bless   to David

1. A Psalm of David. Bless the Lord, O my soul; and all that is within me, bless his holy name.

בָּרְכִי נַפְשִׁי אֶת־יְהֹוָה וְאַל־תִּשְׁכְּחִי כָּל־גְּמוּלָיו׃

his benefits – all   you forgetting – and don't   ihvh – that   my soul   bless

2. Bless the Lord, O my soul, and forget not all his benefits,

הַסֹּלֵחַ לְכָל־עֲוֹנֵכִי הָרֹפֵא לְכָל־תַּחֲלֻאָיְכִי׃

your diseases – to all   the healer   your inequities – to all   the pardoner

3. Who forgives all your iniquities, who heals all your diseases,

הַגּוֹאֵל מִשַּׁחַת חַיָּיְכִי הַמְעַטְּרֵכִי חֶסֶד וְרַחֲמִים׃

and mercies   kindness   the crowning one   your life   from pit   who redeemer

4. Who redeems your life from the pit, who encircles you with loving kindness and compassion,

הַמַּשְׂבִּיעַ בַּטּוֹב עֶדְיֵךְ תִּתְחַדֵּשׁ כַּנֶּשֶׁר נְעוּרָיְכִי׃

your youth   like eagle   you renew   your taste   in good   the satisfies

5. Who satisfies your mouth with good things, so that your youth is renewed like the eagle's.

עֹשֵׂה צְדָקוֹת יְהֹוָה וּמִשְׁפָּטִים לְכָל־עֲשׁוּקִים׃

oppressed ones – to all   and judgments   ihvh   righteousness   doing

6. The Lord executes righteousness and judgment for all who are oppressed.

יוֹדִיעַ דְּרָכָיו לְמֹשֶׁה לִבְנֵי יִשְׂרָאֵל עֲלִילוֹתָיו׃

his acts   Israel   to sons   to Moses   his ways   he made known

7. He made known his ways to Moses, his acts to the children of Israel.

רַחוּם וְחַנּוּן יְהֹוָה אֶרֶךְ אַפַּיִם וְרַב־חָסֶד׃

kindness – and much   angers   slow   ihvh   and gracious   merciful

8. The Lord is merciful and gracious, slow to anger, and bountiful in loving kindness.

לֹא־לָנֶצַח יָרִיב וְלֹא לְעוֹלָם יִטּוֹר׃

will he keep anger   forever   and not   will he contend   forever – not

9. He will not always chide; nor will he keep his anger forever.

לֹא כַחֲטָאֵינוּ עָשָׂה לָנוּ וְלֹא כַעֲוֹנֹתֵינוּ גָּמַל עָלֵינוּ׃

upon us   rewarded   like our inequities   and not   to us   done   like our sins   not

10. He has not dealt with us according to our sins; nor rewarded us according to our iniquities.

כִּי כִגְבֹהַּ שָׁמַיִם עַל־הָאָרֶץ גָּבַר חַסְדּוֹ עַל־יְרֵאָיו:

his fearing - upon   his kindness   great   the earth – upon   heavens   like height   like

11. For as the heaven is high above the earth, so great is his loving kindness toward those who fear him.

כִּרְחֹק מִזְרָח מִמַּעֲרָב הִרְחִיק מִמֶּנּוּ אֶת־פְּשָׁעֵינוּ:

our transgressions – that   from us   he has made far   from west   east   like far

12. As far as the east is from the west, so far has he removed our transgressions from us.

כְּרַחֵם אָב עַל־בָּנִים רִחַם יְהוָה עַל־יְרֵאָיו:

his fearing - upon   ihvh   compassionate   sons – upon   father   like compassionate

13. As a father who pities his children, so the Lord pities those who fear him.

כִּי הוּא יָדַע יִצְרֵנוּ זָכוּר כִּי־עָפָר אֲנָחְנוּ:

we   dust – like   remembering   our fame   knows   he   like

14. For he knows our frame; he remembers that we are dust.

אֱנוֹשׁ כֶּחָצִיר יָמָיו כְּצִיץ הַשָּׂדֶה כֵּן יָצִיץ:

he blossoms   thus   the field   like flower   his days   like grass   man

15. As for man, his days are like grass; he flourishes like a flower of the field.

כִּי רוּחַ עָבְרָה־בּוֹ וְאֵינֶנּוּ וְלֹא־יַכִּירֶנּוּ עוֹד מְקוֹמוֹ:

his place   again   recognized - and not   and isn't   in it - passes   wind   like

16. For the wind passes over it, and it is gone; and its place knows it no more.

וְחֶסֶד יְהוָה מֵעוֹלָם וְעַד־עוֹלָם עַל־יְרֵאָיו

his fearing - upon   forever - and till   from forever   ihvh   and kindness

וְצִדְקָתוֹ לִבְנֵי בָנִים:

sons   to sons   and his righteousness

17. But the loving kindness of the Lord is from everlasting to everlasting upon those who fear him, and his righteousness to children's children,

לְשֹׁמְרֵי בְרִיתוֹ וּלְזֹכְרֵי פִקֻּדָיו לַעֲשׂוֹתָם:

to do them   his precepts   and remembering ones   his covenant   to heeders

18. To those who keep his covenant, and to those who remember to do his commandments.

יְהוָה בַּשָּׁמַיִם הֵכִין כִּסְאוֹ וּמַלְכוּתוֹ בַּכֹּל מָשָׁלָה:

rules   in all   and his kingdom   his throne   established   in heavens   ihvh

19. The Lord has established his throne in the heavens; and his kingdom rules over all.

בָּרֲכוּ יְהוָה מַלְאָכָיו גִּבֹּרֵי כֹחַ עֹשֵׂי דְבָרוֹ

his speakings   doing   strength   mighty   his angels   ihvh   you bless

לִשְׁמֹעַ בְּקוֹל דְּבָרוֹ:

his speaking   in voice   to hear

20. Bless the Lord, O you his angels, you mighty ones, who do his word, listening to the

voice of his word!

בָּרֲכוּ יְהֹוָה כָּל־צְבָאָיו מְשָׁרְתָיו עֹשֵׂי רְצוֹנוֹ:

| you bless | ihvh | all – his legions | his chiefs | doing | his pleasure |

21. Bless the Lord, all his hosts! O you his ministers, who do his will!

בָּרֲכוּ יְהֹוָה כָּל־מַעֲשָׂיו בְּכָל־מְקֹמוֹת מֶמְשַׁלְתּוֹ

| you bless | ihvh | all – his works | in all – places | from his rule |

בָּרֲכִי נַפְשִׁי אֶת־יְהֹוָה:

| bless | my soul | that – ihvh |

22. Bless the Lord, all his works, in all places of his dominion! Bless the Lord, O my soul!

PSALM 104

ספר תהילים פרק קד

בָּרְכִי נַפְשִׁי אֶת־יְהוָֹה יְהוָֹה אֱלֹהַי גָּדַלְתָּ

he great   Elohai   ihvh   ihvh – that   my soul   bless

מְאֹד הוֹד וְהָדָר לָבָשְׁתָּ:

clothed   and majesty   glory   very

1. Bless the Lord, O my soul. O Lord my God, you are very great; you are clothed with glory and majesty,

עֹטֶה אוֹר כַּשַּׂלְמָה נוֹטֶה שָׁמַיִם כַּיְרִיעָה:

like curtain   heavens   stretching   like garments   light   covers

2. Who covers himself with light as with a garment; who stretches out the heavens like a curtain;

הַמְקָרֶה בַמַּיִם עֲלִיּוֹתָיו הַשָּׂם־עָבִים רְכוּבוֹ

and his chariot   clouds – the set   his upper chambers   in waters   the laying beams

הַמְהַלֵּךְ עַל־כַּנְפֵי־רוּחַ:

wind – wings – upon   the stroller

3. Who lays the beams of his chambers in the waters; who makes the clouds his chariot; who walks upon the wings of the wind;

עֹשֶׂה מַלְאָכָיו רוּחוֹת מְשָׁרְתָיו אֵשׁ לֹהֵט:

flaming   fire   his ministers   winds   his messengers   he makes

4. Who makes the winds his messengers; the flames of fire his ministers;

יָסַד אֶרֶץ עַל־מְכוֹנֶיהָ בַּל־תִּמּוֹט עוֹלָם וָעֶד:

and time   forever   be moved – in not   its settlements – upon   earth   he founded

5. Who laid the foundations of the earth, that it should not move forever.

תְּהוֹם כַּלְּבוּשׁ כִּסִּיתוֹ עַל־הָרִים יַעַמְדוּ־מָיִם:

waters – they stood   mountains – upon   his covering   like clothing   deep

6. You covered it with the deep as with a garment; the waters stood above the mountains.

מִן־גַּעֲרָתְךָ יְנוּסוּן מִן־קוֹל רַעַמְךָ יֵחָפֵזוּן:

they hasten away   your thunder   voice – from   they fled   your rebuke - from

7. At your rebuke they fled; at the voice of your thunder they hurried away.

יַעֲלוּ הָרִים יֵרְדוּ בְקָעוֹת אֶל־מְקוֹם זֶה יָסַדְתָּ לָהֶם:

to them   you founded   this   place - unto   valleys   they descend   mountains   they ascended

8. They went up the mountains; they flowed down the valleys to the place which you appointed for them.

גְּבוּל־שַׂמְתָּ בַּל־יַעֲבֹרוּן בַּל־יְשׁוּבוּן לְכַסּוֹת הָאָרֶץ:

the earth   to cover   they return – not   they pass – not   you have set – boundary

9. You have set a bound that they may not pass over, so that they might not again cover the earth.

הַמְשַׁלֵּחַ מַעְיָנִים בַּנְּחָלִים בֵּין הָרִים יְהַלֵּכוּן:

they go | mountains | between | in streams | springs | the sender

10. He sends the springs into the valleys, they flow between the mountains.

יַשְׁקוּ כָּל־חַיְתוֹ שָׂדָי יִשְׁבְּרוּ פְרָאִים צְמָאָם:

their thirst | wild asses | they quench | field | his beasts – all | they give water

11. They give drink to every beast of the field; the wild asses quench their thirst.

עֲלֵיהֶם עוֹף־הַשָּׁמַיִם יִשְׁכּוֹן מִבֵּין עָפָאִים יִתְּנוּ־קוֹל:

voice – they give | branches | from among | they dwell | the heavens – fowl | upon them

12. Beside them dwell the birds of the sky, among the branches they sing.

מַשְׁקֶה הָרִים מֵעֲלִיּוֹתָיו מִפְּרִי מַעֲשֶׂיךָ תִּשְׂבַּע הָאָרֶץ:

the earth | satisfied | your works | from fruit | from his upper chambers | mountains | watering

13. He waters the mountains from his high abode; the earth is satisfied with the fruit of your works.

מַצְמִיחַ חָצִיר לַבְּהֵמָה וְעֵשֶׂב לַעֲבֹדַת הָאָדָם

the Adam | to services | and grass | to beast | plants | grows

לְהוֹצִיא לֶחֶם מִן־הָאָרֶץ:

the earth – from | bread | to bring out

14. He makes the grass grow for the cattle, and plants for the service of man, that he may bring forth food from the earth;

וְיַיִן יְשַׂמַּח לְבַב־אֱנוֹשׁ לְהַצְהִיל פָּנִים מִשָּׁמֶן

from oil | faces | the shine | man – heart | it happy | and wine

וְלֶחֶם לְבַב־אֱנוֹשׁ יִסְעָד:

foundation | man – heart | and bread

15. And wine that gladdens the heart of man, and oil to make his face shine, and bread which strengthens man's heart.

יִשְׂבְּעוּ עֲצֵי יְהוָה אַרְזֵי לְבָנוֹן אֲשֶׁר נָטָע:

planted | which | Lebanon | cedars | ihvh | trees | they satisfied

16. The trees of the Lord have their fill; the cedars of Lebanon, which he has planted,

אֲשֶׁר־שָׁם צִפֳּרִים יְקַנֵּנוּ חֲסִידָה בְּרוֹשִׁים בֵּיתָהּ:

her house | cypress trees | stork | they nest | birds | there – which

17. Where the birds make their nests; as for the stork, the cypress trees are her house.

הָרִים הַגְּבֹהִים לַיְּעֵלִים סְלָעִים מַחְסֶה לַשְׁפַנִּים:

to badgers | refuge | crags | to wild goats | the tall ones | mountains

18. The high mountains are a refuge for the wild goats; and the rocks for the badgers.

עָשָׂה יָרֵחַ לְמוֹעֲדִים שֶׁמֶשׁ יָדַע מְבוֹאוֹ:

its origin | knows | sun | to set times | moon | he made

19. He appointed the moon for seasons; the sun knows its setting time.

תָּשֶׁת חֹשֶׁךְ וִיהִי לָיְלָה בּוֹ־תִרְמֹשׂ כָּל־חַיְתוֹ־יָעַר:

forest – his life - all	stirs – in it	night	and it is	darkness	you set

20. You make darkness, and it is night; when all the beasts of the forest creep forth.

הַכְּפִירִים שֹׁאֲגִים לַטָּרֶף וּלְבַקֵּשׁ מֵאֵל אָכְלָם:

their food	from El	and to seek	to prey	roaring ones	the young lions

21. The young lions roar for their prey, and seek their food from God.

תִּזְרַח הַשֶּׁמֶשׁ יֵאָסֵפוּן וְאֶל־מְעוֹנֹתָם יִרְבָּצוּן:

they crouch	their dens – and unto	they gather	the sun	arise

22. The sun rises, they gather themselves together, and lie down in their dens.

יֵצֵא אָדָם לְפָעֳלוֹ וְלַעֲבֹדָתוֹ עֲדֵי־עָרֶב:

evening – until	and to his service	to his work	Adam	goes out

23. Man goes forth to his work and to his labor until the evening.

מָה־רַבּוּ מַעֲשֶׂיךָ יְהוָה כֻּלָּם בְּחָכְמָה עָשִׂיתָ

you made	in wisdom	all them	ihvh	your works	abundant - how

מָלְאָה הָאָרֶץ קִנְיָנֶךָ:

your possession	the earth	full

24. O Lord, how manifold are your works! In wisdom you have made them all; the earth is full of your creatures.

זֶה הַיָּם גָּדוֹל וּרְחַב יָדָיִם שָׁם רֶמֶשׂ

creeping things	there	hands	and wide	big	the sea	this

וְאֵין מִסְפָּר חַיּוֹת קְטַנּוֹת עִם־גְּדֹלוֹת:

great ones– with	small ones	creatures	number	and isn't

25. So is this great and wide sea, where there are innumerable creeping things, living things, both small and great.

שָׁם אֳנִיּוֹת יְהַלֵּכוּן לִוְיָתָן זֶה יָצַרְתָּ לְשַׂחֶק־בּוֹ:

in it – to play	you formed	this	Leviathan	they go	ships	there

26. There go the ships; and Leviathan which you have made to play in it.

כֻּלָּם אֵלֶיךָ יְשַׂבֵּרוּן לָתֵת אָכְלָם בְּעִתּוֹ:

in season	food	to give	they wait	upon you	all them

27. These wait all upon you; that you may give them their food in due season.

תִּתֵּן לָהֶם יִלְקֹטוּן תִּפְתַּח יָדְךָ יִשְׂבְּעוּן טוֹב:

good	they satisfied	your hand	you open	they gather up	to them	you give

28. When you give to them they gather it up; when you open your hand, they are filled with good.

תַּסְתִּיר פָּנֶיךָ יִבָּהֵלוּן תֹּסֵף רוּחָם יִגְוָעוּן

they die	their spirit	gatherer	they terrified	your face	you will hide

וְאֶל־עֲפָרָם יְשׁוּבוּן:
they return   their dust – and unto

29. When you hide your face, they are troubled; when you take away their breath, they die, and return to

תְּשַׁלַּח רוּחֲךָ יִבָּרֵאוּן וּתְחַדֵּשׁ פְּנֵי אֲדָמָה:
soi   face   and you renew   they created   your breath   you send

30. When you send forth your breath, they are created; and you renew the face of the earth.

יְהִי כְבוֹד יְהוָה לְעוֹלָם יִשְׂמַח יְהוָה בְּמַעֲשָׂיו:
in his works   ihvh   he happy   forever   ihvh   glory   it be

31. May the glory of the Lord endure for ever; may the Lord rejoice in his works.

הַמַּבִּיט לָאָרֶץ וַתִּרְעָד יִגַּע בֶּהָרִים וְיֶעֱשָׁנוּ:
and they smoke   in mountains   he touch   and it trembles   to earth   the beholder

32. He looks on the earth, and it trembles; he touches the mountains, and they smoke.

אָשִׁירָה לַיהוָה בְּחַיָּי אֲזַמְּרָה לֵאלֹהַי בְּעוֹדִי:
in my being   to my Elohim   I will sing psalms   in my life   to ihvh   I will sing

33. I will sing to the Lord as long as I live; I will sing praise to my God while I have my being.

יֶעֱרַב עָלָיו שִׂיחִי אָנֹכִי אֶשְׂמַח בַּיהוָה:
in ihvh   I will be happy   I am   my meditation   upon him   sweet

34. My meditation of him shall be sweet; I will rejoice in the Lord.

יִתַּמּוּ חַטָּאִים מִן־הָאָרֶץ
the earth – from   sinners   they perish

וּרְשָׁעִים עוֹד אֵינָם בָּרְכִי נַפְשִׁי אֶת־יְהוָה הַלְלוּיָהּ:
praise Yah   ihvh – that   my soul   bless   isn't them   again   and wicked ones

35. Let the sinners be consumed from the earth, and let the wicked be no more. Bless the Lord, O my soul. Hallelujah!

PSALM 105

ספר תהילים פרק קה

הוֹדוּ לַיהוָה קִרְאוּ בִשְׁמוֹ הוֹדִיעוּ בָעַמִּים עֲלִילוֹתָיו׃
<small>his deeds   in people   you make known   in his name   you call   to ihvh   you thank</small>

1. O give thanks to the Lord; call upon his name; make known his deeds among the people.

שִׁירוּ לוֹ זַמְּרוּ־לוֹ שִׂיחוּ בְּכָל־נִפְלְאוֹתָיו׃
<small>his mystical works – in all   you meditate   to him – sing psalms   to him   you sing</small>

2. Sing to him, sing psalms to him; talk you of all his wondrous works.

הִתְהַלְלוּ בְּשֵׁם קָדְשׁוֹ יִשְׂמַח לֵב מְבַקְשֵׁי יְהוָה׃
<small>ihvh   seekers   heart   be glad   his holiness   in name   you boast</small>

3. Glory in his holy name; let the heart of those who seek the Lord rejoice.

דִּרְשׁוּ יְהוָה וְעֻזּוֹ בַּקְּשׁוּ פָנָיו תָּמִיד׃
<small>continually   his face   you seek   and his strength   ihvh   you seek</small>

4. Seek the Lord, and his strength; seek his face continually.

זִכְרוּ נִפְלְאוֹתָיו אֲשֶׁר עָשָׂה מֹפְתָיו וּמִשְׁפְּטֵי־פִיו׃
<small>his mouth - and judgments   his wonders   he does   which   his mystical works   you remember</small>

5. Remember his marvelous works that he has done; his wonders, and the judgments of his mouth;

זֶרַע אַבְרָהָם עַבְדּוֹ בְּנֵי יַעֲקֹב בְּחִירָיו׃
<small>his chosen ones   Jacob   sons   his servant   Abraham   seed</small>

6. O seed of Abraham, his servant! O children of Jacob, his chosen!

הוּא יְהוָה אֱלֹהֵינוּ בְּכָל־הָאָרֶץ מִשְׁפָּטָיו׃
<small>his judgments   the earth - in all   our Elohim   ihvh   he</small>

7. He is the Lord our God; his judgments are over all the earth.

זָכַר לְעוֹלָם בְּרִיתוֹ דָּבָר צִוָּה לְאֶלֶף דּוֹר׃
<small>generation   to thousand   he commanded   speakings   his covenant   forever   he remembered</small>

8. He has remembered his covenant for ever, the word which he commanded to a thousand generations.

אֲשֶׁר כָּרַת אֶת־אַבְרָהָם וּשְׁבוּעָתוֹ לְיִשְׂחָק׃
<small>to Isaac   and his oaths   Abraham that   he covenanted   which</small>

9. The covenant which he made with Abraham, and his oath to Isaac;

וַיַּעֲמִידֶהָ לְיַעֲקֹב לְחֹק לְיִשְׂרָאֵל בְּרִית עוֹלָם׃
<small>forever   covenant   to Israel   to statute   to Jacob   and he made it stand</small>

10. And confirmed the same to Jacob for a law, and to Israel for an everlasting covenant;

לֵאמֹר לְךָ אֶתֵּן אֶת־אֶרֶץ כְּנָעַן חֶבֶל נַחֲלַתְכֶם׃
<small>your inheritance   region   Canaan   land - that   I give   to you   saying</small>

11. Saying, To you I will give the land of Canaan, the lot of your inheritance;

בִּהְיוֹתָם מְתֵי מִסְפָּר כִּמְעַט וְגָרִים בָּהּ׃
in it ‎ and sojourners ‎ like little ‎ number ‎ few ‎ in their being

12. When they were but a few men in number; of little account and sojourners there.

וַיִּתְהַלְּכוּ מִגּוֹי אֶל־גּוֹי מִמַּמְלָכָה אֶל־עַם אַחֵר׃
other ‎ people -unto ‎ from kingdom ‎ nation – unto ‎ from nations ‎ and they walked

13. When they went from one nation to another, from one kingdom to another people;

לֹא־הִנִּיחַ אָדָם לְעָשְׁקָם וַיּוֹכַח עֲלֵיהֶם מְלָכִים׃
kings ‎ upon them ‎ and he rebuked ‎ to oppress them ‎ Adam ‎ he suffered - not

14. He did not allow any man to do them wrong; he reproved kings for their sakes;

אַל־תִּגְּעוּ בִמְשִׁיחָי וְלִנְבִיאַי אַל־תָּרֵעוּ׃
you do evil – don't ‎ and to my prophets ‎ in my anointed ones ‎ you touch – don't

15. Saying, Do not touch my anointed, and do not do any harm to my prophets.

וַיִּקְרָא רָעָב עַל־הָאָרֶץ כָּל־מַטֵּה־לֶחֶם שָׁבָר׃
he broke ‎ bread - staff – all ‎ the earth –upon ‎ famine ‎ and he called

16. Moreover he called for a famine upon the land; he broke every staff of bread.

שָׁלַח לִפְנֵיהֶם אִישׁ לְעֶבֶד נִמְכַּר יוֹסֵף׃
Joseph ‎ he was sold ‎ to servant ‎ man ‎ before them ‎ he sent

17. He sent a man before them, Joseph, who was sold as a slave;

עִנּוּ בַכֶּבֶל רַגְלָיו [רַגְלוֹ] בַּרְזֶל בָּאָה נַפְשׁוֹ׃
his soul ‎ came ‎ iron ‎ his foot ‎ in fetter ‎ they afflicted

18. (K) Whose foot they hurt with fetters; he was laid in iron;

עַד־עֵת בֹּא־דְבָרוֹ אִמְרַת יְהוָה צְרָפָתְהוּ׃
tested him ‎ ihvh ‎ word ‎ his word – coming ‎ season - till

19. Until the time that his word came to pass; the word of the Lord had tested him.

שָׁלַח־מֶלֶךְ וַיַּתִּירֵהוּ מֹשֵׁל עַמִּים וַיְפַתְּחֵהוּ׃
and he set him free ‎ peoples ‎ ruler ‎ and he loosed him ‎ king - sent

20. The king sent and released him; the ruler of the people let him go free.

שָׂמוֹ אָדוֹן לְבֵיתוֹ וּמֹשֵׁל בְּכָל־קִנְיָנוֹ׃
his possession – in all ‎ and ruler ‎ to his house ‎ master ‎ he set him

21. He made him lord of his house, and ruler of all his possessions;

לֶאְסֹר שָׂרָיו בְּנַפְשׁוֹ וּזְקֵנָיו יְחַכֵּם׃
he make wise them ‎ and his old men ‎ in his soul ‎ his princes ‎ to bind

22. To bind his princes at his pleasure; and teach his elders wisdom.

וַיָּבֹא יִשְׂרָאֵל מִצְרָיִם וְיַעֲקֹב גָּר בְּאֶרֶץ־חָם׃
Ham – in land ‎ sojourned ‎ and Jacob ‎ Egypt ‎ Israel ‎ and he came

23. And Israel came into Egypt; and Jacob sojourned in the land of Ham.

וַיֶּ֣פֶר אֶת־עַמּ֣וֹ מְאֹ֑ד וַ֝יַּֽעֲצִמֵ֗הוּ מִצָּרָֽיו׃

from his adversaries   and he strengthened them   greatly   his people – that   and he made fruitful

24. And he increased his people greatly; and made them stronger than their enemies.

הָפַ֣ךְ לִ֭בָּם לִשְׂנֹ֣א עַמּ֑וֹ לְ֝הִתְנַכֵּ֗ל בַּעֲבָדָֽיו׃

in his servants   to act craftily   his people   to hate   their hearts   he turned

25. He turned their heart to hate his people, to deal craftily with his servants.

שָׁ֭לַח מֹשֶׁ֣ה עַבְדּ֑וֹ אַ֝הֲרֹ֗ן אֲשֶׁ֣ר בָּֽחַר־בֽוֹ׃

in him – he chose   which   Aaron   his servant   Moses   he sent

26. He sent Moses his servant; and Aaron whom he had chosen.

שָֽׂמוּ־בָ֭ם דִּבְרֵ֣י אֹתוֹתָ֑יו וּ֝מֹפְתִ֗ים בְּאֶ֣רֶץ חָֽם׃

Ham   in land   this wonders   his signs   matters   in them – they set

27. They performed his signs among them, and wonders in the land of Ham.

שָׁ֣לַֽח חֹ֭שֶׁךְ וַיַּחְשִׁ֑ךְ וְלֹֽא־מָ֝ר֗וּ אֶת־דְּבָרָֽיו [דְּבָרֽוֹ]׃

his speakings – that   they rebelled against – and not   it became dark   darkness   he sent

28. (K) He sent darkness, and made it dark; and they did not rebel against his word.

הָפַ֣ךְ אֶת־מֵֽימֵיהֶ֣ם לְדָ֑ם וַ֝יָּ֗מֶת אֶת־דְּגָתָֽם׃

their fish – that   and he killed   to blood   their waters – that   he turned

29. He turned their waters into blood, and caused their fish to die.

שָׁרַ֣ץ אַרְצָ֣ם צְפַרְדְּעִ֑ים בְּ֝חַדְרֵ֗י מַלְכֵיהֶֽם׃

their kings   in chambers   frogs   their land   swarmed

30. Their land swarmed with frogs, in the chambers of their kings.

אָ֭מַר וַיָּבֹ֣א עָרֹ֑ב כִּ֝נִּ֗ים בְּכָל־גְּבוּלָֽם׃

their borders – in all   lice   swarming flies   and it came   he said

31. He spoke, and there came swarms of flies and gnats in all their borders.

נָתַ֣ן גִּשְׁמֵיהֶ֣ם בָּרָ֑ד אֵ֖שׁ לֶהָב֣וֹת בְּאַרְצָֽם׃

in their land   flames   fire   hail   their showers   he gave

32. He gave them hail for rain, and flaming fire in their land.

וַיַּ֣ךְ גַּ֭פְנָם וּתְאֵנָתָ֑ם וַ֝יְשַׁבֵּ֗ר עֵ֣ץ גְּבוּלָֽם׃

their border   trees   and he broke   and their fig trees   their vines   and he smote

33. He struck their vines also and their fig trees; and broke the trees of their country.

אָ֭מַר וַיָּבֹ֣א אַרְבֶּ֑ה וְ֝יֶ֗לֶק וְאֵ֣ין מִסְפָּֽר׃

number   and isn't   and caterpillars   locust   and it came   he said

34. He spoke, and the swarming locusts came, and the hopping locusts without number.

וַיֹּ֣אכַל כָּל־עֵ֣שֶׂב בְּאַרְצָ֑ם וַ֝יֹּ֗אכַל פְּרִ֣י אַדְמָתָֽם׃

their ground   fruit   and it ate   in their land   grass – all   and they ate

35. And they ate up all the plants in their land, and devoured the fruit of their ground.

וַיַּ֣ךְ כָּל־בְּכ֣וֹר בְּאַרְצָ֑ם רֵ֝אשִׁ֗ית לְכָל־אוֹנָֽם׃

their strength – to all   first ones   in their land   first born – all   and he smote

36. And he struck all the firstborn in their land, the first issue of all their strength.

וַיּוֹצִיאֵם   בְּכֶסֶף וְזָהָב וְאֵין בִּשְׁבָטָיו כּוֹשֵׁל:

stumbling   in their tribes   and isn't   and gold   in silver   and he brought out them

37. And he brought them out with silver and gold; and among their tribes there was no one who stumbled.

שָׂמַח   מִצְרַיִם בְּצֵאתָם כִּי־נָפַל פַּחְדָּם עֲלֵיהֶם:

upon them   their fear   fell – like   in their going out   Egypt   was happy

38. Egypt was glad when they departed; for the fear of them had fallen upon them.

פָּרַשׂ עָנָן לְמָסָךְ וְאֵשׁ לְהָאִיר לָיְלָה:

night   to the light   and fire   to covering   cloud   he spread

39. He spread a cloud for a covering; and fire to give light in the night.

שָׁאַל וַיָּבֵא   שְׂלָו וְלֶחֶם שָׁמַיִם יַשְׂבִּיעֵם:

it satisfy them   heaven   and bread   quails   and he brought   asked

40. They asked, and he brought quails, and satisfied them with bread from heaven.

פָּתַח צוּר וַיָּזוּבוּ   מָיִם הָלְכוּ בַּצִּיּוֹת נָהָר:

river   in arid places   it went   waters   and they gushed out   rock   he opened

41. He opened the rock, and the waters gushed out; it ran in the dry places like a river.

כִּי־זָכַר   אֶת־דְּבַר קָדְשׁוֹ אֶת־אַבְרָהָם עַבְדּוֹ:

his servant   Abraham – that   his holiness   word – that   he remembered - like

42. For he remembered his holy promise, and Abraham his servant.

וַיּוֹצִא   עַמּוֹ   בְשָׂשׂוֹן בְּרִנָּה אֶת־בְּחִירָיו:

his chosen ones – that   in shouting   in rejoicing   his people   and he brought out

43. And he brought out his people with joy, and his chosen with gladness;

וַיִּתֵּן   לָהֶם אַרְצוֹת גּוֹיִם וַעֲמַל לְאֻמִּים יִירָשׁוּ:

they possessed it   to peoples   and labor   nations   lands   to them   and he gave

44. And he gave them the lands of the nations; and they seized the labor of the people,

בַּעֲבוּר יִשְׁמְרוּ חֻקָּיו וְתוֹרֹתָיו יִנְצֹרוּ הַלְלוּיָהּ:

Halelujah   they keep   and his torah   his statue   they heed   in sake

45. That they might observe his statutes, and keep his Torot. Hallelujah! Lord.

PSALM 106

ספר תהילים פרק קו

הַלְלוּיָהּ הוֹדוּ לַיהוָה כִּי־טוֹב כִּי לְעוֹלָם חַסְדּוֹ:
his kindness   to forever   like   good – like   to ihvh   give thanks   praise Yah

1. Hallelujah! O give thanks to the Lord; for he is good; for his loving kindness endures for ever.

מִי יְמַלֵּל גְּבוּרוֹת יְהוָה יַשְׁמִיעַ כָּל־תְּהִלָּתוֹ:
his prayer – all   he will hear   ihvh   mighty ones   he utters   who

2. Who can utter the mighty acts of the Lord? Who can declare all his praise?

אַשְׁרֵי שֹׁמְרֵי מִשְׁפָּט עֹשֵׂה צְדָקָה בְכָל־עֵת:
season – in all   righteousness   doing   judgment   heeders   happy

3. Happy are those who maintain justice, and he who does righteousness at all times.

זָכְרֵנִי יְהוָה בִּרְצוֹן עַמֶּךָ פָּקְדֵנִי בִּישׁוּעָתֶךָ:
in your salvation   visit me   your people   in favor   ihvh   remember me

4. Remember me, O Lord, when you show favor to your people. O visit me with your salvation!

לִרְאוֹת בְּטוֹבַת בְּחִירֶיךָ לִשְׂמֹחַ בְּשִׂמְחַת גּוֹיֶךָ
your nation   in gladness   to be happy   your chosen one   in good   to see

לְהִתְהַלֵּל עִם־נַחֲלָתֶךָ:
your inheritance - with   to boast myself

5. That I may see the good of your chosen, that I may rejoice in the gladness of your nation, that I may glory with your inheritance.

חָטָאנוּ עִם־אֲבוֹתֵינוּ הֶעֱוִינוּ הִרְשָׁעְנוּ:
we wicked   we perverse   our fathers – with   we sinned

6. We have sinned with our fathers, we have committed iniquity, we have done wickedly.

אֲבוֹתֵינוּ בְמִצְרַיִם לֹא־הִשְׂכִּילוּ
they understood – not   in Egypt   our fathers

נִפְלְאוֹתֶיךָ לֹא זָכְרוּ אֶת־רֹב חֲסָדֶיךָ
your kindness   multitude – that   they remembered   not   your mysticals

וַיַּמְרוּ עַל־יָם בְּיַם־סוּף:
end – in sea   sea - upon   and they rebelled

7. Our fathers, when they were in Egypt, did not understand your wonders; they did not remember the multitude of your deeds of loving kindness; and they rebelled against you at the sea, the Red Sea.

וַיּוֹשִׁיעֵם לְמַעַן שְׁמוֹ לְהוֹדִיעַ אֶת־גְּבוּרָתוֹ:
his might- that   to make known   his name   to end   and he saved them

8. But he saved them for his name's sake, that he might make known his mighty power.

וַיִּגְעַר בְּיַם־סוּף וַיֶּחֱרָב וַיּוֹלִיכֵם בַּתְּהֹמוֹת כַּמִּדְבָּר׃

<small>like wilderness   in cepths   and he walked them   and it dried up   end – in sea   and he rebuked</small>

9. And he rebuked the Red Sea, and it was dried up; so he led them through the depths, as through the wilderness.

וַיּוֹשִׁיעֵם מִיַּד שׂוֹנֵא וַיִּגְאָלֵם מִיַּד אוֹיֵב׃

<small>enemy   from hand   and he redeemed them   haters   from hand   and he saved them</small>

10. And he saved them from the hard of him who hated them, and redeemed them from the hand of the enemy.

וַיְכַסּוּ־מַיִם צָרֵיהֶם אֶחָד מֵהֶם לֹא נוֹתָר׃

<small>remained   not   from them   one   their adversaries   water - and they covered</small>

11. And the waters covered their enemies; there was not one of them left.

וַיַּאֲמִינוּ בִדְבָרָיו יָשִׁירוּ תְּהִלָּתוֹ׃

<small>his praise   they sang   in his speakings   and they beliefed</small>

12. Then they believed his words; they sang his praise.

מִהֲרוּ שָׁכְחוּ מַעֲשָׂיו לֹא־חִכּוּ לַעֲצָתוֹ׃

<small>to his counsel   they waited - not   his works   they forgot   from soon</small>

13. They soon forgot his works; they did not wait for his counsel;

וַיִּתְאַוּוּ תַאֲוָה בַּמִּדְבָּר וַיְנַסּוּ־אֵל בִּישִׁימוֹן׃

<small>in desolation   unto - and they tried   in wilderness   yearning   and they craved</small>

14. But they had wanton cravings in the wilderness, and put God to the test in the desert.

וַיִּתֵּן לָהֶם שֶׁאֱלָתָם וַיְשַׁלַּח רָזוֹן בְּנַפְשָׁם׃

<small>in their soul   leanness   and he sent   their askings   to them   and he gave</small>

15. And he gave them what they asked; but sent leanness into their soul.

וַיְקַנְאוּ לְמֹשֶׁה בַּמַּחֲנֶה לְאַהֲרֹן קְדוֹשׁ יְהוָה׃

<small>ihvh   holy   to Aaron   in the camp   to Moses   and they envied</small>

16. And they envied Moses in the camp, and Aaron the holy one of the Lord.

תִּפְתַּח־אֶרֶץ וַתִּבְלַע דָּתָן וַתְּכַס עַל־עֲדַת אֲבִירָם׃

<small>Abiram   congregation - upon   and it covered   Dathan   and it swallowed up   earth - it opened</small>

17. The earth opened and swallowed up Dathan, and covered the company of Abiram.

וַתִּבְעַר־אֵשׁ בַּעֲדָתָם לֶהָבָה תְּלַהֵט רְשָׁעִים׃

<small>wicked   it flame   to burn   in their congregation   fire - and kindled</small>

18. And a fire was kindled in their company; the flame burned up the wicked.

יַעֲשׂוּ־עֵגֶל בְּחֹרֵב וַיִּשְׁתַּחֲווּ לְמַסֵּכָה׃

<small>to molten image   and they worshipped   in Horeb   calf - and he did</small>

19. They made a calf in Horeb, and worshipped the molten image.

וַיָּמִירוּ אֶת־כְּבוֹדָם בְּתַבְנִית שׁוֹר אֹכֵל עֵשֶׂב׃

<small>grass   eats   ox   in likeness   their glory - that   and they said</small>

20. Thus they changed their glory for the likeness of an ox that eats grass!

שָׁכְחוּ אֵל מוֹשִׁיעָם עֹשֶׂה גְדֹלוֹת בְּמִצְרָיִם:

in Egypt   greatnesses   doer   saver of them   El   they forgot

21. They forgot God who had saved them, who had done great things in Egypt;

נִפְלָאוֹת בְּאֶרֶץ חָם נוֹרָאוֹת עַל־יַם־סוּף:

end - sea - upon   awesome ones   Ham   in land   wondrous ones

22. Wondrous works in the land of Ham, and awesome things by the Red Sea.

וַיֹּאמֶר לְהַשְׁמִידָם לוּלֵי מֹשֶׁה בְחִירוֹ

his chosen   Moses   unless   to the exterminate them   and he said

עָמַד בַּפֶּרֶץ לְפָנָיו לְהָשִׁיב חֲמָתוֹ מֵהַשְׁחִית:

from the ruining   his wrath   to the turn away   before him   in breach   stood

23. Therefore he said that he would destroy them, had not Moses, his chosen one, stood before him in the breach, to turn away his wrath, lest he should destroy them.

וַיִּמְאֲסוּ בְּאֶרֶץ חֶמְדָּה לֹא־הֶאֱמִינוּ לִדְבָרוֹ:

to his speakings   they believed - not   desirable   in land   and they rejected

24. And they despised the pleasant land, they did not believe his word;

וַיֵּרָגְנוּ בְאָהֳלֵיהֶם לֹא שָׁמְעוּ בְּקוֹל יְהוָה:

ihvh   in voice   they hear   not   in their tents   and they murmured

25. And they murmured in their tents, and did not listen to the voice of the Lord.

וַיִּשָּׂא יָדוֹ לָהֶם לְהַפִּיל אוֹתָם בַּמִּדְבָּר:

in wilderness   to them   to make fall   to them   his hand   and he lifted up

26. And he lifted up his hand against them, to make them fall in the wilderness;

וּלְהַפִּיל זַרְעָם בַּגּוֹיִם וּלְזָרוֹתָם בָּאֲרָצוֹת:

in lands   and to scatter them   in nations   their seed   and to make fall

27. And to make their seed fall among the nations, and to scatter them in the lands.

וַיִּצָּמְדוּ לְבַעַל פְּעוֹר וַיֹּאכְלוּ זִבְחֵי מֵתִים:

dead ones   sacrifices   and they ate   Peor   to Baal   and they joined

28. And they joined themselves to Baal-Peor, and ate the sacrifices of the dead.

וַיַּכְעִיסוּ בְּמַעַלְלֵיהֶם וַתִּפְרָץ־בָּם מַגֵּפָה:

the plague   in them – and broke out   in their actions   and they provoked him

29. Thus they provoked him to anger with their wrong doings; and the plague broke out upon them.

וַיַּעֲמֹד פִּינְחָס וַיְפַלֵּל וַתֵּעָצַר הַמַּגֵּפָה:

the plague   and it was stayed   and meditated   Phinehas   and he stood

30. Then stood up Phinehas, and executed judgment; and so the plague was stayed.

וַתֵּחָשֶׁב לוֹ לִצְדָקָה לְדֹר וָדֹר עַד־עוֹלָם:

forever – till   and generation   to generation   to righteousness   to him   and it was thought

31. And that was counted to him for righteousness to all generations for evermore.

וַיַּקְצִיפוּ עַל־מֵי מְרִיבָה וַיֵּרַע לְמֹשֶׁה בַּעֲבוּרָם׃
<small>in their account · to Moses · and it was evil · Meribah · waters – upon · and they provoked him</small>

32. And they angered him at the waters of Meribah, so that it went ill with Moses for their sakes,

כִּי־הִמְרוּ אֶת־רוּחוֹ וַיְבַטֵּא בִּשְׂפָתָיו׃
<small>in his lips · and he spoke rashly · his spirit – that · they angered – like</small>

33. Because they angered his spirit, so that he spoke rashly with his lips.

לֹא־הִשְׁמִידוּ אֶת־הָעַמִּים אֲשֶׁר אָמַר יְהוָה לָהֶם׃
<small>to them · ihvh · said · which · the peoples – that · they destroy – not</small>

34. They did not destroy the nations, concerning whom the Lord commanded them;

וַיִּתְעָרְבוּ בַגּוֹיִם וַיִּלְמְדוּ מַעֲשֵׂיהֶם׃
<small>their works · and they learned · in nations · and they mingled</small>

35. But they mingled among the nations, and learned to do what they did;

וַיַּעַבְדוּ אֶת־עֲצַבֵּיהֶם וַיִּהְיוּ לָהֶם לְמוֹקֵשׁ׃
<small>to snare · to them · and they were · their idols – that · and they served</small>

36. And they served their idols; which became a snare to them.

וַיִּזְבְּחוּ אֶת־בְּנֵיהֶם וְאֶת־בְּנוֹתֵיהֶם לַשֵּׁדִים׃
<small>to demons · their daughters – and that · their sons – that · and they sacrificed</small>

37. And they sacrificed their sons and their daughters to idols,

וַיִּשְׁפְּכוּ דָם נָקִי דַּם־בְּנֵיהֶם וּבְנוֹתֵיהֶם
<small>and their daughters · their sons – blood · innocent · blood · and they poured out</small>

אֲשֶׁר זִבְּחוּ לַעֲצַבֵּי כְנָעַן וַתֶּחֱנַף הָאָרֶץ בַּדָּמִים׃
<small>in blood · the land · and polluted · Cannan · to idols · they sacrificed · which</small>

38. And shed innocent blood, the blood of their sons and of their daughters, whom they sacrificed to the idols of Canaan; and the land was polluted with blood.

וַיִּטְמְאוּ בְמַעֲשֵׂיהֶם וַיִּזְנוּ בְּמַעַלְלֵיהֶם׃
<small>in their actions · and they whoring · in their works · and they defiled</small>

39. Thus were they defiled with their own works, and played the harlot in their doings.

וַיִּחַר־אַף יְהוָה בְּעַמּוֹ וַיְתָעֵב אֶת־נַחֲלָתוֹ׃
<small>his inheritance – that · and abhorred · in his people · ihvh · anger – and was wroth</small>

40. And the wrath of the Lord was kindled against his people, and he loathed his own heritage.

וַיִּתְּנֵם בְּיַד־גּוֹיִם וַיִּמְשְׁלוּ בָהֶם שֹׂנְאֵיהֶם׃
<small>haters of them · in them · and they ruled · nations – in hand · and he gave them</small>

41. And he gave them into the hand of the nations; and those who hated them ruled over them.

וַיִּלְחָצוּם אוֹיְבֵיהֶם וַיִּכָּנְעוּ תַּחַת יָדָם׃
<small>their hand · under · and they subdued · their enemies · and oppressed them</small>

42. And their enemies oppressed them, and they were brought into subjection under their hand.

פְּעָמִים רַבּוֹת יַצִּילֵם וְהֵמָּה יַמְרוּ בַעֲצָתָם
in their counsel   they rebellious   and they   he delivered them   many   repeating

וַיָּמֹכּוּ בַּעֲוֹנָם:
in their iniquity   and they are reduced

43. Many times he saved them; but they were rebellious in their counsel, and were brought low for their iniquity.

וַיַּרְא בַּצַּר לָהֶם בְּשָׁמְעוֹ אֶת־רִנָּתָם:
their outcry - that   in his hearing   to them   in distress   and he saw

44. Nevertheless, when he heard their cry, he regarded their affliction;

וַיִּזְכֹּר לָהֶם בְּרִיתוֹ וַיִּנָּחֵם כְּרֹב חֲסָדָו [חֲסָדָיו]:
his kindness   like much   and he repented   his covenant   to them   and he remembered

45. And he remembered for them his covenant, and relented according to the abundance of his loving kindness.

וַיִּתֵּן אוֹתָם לְרַחֲמִים לִפְנֵי כָּל־שׁוֹבֵיהֶם:
their captors – all   before   to mercies   to them   and he gave

46. And he caused them to be pitied by all those who held them captive.

הוֹשִׁיעֵנוּ יְהוָה אֱלֹהֵינוּ
our Elohim   ihvh   save us

וְקַבְּצֵנוּ מִן־הַגּוֹיִם לְהֹדוֹת לְשֵׁם קָדְשֶׁךָ לְהִשְׁתַּבֵּחַ בִּתְהִלָּתֶךָ:
in your praise   to triumph   your holiness   to name   to thank   the nations from   and gather us

47. Save us, O Lord our God, and gather us from among the nations, that we may give thanks to your holy name, and to triumph in your praise.

בָּרוּךְ־יְהוָה אֱלֹהֵי יִשְׂרָאֵל מִן־הָעוֹלָם
the forever - from   Israel   my Elohim   ihvh - blessed

וְעַד הָעוֹלָם וְאָמַר כָּל־הָעָם אָמֵן הַלְלוּיָה:
praise Yah   amen   the people – all   and say   the forever   and till

48. Blessed be the Lord God of Israel from everlasting to everlasting; and let all the people say, Amen. Hallelujah!

PSALM 107

ספר תהילים פרק קז

הֹדוּ לַיהֹוָה כִּי־טוֹב כִּי. לְעוֹלָם חַסְדּוֹ:

his kindness   to forever   like   good – like   to ihvh   you give thanks

1. O give thanks to the Lord, for he is good; for his loving kindness endures for ever.

יֹאמְרוּ גְּאוּלֵי יְהֹוָה אֲשֶׁר גְּאָלָם מִיַּד־צָר:

adversary – from hand   redeemed them   which   ihvh   redeemed   they say

2. Let the redeemed of the Lord say so, whom he has redeemed from the hand of the enemy;

וּמֵאֲרָצוֹת קִבְּצָם מִמִּזְרָח וּמִמַּעֲרָב מִצָּפוֹן וּמִיָּם:

and from sea   from north   and from west   from east   he gathered them   and from the lands

3. And gathered them from the lands, from the east, and from the west, from the north, and from the south.

תָּעוּ בַמִּדְבָּר בִּישִׁימוֹן דָּרֶךְ עִיר מוֹשָׁב לֹא מָצָאוּ:

they found   not   habitation   city   way   in desert   in wilderness   they wandered

4. They wandered in the wilderness in a desert way; they found no city to dwell in.

רְעֵבִים גַּם־צְמֵאִים נַפְשָׁם בָּהֶם תִּתְעַטָּף:

it fainted   in them   their souls   thirsty ones – also   hungry ones

5. Hungry and thirsty, their soul fainted in them.

וַיִּצְעֲקוּ אֶל־יְהֹוָה בַּצַּר לָהֶם מִמְּצוּקוֹתֵיהֶם יַצִּילֵם:

he rescuing them   from their afflictions   to them   in distress   ihvh – unto   and they cried

6. Then they cried to the Lord in their trouble, and he saved them from their distresses.

וַיַּדְרִיכֵם בְּדֶרֶךְ יְשָׁרָה לָלֶכֶת אֶל־עִיר מוֹשָׁב:

habitation   city – unto   to go   towards straight   in way   and he guided them

7. And he led them forth by the right way, that they might go to a city of habitation.

יוֹדוּ לַיהֹוָה חַסְדּוֹ וְנִפְלְאוֹתָיו לִבְנֵי אָדָם:

Adam   to sons   and his wondrous works   his kindness   to ihvh   you give thanks

8. Oh that men would praise the Lord for his loving kindness, and for his wonderful works to the children of men!

כִּי־הִשְׂבִּיעַ נֶפֶשׁ שֹׁקֵקָה וְנֶפֶשׁ רְעֵבָה מִלֵּא־טוֹב:

good - fills   hungry   and soul   longing   soul   he satisfied - like

9. For he satisfies the longing soul, and fills the hungry soul with goodness.

יֹשְׁבֵי חֹשֶׁךְ וְצַלְמָוֶת אֲסִירֵי עֳנִי וּבַרְזֶל:

and iron   affliction   bound   and deathly gloom   darkness   dwellers

10. Those who sit in darkness and in the shadow of death, bound in affliction and iron;

כִּי־הִמְרוּ אִמְרֵי־אֵל וַעֲצַת עֶלְיוֹן נָאָצוּ:

they despised   most high   and counsel   El - words   they rebelled - like

11. Because they rebelled against the words of God, and rejected the counsel of the most High;

וַיַּכְנַע בֶּעָמָל לִבָּם כָּשְׁלוּ וְאֵין עֹזֵר:

helper   and isn't   they stumbled   their heart   in travail   and he subdued

12. And he brought down their heart with labor; they fell down, and there was none to help.

וַיִּזְעֲקוּ אֶל־יְהֹוָה בַּצַּר לָהֶם מִמְּצֻקוֹתֵיהֶם יוֹשִׁיעֵם:

he saved them   from their afflictions   to them   in distress   ihvh - unto   and they cried

13. Then they cried to the Lord in their trouble, and he saved them from their distresses.

יוֹצִיאֵם מֵחֹשֶׁךְ וְצַלְמָוֶת וּמוֹסְרוֹתֵיהֶם יְנַתֵּק:

he broke away   and their bands   and deadly gloom   from darkness   he brought them

14. He brought them out of darkness and the shadow of death, and broke their bonds asunder.

יוֹדוּ לַיהֹוָה חַסְדּוֹ וְנִפְלְאוֹתָיו לִבְנֵי אָדָם:

Adam   to sons   and his wondrous works   his kindness   to ihvh   they give thanks

15. Let them praise the Lord for his loving kindness, and for his wonderful works to the children of men!

כִּי־שִׁבַּר דַּלְתוֹת נְחֹשֶׁת וּבְרִיחֵי בַרְזֶל גִּדֵּעַ:

hewed   iron   and bars   brass   big doors   he broke - for

16. For he broke the gates of bronze, and cut the bars of iron asunder.

אֱוִלִים מִדֶּרֶךְ פִּשְׁעָם וּמֵעֲוֹנֹתֵיהֶם יִתְעַנּוּ:

they afflicted   and from their iniquities   their transgressions   from way   fools

17. Fools were afflicted because of their transgression, and because of their iniquities.

כָּל־אֹכֶל תְּתַעֵב נַפְשָׁם וַיַּגִּיעוּ עַד־שַׁעֲרֵי מָוֶת:

death   gates - till   and they drew near   their soul   it abhors   food - all

18. Their soul loathed all manner of food; and they came near to the gates of death.

וַיִּזְעֲקוּ אֶל־יְהֹוָה בַּצַּר לָהֶם מִמְּצֻקוֹתֵיהֶם יוֹשִׁיעֵם:

he saved them   from their afflictions   to them   in distress   ihvh - unto   and they cried

19. Then they cried to the Lord in their trouble, and he saved them out of their distresses.

יִשְׁלַח דְּבָרוֹ וְיִרְפָּאֵם וִימַלֵּט מִשְּׁחִיתוֹתָם:

from their pitfalls   and he deliver them   and he healed them   his words   he sent

20. He sent his word, and healed them, and saved them from their destructions.

יוֹדוּ לַיהֹוָה חַסְדּוֹ וְנִפְלְאוֹתָיו לִבְנֵי אָדָם:

Adam   to sons   and his wondrous works   his kindness   to ihvh   you acclaim

21. Let them praise the Lord for his loving kindness, and for his wonderful works to the children of men!

וְיִזְבְּחוּ זִבְחֵי תוֹדָה וִיסַפְּרוּ מַעֲשָׂיו בְּרִנָּה:

in shouting   his works   and they declare   praise   sacrifices   and they sacrifice

22. And let them sacrifice the sacrifices of thanksgiving, and declare his works with rejoicing.

יוֹרְדֵי   הַיָּם   בָּאֳנִיּוֹת   עֹשֵׂי   מְלָאכָה   בְּמַיִם רַבִּים׃

great	in waters	work	doing	in ships	the sea	who descend

23. Those who go down to the sea in ships, that do business in great waters;

הֵמָּה רָאוּ   מַעֲשֵׂי יְהֹוָה וְנִפְלְאוֹתָיו   בִּמְצוּלָה׃

in depth	and his wondrous works	ihvh	deeds	saw	they

24. Those saw the works of the Lord, and his wonders in the deep.

וַיֹּאמֶר   וַיַּעֲמֵד   רוּחַ סְעָרָה וַתְּרוֹמֵם גַּלָּיו׃

its waves	and it exalted	stormy	wind	and he made stand	and he said

25. For he commands, and raises the stormy wind, which lifts up its waves.

יַעֲלוּ   שָׁמַיִם   יֵרְדוּ   תְהוֹמוֹת נַפְשָׁם בְּרָעָה תִתְמוֹגָג׃

melted	in evil	their soul	deeps	they descend	heavens	they ascend

26. They mount up to the sky, they go down again to the depths; their soul is melted because of trouble.

יָחוֹגּוּ וְיָנוּעוּ כַּשִּׁכּוֹר וְכָל־חָכְמָתָם תִּתְבַּלָּע׃

it swallow up	their wisdom - and all	a drunkard	and stagger	they reel

27. They reel to and fro, and stagger like a drunken man, and are at their wit's end.

וַיִּצְעֲקוּ אֶל־יְהֹוָה בַּצַּר לָהֶם וּמִמְּצוּקֹתֵיהֶם   יוֹצִיאֵם׃

he brings out them	and from their afflictions	to them	in distress	ihvh - unto	and they cry

28. Then they cry to the Lord in their trouble, and he brings them out of their distresses.

יָקֵם סְעָרָה לִדְמָמָה וַיֶּחֱשׁוּ   גַּלֵּיהֶם׃

their waves	and they hushed	to stillness	storm	he calms

29. He calms the storm, so that its waves are still.

וַיִּשְׂמְחוּ כִי־יִשְׁתֹּקוּ וַיַּנְחֵם   אֶל־מְחוֹז חֶפְצָם׃

their delight	haven - unto	and he led them	they quiet - like	and they glad

30. Then they are glad because they have quiet; and he brings them to their desired haven.

יוֹדוּ   לַיהֹוָה חַסְדּוֹ וְנִפְלְאוֹתָיו   לִבְנֵי   אָדָם׃

Adam	to sons	and his wondrous works	his kindness	to ihvh	you thanks

31. Let them praise the Lord for his loving kindness, and for his wonderful works to the children of men!

וִירֹמְמוּהוּ   בִּקְהַל־עָם   וּבְמוֹשַׁב זְקֵנִים יְהַלְלוּהוּ׃

they praise him	old men	and in dwelling	people – in congregation	and they exalt him

32. Let them exalt him also in the congregation of the people, and praise him in the assembly of the elders.

יָשֵׂם נְהָרוֹת לְמִדְבָּר וּמֹצָאֵי מַיִם לְצִמָּאוֹן׃

to dry ground	water	and springs	to wilderness	rivers	he sets

33. He turns rivers into a wilderness, and springs of water into dry ground;

אֶרֶץ פְּרִי לִמְלֵחָה מֵרָעַת יֹשְׁבֵי בָהּ:

in it	dwellers	from evil	to saltness	fruit	land

34. A fruitful land into barrenness, because of the wickedness of its inhabitants.

יָשֵׂם מִדְבָּר לַאֲגַם־מַיִם וְאֶרֶץ צִיָּה לְמֹצָאֵי מָיִם:

water	to springs	dryness	and land	water - to pool	wilderness	he sets

35. He turns the wilderness into a pool of water, and dry ground into springs of water.

וַיּוֹשֶׁב שָׁם רְעֵבִים וַיְכוֹנְנוּ עִיר מוֹשָׁב:

habitation	city	and they establish	hungry ones	there	and he dwells

36. And there he lets the hungry dwell, and they establish a city for habitation;

וַיִּזְרְעוּ שָׂדוֹת וַיִּטְּעוּ כְרָמִים וַיַּעֲשׂוּ פְּרִי תְבוּאָה:

increase	fruit	and they yield	vineyards	and they plant	fields	and they sow

37. And sow the fields, and plant vineyards, which get a fruitful yield.

וַיְבָרֲכֵם וַיִּרְבּוּ מְאֹד וּבְהֶמְתָּם לֹא יַמְעִיט:

he decrease	not	and their cattle	greatly	and multiplied	and he blesses them

38. And he blesses them, so that they are multiplied greatly; and does not let their cattle decrease.

וַיִּמְעֲטוּ וַיָּשֹׁחוּ מֵעֹצֶר רָעָה וְיָגוֹן:

and sorrow	bad	from oppression	and bowed down	and they diminished

39. When they are diminished and brought low through oppression, affliction, and sorrow.

שֹׁפֵךְ בּוּז עַל־נְדִיבִים וַיַּתְעֵם בְּתֹהוּ לֹא־דָרֶךְ:

way - not	in waste	and he makes wonder them	princes – upon	contempt	pours

40. He pours contempt upon nobles, and causes them to wander in the wilderness, where there is no way.

וַיְשַׂגֵּב אֶבְיוֹן מֵעוֹנִי וַיָּשֶׂם כַּצֹּאן מִשְׁפָּחוֹת:

families	like sheep	and he sets them	from affliction	needy	and he set on high

41. But he raises the poor high out of affliction, and makes his families like a flock.

יִרְאוּ יְשָׁרִים וְיִשְׂמָחוּ וְכָל־עַוְלָה קָפְצָה פִּיהָ:

it's mouth	stopped	in equity - and all	and be happy	upright ones	they will see

42. The righteous shall see it, and rejoice; and all iniquity shall stop its mouth.

מִי־חָכָם וְיִשְׁמָר־אֵלֶּה וְיִתְבּוֹנְנוּ חַסְדֵי יְהוָה:

ihvh	kindness	and they consider	these – and it heeds	wise - who

43. Whoever is wise, and will observe these things, let them consider the loving kindness of the Lord.

Psalm 108

ספר תהילים פרק קח

שִׁיר מִזְמוֹר לְדָוִד:

to David psalm song

1. A Song, a Psalm of David.

נָכוֹן לִבִּי אֱלֹהִים אָשִׁירָה וַאֲזַמְּרָה אַף־כְּבוֹדִי:

my glory - thus and will sing psalms I will sing Elohim my heart established

2. O God, my heart is firm; I will sing, I will give praise, also my glory.

עוּרָה הַנֵּבֶל וְכִנּוֹר אָעִירָה שָּׁחַר:

dawn I will arouse and harp lyre the harp awake

3. Awake, O harp and lyre! I will awaken the dawn!

אוֹדְךָ בָעַמִּים יְהֹוָה וַאֲזַמֶּרְךָ בַּל־אֻמִּים:

nations - in not and I will sing psalms ihvh in the people I will give you thanks

4. I will praise you, O Lord, among the peoples; and I will sing praises to you among the nations.

כִּי־גָדוֹל מֵעַל־שָׁמַיִם חַסְדֶּךָ וְעַד־שְׁחָקִים אֲמִתֶּךָ:

your truth skies – and unto your kindness the heavens - above great - like

5. For your loving kindness is great above the heavens; and your truth reaches to the clouds.

רוּמָה עַל־שָׁמַיִם אֱלֹהִים וְעַל כָּל־הָאָרֶץ כְּבוֹדֶךָ:

your glory the earth – all and upon Elohim heavens - upon be exalted

6. Be exalted, O God, above the heavens; and your glory above all the earth;

לְמַעַן יֵחָלְצוּן יְדִידֶיךָ הוֹשִׁיעָה יְמִינְךָ וַעֲנֵנִי:

and answer me your right hand saved your beloved they liberated to end

7. (K) That your beloved ones may be saved; save with your right hand and answer me.

אֱלֹהִים דִּבֶּר בְּקָדְשׁוֹ אֶעְלֹזָה אֲחַלְּקָה שְׁכֶם

Shechem I will divide I will exult in his holiness spoke Elohim

וְעֵמֶק סֻכּוֹת אֲמַדֵּד:

I measure Succoth and valley

8. God has spoken in his holiness; I will rejoice, I will divide Shechem, and measure out the valley of Succoth.

לִי גִלְעָד לִי מְנַשֶּׁה וְאֶפְרַיִם מָעוֹז רֹאשִׁי יְהוּדָה מְחֹקְקִי:

my law giver Judah my head defence and Ephram Manaseth to me Gilead to me

9. Gilead is mine; Manasseh is mine; Ephraim also is the strength of my head; Judah is my scepter;

מוֹאָב סִיר רַחְצִי עַל־אֱדוֹם אַשְׁלִיךְ נַעֲלִי

my shoe I will cast Edom - upon my washing pot Moab

עֲלֵי־פְלֶשֶׁת אֶתְרוֹעָע׃
that I shout   Philistia - over

10. Moab is my washbasin; over Edom I cast my shoe; over Philistia I shout in triumph.

מִי יֹבִלֵנִי עִיר מִבְצָר מִי נָחַנִי עַד־אֱדוֹם׃
Edom – unto   has led me   who   strong hold   city   will bring   who

11. Who will bring me to the fortified city? Who will lead me to Edom?

הֲלֹא־אֱלֹהִים זְנַחְתָּנוּ וְלֹא־תֵצֵא אֱלֹהִים בְּצִבְאֹתֵינוּ׃
in our host   Elohim   you go out - and not   cut off us   Elohim - the not

12. Have you not rejected us, O God? You do not go forth, O God, with our armies.

הָבָה־לָּנוּ עֶזְרָת מִצָּר וְשָׁוְא תְּשׁוּעַת אָדָם׃
Adam   salvation   and vanity   from distress   help   to us - the come

13. Give us help against the enemy; for vain is the help of man.

בֵּאלֹהִים נַעֲשֶׂה־חָיִל וְהוּא יָבוּס צָרֵינוּ׃
our adversaries   will tread down   and he   mightily – we will do   in Elohim

14. Through God we shall do bravely; and he shall trample down our enemies.

PSALM 109

לַמְנַצֵּחַ לְדָוִד מִזְמוֹר אֱלֹהֵי תְהִלָּתִי אַל־תֶּחֱרַשׁ:
be silent – don't   my prayer   my Elohim   psalm   to David   to him that is over

1. To the chief Musician, A Psalm of David. Be not silent, O God of my praise;
1against me deceit and mouth wicked mouth because

כִּי פִי רָשָׁע וּפִי־מִרְמָה עָלַי פָּתָחוּ דִּבְּרוּ אִתִּי לְשׁוֹן שָׁקֶר:
lies   tongue   with me   they spoke   they opened   upon me   deceitful - and mouth   wicked mouth like

2. For the mouth of the wicked and the mouth of the deceitful are opened against me;
they have spoken against me with a lying tongue.

וְדִבְרֵי שִׂנְאָה סְבָבוּנִי וַיִּלָּחֲמוּנִי חִנָּם:
causeless   and they fought   they surrounded me   hatred   and speakings

3. They surrounded me with words of hatred; and fought against me without cause.

תַּחַת־אַהֲבָתִי יִשְׂטְנוּנִי וַאֲנִי תְפִלָּה:
towards prayer   and I   they my adversaries   my love - instead

4. In return for my love they are my accusers; but I give myself to prayer.

וַיָּשִׂימוּ עָלַי רָעָה תַּחַת טוֹבָה וְשִׂנְאָה תַּחַת אַהֲבָתִי:
my love   instead   and hatred   good   instead   evil   upon me   and they set

5. And they have rewarded me evil for good, and hatred for my love.

הַפְקֵד עָלָיו רָשָׁע וְשָׂטָן יַעֲמֹד עַל־יְמִינוֹ:
his right hand – upon   he will stand   and adversary   wicked   him over   appoint

6. Appoint a wicked man over him; and let Satan stand at his right hand.

בְּהִשָּׁפְטוֹ יֵצֵא רָשָׁע וּתְפִלָּתוֹ תִּהְיֶה לַחֲטָאָה:
to the sin   will be   and his prayer   wicked   he will go out   in his being judged

7. When he shall be judged, let him be condemned; and let his prayer become sin.

יִהְיוּ־יָמָיו מְעַטִּים פְּקֻדָּתוֹ יִקַּח אַחֵר:
another   will take   his office   few ones   his days – will be

8. Let his days be few; and let another seize his possessions.

יִהְיוּ־בָנָיו יְתוֹמִים וְאִשְׁתּוֹ אַלְמָנָה:
widow   and his wife   orphans   his sons - will be

9. Let his children become orphans, and his wife a widow.

וְנוֹעַ יָנוּעוּ בָנָיו וְשִׁאֵלוּ וְדָרְשׁוּ מֵחָרְבוֹתֵיהֶם:
from their desolate places   and seek   and they ask   his sons   they wander   and wondering

10. Let his children become vagabonds, and beg; let them seek their bread from their
desolate places.

יְנַקֵּשׁ נוֹשֶׁה לְכָל־אֲשֶׁר־לוֹ וְיָבֹזּוּ זָרִים יְגִיעוֹ:
his touching   strangers   and will spoil   to him   which - to all   extractor   he will lay a snare

11. Let the creditor seize everything that he has; and let strangers plunder his labor.

אַל־יְהִי־לֹו מֹשֵׁךְ חָסֶד וְאַל־יְהִי חֹונֵן לִיתֹומָיו׃

to his orphans gracious let be - and don't kindness one who continue to him - let be - don't

12. Let there be none to extend kindness to him; nor let there be any to favor his orphaned children.

יְהִי־אַחֲרִיתֹו לְהַכְרִית בְּדֹור אַחֵר יִמַּח שְׁמָם׃

their name will be blotted out another in generation to cutting off his posterity - will be

13. Let his posterity be cut off; and in the generation following let their name be blotted out.

יִזָּכֵר עֲוֹן אֲבֹתָיו אֶל־יְהֹוָה וְחַטַּאת אִמֹּו אַל־תִּמָּח׃

be blotted out – don't his mother and sin ihvh - unto his fathers inequity will be remembered

14. Let the iniquity of his fathers be remembered by the Lord; and let not the sin of his mother be blotted out.

יִהְיוּ נֶגֶד־יְהֹוָה תָּמִיד וְיַכְרֵת מֵאֶרֶץ זִכְרָם׃

their memory from earth he will cut off continually ihvh – before they will be

15. Let them be before the Lord continually, that he may cut off the memory of them from the earth.

יַעַן אֲשֶׁר לֹא זָכַר עֲשֹׂות חָסֶד

kindness to do he remembered not which because

וַיִּרְדֹּף אִישׁ־עָנִי וְאֶבְיֹון וְנִכְאֵה לֵבָב לְמֹותֵת׃

to death heart and broken and needy poor – man and he pursued

16. Because he did not remember to perform kindness, but pursued the poor and needy man, and the broken hearted to their death.

וַיֶּאֱהַב קְלָלָה וַתְּבֹואֵהוּ

and it came to him cursing and he loved

וְלֹא־חָפֵץ בִּבְרָכָה וַתִּרְחַק מִמֶּנּוּ׃

from him and it was far off in blessing he delighted and not

17. For he loved cursing, so let it come to him; as he delighted not in blessing, so let it be far from him.

וַיִּלְבַּשׁ קְלָלָה כְּמַדֹּו

like his garment cursing and he was clothed with

וַתָּבֹא כַמַּיִם בְּקִרְבֹּו וְכַשֶּׁמֶן בְּעַצְמֹותָיו׃

in his bones and like oil in his midst like waters and it came

18. And he clothed himself with cursing as his garment, so let it come into his bowels like water, and like oil into his bones.

תְּהִי־לֹו כְּבֶגֶד יַעְטֶה וּלְמֵזַח תָּמִיד יַחְגְּרֶהָ׃

he will gird himself continually and to a girdle he will cover himself like garment to him – let be

19. Let it be to him as the garment which he puts on, and as a girdle with which he is girded continually.

זֹאת פְּעֻלַּת שֹׂטְנַי מֵאֵת יְהֹוָה

this | wages of | my accusers | from that | ihvh

וְהַדֹּבְרִים רָע עַל־נַפְשִׁי:

and the speaking ones | bad | upon – my soul

20. Let this be the reward of my accusers from the Lord, and of those who speak evil against my soul.

וְאַתָּה יְהֹוִה אֲדֹנָי עֲשֵׂה־אִתִּי לְמַעַן שְׁמֶךָ

and you | ihvh | Adoni | do – with me | to end | your name

כִּי־טוֹב חַסְדְּךָ הַצִּילֵנִי:

good – like | your kindness | deliver me

21. But you, O God the Lord, do for me for your name's sake; because your loving kindness is good, save me.

כִּי־עָנִי וְאֶבְיוֹן אָנֹכִי וְלִבִּי חָלַל בְּקִרְבִּי:

poor - like | and needy | I am | and my heart | wounded | my midst

22. For I am poor and needy, and my heart is wounded within me.

כְּצֵל כִּנְטוֹתוֹ נֶהֱלָכְתִּי נִנְעַרְתִּי כָּאַרְבֶּה:

like shadow | like it stretches out | like his shadow | I have gone | I have been shaken | like locust

23. I am gone like the shadow at evening; I am shaken off like a locust.

my knees

בִּרְכַּי כָּשְׁלוּ מִצּוֹם וּבְשָׂרִי כָּחַשׁ מִשָּׁמֶן:

my knees | have stumbled | it weak | from fasting | and my flesh | failed | from fatness

24. My knees are weak through fasting; and my flesh lacks fatness.

וַאֲנִי הָיִיתִי חֶרְפָּה לָהֶם יִרְאוּנִי יְנִיעוּן רֹאשָׁם:

and I | have been | reproach | to them | they will see me | they will shake | their heads

25. I have become a taunt to them; when they see me, they shake their heads.

עָזְרֵנִי יְהֹוָה אֱלֹהָי הוֹשִׁיעֵנִי כְחַסְדֶּךָ:

help me | ihvh | Elohai | save me | like your kindness

26. Help me, O Lord my God; O save me according to your loving kindness;

וְיֵדְעוּ כִּי־יָדְךָ זֹּאת אַתָּה יְהֹוָה עֲשִׂיתָהּ:

and they will know | like – your hand | this | you | ihvh | have done it

27. That they may know that this is your hand; that you, Lord, have done it.

יְקַלְלוּ הֵמָּה וְאַתָּה תְבָרֵךְ קָמוּ וַיֵּבֹשׁוּ וְעַבְדְּךָ יִשְׂמָח:

they curse | they are | and you | you will bless | they arise | and were ashamed | and your servant | he will be glad

28. Let them curse, but you bless; when they arise, let them be ashamed; but let your servant rejoice.

יִלְבְּשׁוּ שׂוֹטְנַי כְּלִמָּה וְיַעֲטוּ כַמְעִיל בָּשְׁתָּם:

they will be clothed | my adversaries | confusion | and they will cover themselves | like the mantle | their shame

29. Let my adversaries be clothed with shame, and let them cover themselves with their own confusion, as with a robe.

אוֹדֶה   יְהֹוָה   מְאֹד   בְּפִי   וּבְתוֹךְ   רַבִּים   אֲהַלְלֶנּוּ׃

I will give thanks to · ihvh · greatly · in my mouth · and in midst · many · I will praise him

30. I will greatly praise the Lord with my mouth; I will praise him among the multitude.

כִּי־יַעֲמֹד   לִימִין   אֶבְיוֹן   לְהוֹשִׁיעַ   מִשֹּׁפְטֵי   נַפְשׁוֹ׃

he will stand - like · to his right hand · needy · to save · those who judge · his soul

31. For he stands at the right hand of the poor, to save him from those who condemn his soul.

PSALM 110

ספר תהילים פרק קי

לְדָוִד מִזְמוֹר נְאֻם יְהוָה לַאדֹנִי
to Adoni   ihvh   declared   psalm   to David

שֵׁב לִימִינִי עַד־אָשִׁית אֹיְבֶיךָ הֲדֹם לְרַגְלֶיךָ:
to your feet   stool   your enemies   I will make- until   to my right hand   sit

1. A Psalm of David. The Lord says to my master, Sit at my right hand, until I make your enemies your footstool.

מַטֵּה עֻזְּךָ יִשְׁלַח יְהוָה מִצִּיּוֹן רְדֵה בְּקֶרֶב אֹיְבֶיךָ:
your enemies   in midst   dominion   from Zion   ihvh   he sends   your strength   staff

2. The Lord sends your mighty scepter from Zion. Rule in the midst of your enemies!

עַמְּךָ נְדָבֹת בְּיוֹם חֵילֶךָ בְּהַדְרֵי־קֹדֶשׁ
holiness - in majesties   your might   in day   offering   your people

מֵרֶחֶם מִשְׁחָר לְךָ טַל יַלְדֻתֶיךָ:
your begattings   dew   to you   dawn   from womb

3. Your people offer themselves willingly on the day of your battle, in the majesty of holiness, from the womb of the morning, when the dew of your youth was upon you.

נִשְׁבַּע יְהוָה וְלֹא יִנָּחֵם אַתָּה־כֹהֵן לְעוֹלָם
to ever   priest – you   will repent   and not   ihvh   sworn

עַל־דִּבְרָתִי מַלְכִּי־צֶדֶק:
Zedek (righteous)-Melchi (kings)   speakings - upon

4. The Lord has sworn, and will not change his mind, You are a priest for ever, after the manner of Melchizedek.

אֲדֹנָי עַל־יְמִינְךָ מָחַץ בְּיוֹם־אַפּוֹ מְלָכִים:
kings   his anger - in day   shatters   your right hand - upon   Adoni

5. The Lord is at your right hand, he shall crush kings in the day of his wrath.

יָדִין בַּגּוֹיִם מָלֵא גְוִיּוֹת מָחַץ רֹאשׁ עַל־אֶרֶץ רַבָּה:
much   earth – upon   head   he shattered   corpses   he filled   in nations   he will judge

6. He shall judge among the nations, he shall fill the places with the dead bodies; he shall shatter heads over many countries.

מִנַּחַל בַּדֶּרֶךְ יִשְׁתֶּה עַל־כֵּן יָרִים רֹאשׁ:
head   he will exalt   thus-upon   he will drink   in way   from brook

7. He shall drink of the brook in the way; therefore he shall lift up the head.

PSALM 111

ספר תהילים פרק קיא

הַלְלוּיָהּ אוֹדֶה יְהוָה בְּכָל־לֵבָב בְּסוֹד יְשָׁרִים וְעֵדָה׃

and knowing upright ones in council heart - in all ihvh I will give thanks praise Ya

1 Praise ye the LORD. I will praise the LORD with *my* whole heart, in the assembly of the upright, and *in* the congregation.

גְּדֹלִים מַעֲשֵׂי יְהוָה דְּרוּשִׁים לְכָל־חֶפְצֵיהֶם׃

delighting them - to all sought out ones ihvh works great ones

2 The works of the LORD are great, sought out of all them that have pleasure therein.

הוֹד־וְהָדָר פָּעֳלוֹ וְצִדְקָתוֹ עֹמֶדֶת לָעַד׃

to ever standing and his righteousness his work and majesty – glory

3 His work is honourable and glorious: and his righteousness endureth for ever.

זֵכֶר עָשָׂה לְנִפְלְאֹתָיו חַנּוּן וְרַחוּם יְהוָה׃

ihvh and compassionate gracious to his mystical he made memorial

4 He hath made his wonderful works to be remembered: the LORD is gracious and full of compassion.

טֶרֶף נָתַן לִירֵאָיו יִזְכֹּר לְעוֹלָם בְּרִיתוֹ׃

his covenant to forever he remembers to his fearing he gave prey

5 He hath given meat unto them that fear him: he will ever be mindful of his covenant.

כֹּחַ מַעֲשָׂיו הִגִּיד לְעַמּוֹ לָתֵת לָהֶם נַחֲלַת גּוֹיִם׃

nations inheritances to them to give to his people the telling his works strength

6 He hath shewed his people the power of his works, that he may give them the heritage of the heathen.

מַעֲשֵׂי יָדָיו אֱמֶת וּמִשְׁפָּט נֶאֱמָנִים כָּל־פִּקּוּדָיו׃

his precepts – all faithful ones and judgment truth his hands works

7 The works of his hands are verity and judgment; all his commandments are sure.

סְמוּכִים לָעַד לְעוֹלָם עֲשׂוּיִם בֶּאֱמֶת וְיָשָׁר׃

and uprightness in truth accomplished ones to forever to time established ones

8 They stand fast for ever and ever, and are done in truth and uprightness.

פְּדוּת שָׁלַח לְעַמּוֹ צִוָּה לְעוֹלָם בְּרִיתוֹ קָדוֹשׁ וְנוֹרָא שְׁמוֹ׃

his name awesome holy his covenant to forever he commanded to his people he sent redemption

9 He sent redemption unto his people: he hath commanded his covenant for ever: holy and reverend is his name.

רֵאשִׁית חָכְמָה יִרְאַת יְהוָה שֵׂכֶל טוֹב לְכָל־עֹשֵׂיהֶם

doing them - to all good understanding ihvh fear wisdom beginning

תְּהִלָּתוֹ עֹמֶדֶת לָעַד׃

forever standing his prayer

10 The fear of the LORD is the beginning of wisdom: a good understanding have all they that do his commandments: his praise endureth for ever.

PSALM 112

ספר תהילים פרק קיב

הַלְלוּיָהּ אַשְׁרֵי־אִישׁ יָרֵא אֶת־יְהוָה בְּמִצְוֹתָיו חָפֵץ מְאֹד׃

greatly   delighting   in his commandments   ihvh – that   fearing   man - happy   praise Ya

1. Hallelujah! Happy is the man who fears the Lord, who delights greatly in his commandments.

גִּבּוֹר בָּאָרֶץ יִהְיֶה זַרְעוֹ דּוֹר יְשָׁרִים יְבֹרָךְ׃

will be blessed   upright ones   generation   his seed   will be   in earth   mighty

2. His seed shall be mighty upon earth; the generation of the upright shall be blessed.

הוֹן־וָעֹשֶׁר בְּבֵיתוֹ וְצִדְקָתוֹ עֹמֶדֶת לָעַד׃

to ever   standing   and his righteousness   in his house   and riches - wealth

3. Wealth and riches shall be in his house; and his righteousness will endure for ever.

זָרַח בַּחֹשֶׁךְ אוֹר לַיְשָׁרִים חַנּוּן וְרַחוּם וְצַדִּיק׃

and righteous   and compassionate   gracious   to upright ones   light   in darkness   shine

4. Light rises in the darkness for the upright; he is gracious, and full of compassion, and righteous.

טוֹב אִישׁ חוֹנֵן וּמַלְוֶה יְכַלְכֵּל דְּבָרָיו בְּמִשְׁפָּט׃

in judgment   his matters   he nourishes   and lending   gracious   man   good

5. A good man lends with a good grace; he conducts his affairs with justice.

כִּי־לְעוֹלָם לֹא יִמּוֹט לְזֵכֶר עוֹלָם יִהְיֶה צַדִּיק׃

righteous   will be   forever   to remembrance   will falter   not   forever - like

6. Surely he shall never be moved; the righteous shall be in everlasting remembrance.

מִשְּׁמוּעָה רָעָה לֹא יִירָא נָכוֹן לִבּוֹ בָּטֻחַ בַּיהוָה׃

in ihvh   trusting   his heart   established   he will fear   not   bad   from report

7. He shall not be afraid of evil tidings; his heart is firm, trusting in the Lord.

סָמוּךְ לִבּוֹ לֹא יִירָא עַד אֲשֶׁר־יִרְאֶה בְצָרָיו׃

in his enemies   he sees – which   till   he will fear   not   his heart   steadfast

8. His heart is steady, he shall not be afraid, until he gazes upon his enemies.

פִּזַּר נָתַן לָאֶבְיוֹנִים צִדְקָתוֹ עֹמֶדֶת לָעַד

to time   standing   his righteousness   to needy ones   he gave   he scattered

קַרְנוֹ תָּרוּם בְּכָבוֹד׃

in glory   will be exalted   his horn

9. He has distributed freely, he has given to the poor; his righteousness endures for ever; his horn shall be exalted with honor.

רָשָׁע יִרְאֶה וְכָעָס שִׁנָּיו

he will gnash   his teeth   and be angered   will see   wicked

יַחֲרֹק֙ וְנָמָ֑ס תַּאֲוַ֖ת רְשָׁעִ֣ים תֹּאבֵֽד׃

will perish   wicked ones   desire   and melt away

10. The wicked man shall see it, and be grieved; he shall gnash his teeth, and melt away; the desire of the wicked comes to naught.

PSALM 113

ספר תהילים פרק קיג

הַלְלוּיָהּ הַלְלוּ עַבְדֵי יְהוָֹה הַלְלוּ אֶת־שֵׁם יְהוָֹה:

ihvh   name – that   praise   ihvh   servants   praise   praise - Ya

1. Hallelujah! Praise, O you servants of the Lord, praise the name of the Lord.

יְהִי שֵׁם יְהוָֹה מְבֹרָךְ מֵעַתָּה וְעַד־עוֹלָם:

forever - and till   from now   blessed   ihvh   name   it be

2. Blessed be the name of the Lord from this time forth and for evermore.

מִמִּזְרַח־שֶׁמֶשׁ עַד־מְבוֹאוֹ מְהֻלָּל שֵׁם יְהוָֹה:

ihvh   name   praised   its setting – till   sun – from rising

3. From sunrise to sunset the Lord's name is to be praised.

רָם עַל־כָּל־גּוֹיִם יְהוָֹה עַל הַשָּׁמַיִם כְּבוֹדוֹ:

his glory   the heavens   upon   ihvh   nations – all – upon   high

4. The Lord is high above all nations, and his glory above the heavens.

מִי כַּיהוָֹה אֱלֹהֵינוּ הַמַּגְבִּיהִי לָשָׁבֶת:

to dwell   the one being elevated   our Elohim   like ihvh   who

5. Who is like the Lord our God, who dwells on high,

הַמַּשְׁפִּילִי לִרְאוֹת בַּשָּׁמַיִם וּבָאָרֶץ:

and in earth   in heavens   to seeing   the one looks far down

6. Who looks far down to behold the things that are on heaven, and on the earth!

מְקִימִי מֵעָפָר דָּל מֵאַשְׁפֹּת יָרִים אֶבְיוֹן:

needy   he rises up   from ash heap   poor   from dust   who raises

7. He raises up the poor from the dust, and lifts the needy from the ash heap,

לְהוֹשִׁיבִי עִם־נְדִיבִים עִם נְדִיבֵי עַמּוֹ:

his peoples   his princes   with   princes – with   to setting

8. That he may set him with nobles, with the nobles of his people.

מוֹשִׁיבִי עֲקֶרֶת הַבַּיִת אֵם־הַבָּנִים שְׂמֵחָה הַלְלוּיָהּ:

praise – Ya   happy   the sons – mother   the house   barren woman   one causing to dwell

9. He gives the barren woman a home, and makes her a joyful mother of children. Hallelujah!

PSALM 114

ספר תהילים פרק קי

בְּצֵאת יִשְׂרָאֵל מִמִּצְרָיִם בֵּית יַעֲקֹב מֵעַם לֹעֵז:

<small>foreign tongue — from people — Jacob — house — from Egypt — Israel — in going out</small>

1. When Israel went from Egypt, the house of Jacob from a people of foreign language;

הָיְתָה יְהוּדָה לְקָדְשׁוֹ יִשְׂרָאֵל מַמְשְׁלוֹתָיו:

<small>from his rulings — Israel — to his holy place — Judah — was</small>

2. Judah was his sanctuary, and Israel his dominion.

הַיָּם רָאָה וַיָּנֹס הַיַּרְדֵּן יִסֹּב לְאָחוֹר:

<small>to backward — it turned — the Jordan — and it fled — saw — the sea</small>

3. The sea saw it, and fled; the Jordan was driven back.

הֶהָרִים רָקְדוּ כְאֵילִים גְּבָעוֹת כִּבְנֵי־צֹאן:

<small>sheep – like sons — hills — like rams — skipped — the mountains</small>

4. The mountains skipped like rams, and the hills like lambs.

מַה־לְּךָ הַיָּם כִּי תָנוּס הַיַּרְדֵּן תִּסֹּב לְאָחוֹר:

<small>to backward — you turned — the Jordan — you flee — like — the sea — to you - what</small>

5. What ails you, O sea, that you flee? O Jordan, that you are driven back?

הֶהָרִים תִּרְקְדוּ כְאֵילִים גְּבָעוֹת כִּבְנֵי־צֹאן:

<small>sheep - like sons — hills — like rams — you skipped — the mountains</small>

6. O mountains, that you skip like rams? And you O hills, like lambs?

מִלִּפְנֵי אָדוֹן חוּלִי אָרֶץ מִלִּפְנֵי אֱלוֹהַּ יַעֲקֹב:

<small>Jacob — Elohim — from before — earth — tremble — Adon — from before</small>

7. Tremble, earth, at the presence of the Lord, at the presence of the God of Jacob;

הַהֹפְכִי הַצּוּר אֲגַם־מָיִם חַלָּמִישׁ לְמַעְיְנוֹ־מָיִם:

<small>waters – to fountain — flint — waters – pool — the rock — the turning</small>

8. Who turned the rock into a pool of water, the flint into a fountain of waters.

PSALM 115

ספר תהילים פרק קטו

לֹא לָנוּ יְהֹוָה לֹא לָנוּ כִּי לְשִׁמְךָ תֵּן כָּבוֹד

| honor | give | to your name | like | to us | not | ihvh | to us | not |

עַל־חַסְדְּךָ עַל־אֲמִתֶּךָ:

| your truth – upon | your mercy - upon |

1. Not to us, O Lord, not to us, but to your name give glory, for your loving kindness, and for your truth's sake.

לָמָּה יֹאמְרוּ הַגּוֹיִם אַיֵּה־נָא אֱלֹהֵיהֶם:

| their Elohim | now – where | the nations | they say | why |

2. Why should the nations say, Where is now their God?

וֵאלֹהֵינוּ בַשָּׁמָיִם כֹּל אֲשֶׁר־חָפֵץ עָשָׂה:

| he does | delights – which | all | in heavens | and our Elohim |

3. But our God is in the heavens; he does whatever he pleases.

עֲצַבֵּיהֶם כֶּסֶף וְזָהָב מַעֲשֵׂה יְדֵי אָדָם:

| Adam | hands | works | and gold | silver | their idols |

4. Their idols are silver and gold, the work of men's hands.

פֶּה־לָהֶם וְלֹא יְדַבֵּרוּ עֵינַיִם לָהֶם וְלֹא יִרְאוּ:

| they see | and not | to them | eyes | they speak | and not | to them - mouth |

5. They have mouths, but they cannot speak; they have eyes, but they can not see;

אָזְנַיִם לָהֶם וְלֹא יִשְׁמָעוּ אַף לָהֶם וְלֹא יְרִיחוּן:

| they smell | and not | to them | nose | they hear | and not | to them | ears |

6. They have ears, but they cannot hear; they have noses, but they can not smell;

יְדֵיהֶם וְלֹא יְמִישׁוּן רַגְלֵיהֶם וְלֹא יְהַלֵּכוּ

| they walk | and not | their feet | they feel | and not | their hands |

לֹא־יֶהְגּוּ בִּגְרוֹנָם:

| in their throats | they sound – not |

7. They have hands, but they cannot feel; they have feet, but they can not walk; and through their throat they cannot speak.

כְּמוֹהֶם יִהְיוּ עֹשֵׂיהֶם כֹּל אֲשֶׁר־בֹּטֵחַ בָּהֶם:

| in them | trusts – which | all | make them | they are | like them |

8. May they who make them become like them, and every one who trusts in them!

יִשְׂרָאֵל בְּטַח בַּיהֹוָה עֶזְרָם וּמָגִנָּם הוּא:

| he | and their shield | their help | in ihvh | trust | Israel |

9. O Israel, trust in the Lord; he is their help and their shield.

בֵּית אַהֲרֹן בִּטְחוּ בַיהֹוָה עֶזְרָם וּמָגִנָּם הוּא:

| he | their shield | their help | in ihvh | you trust | Aaaron | house |

10. O house of Aaron, trust in the Lord; he is their help and their shield.

יִרְאֵי יְהֹוָה בִּטְחוּ בַיהֹוָה עֶזְרָם וּמָגִנָּם הוּא:

| he | and their shield | their help | in ihvh | trust | ihvh | fearers |

11. You who fear the Lord, trust in the Lord; he is their help and their shield.

יְהֹוָה זְכָרָנוּ יְבָרֵךְ יְבָרֵךְ אֶת־בֵּית יִשְׂרָאֵל

| Israel | house – that | he will bless | he will bless | remembered us | ihvh |

יְבָרֵךְ אֶת־בֵּית אַהֲרֹן:

| Aaron | house – that | he will bless |

12. The Lord has been mindful of us; he will bless us; he will bless the house of Israel; he will bless the house of Aaron.

יְבָרֵךְ יִרְאֵי יְהֹוָה הַקְּטַנִּים עִם־הַגְּדֹלִים:

| the big ones – with | the small ones | ihvh | fearers | he will bless |

13. He will bless those who fear the Lord, both small and great.

יֹסֵף יְהֹוָה עֲלֵיכֶם עֲלֵיכֶם וְעַל־בְּנֵיכֶם:

| you – sons – and upon | upon you | upon you | ihvh | he adds |

14. May the Lord increase you more and more, you and your children.

בְּרוּכִים אַתֶּם לַיהֹוָה עֹשֵׂה שָׁמַיִם וָאָרֶץ:

| and earth | heavens | maker | to ihvh | to you | blessed ones |

15. May you be blessed of the Lord who made heaven and earth.

הַשָּׁמַיִם שָׁמַיִם לַיהֹוָה וְהָאָרֶץ נָתַן לִבְנֵי־אָדָם:

| Adam – to sons | he gave | and the earth | to ihvh | heavens | the heavens |

16. The heavens are the heavens of the Lord; but he has given the earth to the children of men.

לֹא־הַמֵּתִים יְהַלְלוּ־יָהּ וְלֹא כָּל־יֹרְדֵי דוּמָה:

| silence | descenders - all | and not | Yah – they praise | the dead ones - not |

17. The dead cannot praise the Lord, nor can any who go down into silence.

וַאֲנַחְנוּ נְבָרֵךְ יָהּ מֵעַתָּה וְעַד־עוֹלָם הַלְלוּיָהּ:

| praise Yah | ever – and till | from now | Yah | will bless | and we |

18. But we will bless the Lord from this time forth and for evermore. Hallelujah!

PSALM 116

ספר תהילים פרק קטז

אָהַבְתִּי כִּי־יִשְׁמַע יְהֹוָה אֶת־קוֹלִי תַּחֲנוּנָי:
my supplications   my voice – that   ihvh   he hears - like   I love

1. I love the Lord, because he has heard my voice and my supplications.

כִּי־הִטָּה אָזְנוֹ לִי וּבְיָמַי אֶקְרָא:
I will call   and in my days   to me   his ear   inclined - like

2. Because he has inclined his ear to me, therefore I will call upon him as long as I live.

אֲפָפוּנִי חֶבְלֵי־מָוֶת וּמְצָרֵי שְׁאוֹל מְצָאוּנִי
found me   Shoel   and confines   death – cords   surrounded me

צָרָה וְיָגוֹן אֶמְצָא:
I found   and sorrow   trouble

3. The cords of death surrounded me, and the pains of Sheol seized me. I found
trouble and sorrow.

וּבְשֵׁם־יְהֹוָה אֶקְרָא אָנָּה יְהֹוָה מַלְּטָה נַפְשִׁי:
my soul   make escape   ihvh   please   I called   ihvh - and in name

4. Then I called upon the name of the Lord; O Lord, I beseech you, save my soul.

חַנּוּן יְהֹוָה וְצַדִּיק וֵאלֹהֵינוּ מְרַחֵם:
merciful   and our Elohim   and righteous   ihvh   gracious

5. Gracious is the Lord, and righteous; our God is merciful.

שֹׁמֵר פְּתָאִים יְהֹוָה דַּלּוֹתִי וְלִי יְהוֹשִׁיעַ:
he saved me   and to me   I brought low   ihvh   simple ones   heeder

6. The Lord preserves the simple; I was brought low, and he saved me.

שׁוּבִי נַפְשִׁי לִמְנוּחָיְכִי כִּי יְהֹוָה גָּמַל עָלָיְכִי:
upon you   rewarded   ihvh   like   to it's rest   my soul   return

7. Return to your rest, O my soul; for the Lord has dealt bountifully with you.

כִּי חִלַּצְתָּ נַפְשִׁי מִמָּוֶת
from death   my soul   you delivered   like

אֶת־עֵינִי מִן־דִּמְעָה אֶת־רַגְלִי מִדֶּחִי:
from stumbling   my feet – that   tears – from   my eye - that

8. For you have saved my soul from death, my eyes from tears, and my feet from falling.

אֶתְהַלֵּךְ לִפְנֵי יְהֹוָה בְּאַרְצוֹת הַחַיִּים:
the living   in lands   ihvh   before   I will walk

9. I will walk before the Lord in the land of the living.

הֶאֱמַנְתִּי כִּי אֲדַבֵּר אֲנִי עָנִיתִי מְאֹד:
again   afflicted   I   I spoke   like   the I believed

10. I kept faith, even when I said, I am greatly afflicted;

אֲנִי אָמַרְתִּי בְחָפְזִי כָּל־הָאָדָם כֹּזֵב

lier the Adam – all in my haste I said I

11. I said in my haste, All men are false.

מָה־אָשִׁיב לַיהוָה כָּל־תַּגְמוּלוֹהִי עָלָי:

upon me his benefits – all to ihvh I will return what

12. How shall I repay the Lord for all his benefits toward me?

כּוֹס־יְשׁוּעוֹת אֶשָּׂא וּבְשֵׁם יְהוָה אֶקְרָא:

call ihvh and in name I will raise salvations - glass

13. I will raise the cup of salvation, and call upon the name of the Lord.

נְדָרַי לַיהוָה אֲשַׁלֵּם נֶגְדָה־נָּא לְכָל־עַמּוֹ:

his people - to all now – presence I will pay to ihvh my vows

14. I will pay my vows to the Lord now in the presence of all his people.

יָקָר בְּעֵינֵי יְהוָה הַמָּוְתָה לַחֲסִידָיו:

to his pious the death ihvh in eyes precious

15. Precious in the sight of the Lord is the death of his pious ones.

אָנָּה יְהוָה כִּי־אֲנִי עַבְדֶּךָ אֲנִי עַבְדְּךָ בֶּן־אֲמָתֶךָ

your handmaid - son your servant I your servant I – like ihvh I beg

פִּתַּחְתָּ לְמוֹסֵרָי:

to my bonds open

16. O Lord, truly I am your servant; I am your servant, the son of your maidservant; you have freed my bonds.

לְךָ־אֶזְבַּח זֶבַח תּוֹדָה וּבְשֵׁם יְהוָה אֶקְרָא:

I will call ihvh and in name thanks offerings I will offer - to you

17. I will offer to you the sacrifice of thanksgiving, and will call upon the name of the Lord.

נְדָרַי לַיהוָה אֲשַׁלֵּם נֶגְדָה־נָּא לְכָל־עַמּוֹ:

his people - to all now – presence I will pay to ihvh my vows

18. I will pay my vows to the Lord now in the presence of all his people,

בְּחַצְרוֹת בֵּית יְהוָה בְּתוֹכֵכִי יְרוּשָׁלָםִ הַלְלוּיָהּ:

praise – Ya Jerusalem in midst you ihvh house in courtyards

19. In the courts of the Lord's house, in the midst of you, O Jerusalem. Hallelujah!

PSALM 117

ספר תהילים פרק קיז

הַלְלוּ אֶת־יְהֹוָה כָּל־גּוֹיִם שַׁבְּחוּהוּ כָּל־הָאֻמִּים:

the peoples – all　　praise him　　nations – all　　ihvh – that　　praise

1. O Praise the Lord, all you nations; praise him, all you peoples.

כִּי גָבַר עָלֵינוּ חַסְדּוֹ וֶאֱמֶת־יְהֹוָה לְעוֹלָם הַלְלוּיָהּ:

praise Ya　　to forever　　ihvh - and truth　　his mercy　　upon us　　endures　　like

2. For his loving kindness is great toward us; and the truth of the Lord endures for ever. Hallelujah!

PSALM 118

ספר תהילים פרק קיח

הוֹדוּ לַיהֹוָה כִּי־טוֹב כִּי לְעוֹלָם חַסְדּוֹ:

his mercy　forever　like　good – like　to ihvh　you give thanks

1. O give thanks to the Lord; for he is good; because his loving kindness endures for ever.

יֹאמַר־נָא יִשְׂרָאֵל כִּי לְעוֹלָם חַסְדּוֹ:

his mercy　forever　like　Israel　now – will say

2. Let Israel now say, that his loving kindness endures for ever.

יֹאמְרוּ נָא בֵית־אַהֲרֹן כִּי לְעוֹלָם חַסְדּוֹ:

his mercy　forever　like　Aaron - house　now　they say

3. Let the house of Aaron now say, that his loving kindness endures for ever.

יֹאמְרוּ נָא יִרְאֵי יְהֹוָה כִּי לְעוֹלָם חַסְדּוֹ:

his mercy　forever　like　ihvh　fearers　now　they say

4. Let now those who fear the Lord say, that his loving kindness endures for ever.

מִן־הַמֵּצַר קָרָאתִי יָּה עָנָנִי בַמֶּרְחָב יָהּ:

Yah　n expanse　answered me　Yah　I called　the distress from

5. In distress I called upon the Lord; the Lord answered me, and set me free.

יְהֹוָה לִי לֹא אִירָא מַה־יַּעֲשֶׂה לִי אָדָם:

Adam　to me　he do – what　I will fear　not　to me　ihvh

6. The Lord is on my side; I will not fear; what can man do to me?

יְהֹוָה לִי בְּעֹזְרָי וַאֲנִי אֶרְאֶה בְשֹׂנְאָי:

in my haters　will see　and I　in help me to me　ihvh

7. The Lord takes my part with those who help me; therefore I shall gaze upon those who hate me.

טוֹב לַחֲסוֹת בַּיהֹוָה מִבְּטֹחַ בָּאָדָם:

in Adam　from trusting　in ihvh　to refuge　good

8. It is better to take refuge in the Lord than to put confidence in man.

טוֹב לַחֲסוֹת בַּיהֹוָה מִבְּטֹחַ בִּנְדִיבִים:

in princes　from trusting　in ihvh　to refuges　good

9. It is better to take refuge in the Lord than to put confidence in princes.

כָּל־גּוֹיִם סְבָבוּנִי בְּשֵׁם יְהֹוָה כִּי אֲמִילַם:

I will cut them off　like　ihvh　in name　surround me　nations - all

10. All nations surround me; but in the name of the Lord I will cut them off.

סַבּוּנִי גַם־סְבָבוּנִי בְּשֵׁם יְהֹוָה כִּי אֲמִילַם:

I will cut them off　like　ihvh　in name　they surround me - also　they surrounded me

11. They surround me; indeed, they surround me; but in the name of the Lord I will cut

them of.

סַבּוּנִי כִדְבוֹרִים דֹּעֲכוּ כְּאֵשׁ קוֹצִים

thorns   like fire   they quenched   like bees   they surround me

בְּשֵׁם יְהֹוָה כִּי אֲמִילַם׃

I will cut them off   like   ihvh   in name

12. They surround me like bees; they are quenched like a fire of thorns; for in the name of the Lord I will cut them off.

דָּחֹה דְּחִיתַנִי לִנְפֹּל וַיהֹוָה עֲזָרָנִי׃

helped me   and ihvh   to fall   you thrusted me   thrusting

13. You pushed me hard that I might fall; but the Lord helped me.

עָזִּי וְזִמְרָת יָהּ וַיְהִי־לִי לִישׁוּעָה׃

to salvation   to me - and was   Yah   and psalm song   my strength

14. The Lord is my strength and song, and he has become my salvation.

קוֹל רִנָּה וִישׁוּעָה בְּאָהֳלֵי צַדִּיקִים יְמִין יְהֹוָה עֹשָׂה חָיִל׃

bravery   does   ihvh   right hand   righteous ones   in tents   and salvation   shouting joy   voice

15. The voice of rejoicing and salvation is in the tents of the righteous; the right hand of the Lord does bravely.

יְמִין יְהֹוָה רוֹמֵמָה יְמִין יְהֹוָה עֹשָׂה חָיִל׃

bravery   does   ihvh   right hand   exalted   ihvh   right hand

16. The right hand of the Lord is exalted; the right hand of the Lord does bravely.

לֹא אָמוּת כִּי־אֶחְיֶה וַאֲסַפֵּר מַעֲשֵׂי יָהּ׃

Yah   works   and I declare   I will live - like   I will die   not

17. I shall not die, but live, and declare the works of the Lord.

יַסֹּר יִסְּרַנִּי יָּהּ וְלַמָּוֶת לֹא נְתָנָנִי׃

he gave me   not   and to death   Yah   he chastened me   chastening

18. The Lord has chastised me severely; but he has not given me over to death.

פִּתְחוּ־לִי שַׁעֲרֵי־צֶדֶק אָבֹא־בָם אוֹדֶה יָהּ׃

Yah   I will praise   in them – I will come   righteous – gates   to me - you open

19. Open to me the gates of righteousness; I will go into them, and I will praise the Lord;

זֶה־הַשַּׁעַר לַיהֹוָה צַדִּיקִים יָבֹאוּ בוֹ׃

in it   they come   righteous ones   to ihvh   the gate - this

20. This is the gate of the Lord, into which the righteous shall enter.

אוֹדְךָ כִּי עֲנִיתָנִי וַתְּהִי־לִי לִישׁוּעָה׃

to salvation   to me – and you were   you answered me   like   I will give you thanks

21. I will give you thanks; for you have answered me, and you have become my salvation.

אֶבֶן מָאֲסוּ הַבּוֹנִים הָיְתָה לְרֹאשׁ פִּנָּה׃

corner   to head   has been   the builder ones   rejected   stone

22. The stone which the builders rejected has become the head stone of the corner.

מֵאֵת יְהֹוָה הָיְתָה זֹּאת הִיא נִפְלָאת בְּעֵינֵינוּ׃

in our eyes   marvelous   it   this   has been   ihvh   from that

23. This is the Lord's doing; it is marvelous in our eyes.

זֶה־הַיּוֹם עָשָׂה יְהֹוָה נָגִילָה וְנִשְׂמְחָה בוֹ׃

in it   and we happy   we will rejoice   ihvh   made   the day - this

24. This is the day which the Lord has made; we will rejoice and be glad in it.

אָנָּא יְהֹוָה הוֹשִׁיעָה נָּא אָנָּא יְהֹוָה הַצְלִיחָה נָּא׃

now   the success   ihvh   I beseech   now   save   ihvh   I beseech

25. Save us, we beseech you, O Lord O Lord, we beseech you, send us prosperity!

בָּרוּךְ הַבָּא בְּשֵׁם יְהֹוָה בֵּרַכְנוּכֶם מִבֵּית יְהֹוָה׃

ihvh   from house   we blessed you   ihvh   in name   the come   blessed

26. Blessed is he who comes in the name of the Lord; we have blessed you from the house of the Lord.

אֵל יְהֹוָה וַיָּאֶר לָנוּ אִסְרוּ־חַג בַּעֲבֹתִים עַד קַרְנוֹת הַמִּזְבֵּחַ׃

the altar   horns   till   in cords   festival – bind you   to us   and light   ihvh   El

27. God is the Lord, who has shown us light; bind the sacrifice with cords, to the horns of the altar.

אֵלִי אַתָּה וְאוֹדֶךָּ אֱלֹהַי אֲרוֹמְמֶךָּ׃

I will exalt you   my Elohim   and I will thank you   you   my El

28. You are my God, and I will praise you; you are my God, I will exalt you.

הוֹדוּ לַיהֹוָה כִּי־טוֹב כִּי לְעוֹלָם חַסְדּוֹ׃

his mercy   forever   like   good - like   to ihvh   you thank

29. O give thanks to the Lord; for he is good; for his loving kindness endures for ever.

PSALM 119

א

אַשְׁרֵי תְמִימֵי דָרֶךְ הַהֹלְכִים בְּתוֹרַת יְהֹוָה׃

ihvh   in Torah   the walking ones   way   perfect   happy

1. Happy are those whose way is blameless, who walk in the Torah of the Lord.

אַשְׁרֵי נֹצְרֵי עֵדֹתָיו בְּכָל־לֵב יִדְרְשׁוּהוּ׃

they seek him   heart - in all   his testimonies   preservers   happy

2. Happy are those who keep his testimonies, and who seek him with the whole heart.

אַף לֹא פָעֲלוּ עַוְלָה בִּדְרָכָיו הָלָכוּ׃

they walk   in his way   inequity   they act   not   then

3. They also do no iniquity; they walk in his ways.

אַתָּה צִוִּיתָה פִקֻּדֶיךָ לִשְׁמֹר מְאֹד׃

greatly   to heed   your precepts   commanded   you

4. You have commanded us to keep your precepts diligently.

אַחֲלַי יִכֹּנוּ דְרָכָי לִשְׁמֹר חֻקֶּיךָ׃

your statutes   to heed   my way   you established   my path

5. O that my ways were directed to keep your statutes!

אָז לֹא אֵבוֹשׁ בְּהַבִּיטִי אֶל כָּל מִצְוֹתֶיךָ׃

your commandments   all   unto   in my observing   I will be ashamed   not   then

6. Then I shall not be ashamed, when I observe to all your commandments.

אוֹדְךָ בְּיֹשֶׁר לֵבָב בְּלָמְדִי מִשְׁפְּטֵי צִדְקֶךָ׃

your righteous   judgments   in my learning   heart   in upright   I thank you

7. I shall give thanks with uprightness of heart, when I learn your righteous judgments.

אֶת חֻקֶּיךָ אֶשְׁמֹר אַל תַּעַזְבֵנִי עַד מְאֹד׃

greatly   till   you forsake me   don't   I will heed   your statutes   that

8. I will keep your statutes; O do not forsake me utterly

ב

בַּמֶּה יְזַכֶּה נַּעַר אֶת אָרְחוֹ לִשְׁמֹר כִּדְבָרֶךָ׃
like your sayings   to heeding   road   that   youth   he clean   in what

9. How can a young man keep his way pure? By guarding it according to your word.

בְּכָל לִבִּי דְרַשְׁתִּיךָ אַל תַּשְׁגֵּנִי מִמִּצְוֹתֶיךָ׃
from your commandments you stray me don't I sought you my heart in all

10. With my whole heart I have sought you; O do not let wander from your commandments!

בְּלִבִּי צָפַנְתִּי אִמְרָתֶךָ לְמַעַן לֹא אֶחֱטָא לָךְ׃
to you   I will sin   not   to end   your word   I have hid   in my heart

11. I have hidden your word in my heart, that I might not sin against you.

בָּרוּךְ אַתָּה יְהוָה לַמְּדֵנִי חֻקֶּיךָ׃
your statutes   teach me   ihvh   you   blessed

12. Blessed are you, O Lord; teach me your statutes.

בִּשְׂפָתַי סִפַּרְתִּי כֹּל מִשְׁפְּטֵי פִיךָ׃
your mouth   judgments   all   I declared   in my lips

13. With my lips I have declared all the judgments of your mouth.

בְּדֶרֶךְ עֵדְוֹתֶיךָ שַׂשְׂתִּי כְּעַל כָּל הוֹן׃
fulfillment   all   like upon   I rejoiced   your testimonies   in way

14. I have rejoiced in the way of your testimonies, as much as in all riches.

בְּפִקֻּדֶיךָ אָשִׂיחָה וְאַבִּיטָה אֹר חֹתֶיךָ׃
your road   light   and I observe   I will meditate   in your precepts

15. I will meditate in your precepts, and observe your ways.

בְּחֻקֹּתֶיךָ אֶשְׁתַּעֲשָׁע לֹא אֶשְׁכַּח דְּבָרֶךָ׃
your sayings   I will forget   not   I will delight   in your statutes

16. I will delight myself in your statutes; I will not forget your word.

ג

גְּמֹל עַל עַבְדְּךָ אֶחְיֶה וְאֶשְׁמְרָה דְבָרֶךָ:

your sayings   and I will heed   I will live   your servant   upon   treat

17. Deal bountifully with your servant, that I may live, and keep your word.

גַּל עֵינַי וְאַבִּיטָה נִפְלָאוֹת מִתּוֹרָתֶךָ:

from your Torah   mysticals   and I will behold   my eye   roll

18. Open my eyes, that I may behold wondrous things in your Torah.

גֵּר אָנֹכִי בָאָרֶץ אַל תַּסְתֵּר מִמֶּנִּי מִצְוֹתֶיךָ:

your commandments   from me   you hide   don't   in earth   I am   stranger

19. I am a stranger on earth; do not hide your commandments from me.

גָּרְסָה נַפְשִׁי לְתַאֲבָה אֶל מִשְׁפָּטֶיךָ בְכָל עֵת:

times   in all   your judgments   unto   to be longing   my soul   consumed

20. My soul is consumed with longing for your judgments at all times.

גָּעַרְתָּ זֵדִים אֲרוּרִים הַשֹּׁגִים מִמִּצְוֹתֶיךָ:

from your commandments   erring ones   cursed ones   arrogant ones   you rebuked

21. You have rebuked the arrogant who are cursed, who wander from your commandments.

גַּל מֵעָלַי חֶרְפָּה וָבוּז כִּי עֵדֹתֶיךָ נָצָרְתִּי:

I kept   your testimonies   like   and contempt   insult   from upon me   roll

22. Remove from me insult and contempt; for I have kept your testimonies.

גַּם יָשְׁבוּ שָׂרִים בִּי נִדְבָּרוּ עַבְדְּךָ יָשִׂיחַ בְּחֻקֶּיךָ:

in your statutes   meditated   your servant   they spoke   in me   princes   they sat   also

23. Princes also sat and spoke against me; but your servant meditated in your statutes.

גַּם עֵדֹתֶיךָ שַׁעֲשֻׁעָי אַנְשֵׁי עֲצָתִי:

my advisories   my men   my delight   your testimonies   also

24. Your testimonies also are my delight and my counselors.

ד

דָּבְקָה לֶעָפָר נַפְשִׁי חַיֵּנִי כִּדְבָרֶךָ׃
like your sayings   give me life   my soul   to dust   clings

25. My soul cleaves to the dust; revive me according to your word.

דְּרָכַי סִפַּרְתִּי וַתַּעֲנֵנִי לַמְּדֵנִי חֻקֶּיךָ׃
your statutes   teach me   and you answered   I declared   my path

26. I have declared my ways, and you heard me; teach me your statutes.

דֶּרֶךְ פִּקּוּדֶיךָ הֲבִינֵנִי וְאָשִׂיחָה בְּנִפְלְאוֹתֶיךָ׃
in your wonders   and I will meditate   the my understand   your precepts   path

27. Make me understand the way of your precepts; so I shall talk of your wondrous works.

דָּלְפָה נַפְשִׁי מִתּוּגָה קַיְּמֵנִי כִּדְבָרֶךָ׃
like your speakings   raise me   from sorrow   my soul   melts

28. My soul melts away for sorrow; strengthen me according to your word.

דֶּרֶךְ שֶׁקֶר הָסֵר מִמֶּנִּי וְתוֹרָתְךָ חָנֵּנִי׃
grant me   and your torah   from me   remove   lie   the path

29. Put the ways of falsehood away from me; and grant me your Torah graciously.

דֶּרֶךְ אֱמוּנָה בָחָרְתִּי מִשְׁפָּטֶיךָ שִׁוִּיתִי׃
laic before me   your judgments   I chose   truth   path

30. I have chosen the way of truth; your judgments have I laid before me.

דָּבַקְתִּי בְעֵדְוֹתֶיךָ יְהֹוָה אַל תְּבִישֵׁנִי׃
you shame me   don't   ihvh   in your testimonies   I cleaved

31. I cleave to your testimonies; O Lord, put me not to shame.

דֶּרֶךְ מִצְוֹתֶיךָ אָרוּץ כִּי תַרְחִיב לִבִּי׃
my heart   it will enlarge   like   I run   your commandments   the path

32. I will run the way of your commandments, when you shall enlarge my heart.

ה

הוֹרֵנִי יְהֹוָה דֶּרֶךְ חֻקֶּיךָ וְאֶצְּרֶנָּה עֵקֶב:

teach me   ihvh   path   your statutes   and I will keep   end

33. Teach me, O Lord, the way of your statutes; and I shall keep it to the end.

הֲבִינֵנִי וְאֶצְּרָה תוֹרָתֶךָ וְאֶשְׁמְרֶנָּה בְכָל לֵב:

the my understanding   and I will keep   your Torah   and I will heed it   in all   heart

34. Give me understanding, and I shall keep your Torah; I shall observe it with my whole heart.

הַדְרִיכֵנִי בִּנְתִיב מִצְוֹתֶיךָ כִּי בוֹ חָפָצְתִּי:

the path of me   in lead   your commandments   like   in it   I delight

35. Lead me in the path of your commandments; for I delight in it.

הַט לִבִּי אֶל עֵדְוֹתֶיךָ וְאַל אֶל בָּצַע:

incline my heart   unto   your testimonies   and don't   unto   unjust gain

36. Incline my heart to your testimonies, and not to unjust gain.

הַעֲבֵר עֵינַי מֵרְאוֹת שָׁוְא בִּדְרָכֶךָ חַיֵּנִי:

the pass   my eyes   from seeing   vanity   in your way   give me life

37. Turn away my eyes from beholding vanity; and give me life in your way.

הָקֵם לְעַבְדְּךָ אִמְרָתֶךָ אֲשֶׁר לְיִרְאָתֶךָ:

confirm   to your servant   your word   which   to fearing you

38. Confirm to your servant your word. which is for those who fear you.

הַעֲבֵר חֶרְפָּתִי אֲשֶׁר יָגֹרְתִּי כִּי מִשְׁפָּטֶיךָ טוֹבִים:

the pass   my insult   which   I feared   like   your judgments   good ones

39. Turn away my insult which I fear; for your judgments are good.

הִנֵּה תָּאַבְתִּי לְפִקֻּדֶיךָ בְּצִדְקָתְךָ חַיֵּנִי:

here is   I longed   to your precepts   in your righteousness   give me life

40. Behold, I have longed after your precepts; give me life in your righteousness.

וֹ

וִיבֹאֻנִי   חֲסָדֶךָ   יְהֹוָה   תְּשׁוּעָתְךָ   כְּאִמְרָתֶךָ:
and come to me   your mercies   ihvh   your salvation   like your word

41. Let your loving kindness come also to me, O Lord, your salvation, according to your word.

וְאֶעֱנֶה   חֹרְפִי   דָבָר   כִּי   בָטַחְתִּי   בִּדְבָרֶךָ:
and I will answer   my insulter   speech   like   my trust   in your sayings

42. So shall I have an answer for him who insults me; for I trust in your word.

וְאַל   תַּצֵּל   מִפִּי   דְבַר   אֱמֶת   עַד   מְאֹד
and don't   take away   from my mouth   speech   truth   till   again

כִּי   לְמִשְׁפָּטֶךָ   יִחָלְתִּי:
like   to your judgments   I hoped

43. And do not take the word of truth utterly from my mouth; for I have hoped in your judgments.

וְאֶשְׁמְרָה   תוֹרָתְךָ   תָמִיד   לְעוֹלָם   וָעֶד:
and I will heed   your Torah   always   to forever   and time

44. So shall I keep your Torah continually for ever and ever.

וְאֶתְהַלְּכָה   בָרְחָבָה   כִּי   פִקֻּדֶיךָ   דָרָשְׁתִּי:
and I will walk   in liberty   like   your precepts   I seek

45. And I will walk at liberty; for I seek your precepts.

וַאֲדַבְּרָה   בְעֵדֹתֶיךָ   נֶגֶד   מְלָכִים   וְלֹא   אֵבוֹשׁ:
and I will speak   in testimonies   before   kings   and not   I will be ashamed

46. I will also speak of your testimonies before kings, and will not be ashamed.

וְאֶשְׁתַּעֲשַׁע   בְּמִצְוֹתֶיךָ   אֲשֶׁר   אָהָבְתִּי:
and I will delight   in your commandments   which   I loved

47. And I will delight myself in your commandments, which I have loved.

וְאֶשָּׂא   כַפַּי   אֶל   מִצְוֹתֶיךָ   אֲשֶׁר   אָהָבְתִּי   וְאָשִׂיחָה   בְחֻקֶּיךָ:
and I will lift   my palms   onto   your commandments   which   I loved   and I will meditate   in your statutes

48. My hands also I will lift up to your commandments, which I have loved; and I will meditate in your statutes.

ז

זְכֹר דָּבָר לְעַבְדֶּךָ עַל אֲשֶׁר יִחַלְתָּנִי:
it [gives] hope to me   which   upon   to your servant   speak   remember

49. Remember the word to your servant, whereby you have given me hope.

זֹאת נֶחָמָתִי בְעָנְיִי כִּי אִמְרָתְךָ חִיָּתְנִי:
life [to] me   your word   like   in my affliction   I comforted   this is

50. This is my comfort in my affliction; for your word has revived me.

זֵדִים הֱלִיצֻנִי עַד מְאֹד מִתּוֹרָתְךָ לֹא נָטִיתִי:
I turned away   not   from your torah   greatly   till   cause me derision   the proud ones

51. The arrogant have had me greatly in derision; but I have not turned away from your Torah.

זָכַרְתִּי מִשְׁפָּטֶיךָ מֵעוֹלָם יְהֹוָה וָאֶתְנֶחָם:
and I am comforted   ihvh   from forever   your judgments   I remembered

52. I remembered your judgments of old, O Lord; and have comforted myself.

זַלְעָפָה אֲחָזַתְנִי מֵרְשָׁעִים עֹזְבֵי תוֹרָתֶךָ:
your Torah   forsakers   from wicked ones   took hold of me   horror

53. Horror has taken hold of me because of the wicked who forsake your Torah.

זְמִרוֹת הָיוּ לִי חֻקֶּיךָ בְּבֵית מְגוּרָי:
my pilgrimage   in house   your statutes   to me   have been   songs

54. Your statutes have been my songs in the house of my pilgrimage.

זָכַרְתִּי בַלַּיְלָה שִׁמְךָ יְהֹוָה וָאֶשְׁמְרָה תּוֹרָתֶךָ:
your Torah   and I heeded   ihvh   your name   in night   I remembered

55. I have remembered your name, O Lord, in the night, and have kept your Torah.

זֹאת הָיְתָה לִּי כִּי פִקֻּדֶיךָ נָצָרְתִּי:
I kept   your precepts   like   to me   I had   this

56. This I had, because I kept your precepts.

ח

חֶלְקִי יְהֹוָה אָמַרְתִּי לִשְׁמֹר דְּבָרֶיךָ׃
your sayings   to heed   I said   ihvh   my portion

57. You are my portion, O Lord; I have said that I would keep your words.

חִלִּיתִי פָנֶיךָ בְכָל־לֵב חָנֵּנִי כְּאִמְרָתֶךָ׃
like your word   grant me   heart - in all   your face   I entreated

58. I entreated your favor with my whole heart; be merciful to me according to your word.

חִשַּׁבְתִּי דְרָכָי וָאָשִׁיבָה רַגְלַי אֶל עֵדֹתֶיךָ׃
your testimonies unto   my feet   and returned toward   my ways   I thought

59. I thought on my ways, and turned my feet to your testimonies.

חַשְׁתִּי וְלֹא הִתְמַהְמָהְתִּי לִשְׁמֹר מִצְוֹתֶיךָ׃
your commandments   to heed   I delayed   and not   I hastened

60. I made haste, and did not delay to keep your commandments.

חֶבְלֵי רְשָׁעִים עִוְּדֻנִי תּוֹרָתְךָ לֹא שָׁכָחְתִּי׃
I forgot   not   your Torah   robbed me   wicked ones   bands

61. Bands of wicked men have robbed me; but I have not forgotten your Torah.

חֲצוֹת־לַיְלָה אָקוּם לְהוֹדוֹת לָךְ עַל מִשְׁפְּטֵי צִדְקֶךָ׃
your righteous   judgments   upon   to you   to thankings   I will rise   night - mid

62. At midnight I will rise to give thanks to you because of your righteous judgments.

חָבֵר אָנִי לְכָל־אֲשֶׁר יְרֵאוּךָ וּלְשֹׁמְרֵי פִּקּוּדֶיךָ׃
your precepts   and to heeders   they fear you   which - to all   I   friend

63. I am a companion of all those who fear you, and of those who keep your precepts.

חַסְדְּךָ יְהֹוָה מָלְאָה הָאָרֶץ חֻקֶּיךָ לַמְּדֵנִי׃
teach me   your statutes   the earth   full   ihvh   your mercy

64. The earth, O Lord, is full of your loving kindness; teach me your statutes.

ט

טוֹב עָשִׂיתָ עִם־עַבְדְּךָ יְהֹוָה כִּדְבָרֶךָ׃
like your sayings   ihvh   your servant - with   you did   good

65. You have dealt well with your servant, O Lord, according to your word.

טוֹב טַעַם וָדַעַת לַמְּדֵנִי כִּי בְמִצְוֹתֶיךָ הֶאֱמָנְתִּי׃
the I believed   in your commandments   like   teach me   and knowledge   reason   good

66. Teach me good judgment and knowledge; for I have believed your commandments.

טֶרֶם אֶעֱנֶה אֲנִי שֹׁגֵג וְעַתָּה אִמְרָתְךָ שָׁמָרְתִּי׃
I heed   your word   and now   astray one   I   I afflicted   before

67. Before I was afflicted I went astray; but now I observe your word.

טוֹב־אַתָּה וּמֵטִיב לַמְּדֵנִי חֻקֶּיךָ׃
your statutes   teach me   and beneficial   you - good

68. You are good, and you do good; teach me your statutes.

טָפְלוּ עָלַי שֶׁקֶר זֵדִים אֲנִי בְּכָל־לֵב אֶצֹּר פִּקּוּדֶיךָ׃
your precepts   I will keep   heart - in all   I   arrogant ones   lies   upon me   they smear

69. The arrogant smear me with lies; but I will keep your precepts with my whole heart.

טָפַשׁ כַּחֵלֶב לִבָּם אֲנִי תּוֹרָתְךָ שִׁעֲשָׁעְתִּי׃
my delight   your torah   I   their heart   like fat   gross

70. Their heart is gross like fat; but I delight in your Torah.

טוֹב־לִי כִי־עֻנֵּיתִי לְמַעַן אֶלְמַד חֻקֶּיךָ׃
your statutes   I will learn   to end   I afflicted - like   to me - Good

71. It is good for me that I have been afflicted; that I might learn your statutes.

טוֹב־לִי תוֹרַת פִּיךָ מֵאַלְפֵי זָהָב וָכָסֶף׃
and silver   gold   from thousand   your mouth   Torah   to me - good

72. The Torah of your mouth is better to me than thousands of gold and silver.

י

יָדֶיךָ   עָשׂוּנִי   וַיְכוֹנְנוּנִי   הֲבִינֵנִי   וְאֶלְמְדָה מִצְוֹתֶיךָ:

your commandments   and I will learn   the my understanding   and they established me   made me   your hands

73. Your hands have made me and fashioned me; give me understanding, that I may learn your commandments.

יְרֵאֶיךָ   יִרְאוּנִי   וְיִשְׂמָחוּ   כִּי   לִדְבָרְךָ   יִחָלְתִּי:

I hoped   to your saying   like   and they will be happy   they will see me   your fearing

74. Those who fear you will be glad when they see me; because I have hoped in your word.

יָדַעְתִּי   יְהֹוָה   כִּי־צֶדֶק   מִשְׁפָּטֶיךָ   וֶאֱמוּנָה   עִנִּיתָנִי:

afflicted me   and faithfulness   your judgments   righteous - like   ihvh   I know

75. I know, O Lord, that your judgments are right, and that you in faithfulness have afflicted me.

יְהִי־נָא   חַסְדְּךָ   לְנַחֲמֵנִי   כְּאִמְרָתְךָ   לְעַבְדֶּךָ:

to your servant   like your word   to comfort me   your mercy   now - it be

76. Let, I pray you, your loving kindness be for my comfort, according to your word to your servant.

יְבֹאוּנִי   רַחֲמֶיךָ   וְאֶחְיֶה   כִּי   תוֹרָתְךָ   שַׁעֲשֻׁעָי:

my delight   your Torah   like   and I will live   your mercies   they come to me

77. Let your mercies come to me, that I may live; for your Torah is my delight.

יֵבֹשׁוּ   זֵדִים   כִּי־שֶׁקֶר   עִוְּתוּנִי   אֲנִי   אָשִׂיחַ   בְּפִקּוּדֶיךָ:

in your precepts   will meditate   I   dealt perversely to me   lies - like   arrogant ones   they ashamed

78. Let the arrogant be ashamed; for they dealt perversely with me without a cause; but I will meditate on your precepts.

יָשׁוּבוּ־לִי   יְרֵאֶיךָ   וְיֹדְעֵו   עֵדֹתֶיךָ:

your testimonies   and his knowing   your fearing ones   to me - they return

79. (K) Let those who fear you turn to me, and those who have known your testimonies.

יְהִי־לִבִּי   תָמִים   בְּחֻקֶּיךָ   לְמַעַן   לֹא   אֵבוֹשׁ:

I ashamed   not   to end   in your statutes   perfect   my heart - it be

80. Let my heart be sound in your statutes; that I be not ashamed.

כ

כָּלְתָה לִתְשׁוּעָתְךָ נַפְשִׁי לִדְבָרְךָ יִחָלְתִּי׃

<small>I hope   to your saying   my soul   to your salvation   languishes</small>

81. My soul languishes for your salvation; I hope in your word.

כָּלוּ עֵינַי לְאִמְרָתֶךָ לֵאמֹר מָתַי תְּנַחֲמֵנִי׃

<small>you will comfort me   when   to say   to your word   my eyes   fails</small>

82. My eyes fail longing for your word, saying, When will you comfort me?

כִּי־הָיִיתִי כְּנֹאד בְּקִיטוֹר חֻקֶּיךָ לֹא שָׁכָחְתִּי׃

<small>I forgot   not   your statutes   in smoke   like wineskin   I was - like</small>

83. For I have become like a wineskin in the smoke; yet I do not forget your statutes.

כַּמָּה יְמֵי עַבְדֶּךָ מָתַי תַּעֲשֶׂה בְרֹדְפַי מִשְׁפָּט׃

<small>judgment   in my persecutors   will you do   how long   your servant   days   how many</small>

84. How many are the days of your servant? When will you execute judgment on those who persecute me?

כָּרוּ־לִי זֵדִים שִׁיחוֹת אֲשֶׁר לֹא כְתוֹרָתֶךָ׃

<small>like to your torah   not   which   pits   proud ones   to me - they dug</small>

85. The arrogant dug pits for me, which are not according to your Torah.

כָּל־מִצְוֺתֶיךָ אֱמוּנָה שֶׁקֶר רְדָפוּנִי עָזְרֵנִי׃

<small>help me   they persecute me   lies   faithful   your commandments - all</small>

86. All your commandments are faithful; they persecute me wrongfully; help me.

כִּמְעַט כִּלּוּנִי בָאָרֶץ וַאֲנִי לֹא עָזַבְתִּי פִּקּוּדֶיךָ׃

<small>your precepts   have forsaken   not   and I   in earth   consumed me   like a little</small>

87. They had almost consumed me on earth; but I have not forsaken your precepts.

כְּחַסְדְּךָ חַיֵּנִי וְאֶשְׁמְרָה עֵדוּת פִּיךָ׃

<small>your mouth   testimonies   and I will heed   give me life   like your kindness</small>

88. In your loving kindness spare my life; so I shall keep the testimony of your mouth.

לְ

לְעוֹלָם יְהוָה דְּבָרְךָ נִצָּב בַּשָּׁמָיִם:
in heavens   fixed   your sayings   ihvh   to forever

89. For ever, O Lord, your word is fixed in heaven.

לְדֹר וָדֹר אֱמוּנָתֶךָ כּוֹנַנְתָּ אֶרֶץ וַתַּעֲמֹד:
and it stands   earth   you established   your faithfulness   and generation   to generation

90. Your faithfulness endures to all generations; you have established the earth, and it stands firm.

לְמִשְׁפָּטֶיךָ עָמְדוּ הַיּוֹם כִּי הַכֹּל עֲבָדֶיךָ:
your servants   the all   like   the day   they stand   to your judgements

91. They continue this day according to your ordinances; for all are your servants.

לוּלֵי תוֹרָתְךָ שַׁעֲשֻׁעָי אָז אָבַדְתִּי בְעָנְיִי:
in my affliction   I perished   then   my delight   your torah   had it not been

92. If your Torah had not been my delight, I should have perished in my affliction.

לְעוֹלָם לֹא אֶשְׁכַּח פִּקּוּדֶיךָ כִּי בָם חִיִּיתָנִי:
life to me   in them   like   your precepts   I will forget   not   to forever

93. I will never forget your precepts; for with them you have given me life.

לְךָ אֲנִי הוֹשִׁיעֵנִי כִּי פִקּוּדֶיךָ דָרָשְׁתִּי:
I sought   your precepts   like   save me   I   to you

94. I am yours, save me; for I have sought your precepts.

לִי קִוּוּ רְשָׁעִים לְאַבְּדֵנִי עֵדֹתֶיךָ אֶתְבּוֹנָן:
I will consider   your testimonies   to destroy me   the wicked   they waited   to me

95. The wicked have waited for me to destroy me; but I will consider your testimonies.

לְכָל תִּכְלָה רָאִיתִי קֵץ רְחָבָה מִצְוָתְךָ מְאֹד:
greatly   your commandment   broad   limits   I saw   perfection   to all

96. I have seen a limit to all perfection; but your commandment is exceedingly broad.

מ

מָה אָהַבְתִּי תוֹרָתֶךָ כָּל הַיּוֹם הִיא שִׂיחָתִי:

how | I loved | your torah | all | the day | it | my meditation

97. O how I love your Torah! It is my meditation all the day.

מֵאֹיְבַי תְּחַכְּמֵנִי מִצְוֺתֶךָ כִּי לְעוֹלָם הִיא לִי:

from my enemies | it made me wise | your commandments | like - | to forever | it | to me

98. Your commandments have made me wiser than my enemies; for they are always with me.

מִכָּל מְלַמְּדַי הִשְׂכַּלְתִּי כִּי עֵדְוֺתֶיךָ שִׂיחָה לִי:

from all | my teachers | I comprehended | like | your testimonies | meditation | to me

99. I have more understanding than all my teachers; for your testimonies are my meditation.

מִזְּקֵנִים אֶתְבּוֹנָן כִּי פִקּוּדֶיךָ נָצָרְתִּי:

from elder ones | I understand | like | your precepts | I keep

100. I understand more than the elders, because I keep your precepts.

מִכָּל אֹרַח רָע כָּלִאתִי רַגְלָי לְמַעַן אֶשְׁמֹר דְּבָרֶךָ:

from all | way | bad | I refrained | my feet | to end | I will heed | your sayings

101. I have refrained my feet from every evil way, that I might keep your word.

מִמִּשְׁפָּטֶיךָ לֹא סָרְתִּי כִּי אַתָּה הוֹרֵתָנִי:

from your judgments | not | I departed | like | you | taught me

102. I have not departed from your judgments; for you have taught me.

מָה נִּמְלְצוּ לְחִכִּי אִמְרָתֶךָ מִדְּבַשׁ לְפִי:

how | they sweet | to my taste | your words | from honey | to my mouth

103. How sweet are your words to my taste! Sweeter than honey to my mouth!

מִפִּקּוּדֶיךָ אֶתְבּוֹנָן עַל כֵּן שָׂנֵאתִי כָּל אֹרַח שָׁקֶר:

from your precepts | I understand | upon | thus | I hate | all | roads | lies

104. Through your precepts I get understanding; therefore I hate every false way.

נ

נֵר לְרַגְלִי דְבָרֶךָ וְאוֹר לִנְתִיבָתִי:

to my path   and light   your sayings   to my feet   lamp

105. Your word is a lamp to my feet, and a light to my path.

נִשְׁבַּעְתִּי וָאֲקַיֵּמָה לִשְׁמֹר מִשְׁפְּטֵי צִדְקֶךָ:

your righteous   judgments   to heed   and I will execute   I swore

106. I have sworn, and I will perform it, that I will keep your righteous judgments.

נַעֲנֵיתִי עַד מְאֹד יְהוָה חַיֵּנִי כִדְבָרֶךָ:

like your word   give me life   ihvh   greatly   till   'm afflicted

107. I am very much afflicted; revive me, O Lord, according to your word.

נִדְבוֹת פִּי רְצֵה נָא יְהוָה וּמִשְׁפָּטֶיךָ לַמְּדֵנִי:

teach me   and your judgements   ihvh   now   accept   mouth   freewill offerings

108. Accept, I beseech you, the freewill offerings of my mouth, O Lord, and teach me your ordinances.

נַפְשִׁי בְכַפִּי תָמִיד וְתוֹרָתְךָ לֹא שָׁכָחְתִּי:

I forget   not   and your torah   always   in my palm   my soul

109. My soul is continually in my hand; yet I do not forget your Torah.

נָתְנוּ רְשָׁעִים פַּח לִי וּמִפִּקּוּדֶיךָ לֹא תָעִיתִי:

I strayed   not   and from your precepts   to me   snare   the wicked   they gave

110. The wicked have laid a snare for me; yet I have not strayed from your precepts.

נָחַלְתִּי עֵדְוֹתֶיךָ לְעוֹלָם כִּי שְׂשׂוֹן לִבִּי הֵמָּה:

they are   my heart   rejoicing   like   to forever   your testimonies   my heritage

111. Your testimonies I have taken as a heritage for ever; for they are the rejoicing of my heart.

נָטִיתִי לִבִּי לַעֲשׂוֹת חֻקֶּיךָ לְעוֹלָם עֵקֶב:

very end   to forever   your statutes   to doing   my heart   I inclined

112. I have inclined my heart to perform your statutes always, to the end.

ס

סֵעֲפִים שָׂנֵאתִי וְתוֹרָתְךָ אָהָבְתִּי׃

| vain thoughts | I hate | and your Torah | I loved |

113. I hate vain thoughts; but I love your Torah.

סִתְרִי   וּמָגִנִּי אַתָּה לִדְבָרְךָ יִחָלְתִּי׃

| my hiding place | and my shield | you | to your saying | I hope |

114. You are my hiding place and my shield; I hope in your word.

סוּרוּ מִמֶּנִּי מְרֵעִים וְאֶצְּרָה מִצְוֹת אֱלֹהָי׃

| you depart | from me | evil doers | I will keep | commandments | my Elohim |

115. Depart from me, you evil doers; for I will keep the commandments of my God.

סָמְכֵנִי כְאִמְרָתְךָ וְאֶחְיֶה וְאַל תְּבִישֵׁנִי מִשִּׂבְרִי׃

| uphold me | like to your word | and I will live | and don't | you ashamed me | from my hope |

116. Uphold me according to your word, that I may live; and do not let me be ashamed of my hope.

סְעָדֵנִי וְאִוָּשֵׁעָה וְאֶשְׁעָה בְחֻקֶּיךָ תָמִיד׃

| support me | and I will be safe | and I will observe | in your statutes | continually |

117. Hold me up, and I shall be safe; and I will observe your statutes continually.

סָלִיתָ כָּל שׁוֹגִים מֵחֻקֶּיךָ כִּי שֶׁקֶר תַּרְמִיתָם׃

| you trampled | all | stray ones | from your statutes | like | lies | their vanity |

118. You have trampled down all those who stray from your statutes; for their deceit is vain.

סִגִים הִשְׁבַּתָּ כָל רִשְׁעֵי אָרֶץ לָכֵן אָהַבְתִּי עֵדֹתֶיךָ׃

| drosses | you put to rest | all | wicked | earth | to thus | I love | your testimonies |

119. You put away all the wicked of the earth like dross; therefore I love your testimonies.

סָמַר מִפַּחְדְּךָ בְשָׂרִי וּמִמִּשְׁפָּטֶיךָ יָרֵאתִי׃

| trembles | from your awe fear | my flesh | and from your judgments | I am afraid |

120. My flesh trembles for fear of you; and I am afraid of your judgments.

ע

עָשִׂיתִי מִשְׁפָּט וָצֶדֶק   בַּל תַּנִּיחֵנִי   לְעֹשְׁקָי:

to my oppressors   you leave me   in not   and righteousness   justice   I did

121. I have done what is just and right; do not leave me to my oppressors.

עֲרֹב עַבְדְּךָ לְטוֹב אַל יַעַשְׁקֻנִי זֵדִים:

arrogant ones   they oppress me   don't   to good   your servant   be surety

122. Be surety for your servant for good; do not let the arrogant oppress me.

עֵינַי כָּלוּ לִישׁוּעָתֶךָ וּלְאִמְרַת צִדְקֶךָ:

your righteousness   and to words   to your salvation   they failed   my eyes

123. My eyes fail with watching for your salvation, and for the word of your righteousness.

עֲשֵׂה עִם עַבְדְּךָ כְחַסְדֶּךָ וְחֻקֶּיךָ לַמְּדֵנִי:

teach me   your statutes   like your mercy   your servant   with   do

124. Deal with your servant according to your loving kindness, and teach me your statutes.

עַבְדְּךָ אָנִי הֲבִינֵנִי וְאֵדְעָה עֵדֹתֶיךָ:

your testimonies   and I know   the give me understanding   I   your servant

125. I am your servant; give me understanding, that I may know your testimonies.

עֵת לַעֲשׂוֹת לַיהוָה הֵפֵרוּ תּוֹרָתֶךָ:

your torah   they voided   to ihvh   to act   time

126. It is time for you, Lord, to act; for they have made void your Torah.

עַל כֵּן אָהַבְתִּי מִצְוֹתֶיךָ מִזָּהָב וּמִפָּז:

and from pure gold   from love   your commandments   I loved   thus   upon

127. Therefore I love your commandments above gold; above fine gold.

עַל כֵּן כָּל פִּקּוּדֵי כֹל יִשָּׁרְתִּי כָּל אֹרַח שֶׁקֶר שָׂנֵאתִי:

I hate   lies   roads   all   my uprights   all   precepts   all   thus   upon

128. Therefore I esteem all your precepts to be entirely right; and I hate every false way.

פ

פְּלָאוֹת עֵדְוֺתֶיךָ עַל כֵּן נְצָרָתַם נַפְשִׁי:

my soul　　kept them　　thus　upon　your testimonies　mystical

129. Your testimonies are wonderful; therefore my soul keeps them.

פֵּתַח דְּבָרֶיךָ יָאִיר מֵבִין פְּתָיִים:

simple ones　from understanding　it shines　your sayings　opening

130. The unfolding of your words gives light; it gives understanding to the simple.

פִּי פָעַרְתִּי וָאֶשְׁאָפָה כִּי לְמִצְוֺתֶיךָ יָאָבְתִּי:

it I love　to your commandment　like　and pant　I open　mouth

131. I open my mouth and pant; because I long for your commandments.

פְּנֵה אֵלַי וְחָנֵּנִי כְּמִשְׁפָּט לְאֹהֲבֵי שְׁמֶךָ:

your name　to lovers　like judgment　and be merciful to me　unto me　face

132. Look upon me, and be merciful to me, as you are to those who love your name.

פְּעָמַי הָכֵן בְּאִמְרָתֶךָ וְאַל תַּשְׁלֶט בִּי כָל אָוֶן:

inequity　all　in me　it dominated　and don't　in your word　the thus　my steps

133. Order my steps in your word; and do not let any iniquity have dominion over me.

פְּדֵנִי מֵעֹשֶׁק אָדָם וְאֶשְׁמְרָה פִּקּוּדֶיךָ:

your precepts　and I will heed　Adam　from oppression　deliver me

134. Save me from the oppression of man; and I will keep your precepts.

פָּנֶיךָ הָאֵר בְּעַבְדֶּךָ וְלַמְּדֵנִי אֶת חֻקֶּיךָ:

your statutes　that　and teach me　in your servant　the shine　your face

135. Let your face shine upon your servant; and teach me your statutes.

פַּלְגֵי מַיִם יָרְדוּ עֵינָי עַל לֹא שָׁמְרוּ תוֹרָתֶךָ:

your Torah　they heeded　not　upon　my eyes　they descend　water　rivers

136. Rivers of water run down my eyes, because they do not keep your Torah.

צ

צַדִּיק אַתָּה יְהוָה וְיָשָׁר מִשְׁפָּטֶיךָ:
your judgments and upright ihvh you righteous

137. You are righteous, O Lord, and upright are your judgments.

צִוִּיתָ צֶדֶק עֵדֹתֶיךָ וֶאֱמוּנָה מְאֹד:
greatly and faithful your testimonies righteous you commanded

138. You have commanded your testimonies in righteousness and in all faithfulness.

צִמְּתַתְנִי קִנְאָתִי כִּי־שָׁכְחוּ דְבָרֶיךָ צָרָי:
my enemies your sayings they forgot like my zeal consumes me

139. My zeal consumes me, because my enemies have forgotten your words.

צְרוּפָה אִמְרָתְךָ מְאֹד וְעַבְדְּךָ אֲהֵבָהּ:
loves it and your servant greatly your word very pure

140. Your word is very pure; therefore your servant loves it.

צָעִיר אָנֹכִי וְנִבְזֶה פִּקֻּדֶיךָ לֹא שָׁכָחְתִּי:
I forget not your precepts and despised I am small

141. I am small and despised; yet I do not forget your precepts.

צִדְקָתְךָ צֶדֶק לְעוֹלָם וְתוֹרָתְךָ אֱמֶת:
truth and your Torah to forever right your righteousness

142. Your righteousness is an everlasting righteousness, and your Torah is the truth.

צַר־וּמָצוֹק מְצָאוּנִי מִצְוֺתֶיךָ שַׁעֲשֻׁעָי:
my delights your commandments took hold of me and anguish - trouble

143. Trouble and anguish have taken hold of me; yet your commandments are my delights.

צֶדֶק עֵדְוֺתֶיךָ לְעוֹלָם הֲבִינֵנִי וְאֶחְיֶה:
and I will live the give me understanding to forever your testimonies righteous

144. The righteousness of your testimonies is everlasting; give me understanding, and I shall live.

ק

קָרָאתִי בְכָל־לֵב עֲנֵנִי יְהֹוָה חֻקֶּיךָ אֶצֹּרָה׃
I will keep   your statutes   ihvh   answer me   heart - in all   I cry

145. I cry with my whole heart; answer me, O Lord; I will keep your statutes.

קְרָאתִיךָ הוֹשִׁיעֵנִי וְאֶשְׁמְרָה עֵדֹתֶיךָ׃
your testimonies   I will heed   save me   I cried to you

146. I cry to you: save me, and I shall keep your testimonies.

קִדַּמְתִּי בַנֶּשֶׁף וָאֲשַׁוֵּעָה לִדְבָרְךָ יִחָלְתִּי׃
I hope   to your sayings   and I cry out   in before dawn   I awake

147. (K) I rise before dawn, and I cry out; my hope is in your word.

קִדְּמוּ עֵינַי אַשְׁמֻרוֹת לָשִׂיחַ בְּאִמְרָתֶךָ׃
in your word   to meditate   watches of night   my eyes   they awake

148. My eyes open before the watches of the night, that I may meditate on your saying.

קוֹלִי שִׁמְעָה כְחַסְדֶּךָ יְהֹוָה כְּמִשְׁפָּטֶךָ חַיֵּנִי׃
give me life   like your judgment   ihvh   like your mercy   hear   my voice

149. Hear my voice according to your loving kindness; O Lord, revive me according to your judgment.

קָרְבוּ רֹדְפֵי זִמָּה מִתּוֹרָתְךָ רָחָקוּ׃
they far   from the torah   mischief   perusers   they near

150. Those who follow after mischief draw near; they are far from your Torah.

קָרוֹב אַתָּה יְהֹוָה וְכָל־מִצְוֹתֶיךָ אֱמֶת׃
truth   your commandments - and all   ihvh   you   near

151. You are near, O Lord; and all your commandments are truth.

קֶדֶם יָדַעְתִּי מֵעֵדֹתֶיךָ כִּי לְעוֹלָם יְסַדְתָּם׃
you founded them   to forever   like   from your testimonies   I knew   of ancient time

152. Concerning your testimonies, I have known of old that you have founded them for ever.

ר

רְאֵה־עָנְיִי וְחַלְּצֵנִי כִּי־תוֹרָתְךָ לֹא שָׁכָחְתִּי:

I forget	not	your Torah – like	and rescue me	my affliction – see

153. Consider my affliction and save me; for I do not forget your Torah.

רִיבָה רִיבִי וּגְאָלֵנִי לְאִמְרָתְךָ חַיֵּנִי:

give me life	to your word	and save me	my cause	plead

154. Plead my cause, and save me; give me life according to your word.

רָחוֹק מֵרְשָׁעִים יְשׁוּעָה כִּי־חֻקֶּיךָ לֹא דָרָשׁוּ:

they seek	not	statutes - like	salvation	from wicked ones	far

155. Salvation is far from the wicked; for they do not seek your statutes.

רַחֲמֶיךָ רַבִּים יְהוָה כְּמִשְׁפָּטֶיךָ חַיֵּנִי:

give me life	like your judgments	ihvh	many ones	your compassion

156. Great is your compassion, O Lord; give me life according to your justice.

רַבִּים רֹדְפַי וְצָרָי מֵעֵדְוֹתֶיךָ לֹא נָטִיתִי:

I turned	not	from your testimonies	my enemies	my persecutors	many

157. Many are my persecutors and my enemies; yet I do not swerve from your testimonies.

רָאִיתִי בֹגְדִים וָאֶתְקוֹטָטָה אֲשֶׁר אִמְרָתְךָ לֹא שָׁמָרוּ:

they heeded	not	your word	which	and I am grieved	transgressor ones	I see

158. I look at the transgressors, and I am grieved; because they do not keep your saying.

רְאֵה כִּי־פִקּוּדֶיךָ אָהָבְתִּי יְהוָה כְּחַסְדְּךָ חַיֵּנִי:

give me life	like your kindness	ihvh	I loved	your precepts - like	you see

159. Consider how I love your precepts; revive me, O Lord, according to your loving kindness.

רֹאשׁ־דְּבָרְךָ אֱמֶת וּלְעוֹלָם כָּל־מִשְׁפַּט צִדְקֶךָ:

your righteous	judgment - all	and to forever	truth	your sayings - beginning

160. The sum of your word is truth: and every one of your righteous judgments endures for ever.

שׁ

שָׂרִים רְדָפוּנִי חִנָּם וּמִדְּבָרֶיךָ פָּחַד לִבִּי:
my heart   awe   and from your sayings   without cause   persecuted me   princes

161. (K) Princes have persecuted me without cause; but my heart in awe of your word.

שָׂשׂ אָנֹכִי עַל־אִמְרָתֶךָ כְּמוֹצֵא שָׁלָל רָב:
much   booty   like finding   your word – upon   I am   rejoice

162. I rejoice at your word, like one who finds great booty.

שֶׁקֶר שָׂנֵאתִי וַאֲתַעֵבָה תּוֹרָתְךָ אָהָבְתִּי:
I loved   your torah   and I loathe   I hate   lies

163. I hate and loathe lying; but I love your Torah.

שֶׁבַע בַּיּוֹם הִלַּלְתִּיךָ עַל מִשְׁפְּטֵי צִדְקֶךָ:
your righteous   judgments   upon   I praise you   in day   seven

164. Seven times a day I praise you because of your righteous judgments.

שָׁלוֹם רָב לְאֹהֲבֵי תוֹרָתֶךָ וְאֵין לָמוֹ מִכְשׁוֹל:
stumbling   to them   and isn't   your torah   to lovers   much   peace

165. Great peace have those who love your Torah; and nothing can make them stumble.

שִׂבַּרְתִּי לִישׁוּעָתְךָ יְהֹוָה וּמִצְוֹתֶיךָ עָשִׂיתִי:
I have done   and your commandments   ihvh   to your salvation   I longed

166. Lord, I have hoped for your salvation, and done your commandments.

שָׁמְרָה נַפְשִׁי עֵדֹתֶיךָ וָאֹהֲבֵם מְאֹד:
greatly   and I love them   your testimonies   my soul   heeded

167. My soul has kept your testimonies; and I love them exceedingly.

שָׁמַרְתִּי פִקּוּדֶיךָ וְעֵדֹתֶיךָ כִּי כָל־דְּרָכַי נֶגְדֶּךָ:
before you   my ways – all   like   and your testimonies   your precepts   I heeded

168. I have kept your precepts and your testimonies; for all my ways are before you.

ת

תִּקְרַב רִנָּתִי לְפָנֶיךָ יְהֹוָה כִּדְבָרְךָ הֲבִינֵנִי׃
the give understanding to me   like your sayings   ihvh   to your presence   my joy cry   will near

169. Let my cry come before you, O Lord; give me understanding according to your word.

תָּבוֹא תְּחִנָּתִי לְפָנֶיךָ כְּאִמְרָתְךָ הַצִּילֵנִי׃
rescue me   like your word   to your face   my supplication   will come

170. Let my supplication come before you; save me according to your word.

תַּבַּעְנָה שְׂפָתַי תְּהִלָּה כִּי תְלַמְּדֵנִי חֻקֶּיךָ׃
your statutes   you taught me   like   praise   my lips   will utter

171. My lips shall utter praise, when you have taught me your statutes.

תַּעַן לְשׁוֹנִי אִמְרָתֶךָ כִּי כָל־מִצְוֺתֶיךָ צֶּדֶק׃
just   commandments - all   like   your word   my tongue   will answer

172. My tongue shall speak of your word; for all your commandments are just.

תְּהִי־יָדְךָ לְעָזְרֵנִי כִּי פִקּוּדֶיךָ בָחָרְתִּי׃
I've chosen   your precepts   like   to help me   your hand - let be

173. Let your hand help me; for I have chosen your precepts.

תָּאַבְתִּי לִישׁוּעָתְךָ יְהֹוָה וְתוֹרָתְךָ שַׁעֲשֻׁעָי׃
my delight   and your Torah   ihvh   your salvation   I long

174. I long for your salvation, O Lord; and your Torah is my delight.

תְּחִי־נַפְשִׁי וּתְהַלְלֶךָּ וּמִשְׁפָּטֶךָ יַעְזְרֻנִי׃
they help me   and your judgments   and will praise you   my soul - you let live

175. Let my soul live, and it shall praise you; and let your judgments help me.

תָּעִיתִי כְּשֶׂה אֹבֵד בַּקֵּשׁ עַבְדֶּךָ כִּי מִצְוֺתֶיךָ לֹא שָׁכָחְתִּי׃
I forget   not   your commandments   like   your servant   seek   lost   like a sheep   I went astray

176. I have gone astray like a lost sheep; seek your servant; for I do not forget your commandments.

Psalm 120

ספר תהילים פרק קכ

שִׁיר הַמַּעֲלוֹת
the assents   song

אֶל־יְהֹוָה בַּצָּרָתָה לִּי קָרָאתִי וַיַּעֲנֵנִי׃
and he answered me   I called   to me   in distress   ihvh - onto

1. A Song of Maalot. In my distress I cried to the Lord, and he answered me.

יְהֹוָה הַצִּילָה נַפְשִׁי מִשְּׂפַת־שֶׁקֶר מִלָּשׁוֹן רְמִיָּה׃
deceitful   from tongue   lying - from lip   my soul   the deliver   ihvh

2. Save my soul, O Lord, from lying lips, and from a deceitful tongue.

מַה־יִּתֵּן לְךָ וּמַה־יֹּסִיף לָךְ לָשׁוֹן רְמִיָּה׃
deceitful   tongue   to you   he will add - and what   to you   he will give - what

3. What shall be given to you? What shall be done to you, O false tongue?

חִצֵּי גִבּוֹר שְׁנוּנִים עִם גַּחֲלֵי רְתָמִים׃
Rathem   coals   with   sharpened   mighty   arrows

4. Sharp arrows of the mighty, with coals of the broom tree.

אוֹיָה לִי כִּי־גַרְתִּי מֶשֶׁךְ
Mesheck   I have sojourned – like   to me   alas

שָׁכַנְתִּי עִם־אָהֳלֵי קֵדָר׃
Kedar   my tent - with   my dwelling

5. Woe is me, that I sojourn in Meshech, that I dwell in the tents of Kedar!

רַבַּת שָׁכְנָה־לָּהּ נַפְשִׁי עִם שׂוֹנֵא שָׁלוֹם׃
peace   he hates   with   my soul   to itself - dwells   much

6. My soul has long dwelt with those who hate peace.

אֲנִי־שָׁלוֹם וְכִי אֲדַבֵּר הֵמָּה לַמִּלְחָמָה׃
to the war   they are   I speak   and like   peace - I

7. I am for peace; but when I speak, they are for war.

PSALM 121

שִׁיר לַמַּעֲלוֹת
to ascents   song

אֶשָּׂא עֵינַי אֶל־הֶהָרִים מֵאַיִן יָבֹא עֶזְרִי:
my help   comes   from isn't   the mountains - onto   my eyes   I will lift

1. A Song of Maalot. I will lift up my eyes to the mountains. From where does my help come?

עֶזְרִי מֵעִם יְהוָֹה עֹשֵׂה שָׁמַיִם וָאָרֶץ:
and earth   heaven   maker   ihvh   from with   my help

2. My help comes from the Lord, who made heaven and earth.

אַל־יִתֵּן לַמּוֹט רַגְלֶךָ אַל־יָנוּם שֹׁמְרֶךָ:
your heeding   slumber – don't   your foot   to wavering   he will give - don't

3. He will not let your foot be moved; he who watches you will not slumber.

הִנֵּה לֹא יָנוּם וְלֹא יִישָׁן שׁוֹמֵר יִשְׂרָאֵל:
Israel   heeder   he will sleep   and not   he will slumber   not   here

4. Behold, he who watches Israel shall neither slumber nor sleep.

יְהוָֹה שֹׁמְרֶךָ יְהוָֹה צִלְּךָ עַל־יַד יְמִינֶךָ:
your right   hand – upon   your shade   ihvh   your heeder   ihvi

5. The Lord is your keeper; the Lord is your shade upon your right hand.

יוֹמָם הַשֶּׁמֶשׁ לֹא־יַכֶּכָּה וְיָרֵחַ בַּלָּיְלָה:
in the night   and moon   strike – not   the sun   by day

6. The sun shall not strike you by day, nor the moon by night.

יְהוָֹה יִשְׁמָרְךָ מִכָּל־רָע יִשְׁמֹר אֶת־נַפְשֶׁךָ:
your soul - that   he will heed   bad - of all   he will be your heeder   ihvh

7. The Lord shall preserve you from all evil; he shall preserve your soul.

יְהוָֹה יִשְׁמָר־צֵאתְךָ וּבוֹאֶךָ מֵעַתָּה וְעַד־עוֹלָם:
forever – and until   from now   and your coming   your going out - he will heed   ihvh

8. The Lord shall preserve your going out and your coming in from this time forth, and for evermore.

PSALM 122

ספר תהילים פרק קכב

שִׁיר הַמַּעֲלוֹת לְדָוִד
to David   the assents   song

שָׂמַחְתִּי בְּאֹמְרִים לִי בֵּית יְהֹוָה נֵלֵךְ׃
let's go   ihvh   house   to me   in them saying   I was glad

1. A Song of Maalot of David. I was glad when they said to me, Let us go into the house of the Lord.

עֹמְדוֹת הָיוּ רַגְלֵינוּ בִּשְׁעָרַיִךְ יְרוּשָׁלָ͏ִם׃
Jerusalem   in your gates   our feet   have been   we will stand

2. Our feet shall stand inside your gates, O Jerusalem.

יְרוּשָׁלַ͏ִם הַבְּנוּיָה כְּעִיר שֶׁחֻבְּרָה־לָּהּ יַחְדָּו׃
together   to it - that joined firmly   like city   the built one   Jerusalem

3. Jerusalem is built as a city which is bound firmly together;

שֶׁשָּׁם עָלוּ שְׁבָטִים
tribes   ascended   that them

שִׁבְטֵי־יָהּ עֵדוּת לְיִשְׂרָאֵל לְהֹדוֹת לְשֵׁם יְהֹוָה׃
ihvh   to name   to give thanks   to Israel   testimony   Ya - tribes

4. There the tribes go up, the tribes of the Lord, as was decreed for Israel, to give thanks to the name of the Lord.

כִּי שָׁמָּה יָשְׁבוּ כִסְאוֹת לְמִשְׁפָּט
to judgment   thrones   they will sit   there   like

כִּסְאוֹת לְבֵית דָּוִיד׃
David   to house   thrones

5. For thrones of judgment were set there, the thrones of the house of David.

שַׁאֲלוּ שְׁלוֹם יְרוּשָׁלָ͏ִם יִשְׁלָיוּ אֹהֲבָיִךְ׃
lovers of you   they will prosper   Jerusalem   peace   you request

6. Pray for the peace of Jerusalem; those who love you shall prosper.

יְהִי־שָׁלוֹם בְּחֵילֵךְ שַׁלְוָה בְּאַרְמְנוֹתָיִךְ׃
in your palaces   prosperity   in your fort   peace - there be

7. Peace be within your walls, and prosperity within your palaces.

לְמַעַן־אַחַי וְרֵעָי אֲדַבְּרָה־נָּא שָׁלוֹם בָּךְ׃
in you   Peace   now – I will say   and witnesses   brothers - to the end

8. For my brothers and companions' sakes, I will now say, Peace be within you.

לְמַעַן בֵּית־יְהֹוָה אֱלֹהֵינוּ אֲבַקְשָׁה טוֹב לָךְ׃
to you   good   I will seek   our Elohim   ihvh - house   to end

9. Because of the house of the Lord our God I will seek your good.

PSALM 123

ספר תהילים פרק קכג

שִׁיר הַמַּעֲלוֹת
<small>the ascensions   song</small>

אֵלֶיךָ נָשָׂאתִי אֶת־עֵינַי הַיֹּשְׁבִי בַּשָּׁמָיִם:
<small>in heaven   the sitting one   my eyes - that   I lift up   unto you</small>

1. A Song of Maalot. To you lift I up my eyes, O you who are enthroned in the heavens.

הִנֵּה כְעֵינֵי עֲבָדִים אֶל־יַד אֲדוֹנֵיהֶם
<small>their masters   hand - onto   servants ones   like eyes   here</small>

כְּעֵינֵי שִׁפְחָה אֶל־יַד גְּבִרְתָּהּ
<small>lady   hand – onto   maid   like eyes</small>

כֵּן עֵינֵינוּ אֶל־יְהוָה אֱלֹהֵינוּ עַד שֶׁיְּחָנֵּנוּ:
<small>that will be gracious to us   until   our Elohim   ihvh - unto   our eyes   thus</small>

2. Behold, as the eyes of servants look to the hand of their masters, and as the eyes of
a maid to the hand of her mistress; so our eyes wait upon the Lord our God, until he
shall be gracious to us.

חָנֵּנוּ יְהוָה חָנֵּנוּ כִּי־רַב שָׂבַעְנוּ בוּז:
<small>contempt   we satiated   much - like   be gracious to us   ihvh   be gracious to us</small>

3. Be gracious to us, O Lord, be gracious to us; for we are overfilled with contempt.

רַבַּת שָׂבְעָה־לָּהּ נַפְשֵׁנוּ
<small>our soul   to itself - satisfied   abundant</small>

הַלַּעַג הַשַּׁאֲנַנִּים הַבּוּז לִגְאֵיוֹנִים:
<small>to arrogant ones   the contempt   the tranquil ones   the mocking</small>

4. (K) Our soul is overfilled with the scorn of those who are at ease, and with the
contempt of the arrogant.

PSALM 124

ספר תהילים פרק קכד

שִׁיר הַמַּעֲלוֹת לְדָוִד

to David   the ascents   Song

לוּלֵי   יְהֹוָה שֶׁהָיָה לָנוּ יֹאמַר־נָא יִשְׂרָאֵל:

Israel   now - will say   to us   that was   ihvh   had it not been

1. A Song of Maalot of David. If it had not been the Lord who was on our side, let
Israel now say;

לוּלֵי   יְהֹוָה שֶׁהָיָה לָנוּ בְּקוּם עָלֵינוּ אָדָם:

Adam   upon us   in risen   to us   that was   ihvh   it had not been

2. If it had not been the Lord who was on our side, when men rose up against us;

אֲזַי חַיִּים בְּלָעוּנוּ בַּחֲרוֹת אַפָּם בָּנוּ:

in us   anger   in blazings   in swallowing us   live ones   then

3. Then they would have swallowed us up alive, when their wrath was kindled against us;

אֲזַי הַמַּיִם שְׁטָפוּנוּ נַחְלָה עָבַר עַל־נַפְשֵׁנוּ:

our soul - upon   cover   stream   overwhelmed   the waters   then

4. Then the waters would have overwhelmed us, the stream would have gone over our
soul;

אֲזַי עָבַר עַל־נַפְשֵׁנוּ הַמַּיִם הַזֵּידוֹנִים:

the arrogant ones   the waters   our soul - upon   cover   then

5. Then the proud waters would have gone over our soul.

בָּרוּךְ יְהֹוָה שֶׁלֹּא נְתָנָנוּ טֶרֶף לְשִׁנֵּיהֶם:

to their teeth   prey   given us   that not   ihvh   blessed

6. Blessed be the Lord, who has not given us as a prey to their teeth.

נַפְשֵׁנוּ כְּצִפּוֹר נִמְלְטָה מִפַּח יוֹקְשִׁים

fowlers   from snare   escaped   like small bird   our soul

הַפַּח נִשְׁבָּר וַאֲנַחְנוּ נִמְלָטְנוּ:

we have escaped   and we   burst   the snare

7. Our soul has escaped as a bird from the snare of the fowlers; the snare is broken, and
we have escaped.

עֶזְרֵנוּ בְּשֵׁם יְהֹוָה עֹשֵׂה שָׁמַיִם וָאָרֶץ:

and earth   heaven   made   ihvh   in name   our help

8. Our help is in the name of the Lord, who made heaven and earth.

PSALM 125

ספר תהילים פרק קכה

שִׁיר הַמַּעֲלוֹת
the assents   song

הַבֹּטְחִים בַּיהֹוָה כְּהַר־צִיּוֹן לֹא־יִמּוֹט לְעוֹלָם יֵשֵׁב׃
it dwells   to forever   it moved - not   Zion - like mountain   in ihvh   the trusting ones

1. A Song of Maalot. Those who trust in the Lord shall be like Mount Zion, which cannot be removed, but abides for ever.

יְרוּשָׁלַם הָרִים סָבִיב לָהּ
to her   around   mountains   Jerusalem

וַיהֹוָה סָבִיב לְעַמּוֹ מֵעַתָּה וְעַד־עוֹלָם׃
forever - and until   from now   to his people   around   and ihvh

2. As the mountains are around Jerusalem, so the Lord surrounds his people from this time forth and for evermore.

כִּי לֹא יָנוּחַ שֵׁבֶט הָרֶשַׁע עַל גּוֹרַל הַצַּדִּיקִים
the righteous ones   lot   upon   the wickedness   rod   will rest   not   like

לְמַעַן לֹא־יִשְׁלְחוּ הַצַּדִּיקִים בְּעַוְלָתָה יְדֵיהֶם׃
their hands   in iniquity   the righteous ones   will send - not   to end

3. For the scepter of the wicked shall not rest upon the share allotted to the righteous; lest the righteous put forth their hands to do wrong.

הֵיטִיבָה יְהֹוָה לַטּוֹבִים וְלִישָׁרִים בְּלִבּוֹתָם׃
in their hearts   and to upright ones   to good ones   ihvh   cause good

4. Do good, O Lord, to those who are good, and to those who are upright in their hearts.

וְהַמַּטִּים עֲקַלְקַלּוֹתָם יוֹלִיכֵם יְהֹוָה אֶת־פֹּעֲלֵי הָאָוֶן
the inequity   workers - that   ihvh   you will walk   their crooked ways   and the inclining ones

שָׁלוֹם עַל־יִשְׂרָאֵל׃
Israel - upon   peace

5. As for those who turn aside to their crooked ways, the Lord shall lead them away with the evil doers; but peace shall be upon Israel.

PSALM 126

ספר תהילים פרק קכו

שִׁיר הַמַּעֲלוֹת

the assents   song

בְּשׁוּב יְהֹוָה אֶת־שִׁיבַת צִיּוֹן הָיִינוּ כְּחֹלְמִים:

like dreamer ones   we were   Zion   captivity - that   ihvh   in returning

1. A Song of Maalot. When the Lord brought back the captivity of Zion, we were like men who dream.

אָז יִמָּלֵא שְׂחוֹק פִּינוּ וּלְשׁוֹנֵנוּ רִנָּה

shouting   and our tongues   our mouth   laughter   it filled   then

אָז יֹאמְרוּ בַגּוֹיִם הִגְדִּיל יְהֹוָה לַעֲשׂוֹת עִם־אֵלֶּה:

these - with   to doings   ihvh   magnified   in nations   they said   then

2. Then our mouth was filled with laughter, and our tongue with singing; then they said among the nations, The Lord has done great things for them.

הִגְדִּיל יְהֹוָה לַעֲשׂוֹת עִמָּנוּ הָיִינוּ שְׂמֵחִים:

happy ones   we were   with us   to doings   ihvh   magnified

3. The Lord has done great things for us; we are glad.

שׁוּבָה יְהֹוָה אֶת־שְׁבוּתֵנוּ [שְׁבִיתֵנוּ] כַּאֲפִיקִים בַּנֶּגֶב:

in the Negev   like brooks   which our captivity - that   ihvh   return

4. (K) Bring back our captivity, O Lord, like the streams in the Negev.

הַזֹּרְעִים בְּדִמְעָה בְּרִנָּה יִקְצֹרוּ:

they will reap   in shouting   in tears   the sowing ones

5. Those who sow in tears shall reap in joy.

הָלוֹךְ יֵלֵךְ וּבָכֹה נֹשֵׂא מֶשֶׁךְ־הַזָּרַע

the seed - basket   bearing   and in weeping   he walks   walk

בֹּא־יָבוֹא בְרִנָּה נֹשֵׂא אֲלֻמֹּתָיו:

his sheaves   bearing   in shouting   he comes - come

6. He who goes forth weeping, bearing the seed for sowing, shall come back with shouts of joy, bringing his sheaves with him.

PSALM 127

ספר תהילים פרק קכז

שִׁיר הַמַּעֲלוֹת לִשְׁלֹמֹה
to Solomon   the from assents   song

אִם־יְהוָה לֹא־יִבְנֶה בַיִת שָׁוְא עָמְלוּ בוֹנָיו בּוֹ
in it   its builders   toiled   vain   house   he builds - not   ihvh - with

אִם־יְהוָה לֹא־יִשְׁמָר־עִיר
city - he heeds - not   ihvh - if

שָׁוְא שָׁקַד שׁוֹמֵר׃
heeder   watchman   vanity

1. A Song of Maalot for Solomon. Unless the Lord builds the house, those who build it labor in vain; unless the Lord watches over the city, the watchman stays awake in vain.

שָׁוְא לָכֶם מַשְׁכִּימֵי קוּם
rise   ones rising early   to them   vanity

מְאַחֲרֵי־שֶׁבֶת אֹכְלֵי לֶחֶם הָעֲצָבִים
the sorrows   bread   eating   sitting - from after

כֵּן יִתֵּן לִידִידוֹ שֵׁנָא׃
sleep   to his loved   he gives   thus

2. It is vain for you to rise up early, to sit up late, to eat the bread of toil; for truly to his beloved he gives sleep.

הִנֵּה נַחֲלַת יְהוָה בָּנִים שָׂכָר פְּרִי הַבָּטֶן׃
the belly   fruit   reward   sons   ihvh   inheritance   here

3. Behold, children are a heritage of the Lord; and the fruit of the womb is a reward.

כְּחִצִּים בְּיַד־גִּבּוֹר כֵּן בְּנֵי הַנְּעוּרִים׃
the youth ones   sons   thus   mighty - in hand   like arrows

4. As arrows are in the hand of a mighty man; so are the children of one's youth.

אַשְׁרֵי הַגֶּבֶר אֲשֶׁר מִלֵּא אֶת־אַשְׁפָּתוֹ
his quiver - that   full   which   the gentlemen   he happy

מֵהֶם לֹא יֵבֹשׁוּ כִּי־יְדַבְּרוּ אֶת־אוֹיְבִים בַּשָּׁעַר׃
in the gate   enemy ones - that   they will speak - like   they ashamed   not   with them

5. Happy is the man who has his quiver full of them; they shall not be put to shame, but they shall speak with the enemies in the gate.

PSALM 128

ספר תהילים פרק קכח

שִׁיר הַמַּעֲלוֹת
song   the assents

אַשְׁרֵי כָּל־יְרֵא יְהוָה הַהֹלֵךְ בִּדְרָכָיו:
happy   fearing - all   ihvh   the walk   in his ways

1. A Song of Maalot. Happy is every one who fears the Lord; who walks in his ways.

יְגִיעַ כַּפֶּיךָ כִּי תֹאכֵל אַשְׁרֶיךָ וְטוֹב לָךְ:
it effort   like your palms   you will eat   your praises   and good   to you

2. For you shall eat the labor of your hands; happy shall you be, and it shall be well with you.

אֶשְׁתְּךָ כְּגֶפֶן פֹּרִיָּה בְּיַרְכְּתֵי בֵיתֶךָ
your wife   like vine   fruitful   in recesses   your house

בָּנֶיךָ כִּשְׁתִלֵי זֵיתִים סָבִיב לְשֻׁלְחָנֶךָ:
your sons   like plants   olives   around   to your table

3. Your wife shall be like a fruitful vine in the recesses of your house; your children like olive shoots around your table.

הִנֵּה כִי־כֵן יְבֹרַךְ גָּבֶר יְרֵא יְהוָה:
here   thus - like   will be blessed   gentleman   fearing   ihvh

4. Behold, thus shall the man be blessed who fears the Lord.

יְבָרֶכְךָ יְהוָה מִצִּיּוֹן
he will bless you   ihvh   from Zion

וּרְאֵה בְּטוֹב יְרוּשָׁלָם כֹּל יְמֵי חַיֶּיךָ:
and you will see   in good   Jerusalem   all   days   your life

5. The Lord shall bless you from Zion; and you shall see the good of Jerusalem all the days of your life.

וּרְאֵה־בָנִים לְבָנֶיךָ
and you will see - sons   sons   to your sons

שָׁלוֹם עַל־יִשְׂרָאֵל:
peace   Israel - upon

6. And you shall see your children's children, and peace upon Israel.

Psalm 129

ספר תהילים פרק קכט

שִׁיר הַמַּעֲלוֹת

the assents   song

רַבַּת צְרָרוּנִי מִנְּעוּרַי יֹאמַר־נָא יִשְׂרָאֵל:

Israel   now – say   from my youth   they distressed me   much

1. A Song of Maalot. Many a time have they afflicted me from my youth, let Israel now say;

רַבַּת צְרָרוּנִי מִנְּעוּרָי גַּם לֹא יָכְלוּ־לִי:

to me - they prevailed   not   also   from my youth   they oppressed me   much

2. Many a time have they afflicted me from my youth; yet they have not prevailed against me.

עַל־גַּבִּי חָרְשׁוּ חֹרְשִׁים הֶאֱרִיכוּ לְמַעֲנוֹתָם [לְמַעֲנִיתָם]:

to their furrows   they lengthened   plower ones   they plowed   my back - upon

3. (K) The plowers plowed upon my back; they made long their furrows.

יְהֹוָה צַדִּיק קִצֵּץ עֲבוֹת רְשָׁעִים:

wicked ones   cord   he cut asunder   righteous   ihvh

4. The Lord is righteous; he has cut the cords of the wicked.

יֵבֹשׁוּ וְיִסֹּגוּ אָחוֹר כֹּל שֹׂנְאֵי צִיּוֹן:

Zion   haters   all   backward   and they be driven   they will be ashamed

5. Let them all who hate Zion be put to shame and turned backward.

יִהְיוּ כַּחֲצִיר גַּגּוֹת שֶׁקַּדְמַת שָׁלַף יָבֵשׁ:

it cut   grows up   that precedes   roofs   like grass   they will be

6. Let them be like the grass on the roof tops, which withers before it is plucked;

שֶׁלֹּא מִלֵּא כַפּוֹ קוֹצֵר וְחִצְנוֹ מְעַמֵּר:

from binder ones of sheaves   and his pocket   reaper   his palm   filled   that not

7. With which the reaper does not fill his hand; nor he who binds sheaves his bosom.

וְלֹא אָמְרוּ הָעֹבְרִים בִּרְכַּת יְהֹוָה אֲלֵיכֶם

upon you   ihvh   blessing   the passing ones   they said   and not

בֵּרַכְנוּ אֶתְכֶם בְּשֵׁם יְהֹוָה:

ihvh   in name   that you   we blessing

8. And those who pass by do not say, The blessing of the Lord be upon you; we bless you in the name of the Lord.

PSALM 130

ספר תהילים פרק קל

שִׁיר הַמַּעֲלוֹת
the from assents   song

מִמַּעֲמַקִּים קְרָאתִיךָ יְהוָֹה:
ihvh   I call you   from deep places

1. A Song of Maalot. Out of the depths have I cry to you, O Lord.

אֲדֹנָי שִׁמְעָה בְקוֹלִי
in my voice   hear   Adoni

תִּהְיֶינָה אָזְנֶיךָ קַשֻּׁבוֹת לְקוֹל תַּחֲנוּנָי:
my supplications   to voice   attentive   your ears   let be now

2. Lord, hear my voice; let your ears be attentive to the voice of my supplications.

אִם־עֲוֹנוֹת תִּשְׁמָר־יָהּ אֲדֹנָי מִי יַעֲמֹד:
he will stand   who   Adoni   Ya - you will heed   iniquities - if

3. If you, Lord, should mark iniquities, O Lord, who could stand?

כִּי־עִמְּךָ הַסְּלִיחָה לְמַעַן תִּוָּרֵא:
you will be feared   to end   the pardon   with you - like

4. But there is forgiveness with you, that you may be feared.

קִוִּיתִי יְהוָֹה קִוְּתָה נַפְשִׁי
my soul   expects   ihvh   my expectation

וְלִדְבָרוֹ הוֹחָלְתִּי:
I hope   and to his speech

5. I wait for the Lord, my soul waits, and in his word I hope.

נַפְשִׁי לַאדֹנָי מִשֹּׁמְרִים לַבֹּקֶר
to morning   from heeding ones   to Adoni   my nephesh

שֹׁמְרִים לַבֹּקֶר:
to morning   heeding ones

6. My soul waits for the Lord more than those who watch for the morning watch for the morning.

יַחֵל יִשְׂרָאֵל אֶל־יְיָהוָֹה
ihvh - unto   Israel   will hope

כִּי־עִם־יְהוָֹה הַחֶסֶד וְהַרְבֵּה עִמּוֹ פְדוּת:
redemption   with him   and the much   the mercy   ihvh - with - like

7. Let Israel hope in the Lord; for with the Lord there is loving kindness, and with him is bountiful redemption.

וְהוּא יִפְדֶּה אֶת־יִשְׂרָאֵל מִכֹּל עֲוֺנֹתָיו:

his iniquities   from all   Israel - that   will redeem   and he

8. And he shall redeem Israel from all his iniquities.

PSALM 131

ספר תהילים פרק קלא

שִׁיר הַמַּעֲלוֹת לְדָוִד

    to David   the assents   song

הֹוָה לֹא־גָבַהּ לִבִּי וְלֹא־רָמוּ עֵינַי

my eyes been high - and not my heart elevated – not ihvh

וְלֹא־הִלַּכְתִּי בִּגְדֹלוֹת וּבְנִפְלָאוֹת מִמֶּנִּי׃

from me and in mysticals in great ones I walked - and not

1. A Song of Maalot of David. Lord, my heart is not haughty, nor my eyes lofty; nor do I exercise myself in great matters, or in things too high for me.

אִם־לֹא שִׁוִּיתִי וְדוֹמַמְתִּי נַפְשִׁי

my soul and made silent I set not - if

כְּגָמֻל עֲלֵי אִמּוֹ כַּגָּמֻל עָלַי נַפְשִׁי׃

my soul upon me like weaned his mother upon me like weaned

2. Surely I have behaved and quieted myself, like a child who is weaned from his mother; my soul is like a weaned child.

יַחֵל יִשְׂרָאֵל אֶל־יְיהוָה מֵעַתָּה וְעַד־עוֹלָם׃

forever - and until from now ihvh - unto Israel will hope

3. Let Israel hope in the Lord from this time forth and for evermore.

PSALM 132

ספר תהילים פרק קלב

שִׁיר הַמַּעֲלוֹת
<small>the assents   song</small>

זְכוֹר־יְהוָֹה לְדָוִד אֵת כָּל־עֻנּוֹתוֹ:
<small>his afflictions - all   that   to David   ihvh - remember</small>

1. A Song of Maalot. Lord, remember in David's favor all his afflictions;

אֲשֶׁר נִשְׁבַּע לַיהוָֹה נָדַר לַאֲבִיר יַעֲקֹב:
<small>Jacob   to mighty one   he vowed   to ihvh   he swore   which</small>

2. How he swore to the Lord, and vowed to the mighty God of Jacob;

אִם־אָבֹא בְּאֹהֶל בֵּיתִי
<small>my house   in tent   I will go – if</small>

אִם־אֶעֱלֶה עַל־עֶרֶשׂ יְצוּעָי:
<small>my bed   spread - upon   I will get up - if</small>

3. Surely I will not come into the tent of my house, nor get into my bed;

אִם־אֶתֵּן שְׁנָת לְעֵינָי לְעַפְעַפַּי תְּנוּמָה:
<small>will slumber   to my eyelids   to my eyes   sleep   I will give - if</small>

4. I will not give sleep to my eyes, or slumber to my eyelids,

עַד־אֶמְצָא מָקוֹם לַיהוָֹה מִשְׁכָּנוֹת לַאֲבִיר יַעֲקֹב:
<small>Jacob   to mighty one   tabernacles   to ihvh   place   I find - until</small>

5. Until I find out a place for the Lord, a habitation for the mighty One of Jacob.

הִנֵּה־שְׁמַעֲנוּהָ בְאֶפְרָתָה מְצָאנוּהָ בִּשְׂדֵי־יָעַר:
<small>Jaar - in fields   we found it   in Ephratah   we heard it - here</small>

6. Behold, we heard of it at Ephratah; we found it in the fields of Jaar;

נָבוֹאָה לְמִשְׁכְּנוֹתָיו נִשְׁתַּחֲוֶה לַהֲדֹם רַגְלָיו:
<small>his feet   to the stool   we will bow down   to his tabernacles   we will come</small>

7. We will go into his dwelling places; we will worship at his footstool.

קוּמָה יְהוָֹה לִמְנוּחָתֶךָ אַתָּה וַאֲרוֹן עֻזֶּךָ:
<small>your strength   and ark   you   to your rest   ihvh   arise</small>

8. Arise, O Lord, and go to your resting place; you, and the ark of your might.

כֹּהֲנֶיךָ יִלְבְּשׁוּ־צֶדֶק וַחֲסִידֶיךָ יְרַנֵּנוּ:
<small>sing joyfully   and your devout   righteousness - they clothed   your priests</small>

9. Let your priests be clothed with righteousness; and let your pious ones shout for joy.

בַּעֲבוּר דָּוִד עַבְדֶּךָ אַל־תָּשֵׁב פְּנֵי מְשִׁיחֶךָ:
<small>from your anointed   face   you turn away - don't   your servant   David   in favor</small>

10. For your servant David's sake do not turn away the face of your anointed.

נִשְׁבַּע יְהוָה לְדָוִד אֱמֶת לֹא־יָשׁוּב מִמֶּנָּה

from it   he will turn - not   truth   to David   ihvh   swore

מִפְּרִי בִטְנְךָ אָשִׁית לְכִסֵּא־לָךְ׃

to you - to throne   I will set   your belly   from fruit

11. The Lord has sworn in truth to David; he will not turn from it; One of the sons of your body I will set on your throne.

אִם־יִשְׁמְרוּ בָנֶיךָ בְּרִיתִי וְעֵדֹתִי זוֹ אֲלַמְּדֵם

I will teach them   this   and my testimony   my covenant   your sons   will heed - if

גַּם־בְּנֵיהֶם עֲדֵי־עַד יֵשְׁבוּ לְכִסֵּא־לָךְ׃

to you - to throne   they will sit   ever - until   their sons - also

12. If your children will keep my covenant and my testimony that I shall teach them, their children shall also sit upon your throne for evermore.

כִּי־בָחַר יְהוָה בְּצִיּוֹן אִוָּהּ לְמוֹשָׁב לוֹ׃

to him   to dwelling   he desired   in Zion   ihvh   chosen - like

13. For the Lord has chosen Zion; he has desired it for his habitation.

זֹאת־מְנוּחָתִי עֲדֵי־עַד פֹּה אֵשֵׁב כִּי אִוִּתִיהָ׃

I desired it   like   I will dwell   here   time - until   my rest place - this

14. This is my resting place for ever; here I will dwell; for I have desired it.

צֵידָהּ בָּרֵךְ אֲבָרֵךְ אֶבְיוֹנֶיהָ אַשְׂבִּיעַ לָחֶם׃

bread   I will satisfy   her needy   I will bless   blessing   Its provision

15. I will abundantly bless her provision; I will satisfy her poor with bread.

וְכֹהֲנֶיהָ אַלְבִּישׁ יֶשַׁע וַחֲסִידֶיהָ רַנֵּן יְרַנֵּנוּ׃

we will sing joy   shouting joy   and her devout   salvation   I will clothe   and her priests

16. I will also clothe her priests with salvation; and her pious ones shall shout aloud for joy.

שָׁם אַצְמִיחַ קֶרֶן לְדָוִד עָרַכְתִּי נֵר לִמְשִׁיחִי׃

to my anointed   lamp   I prepared   to David   horn   I will make sprout   there

17. There I will make the horn of David to bud; I have prepared a lamp for my anointed.

אוֹיְבָיו אַלְבִּישׁ בֹּשֶׁת וְעָלָיו יָצִיץ נִזְרוֹ׃

his crown   will flourish   and upon him   shame   I will clothe   his enemies

18. His enemies I will clothe with shame; but upon himself his crown shall flourish.

PSALM 133

ספר תהילים פרק קלג

שִׁיר הַמַּעֲלוֹת לְדָוִד
Song   the assents   to David

הִנֵּה מַה־טּוֹב וּמַה־נָּעִים שֶׁבֶת אַחִים גַּם־יָחַד׃
here   good - how   pleasant - and what   dwelling   brothers   together - also

1. A Song of Maalot of David. Behold, how good and how pleasant it is for brothers to
dwell together in unity!

כַּשֶּׁמֶן הַטּוֹב עַל־הָרֹאשׁ יֹרֵד עַל־הַזָּקָן
like oil   the good   the head - upon   descending   the beard - upon

זְקַן אַהֲרֹן שֶׁיֹּרֵד עַל־פִּי מִדּוֹתָיו׃
beard   Aaron   that descends   mouth - upon   from his garments

2. It is like the precious ointment upon the head, that runs down upon the beard,
Aaron's beard, that runs down to the hem of his garments.

כְּטַל־חֶרְמוֹן שֶׁיֹּרֵד עַל־הַרְרֵי צִיּוֹן
Hermon - like dew   that descends   mountains - upon   Zion

כִּי שָׁם צִוָּה יְהוָה אֶת־הַבְּרָכָה חַיִּים עַד־הָעוֹלָם׃
like   there   commanded   ihvh   the blessing - that   life   the forever - until

3. Like the dew of Hermon descending upon the mountains of Zion; for there the Lord
has commanded the blessing, life for evermore.

PSALM 134

ספר תהילים פרק קלד

שִׁיר הַמַּעֲלוֹת
the from assent Song

הִנֵּה בָּרֲכוּ אֶת־יְהוָה כָּל־עַבְדֵי יְהוָה
ihvh servants - all ihvh - that bless here

הָעֹמְדִים בְּבֵית־יְהוָה בַּלֵּילוֹת:
in the nights ihvh – in house the standing ones

1. A Song of Maalot. Behold, bless the Lord, all you servants of the Lord, who by night stand in the house of the Lord.

שְׂאוּ־יְדֵכֶם קֹדֶשׁ וּבָרֲכוּ אֶת־יְהוָה:
ihvh - that and bless holy your hands - lift up

2. Lift up your hands in the sanctuary, and bless the Lord.

יְבָרֶכְךָ יְהוָה מִצִּיּוֹן עֹשֵׂה שָׁמַיִם וָאָרֶץ:
and earth heavens maker from Zion ihvh he will blessing you

3. May the Lord who made heaven and earth bless you from Zion!

Psalm 135

ספר תהילים פרק קלה

הַלְלוּיָהּ
praise Ya

הַלְלוּ אֶת־שֵׁם יְהֹוָה הַלְלוּ עַבְדֵי יְהֹוָה׃
you praise / name - to that / ihvh / praise / servants / ihvh

1 Praise ye the LORD. Praise ye the name of the LORD; praise *him*, O ye servants of the LORD.

שֶׁעֹמְדִים בְּבֵית יְהֹוָה בְּחַצְרוֹת בֵּית אֱלֹהֵינוּ׃
that you standing / in house / ihvh / in courtyards / house / our Elohim

2 Ye that stand in the house of the LORD, in the courts of the house of our God,

הַלְלוּיָהּ כִּי־טוֹב יְהֹוָה זַמְּרוּ לִשְׁמוֹ כִּי נָעִים׃
praise Ya / good – like / ihvh / you sing psalms / to his name / like / delightful

3 Praise the LORD; for the LORD *is* good: sing praises unto his name; for *it is* pleasant.

כִּי־יַעֲקֹב בָּחַר לוֹ יָהּ יִשְׂרָאֵל לִסְגֻלָּתוֹ׃
Jacob – like / chose / to him / Ya / Israel / to his treasure

4 For the LORD hath chosen Jacob unto himself, *and* Israel for his peculiar treasure.

כִּי אֲנִי יָדַעְתִּי כִּי־גָדוֹל יְהֹוָה וַאֲדֹנֵינוּ מִכָּל־אֱלֹהִים׃
like / I / I know / great – like / ihvh / and our Adonei / Elohim - from all

5 For I know that the LORD *is* great, and *that* our Lord *is* above all gods.

כֹּל אֲשֶׁר־חָפֵץ יְהֹוָה עָשָׂה בַּשָּׁמַיִם וּבָאָרֶץ בַּיַּמִּים
all / desires – which / ihvh / did / in heaven / and in earth / in seas

וְכָל־תְּהוֹמוֹת׃
deep places - and all

6 Whatsoever the LORD pleased, *that* did he in heaven, and in earth, in the seas, and all deep places.

מַעֲלֶה נְשִׂאִים מִקְצֵה הָאָרֶץ
ascending / vapors / from extremities / the earth

בְּרָקִים לַמָּטָר עָשָׂה מוֹצֵא־רוּחַ מֵאוֹצְרוֹתָיו׃
lightnings / to the rain / makes / wind – brings forth / from his storehouses

7 He causeth the vapours to ascend from the ends of the earth; he maketh lightnings for the rain; he bringeth the wind out of his treasuries.

שֶׁהִכָּה בְּכוֹרֵי מִצְרָיִם מֵאָדָם עַד־בְּהֵמָה׃
that striking / in firstborn / Egypt / from Adam / beast – until

8 Who smote the firstborn of Egypt, both of man and beast.

שָׁלַח אֹתֹת וּמֹפְתִים בְּתוֹכֵכִי מִצְרָיִם בְּפַרְעֹה וּבְכָל־עֲבָדָיו:

his servants - and in all   in Pharaoh   Egypt   in midst   and wonders   signs   he sent

9 *Who* sent tokens and wonders into the midst of thee, O Egypt, upon Pharaoh, and upon all his servants.

שֶׁהִכָּה גּוֹיִם רַבִּים וְהָרַג מְלָכִים עֲצוּמִים:

mighty ones   kings   and killed   many   nations   that struck

10 Who smote great nations, and slew mighty kings;

לְסִיחוֹן מֶלֶךְ הָאֱמֹרִי וּלְעוֹג מֶלֶךְ הַבָּשָׁן

the Bashan   king   and to Og   the Amorites   king   to Sihon

וּלְכֹל מַמְלְכוֹת כְּנָעַן:

Canaan   from kingdoms   and to all

11 Sihon king of the Amorites, and Og king of Bashan, and all the kingdoms of Canaan:

וְנָתַן אַרְצָם נַחֲלָה נַחֲלָה לְיִשְׂרָאֵל עַמּוֹ:

his people   to Israel   inheritance   inheritance   land   and he gave

12 And gave their land *for* an heritage, an heritage unto Israel his people.

יְהֹוָה שִׁמְךָ לְעוֹלָם יְהֹוָה זִכְרְךָ לְדֹר־וָדֹר:

and generation - to generation   your remembrance   ihvh   forever   your name   ihvh

13 Thy name, O LORD, *endureth* for ever; *and* thy memorial, O LORD, throughout all generations.

כִּי־יָדִין יְהֹוָה עַמּוֹ וְעַל־עֲבָדָיו יִתְנֶחָם:

sigh sorry like   his servants - and upon   his people   ihvh   will judge – like

14 For the LORD will judge his people, and he will repent himself concerning his servants.

עֲצַבֵּי הַגּוֹיִם כֶּסֶף וְזָהָב מַעֲשֵׂה יְדֵי אָדָם:

Adam   hands   works   and gold   silver   the nations   idols

15 The idols of the heathen *are* silver and gold, the work of men's hands.

פֶּה־לָהֶם וְלֹא יְדַבֵּרוּ עֵינַיִם לָהֶם וְלֹא יִרְאוּ:

they see   and not   to them   eyes   they speak   and not   to them – mouths

16 They have mouths, but they speak not; eyes have they, but they see not;

אָזְנַיִם לָהֶם וְלֹא יַאֲזִינוּ אַף אֵין־יֶשׁ־רוּחַ בְּפִיהֶם:

in their mouths   spirit –there is - isn't   then   they hear   and not   to them   ears

17 They have ears, but they hear not; neither is there *any* breath in their mouths.

כְּמוֹהֶם יִהְיוּ עֹשֵׂיהֶם כֹּל אֲשֶׁר־בֹּטֵחַ בָּהֶם:

in them   trust – which   all   their makers   they be   like them

18 They that make them are like unto them: *so is* every one that trusteth in them.

בֵּית יִשְׂרָאֵל בָּרְכוּ אֶת־יְהֹוָה בֵּית אַהֲרֹן

Aaron   house   ihvh – that   bless   Israel   house

בָּרְכוּ אֶת־יְהֹוָה:

ihvh - that   bless

19 Bless the LORD, O house of Israel: bless the LORD, O house of Aaron:

בֵּית הַלֵּוִי בָּרְכוּ אֶת־יְהֹוָה יִרְאֵי יְהֹוָה בָּרְכוּ אֶת־יְהֹוָה:

ihvh – that   bless   ihvh   those fearing   ihvh – that   bless   the Levi   house

20 Bless the LORD, O house of Levi: ye that fear the LORD, bless the LORD.

בָּרוּךְ יְהֹוָה מִצִּיּוֹן שֹׁכֵן יְרוּשָׁלִָם

Jerusalem   he dwells   from Zion   ihvh   blessed

הַלְלוּיָהּ:

praise Ya

21 Blessed be the LORD out of Zion, which dwelleth at Jerusalem. Praise ye the LORD.

PSALM 136

ספר תהילים פרק קלו

הוֹדוּ לַיהוָה כִּי־טוֹב כִּי לְעוֹלָם חַסְדּוֹ:

<small>his mercy   to forever   like   good – like   to ihvh   you give thanks</small>

1 O give thanks unto the LORD; for he is good: for his mercy endureth for ever.

הוֹדוּ לֵאלֹהֵי הָאֱלֹהִים כִּי לְעוֹלָם חַסְדּוֹ:

<small>his mercy   to forever   like   the Elohim   to Elohim   you give thanks</small>

2 O give thanks unto the God of gods: for his mercy endureth for ever.

הוֹדוּ לַאֲדֹנֵי הָאֲדֹנִים כִּי לְעוֹלָם חַסְדּוֹ:

<small>his mercy   to forever   like   the Master ones   to Masters   you give thanks</small>

3 O give thanks to the Lord of lords: for his mercy endureth for ever.

לְעֹשֵׂה נִפְלָאוֹת גְּדֹלוֹת לְבַדּוֹ כִּי לְעוֹלָם חַסְדּוֹ:

<small>his mercy   to forever   like   alone   great ones   mystical ones   to maker</small>

4 To him who alone doeth great wonders: for his mercy endureth for ever.

לְעֹשֵׂה הַשָּׁמַיִם בִּתְבוּנָה כִּי לְעוֹלָם חַסְדּוֹ:

<small>his mercy   to forever   like   in understanding   the heavens   to maker</small>

5 To him that by wisdom made the heavens: for his mercy endureth for ever.

לְרֹקַע הָאָרֶץ עַל־הַמָּיִם כִּי לְעוֹלָם חַסְדּוֹ:

<small>his mercy   to forever   like   the waters – upon   the earth   to spread</small>

6 To him that stretched out the earth above the waters: for his mercy endureth for ever.

לְעֹשֵׂה אוֹרִים גְּדֹלִים כִּי לְעוֹלָם חַסְדּוֹ:

<small>his mercy   to forever   like   great ones   lights   to maker</small>

7 To him that made great lights: for his mercy endurethfor ever:

אֶת־הַשֶּׁמֶשׁ לְמֶמְשֶׁלֶת בַּיּוֹם כִּי לְעוֹלָם חַסְדּוֹ:

<small>his mercy   to forever   like   in day   to rule   the sun – that</small>

8 The sun to rule by day: for his mercy endureth for ever:

אֶת־הַיָּרֵחַ וְכוֹכָבִים לְמֶמְשָׁלוֹת בַּלָּיְלָה כִּי לְעוֹלָם חַסְדּוֹ:

<small>his mercy   to forever   like   in night   to rule   and stars   the moon – that</small>

9 The moon and stars to rule by night: for his mercy endureth for ever.

לְמַכֵּה מִצְרַיִם בִּבְכוֹרֵיהֶם כִּי לְעוֹלָם חַסְדּוֹ:

<small>his mercy   to forever   like   in their firstborn   Egypt   to strike</small>

10 To him that smote Egypt in their firstborn: for his mercy endureth for ever:

וַיּוֹצֵא יִשְׂרָאֵל מִתּוֹכָם כִּי לְעוֹלָם חַסְדּוֹ:

<small>his mercy   to forever   like   from their midst   Israel   and came out</small>

11 And brought out Israel from among them: for his mercy endureth for ever:

בְּיָד חֲזָקָה וּבִזְרוֹעַ נְטוּיָה כִּי לְעוֹלָם חַסְדּוֹ:

<small>his mercy   to forever   like   stretched out   and in arm   strong   in hand</small>

12 With a strong hand, and with a stretched out arm: for his mercy endureth for ever.

לְגֹזֵר   יַם־סוּף   לִגְזָרִים   כִּי לְעוֹלָם חַסְדּוֹ׃

to part-er of   reeds – sea   to parts   like   to forever   his mercy

13 To him which divided the Red sea into parts: for his mercy endureth for ever:

וְהֶעֱבִיר   יִשְׂרָאֵל   בְּתוֹכוֹ   כִּי לְעוֹלָם חַסְדּוֹ׃

and caused to pass   Israel   in its midst   like   to forever   his mercy

14 And made Israel to pass through the midst of it: for his mercy endureth for ever:

וְנִעֵר   פַּרְעֹה   וְחֵילוֹ   בְיַם־סוּף   כִּי לְעוֹלָם חַסְדּוֹ׃

and threw   Pharaoh   and his army   end – in sea   like   to forever   his mercy

15 But overthrew Pharaoh and his host in the Red sea: for his mercy endureth for ever.

לְמוֹלִיךְ   עַמּוֹ   בַּמִּדְבָּר   כִּי לְעוֹלָם חַסְדּוֹ׃

to lead   his people   in desert   like   to forever   his mercy

16 To him which led his people through the wilderness: for his mercy endureth for ever.

לְמַכֵּה   מְלָכִים   גְּדֹלִים   כִּי לְעוֹלָם חַסְדּוֹ׃

to striking   kings   great ones   like   to forever   his mercy

17 To him which smote great kings: for his mercy endureth for ever:

וַיַּהֲרֹג   מְלָכִים   אַדִּירִים   כִּי לְעוֹלָם חַסְדּוֹ׃

and he slew   kings   excellent ones   like   to forever   his mercy

18 And slew famous kings: for his mercy endureth for ever:

לְסִיחוֹן   מֶלֶךְ   הָאֱמֹרִי   כִּי לְעוֹלָם חַסְדּוֹ׃

to Sion   king   the Amori   like   to forever   his mercy

19 Sihon king of the Amorites: for his mercy endureth for ever:

וּלְעוֹג   מֶלֶךְ   הַבָּשָׁן   כִּי לְעוֹלָם חַסְדּוֹ׃

and to Og   king   the Bashan   like   to forever   his mercy

20 And Og the king of Bashan: for his mercy endureth for ever:

וְנָתַן   אַרְצָם   לְנַחֲלָה   כִּי לְעוֹלָם חַסְדּוֹ׃

and gave   their land   to inheritance   like   to forever   his mercy

21 And gave their land for an heritage: for his mercy endureth for ever:

נַחֲלָה   לְיִשְׂרָאֵל   עַבְדּוֹ   כִּי לְעוֹלָם חַסְדּוֹ׃

heritage   to Israel   his servant   like   to forever   his mercy

22 Even an heritage unto Israel his servant: for his mercy endureth for ever.

שֶׁבְּשִׁפְלֵנוּ   זָכַר־לָנוּ   כִּי לְעוֹלָם חַסְדּוֹ׃

that in our low rank   to us – remembered   like   to forever   his mercy

23 Who remembered us in our low estate: for his mercy endureth for ever:

וַיִּפְרְקֵנוּ   מִצָּרֵינוּ   כִּי לְעוֹלָם חַסְדּוֹ׃

and he redeemed us   from our enemies   like   to forever   his mercy

24 And hath redeemed us from our enemies: for his mercy endureth for ever.

נֹתֵן לֶחֶם לְכָל־בָּשָׂר   כִּי לְעוֹלָם חַסְדּוֹ:
he gives   bread   flesh – to all   like   to forever   his mercy

25 Who giveth food to all flesh: for his mercy endurethfor ever.

הוֹדוּ לְאֵל הַשָּׁמָיִם   כִּי לְעוֹלָם חַסְדּוֹ:
you give thanks   to El   the heavens   like   to forever   his mercy

26 O give thanks unto the God of heaven: for his mercy endureth for ever.

Psalm 137

ספר תהילים פרק קלז

עַל־נַהֲרוֹת בָּבֶל שָׁם יָשַׁבְנוּ גַּם־בָּכִינוּ בְּזָכְרֵנוּ אֶת־צִיּוֹן:
Zion - that   in we remembered   we wept - also   we sat   there   in Babylon   rivers - upon

1. By the rivers of Babylon, there we sat down, we also wept, when we remembered Zion.

עַל־עֲרָבִים בְּתוֹכָהּ תָּלִינוּ כִּנֹּרוֹתֵינוּ
our harps   we hung   in midst   the willows - upon

2. We hung our lyres on the willows in its midst.

כִּי שָׁם שְׁאֵלוּנוּ שׁוֹבֵינוּ דִּבְרֵי־שִׁיר
song – words   our captors   asked us   there   like

וְתוֹלָלֵינוּ שִׂמְחָה שִׁירוּ לָנוּ מִשִּׁיר צִיּוֹן:
Zion   from song   to us   you sing   happy   and our enslavers

3. For there those who carried us away captive required of us a song; and those who tormented us required of us mirth, saying, Sing us one of the songs of Zion.

אֵיךְ נָשִׁיר אֶת־שִׁיר יְהוָה עַל אַדְמַת נֵכָר:
foreign   lands   upon   ihvh   song – that   we sing   how

4. How shall we sing the Lord's song in a foreign land?

אִם־אֶשְׁכָּחֵךְ יְרוּשָׁלָם תִּשְׁכַּח יְמִינִי:
my right hand   I forget   Jerusalem   I forget you - if

5. If I forget you, O Jerusalem, let my right hand forget her cunning.

תִּדְבַּק־לְשׁוֹנִי לְחִכִּי אִם־לֹא אֶזְכְּרֵכִי
I remember you   not - if   to my palate   my tongue - adhere

אִם־לֹא אַעֲלֶה אֶת־יְרוּשָׁלַם עַל רֹאשׁ שִׂמְחָתִי:
my happiness   head   upon   Jerusalem – that   I ascend   not - if

6. If I do not remember you, let my tongue cleave to the roof of my mouth; if I do not set Jerusalem above my highest joy.

זְכֹר יְהוָה לִבְנֵי אֱדוֹם אֵת יוֹם יְרוּשָׁלָם
Jerusalem   day   that   Edomites   to sons   ihvh   remember

הָאֹמְרִים עָרוּ עָרוּ עַד הַיְסוֹד בָּהּ:
in it   the foundation   till   raze it   raze it   the saying ones

7. Remember, O Lord, against the Edomites, the day of Jerusalem; who said, Raze it, raze it, to its foundation.

בַּת־בָּבֶל הַשְּׁדוּדָה
the violated   Babylon - daughter

אַשְׁרֵי שֶׁיְשַׁלֶּם־לָךְ אֶת־גְּמוּלֵךְ שֶׁגָּמַלְתְּ לָנוּ:
to us   that you rewarded   your reward – that   to you – that will pay them   happy

8. O daughter of Babylon, you are to be destroyed! Happy shall he be, who repays you for what you have done to us!

אַשְׁרֵי שֶׁיֹּאחֵז וְנִפֵּץ אֶת־עֹלָלַיִךְ אֶל־הַסָּלַע:

the crag – onto   your babes – that   and dash   that he grab   happy

9. Happy shall he be, who takes your little ones and dashes them against the rock.

Psalm 138

ספר תהילים פרק קלח

לְדָוִד   אוֹדְךָ   בְּכָל־לִבִּי   נֶגֶד   אֱלֹהִים   אֲזַמְּרֶךָּ:
I will sing you melody   Elohim   before   my heart – in all   I will praise you   to David

1. Of David. I will praise you with my whole heart; before princes I will sing praise to
you.

אֶשְׁתַּחֲוֶה   אֶל־הֵיכַל   קָדְשְׁךָ   וְאוֹדֶה   אֶת־שְׁמֶךָ
your name – that   and I praise   your holiness   the temple – unto   I will bow down

עַל־חַסְדְּךָ   וְעַל־אֲמִתֶּךָ   כִּי־הִגְדַּלְתָּ
you magnified - like   your fullness - and upon   your mercy – upon

עַל־כָּל־שִׁמְךָ   אִמְרָתֶךָ:
your word   your name – all – upon

2. I will worship toward your holy temple, and praise your name for your loving
kindness and for your truth; for you have magnified your word above all your name.

בְּיוֹם   קָרָאתִי   וַתַּעֲנֵנִי   תַּרְהִבֵנִי   בְנַפְשִׁי   עֹז:
strength   in my soul   you empowered   and you answered me   I called   in day

3. In the day when I cried you answered me, and strengthened me with strength in my
soul.

יוֹדוּךָ   יְהֹוָה   כָּל־מַלְכֵי־אָרֶץ   כִּי   שָׁמְעוּ   אִמְרֵי־פִיךָ:
your mouth - words   they hear   like   earth – kings – all   ihvh   will thank

4. All the kings of the earth shall give you thanks, O Lord, when they hear the words of
your mouth.

וְיָשִׁירוּ   בְּדַרְכֵי   יְהֹוָה   כִּי   גָדוֹל   כְּבוֹד   יְהֹוָה:
ihvh   glory   big   like   ihvh   in ways   and they will sing

5. And they shall sing in the ways of the Lord; for great is the glory of the Lord.

כִּי־רָם   יְהֹוָה   וְשָׁפָל   יִרְאֶה   וְגָבֹהַּ   מִמֶּרְחָק   יְיֵדָע:
he knows   from far   and proud   he sees   and lowly   ihvh   exalted - like

6. Though the Lord is high, he regards the lowly; but the arrogant he knows from far
away.

אִם־אֵלֵךְ   בְּקֶרֶב   צָרָה   תְּחַיֵּנִי
you give life   distress   in midst   I will walk - if

עַל   אַף   אֹיְבַי   תִּשְׁלַח   יָדֶךָ   וְתוֹשִׁיעֵנִי   יְמִינֶךָ:
your right hand   and will save me   your hand   you send   my enemies   anger   upon

7. Though I walk in the midst of trouble, you will revive me; you shall stretch forth your
hand against the wrath of my enemies, and your right hand shall save me.

יְהֹוָה   יִגְמֹר   בַּעֲדִי   יְהֹוָה   חַסְדְּךָ
your mercy   ihvh   in my being   he complete   ihvh

לְעוֹלָם מַעֲשֵׂי יָדֶיךָ אַל־תֶּרֶף:
to forever   works   your hands   foresake – don't

8. May the Lord fulfil his purpose for me! Your loving kindness, O Lord, endures for ever; do not forsake the works of your own hands.

Psalm 139

ספר תהילים פרק קלט

לַמְנַצֵּחַ לְדָוִד מִזְמוֹר יְהֹוָה חֲקַרְתַּנִי וַתֵּדָע:
<small>and you know   you searched me   ihvh   psalm   to David   to him that is over</small>

1. To the chief Musician, A Psalm of David. O Lord, you have searched me, and known me.

אַתָּה יָדַעְתָּ שִׁבְתִּי וְקוּמִי בַּנְתָּה לְרֵעִי מֵרָחוֹק:
<small>from afar   my thoughts   you understood   and my rising   my sitting   known   you</small>

2. You know when I sit down and when I rise up, you understand my thoughts from far away.

אָרְחִי וְרִבְעִי זֵרִיתָ וְכָל־דְּרָכַי הִסְכַּנְתָּה:
<small>you acquainted   my ways - and all   you scattered   and my lying down   my path</small>

3. You have measured my going and my lying down, and you are acquainted with all my ways.

כִּי אֵין מִלָּה בִּלְשׁוֹנִי הֵן יְהֹוָה יָדַעְתָּ כֻלָּהּ:
<small>it all   you know   ihvh   behold   in my tongue   word   isn't   like</small>

4. For before a word is in my tongue, behold, O Lord, you know it all.

אָחוֹר וָקֶדֶם צַרְתָּנִי וַתָּשֶׁת עָלַי כַּפֶּכָה:
<small>your hand   upon me   and you set   you besieged me   and before   behind</small>

5. You have beset me behind and before, and laid your hand upon me.

פְּלִאיָה [פְּלִיאָה] דַעַת מִמֶּנִּי נִשְׂגְּבָה לֹא־אוּכַל לָהּ:
<small>to it   I able – not   set on high   from me   knowledge   wonderful</small>

6. (K) Such knowledge is too wonderful for me; it is high, I cannot attain it.

אָנָה אֵלֵךְ מֵרוּחֶךָ וְאָנָה מִפָּנֶיךָ אֶבְרָח:
<small>I will flee   from your face   and whither   from your spirit   will I go   whither</small>

7. Where shall I go from your spirit? Where shall I flee from your presence?

אִם־אֶסַּק שָׁמַיִם שָׁם אָתָּה וְאַצִּיעָה שְּׁאוֹל הִנֶּךָ:
<small>behold you   Sheol   and I spread a bed   you   there   heavens   I ascend - if</small>

8. If I ascend up to heaven, you are there! If I make my bed in Sheol, behold, you are there!

אֶשָּׂא כַנְפֵי־שָׁחַר אֶשְׁכְּנָה בְּאַחֲרִית יָם:
<small>sea   in back most   I dwell   down - wings   I take</small>

9. If I take the wings of the morning, and dwell in the uttermost parts of the sea,

גַּם־שָׁם יָדְךָ תַנְחֵנִי וְתֹאחֲזֵנִי יְמִינֶךָ:
<small>your right hand   and will take hold of me   will lead me   your hand   there- also</small>

10. Even there shall your hand lead me, and your right hand shall hold me.

וָאֹמַר אַךְ־חֹשֶׁךְ יְשׁוּפֵנִי וְלַיְלָה אוֹר בַּעֲדֵנִי׃

| and I said | darkness – surely | will cover me | and night | light | in about me |

11. If I say, Surely the darkness shall cover me, the light shall be night about me.

גַּם־חֹשֶׁךְ לֹא־יַחְשִׁיךְ מִמֶּךָ וְלַיְלָה כַּיּוֹם יָאִיר

| darkness - also | make dark – not | from you | and night | like day | shine |

כַּחֲשֵׁיכָה כָּאוֹרָה׃

| like darkness | like light |

12. Even the darkness is not dark for you; but the night shines like the day; darkness is
as light with you.

כִּי־אַתָּה קָנִיתָ כִלְיֹתָי תְּסֻכֵּנִי בְּבֶטֶן אִמִּי׃

| you - like | possessed | my reins | you cover me | in belly | my mother |

13. For you have formed my insides; you knit me together in my mother's womb.

אוֹדְךָ עַל כִּי נוֹרָאוֹת נִפְלֵיתִי

| I will give you thanks | upon | like | terrible things | my wonderful |

נִפְלָאִים מַעֲשֶׂיךָ וְנַפְשִׁי יֹדַעַת מְאֹד׃

| wonderful ones | your works | and my soul | knowing | greatly |

14. I will praise you; for I am fearfully and wonderfully made. Marvelous are your works!
And my soul knows that right well.

לֹא־נִכְחַד עָצְמִי מִמֶּךָ אֲשֶׁר־עֻשֵּׂיתִי

| was concealed - not | my bone | from you | which | I was made – which |

בַּסֵּתֶר רֻקַּמְתִּי בְּתַחְתִּיּוֹת אָרֶץ׃

| in hiding place | I embroidered | in depths | earth |

15. My frame was not hidden from you, when I was made in secret, and finely wrought
in the depths of the earth.

גָּלְמִי רָאוּ עֵינֶיךָ וְעַל־סִפְרְךָ כֻּלָּם יִכָּתֵבוּ

| my unformed substance | saw | your eyes | your book – and upon | all them | were written |

יָמִים יֻצָּרוּ וְלֹא [וְלוֹ] אֶחָד בָּהֶם׃

| days | they fashioned | and not | [and to him] | one | among them |

16. (K) Your eyes saw my unformed substance; and in your book all things were written;
also the days in which they are to be fashioned, and for it too there was one of them.

וְלִי מַה־יָּקְרוּ רֵעֶיךָ אֵל מֶה עָצְמוּ רָאשֵׁיהֶם׃

| and to me | they precious – how | your thoughts | El | how | they strong | their sums |

17. How precious also are your thoughts to me, O God! How vast is their sum!

אֶסְפְּרֵם מֵחוֹל יִרְבּוּן הֱקִיצֹתִי וְעוֹדִי עִמָּךְ׃

| I will count them | from sand | they many | I awake | and still I | with you |

18. If I should count them, they are more in number than the sand; when I awake, I am
still with you.

אִם־תִּקְטֹל אֱלוֹהַּ רָשָׁע וְאַנְשֵׁי דָמִים סוּרוּ מֶנִּי׃

from me depart you bloods and peoples wicked Elohim you will slay - if

19. Surely you will slay the wicked, O God! Depart from me therefore, you bloody men!

אֲשֶׁר יֹאמְרֻךָ לִמְזִמָּה נָשָׂא לַשָּׁוְא עָרֶיךָ׃

your enemy to vanity bear to scheme they say to you which

20. For they speak against you wickedly, and your enemies take your name in vain.

הֲלוֹא־מְשַׂנְאֶיךָ יְהוָה אֶשְׂנָא וּבִתְקוֹמְמֶיךָ אֶתְקוֹטָט׃

I be disgusted and in those who rise against you I hate ihvh from haters of you - the him

21. Do I not hate them, O Lord, those who hate you? And do I not strive with those who rise up against you?

תַּכְלִית שִׂנְאָה שְׂנֵאתִים לְאוֹיְבִים הָיוּ לִי׃

to me they were to enemies I hate them hate perfection

22. I hate them with the utmost hatred; I count them my enemies.

חָקְרֵנִי אֵל וְדַע לְבָבִי בְּחָנֵנִי וְדַע שַׂרְעַפָּי׃

my thoughts and know prove my heart and know El search me

23. Search me, O God, and know my heart! Test me, and know my thoughts!

וּרְאֵה אִם־דֶּרֶךְ־עֹצֶב בִּי וּנְחֵנִי בְּדֶרֶךְ עוֹלָם׃

forever in way and lead me in me grieving – way – if and see

24. And see if there is any wicked way in me, and lead me in the way everlasting.

PSALM 140

ספר תהילים פרק קמ

לַמְנַצֵּחַ מִזְמוֹר לְדָוִד׃

to David   Psalm   to chief Musician

1. To the chief Musician, A Psalm of David.

חַלְּצֵנִי יְהוָה מֵאָדָם רָע מֵאִישׁ חֲמָסִים תִּנְצְרֵנִי׃

preserve me   violent ones   from man   evil   from Adam   ihvh   deliver me

2. Save me, O Lord from the evil man; preserve me from the violent man;

אֲשֶׁר חָשְׁבוּ רָעוֹת בְּלֵב כָּל־יוֹם יָגוּרוּ מִלְחָמוֹת׃

wars   they stir up   day – all   in heart   evils   they devised   which

3. Who plot evil plans in their heart; and stir up wars continually.

שָׁנֲנוּ לְשׁוֹנָם כְּמוֹ־נָחָשׁ חֲמַת עַכְשׁוּב תַּחַת שְׂפָתֵימוֹ סֶלָה׃

sela   their lips   under   adder   wrath   serpent - like   their tongue   they whetted

4. They have sharpened their tongues like a serpent; spiders' poison is under their lips.
Selah.

שָׁמְרֵנִי יְהוָה מִידֵי רָשָׁע מֵאִישׁ חֲמָסִים

violent ones   from man   wicked   from hands   ihvh   keep me

תִּנְצְרֵנִי אֲשֶׁר חָשְׁבוּ לִדְחוֹת פְּעָמָי׃

my steps   to thrust down   they devised   which   you preserve me

5. Keep me, O Lord, from the hands of the wicked; preserve me from the violent man;
who intend to trip up my feet.

טָמְנוּ גֵאִים פַּח־לִי וַחֲבָלִים פָּרְשׂוּ רֶשֶׁת

net   they spread   and cords   to me – trap   proud   have hid

לְיַד מַעְגָּל מֹקְשִׁים שָׁתוּ־לִי סֶלָה׃

sela   to me - they set   snares   track   to side

6. Arrogant men have hidden a snare for me, and cords; they have spread a net by the
wayside; they have set traps for me. Selah.

אָמַרְתִּי לַיהוָה אֵלִי אָתָּה הַאֲזִינָה יְהוָה קוֹל תַּחֲנוּנָי׃

my supplications   voice   ihvh   the give ear   you   my El   to ihvh   I said

7. I said to the Lord, You are my God; hear the voice of my supplications, O Lord.

יְהוִֹה אֲדֹנָי עֹז יְשׁוּעָתִי סַכּוֹתָה לְרֹאשִׁי בְּיוֹם נָשֶׁק׃

armor   in day   to my head   you covered   my salvation   strength   Adoni   ihvh

8. O God the Lord, the strength of my salvation, you have covered my head in the day
of battle.

אַל־תִּתֵּן יְהוָה מַאֲוַיֵּי רָשָׁע זְמָמוֹ אַל־תָּפֵק יָרוּמוּ סֶלָה׃

sela   they exalt   further – don't   his devices   wicked   from desires   ihvh   give - don't

9. Do not grant, O Lord, the desires of the wicked man; do not further his evil plot; lest

they exalt themselves. Selah.

רֹאשׁ מְסִבָּי   עֲמַל שְׂפָתֵימוֹ יְכַסֵּימוֹ [יְכַסֵּמוֹ]׃

it cover them	their lips	grievous	from around me	head

10. (K) As for the head of those who surround me, let the mischief of their own lips cover them.

יָמִיטוּ [יִמּוֹטוּ] עֲלֵיהֶם גֶּחָלִים בָּאֵשׁ יַפִּלֵם

it falls them	in fire	coals	upon them	they will slip

בְּמַהֲמֹרוֹת בַּל־יָקוּמוּ׃

they will rise - not	in pits

11. (K) Let burning coals fall upon them; let them be cast into the fire; into deep pits, so that they should not rise up again.

אִישׁ לָשׁוֹן בַּל־יִכּוֹן בָּאָרֶץ אִישׁ־חָמָס רָע

evil	violence – man	in earth	be established – not	tongue	man

יְצוּדֶנּוּ לְמַדְחֵפֹת׃

to overthrowing	it hunt him

12. Let not a slanderer be established in the earth; let evil hunt down the violent man to overthrow him.

יָדַעְתָּ [יָדַעְתִּי] כִּי־יַעֲשֶׂה יְהוָה דִּין עָנִי מִשְׁפַּט אֶבְיֹנִים׃

needy ones	judgment	poor	judge	ihvh	he does - like	I know

13. I know that the Lord maintains the cause of the afflicted, and the right of the poor.

אַךְ צַדִּיקִים יוֹדוּ לִשְׁמֶךָ יֵשְׁבוּ יְשָׁרִים אֶת־פָּנֶיךָ׃

your face - that	upright ones	they will dwell	to your name	they will give thanks	righteous ones	surely

14. Surely the righteous shall give thanks to your name; the upright shall dwell in your presence.

Psalm 141

ספר תהילים פרק קמא

מִזְמֹ֗ור לְדָ֫וִ֥ד

to David   psalm

יְהֹוָ֣ה קְרָאתִ֖יךָ ח֣וּשָׁה לִּ֑י הַאֲזִ֥ינָה קֹ֝ולִ֗י בְּקָרְאִי־לָֽךְ׃

to you – in my call   my voice   the ear it   to me   hasten   I call you   ihvh

1. A Psalm of David. Lord, I cry to you; make haste to me; give ear to my voice, when I cry to you.

תִּכֹּ֤ון תְּפִלָּתִ֣י קְטֹ֣רֶת לְפָנֶ֑יךָ מַשְׂאַ֥ת כַּ֝פַּ֗י מִנְחַת־עָֽרֶב׃

evening – offering   my palms   lifting up   before you   incense   my prayer   establish

2. Let my prayer be set forth before you like incense; and the lifting up of my hands like the evening sacrifice.

שִׁיתָ֣ה יְ֭הֹוָה שָׁמְרָ֣ה לְפִ֑י נִ֝צְּרָ֗ה עַל־דַּ֥ל שְׂפָתָֽי׃

my lips   door - upon   preserve   to my mouth   heeding   ihvh   set

3. Set a guard, O Lord, over my mouth; keep watch over the door of my lips.

אַל־תַּ֥ט לִבִּ֨י לְדָבָ֪ר רָ֡ע לְהִתְעֹ֘ולֵ֤ל

to practice   evil   to matter   my heart   incline - don't

עֲלִלֹ֨ות בְּרֶ֗שַׁע אֶת־אִישִׁ֥ים פֹּֽעֲלֵי־אָ֑וֶן

inequity – working   men – that   in wickedness   acts

וּבַל־אֶ֝לְחַ֗ם בְּמַנְעַמֵּיהֶֽם׃

in their pleasure   let me eat – and in not

4. Do not incline my heart to any evil thing, to practice wicked deeds with men who work iniquity; and do not let me eat of their dainties.

יֶֽהֶלְמֵֽנִי־צַדִּ֨יק חֶ֡סֶד וְֽיֹוכִיחֵ֗נִי שֶׁ֣מֶן רֹ֭אשׁ

head   oil   and he rebuke me   mercy   righteous – it strike me

אַל־יָנִ֣י רֹאשִׁ֑י כִּי־עֹ֥וד וּ֝תְפִלָּתִ֗י בְּרָעֹותֵיהֶֽם׃

in their evil deeds   and my prayer   still   like   my head   refuse – don't

5. Let the righteous strike me in loving kindness, and let him rebuke me; it shall be as oil for my head; let not my head refuse it; but my prayer shall still be against their evil deeds.

נִשְׁמְט֣וּ בִֽידֵי־סֶ֭לַע שֹׁפְטֵיהֶ֑ם וְשָׁמְע֥וּ אֲ֝מָרַ֗י כִּ֣י נָעֵֽמוּ׃

they pleasant   like   my words   and they heard   their judges   crag – in side   stumbled

6. When their judges are thrown down to stony places, then they will hear how sweet were my words.

כְּמֹ֤ו פֹלֵ֣חַ וּבֹקֵ֣עַ בָּאָ֑רֶץ נִפְזְר֥וּ עֲ֝צָמֵ֗ינוּ לְפִ֣י שְׁאֹֽול׃

Shoel   to mouth   our bones   scattered   in earth   and clearing   cutting   like

7. As when one cuts and breaks up wood on the earth, so are our bones scattered at the

mouth of Sheol.

כִּי אֵלֶיךָ יְהוָֹה אֲדֹנָי עֵינָי בְּכָה חָסִיתִי אַל־תְּעַר נַפְשִׁי׃

my soul　make empty – don't　I take refuge　I trusted　my eyes　Adoni　Ihvh　unto you　like

8. But my eyes are toward you, O God the Lord; in you is my trust; do not leave my soul destitute.

שָׁמְרֵנִי מִידֵי־פַח יָקְשׁוּ לִי וּמֹקְשׁוֹת פֹּעֲלֵי אָוֶן׃

inequity　workers　and traps　to me　they laid　trap – from hands　heed me

9. Keep me from the snare which they have laid for me, and the traps of the evil doers.

יִפְּלוּ בְמַכְמֹרָיו רְשָׁעִים יַחַד אָנֹכִי עַד־אֶעֱבוֹר׃

I pass – till　I am　together　wicked　in his nets　they fall

10. Let the wicked fall together into their own nets, while I escape.

PSALM 142

ספר תהילים פרק קמב

מַשְׂכִּיל לְדָוִד בִּהְיוֹתוֹ בַמְּעָרָה תְפִלָּה:

prayer   in cave   in his being   to David   Mashkil

1. A Maskil of David; A Prayer when he was in the cave.

קוֹלִי אֶל־יְהֹוָה אֶזְעָק קוֹלִי אֶל־יְהֹוָה אֶתְחַנָּן:

I plead   ihvh - unto   my voice   I cry   ihvh – unto   my voice

2. I cry to the Lord with my voice; with my voice I make my supplication to the Lord.

אֶשְׁפֹּךְ לְפָנָיו שִׂיחִי צָרָתִי לְפָנָיו אַגִּיד:

I declare   before him   my distress   my meditation   before him   I pour out

3. I pour out my complaint before him; I declare my trouble before him.

בְּהִתְעַטֵּף עָלַי רוּחִי וְאַתָּה יָדַעְתָּ נְתִיבָתִי בְּאֹרַח־זוּ אֲהַלֵּךְ

I walk   this – in road   my paths   you know   and you   my spirit   upon me   in faint

טָמְנוּ פַח לִי:

to me   trap   they hid

4. When my spirit is faint inside me, you know my path. In the path where I walk they have secretly laid a snare for me.

הַבֵּיט יָמִין וּרְאֵה וְאֵין־לִי מַכִּיר אָבַד מָנוֹס מִמֶּנִּי

from me   refuge   remains   acquaintance   to me – and isn't   and see   right hand   look

אֵין דּוֹרֵשׁ לְנַפְשִׁי:

to my soul   seeks   isn't

5. I look on my right hand, and behold, but there is no man who knows me; no refuge remains to me; no man cares for my soul.

זָעַקְתִּי אֵלֶיךָ יְהֹוָה אָמַרְתִּי אַתָּה מַחְסִי חֶלְקִי בְּאֶרֶץ הַחַיִּים:

the living   in land   my portion   my refuge   you   I said   ihvh   unto you   I cry

6. I cry to you, O Lord; I say, You are my refuge and my portion in the land of the living.

הַקְשִׁיבָה אֶל־רִנָּתִי כִּי־דַלּוֹתִי מְאֹד הַצִּילֵנִי מֵרֹדְפַי

from my pursuers   deliver me   greatly   I brought low - like   my outcry – unto   the attention

כִּי אָמְצוּ מִמֶּנִּי:

from I   they strong   like

7. Attend to my cry; for I am brought very low; save me from my persecutors; for they are too strong for me.

הוֹצִיאָה מִמַּסְגֵּר נַפְשִׁי לְהוֹדוֹת אֶת־שְׁמֶךָ בִּי יַכְתִּרוּ

they encompass   in me   your name – that   to thanking   my soul   from prison   bring out

צַדִּיקִים כִּי תִגְמֹל עָלָי׃

upon me you reward like righteous ones

8. Bring my soul out of prison, that I may give thanks to your name; the righteous shall surround me; for you shall deal bountifully with me.

PSALM 143

מִזְמוֹר לְדָוִד יְהוָה שְׁמַע תְּפִלָּתִי

psalm   to David   ihvh   hear   my prayer

הַאֲזִינָה אֶל־תַּחֲנוּנַי בֶּאֱמֻנָתְךָ עֲנֵנִי בְּצִדְקָתֶךָ:

the ear   my supplications - unto   in your faithfulness   answer me   in our rightness

. A Psalm of David. Hear my prayer, O Lord, give ear to my supplications; in your faithfulness answer me, and in your righteousness.

וְאַל־תָּבוֹא בְמִשְׁפָּט אֶת־עַבְדֶּךָ

and not - you come   in judgment   that - your servant

כִּי לֹא־יִצְדַּק לְפָנֶיךָ כָל־חָי:

like   not - will be justified   before you   all - living

2. And do not enter into judgment with your servant; for in your sight no living man shall be justified.

כִּי רָדַף אוֹיֵב נַפְשִׁי דִּכָּא לָאָרֶץ

like   pursued   enemies   my soul   he crushed   to earth

חִיָּתִי הוֹשִׁיבַנִי בְמַחֲשַׁכִּים כְּמֵתֵי עוֹלָם:

my life   made me dwell   in dark places   like dead   forever

3. For the enemy has persecuted my soul; he has crushed my life down to the ground; he has made me dwell in darkness, like those who have been long dead.

וַתִּתְעַטֵּף עָלַי רוּחִי בְּתוֹכִי יִשְׁתּוֹמֵם לִבִּי:

and it droops   upon me   my spirit   in midst me   dejected them   my heart

4. Therefore my spirit faints inside me; my heart inside me is appalled.

זָכַרְתִּי יָמִים מִקֶּדֶם הָגִיתִי בְכָל־פָּעֳלֶךָ

I remember   days   from old   I meditate   in all - your deeds

בְּמַעֲשֵׂה יָדֶיךָ אֲשׂוֹחֵחַ:

in work   your hands   I meditate

5. I remember the days of old; I meditate on all your works; I muse on the work of your hands.

פֵּרַשְׂתִּי יָדַי אֵלֶיךָ נַפְשִׁי כְּאֶרֶץ־עֲיֵפָה לְךָ סֶלָה:

I stretch   my hands   unto you   my soul   weary - like land   to you   Sela

6. I stretch forth my hands to you; my soul thirsts after you, like a parched land. Selah.

מַהֵר עֲנֵנִי יְהוָה כָּלְתָה רוּחִי אַל־תַּסְתֵּר פָּנֶיךָ מִמֶּנִּי

hasten   answer me   ihvh   consumed   my spirit   don't - hide   your face   from me

וְנִמְשַׁלְתִּי עִם־יֹרְדֵי בוֹר:

and I be cast   with - those descending   pit

7. Answer me speedily, O Lord; my spirit fails; do not hide your face from me, lest I be

like those who go down into the pit.

הַשְׁמִיעֵנִי בַבֹּקֶר חַסְדֶּךָ כִּי־בְךָ בָטָחְתִּי

I trust   in you – like   your mercy   in morning   the hear me

הוֹדִיעֵנִי דֶּרֶךְ־זוּ אֵלֵךְ כִּי־אֵלֶיךָ נָשָׂאתִי נַפְשִׁי:

my soul   I lift   unto you – like   I walk   this – way   let me know

8. Let me hear your loving kindness in the morning; for in you I trust; let me know the path where I should walk; for I lift up my soul to you.

הַצִּילֵנִי מֵאֹיְבַי יְהוָה אֵלֶיךָ כִסִּתִי:

I hide   unto you   ihvh   from my enemies   deliver me

9. Save me, O Lord, from my enemies; I flee to you to hide me.

לַמְּדֵנִי לַעֲשׂוֹת רְצוֹנֶךָ כִּי־אַתָּה אֱלוֹהָי

m√ Elohim   you – like   your pleasure   to do   teach me

רוּחֲךָ טוֹבָה תַּנְחֵנִי בְּאֶרֶץ מִישׁוֹר:

level   in land   you lead me   good   your spirit

10. Teach me to do your will; for you are my God; let your good spirit lead me to a level land.

לְמַעַן־שִׁמְךָ יְהוָה תְּחַיֵּנִי בְּצִדְקָתְךָ תוֹצִיא מִצָּרָה נַפְשִׁי:

my soul   from distress   remove   in your righteousness   you revive me   ihvh   your name – to end

11. Revive me, O Lord, for your name's sake; for your righteousness' sake bring my soul out of trouble.

וּבְחַסְדְּךָ תַּצְמִית אֹיְבָי וְהַאֲבַדְתָּ כָּל־צֹרֲרֵי

oppressors – all   and the destroy   my enemies   you cut off   and in your mercy

נַפְשִׁי כִּי אֲנִי עַבְדֶּךָ:

your servant   I   like   my soul

12. And in your loving kindness cut off my enemies, and destroy all those who afflict my soul; for I am your servant.

PSALM 144

ספר תהילים פרק קמד

לְדָוִד
to David

בָּרוּךְ יְהֹוָה צוּרִי הַמְלַמֵּד יָדַי לַקְרָב אֶצְבְּעוֹתַי לַמִּלְחָמָה:
blessed   ihvh   my rock   the teaching   my hands   to attack   my fingers   to war

1. A Psalm of David. Blessed be the Lord my strength, who teaches my hands to war,
and my fingers to fight;

חַסְדִּי וּמְצוּדָתִי מִשְׂגַּבִּי וּמְפַלְטִי לִי מָגִנִּי
my mercy   and my fortress   my high tower   and my deliverer   to me   my shield

וּבוֹ חָסִיתִי הָרוֹדֵד עַמִּי תַחְתָּי:
and in him   I take refuge   the subduing   my people   under me

2. My gracious one, and my fortress; my high tower, and my savior; my shield, and he in
whom I trust; who subdues my people under me.

יְהֹוָה מָה־אָדָם וַתֵּדָעֵהוּ בֶּן־אֱנוֹשׁ וַתְּחַשְּׁבֵהוּ:
ihvh   Adam – what   and you know him   Enosh – son   and you reckoned him

3. Lord, what is man, that you should take knowledge of him, or the son of man, that
you should make account of him?

אָדָם לַהֶבֶל דָּמָה יָמָיו כְּצֵל עוֹבֵר:
Adam   to vanity   compared   his days   like shadow   passing

4. Man is like a breath; his days are like a passing shadow.

יְהֹוָה הַט־שָׁמֶיךָ וְתֵרֵד גַּע בֶּהָרִים וְיֶעֱשָׁנוּ:
ihvh   your heavens – bow   and you descend   touch   in mountains   and they will smoke

5. Bow your heavens, O Lord, and come down; touch the mountains, and they shall
smoke.

בְּרוֹק בָּרָק וּתְפִיצֵם שְׁלַח חִצֶּיךָ וּתְהֻמֵּם:
flash   lightning   and scatter them   send   your arrows   and discomfort them

6. Cast forth lightning, and scatter them; shoot out your arrows, and destroy them.

שְׁלַח יָדֶיךָ מִמָּרוֹם פְּצֵנִי וְהַצִּילֵנִי מִמַּיִם רַבִּים
send   your hand   from on high   rescue me   and deliver me   from waters   many

מִיַּד בְּנֵי נֵכָר:
from hand   sons   stranger

7. Send your hand from above; rescue me, and save me from great waters, from the
hand of strangers;

אֲשֶׁר פִּיהֶם דִּבֶּר־שָׁוְא וִימִינָם יְמִין שָׁקֶר:
which   their mouth   vanity – speaks   and their right hand   right hand   lie

8. Whose mouth speak vanity, and their right hand is a right hand of falsehood.

אֱלֹהִים שִׁיר חָדָשׁ אָשִׁירָה לָּךְ בְּנֵבֶל עָשׂוֹר אֲזַמְּרָה־לָּךְ:

| to you - I will sing psalms | ten strings | in lyre | to you | I will sing | new | song | Elohim |

9. I will sing a new song to you, O God; on a harp of ten strings will I sing praises to you.

הַנּוֹתֵן תְּשׁוּעָה לַמְּלָכִים הַפּוֹצֶה אֶת־דָּוִד עַבְדּוֹ מֵחֶרֶב רָעָה:

| evil | from sword | his servant | David - that | the releaser | to kings | salvation | the giver |

10. It is he who gives salvation to kings; who saves David his servant from the harmful sword.

פְּצֵנִי וְהַצִּילֵנִי מִיַּד בְּנֵי־נֵכָר אֲשֶׁר־פִּיהֶם דִּבֶּר־שָׁוְא

| vanity – speaks | their mouths - which | stranger – sons | from hand | and deliver me | release me |

וִימִינָם יְמִין שָׁקֶר:

| lie | right hand | and their right hand |

11. Rescue and save me from the hand of strangers, whose mouth speaks vanity, and their right hand is a right hand of falsehood;

אֲשֶׁר בָּנֵינוּ כִּנְטִעִים מְגֻדָּלִים בִּנְעוּרֵיהֶם

| in their youths | grown up | like plants | our sons | which |

בְּנוֹתֵינוּ כְזָוִיֹּת מְחֻטָּבוֹת תַּבְנִית הֵיכָל:

| palace | structure | hewn | like corner stones | our daughters |

12. May our sons be like plants grown up in their youth! May our daughters be like corner stones, cut for the structure of a palace!

מְזָוֵינוּ מְלֵאִים מְפִיקִים מִזַּן אֶל־זַן

| sort – unto | from sort | providing | full ones | our corners |

צֹאונֵנוּ מַאֲלִיפוֹת מְרֻבָּבוֹת בְּחוּצוֹתֵינוּ:

| in our outsides | from many ones | from thousands | our sheep |

13. May our garners be full, affording all manner of store! May our sheep bring forth thousands and ten thousands in our fields!

אַלּוּפֵינוּ מְסֻבָּלִים אֵין פֶּרֶץ וְאֵין יוֹצֵאת

| going out | and isn't | breach | and isn't | laden ones | our oxen |

וְאֵין צְוָחָה בִּרְחֹבֹתֵינוּ:

| in our streets | wailing | and isn't |

14. May our oxen be heavy laden, so there should be no breach or migration! May there be no loud cry in our in our streets!

אַשְׁרֵי הָעָם שֶׁכָּכָה לּוֹ אַשְׁרֵי הָעָם שֶׁיֲהוָה אֱלֹהָיו:

| its Elohim | which ihvh | the people | happy | to it | which this | the people | happy |

15. Happy is the people to whom that is the case! Happy is the people whose God is the Lord!

PSALM 145

ספר תהילים פרק קמה

תְּהִלָּה לְדָוִד
prayer   to David

1 David's *Psalm* of praise.

אֲרוֹמִמְךָ אֱלוֹהַי הַמֶּלֶךְ וַאֲבָרֲכָה שִׁמְךָ לְעוֹלָם וָעֶד:
and again   forever   your name   and I bless   the king   my Elohim   I exalt you

I will extol thee, my God, O king; and I will bless thy name for ever and ever.

בְּכָל־יוֹם אֲבָרֲכֶךָּ וַאֲהַלְלָה שִׁמְךָ לְעוֹלָם וָעֶד:
and again   forever   your name   and I praise   I bless you   day - in all

2 Every day will I bless thee; and I will praise thy name for ever and ever.

גָּדוֹל יְהוָֹה וּמְהֻלָּל מְאֹד וְלִגְדֻלָּתוֹ אֵין חֵקֶר:
searchable   isn't   and to his greatness   very   and from praised   ihvh   great

3 Great is the LORD, and greatly to be praised; and his greatness is unsearchable.

דּוֹר לְדוֹר יְשַׁבַּח מַעֲשֶׂיךָ וּגְבוּרֹתֶיךָ יַגִּידוּ:
they expound   and your mighty acts   your works   I laud   to generation   generation

4 One generation shall praise thy works to another, and shall declare thy mighty acts.

הֲדַר כְּבוֹד הוֹדֶךָ וְדִבְרֵי נִפְלְאֹתֶיךָ אָשִׂיחָה:
meditation   your mystical   and speakings   your splendor   glorious   splendor

5 I will speak of the glorious honour of thy majesty, and of thy wondrous works.

וֶעֱזוּז נוֹרְאֹתֶיךָ יֹאמֵרוּ וּגְדוּלָּתֶיךָ [וּגְדוּלָּתְךָ] אֲסַפְּרֶנָּה:
I declare   and your great acts   they say   your awesome acts   and forcefully

6 And *men* shall speak of the might of thy terrible acts: and I will declare thy greatness.

זֵכֶר רַב־טוּבְךָ יַבִּיעוּ וְצִדְקָתְךָ יְרַנֵּנוּ:
they shout joy   and your righteousness   they utter   your goodness - many   recalling

7 They shall abundantly utter the memory of thy great goodness, and shall sing of thy righteousness.

חַנּוּן וְרַחוּם יְהוָֹה אֶרֶךְ אַפַּיִם וּגְדָל־חָסֶד:
mercy - and great   to angers   long   ihvh   and merciful   gracious

8 The LORD *is* gracious, and full of compassion; slow to anger, and of great mercy.

טוֹב־יְהוָֹה לַכֹּל וְרַחֲמָיו עַל־כָּל־מַעֲשָׂיו:
his works – all – upon   and his compassion   to all   ihvh – good

9 The LORD is good to all: and his tender mercies are over all his works.

יוֹדוּךָ יְהוָֹה כָּל־מַעֲשֶׂיךָ וַחֲסִידֶיךָ יְבָרֲכוּכָה:
they bless you   and your pious ones   your works – all   ihvh   they acclaim you

10 All thy works shall praise thee, O LORD; and thy saints shall bless thee.

כְּבוֹד מַלְכוּתְךָ יֹאמֵרוּ וּגְבוּרָתְךָ יְדַבֵּרוּ:

<small>they speak   and your might   they say   your kingdom   glorious</small>

11 They shall speak of the glory of thy kingdom, and talk of thy power;

לְהוֹדִיעַ לִבְנֵי הָאָדָם גְּבוּרֹתָיו וּכְבוֹד הֲדַר מַלְכוּתוֹ:

<small>his kingdom   splendor   and glory   his mighty acts   the Adam   to sons   to inform</small>

12 To make known to the sons of men his mighty acts, and the glorious majesty of his kingdom.

מַלְכוּתְךָ מַלְכוּת כָּל־עֹלָמִים וּמֶמְשַׁלְתְּךָ בְּכָל־דּוֹר וָדוֹר:

<small>and generation   generation - in all   and your ruling   forevers – all   kingdom   your kingdom</small>

13 Thy kingdom is an everlasting kingdom, and thy dominion endureth throughout all generations.

סוֹמֵךְ יְהֹוָה לְכָל־הַנֹּפְלִים וְזוֹקֵף לְכָל־הַכְּפוּפִים:

<small>bowed ones - to all   and straightens   the fallen ones – to all   ihvh   supports</small>

14 The LORD upholdeth all that fall, and raiseth up all those that be bowed down.

עֵינֵי־כֹל אֵלֶיךָ יְשַׂבֵּרוּ וְאַתָּה נוֹתֵן־לָהֶם אֶת־אָכְלָם בְּעִתּוֹ:

<small>in its season   their food - that   to them - giver   and you   they look forward   unto you   all – eyes</small>

15 The eyes of all wait upon thee; and thou givest them their meat in due season.

פּוֹתֵחַ אֶת־יָדֶךָ וּמַשְׂבִּיעַ לְכָל־חַי רָצוֹן:

<small>desire   life - to all   and satisfy   your hand - that   open</small>

16 Thou openest thine hand, and satisfiest the desire of every living thing.

צַדִּיק יְהֹוָה בְּכָל־דְּרָכָיו וְחָסִיד בְּכָל־מַעֲשָׂיו:

<small>his works - in all   and merciful   his ways - in all   ihvh   righteous</small>

17 The LORD is righteous in all his ways, and holy in all his works.

קָרוֹב יְהֹוָה לְכָל־קֹרְאָיו לְכֹל אֲשֶׁר יִקְרָאֻהוּ בֶאֱמֶת:

<small>in truth   they call him   which   to all   his callers – to all   ihvh   near</small>

18 The LORD is nigh unto all them that call upon him, to all that call upon him in truth.

רְצוֹן־יְרֵאָיו יַעֲשֶׂה וְאֶת־שַׁוְעָתָם יִשְׁמַע וְיוֹשִׁיעֵם:

<small>and he saves them   he hears   their cry - and that   he does   his fearing – desire</small>

19 He will fulfil the desire of them that fear him: he also will hear their cry, and will save them.

שׁוֹמֵר יְהֹוָה אֶת־כָּל־אֹהֲבָיו וְאֵת כָּל־הָרְשָׁעִים יַשְׁמִיד:

<small>he destroys   the wicked – all   and that   his loving ones - all - that   ihvh   heeds</small>

20 The LORD preserveth all them that love him: but all the wicked will he destroy.

תְּהִלַּת יְהֹוָה יְדַבֶּר־פִּי

<small>my mouth - he speaks   ihvh   prayers</small>

וִיבָרֵךְ כָּל־בָּשָׂר שֵׁם קָדְשׁוֹ לְעוֹלָם וָעֶד:

<small>and again   forever   his holy   name   flesh - all   and he blesses</small>

21 My mouth shall speak the praise of the LORD: and let all flesh bless his holy name for ever and ever.

PSALM 146

ספר תהילים פרק קמו

הַלְלוּיָהּ
praise Ya

הַלְלִי נַפְשִׁי אֶת־יְהֹוָה:
ihvh - that   my soul   praise

1 Praise ye the LORD. Praise the LORD, O my soul.

אֲהַלְלָה יְהֹוָה בְּחַיָּי אֲזַמְּרָה לֵאלֹהַי בְּעוֹדִי:
in my being   to my Elohim   I sing psalms   in my life   ihvh   I praise

2 While I live will I praise the LORD: I will sing praises unto my God while I have any being.

אַל־תִּבְטְחוּ בִנְדִיבִים בְּבֶן־אָדָם שֶׁאֵין לוֹ תְשׁוּעָה:
salvation   to him   that isn't   Adam - in son   in princes   you trust - don't

3 Put not your trust in princes, *nor* in the son of man, in whom *there is* no help.

תֵּצֵא רוּחוֹ יָשֻׁב לְאַדְמָתוֹ בַּיּוֹם הַהוּא אָבְדוּ עֶשְׁתֹּנֹתָיו:
his plans   perish   the he   in day   to his soil   he returns   his spirit   go out

4 His breath goeth forth, he returneth to his earth; in that very day his thoughts perish.

אַשְׁרֵי שֶׁאֵל יַעֲקֹב בְּעֶזְרוֹ שִׂבְרוֹ עַל־יְהֹוָה אֱלֹהָיו:
his Elohim   ihvh -- upon   his hope   in his help   Jacob   that El   praiseworthy

5 Happy is he that hath the God of Jacob for his help, whose hope *is* in the LORD his God:

עֹשֶׂה שָׁמַיִם וָאָרֶץ אֶת־הַיָּם וְאֶת־כָּל־אֲשֶׁר־בָּם
in them - which - all - and that   the sea - that   and earth   heavens   maker

הַשֹּׁמֵר אֱמֶת לְעוֹלָם:
forever   truth   the heeder

6 Which made heaven, and earth, the sea, and all that therein is: which keepeth truth for ever:

עֹשֶׂה מִשְׁפָּט לַעֲשׁוּקִים נֹתֵן לֶחֶם לָרְעֵבִים
to hungry ones   bread   he gives   to oppressed ones   judgment   he made

יְהֹוָה מַתִּיר אֲסוּרִים:
bound ones   loosing   ihvh

7 Which executeth judgment for the oppressed: which giveth food to the hungry. The LORD looseth the prisoners:

יְהֹוָה פֹּקֵחַ עִוְרִים יְהֹוָה זֹקֵף כְּפוּפִים יְהֹוָה אֹהֵב צַדִּיקִים:
righteous ones   loves   ihvh   bowed down ones   straightens   ihvh   blind ones   opening   ihvh

8 The LORD openeth the eyes of the blind: the LORD raiseth them that are bowed down: the LORD loveth the righteous:

יְהֹוָה שֹׁמֵר אֶת־גֵּרִים יָתוֹם וְאַלְמָנָה יְעוֹדֵד

he restores   and widow   orphan   strangers - that   heeder   ihvh

וְדֶרֶךְ רְשָׁעִים יְעַוֵּת:

he perverts   wicked   and path

9 The LORD preserveth the strangers; he relieveth the fatherless and widow: but the way of the wicked he turneth upside down.

יִמְלֹךְ יְהֹוָה לְעוֹלָם אֱלֹהַיִךְ צִיּוֹן לְדֹר וָדֹר

and generation   to generation   Zion   your Elohim   forever   ihvh   he reigns

הַלְלוּיָהּ:

praise Ya

10 The LORD shall reign for ever, even thy God, O Zion, unto all generations. Praise ye the LORD.

PSALM 147

ספר תהילים פרק קמז

הַלְלוּיָהּ
Praise Ya

כִּי־טוֹב זַמְּרָה אֱלֹהֵינוּ כִּי־נָעִים נָאוָה תְהִלָּה׃
prayer · pleasantly · pleasant ones – like · our Elohim · sing psalm · good – like

1 Praise ye the LORD: for *it is* good to sing praises unto our God; for *it is* pleasant; *and* praise is comely.

בּוֹנֵה יְרוּשָׁלַ͏ִם יְהֹוָה נִדְחֵי יִשְׂרָאֵל יְכַנֵּס׃
he gathers · Israel · outcasts · ihvh · Jerusalem · builder

2 The LORD doth build up Jerusalem: he gathereth together the outcasts of Israel.

הָרֹפֵא לִשְׁבוּרֵי לֵב וּמְחַבֵּשׁ לְעַצְּבוֹתָם׃
to wounds · and bandages · heart · to broken · the healer

3 He healeth the broken in heart, and bindeth up their wounds.

מוֹנֶה מִסְפָּר לַכּוֹכָבִים לְכֻלָּם שֵׁמוֹת יִקְרָא׃
he calls · names · to all them · to the stars · numbers · one counting

4 He telleth the number of the stars; he calleth them all by *their* names.

גָּדוֹל אֲדוֹנֵינוּ וְרַב־כֹּחַ לִתְבוּנָתוֹ אֵין מִסְפָּר׃
numbering · isn't · to his understanding · power—and many · our Adonei · great

5 Great *is* our Lord, and of great power: his understanding *is* infinite.

מְעוֹדֵד עֲנָוִים יְהֹוָה מַשְׁפִּיל רְשָׁעִים עֲדֵי־אָרֶץ׃
earth – till · wicked · lowering · ihvh · humble ones · encouraging

6 The LORD lifteth up the meek: he casteth the wicked down to the ground.

עֱנוּ לַיהֹוָה בְּתוֹדָה זַמְּרוּ לֵאלֹהֵינוּ בְכִנּוֹר׃
in harp · to our Elohim · sing psalms · in thanks · to ihvh · you answer

7 Sing unto the LORD with thanksgiving; sing praise upon the harp unto our God:

הַמְכַסֶּה שָׁמַיִם בְּעָבִים הַמֵּכִין לָאָרֶץ מָטָר
rain · to earth · the prepares · in clouds · heavens · the covering

הַמַּצְמִיחַ הָרִים חָצִיר׃
grass · mountains · the sprouting

8 Who covereth the heaven with clouds, who prepareth rain for the earth, who maketh grass to grow upon the mountains.

נוֹתֵן לִבְהֵמָה לַחְמָהּ לִבְנֵי עֹרֵב אֲשֶׁר יִקְרָאוּ׃
they call · which · raven · to sons · bread · to beasts · he gives

9 He giveth to the beast his food, *and* to the young ravens which cry.

לֹא בִגְבוּרַת הַסּוּס יֶחְפָּץ לֹא־בְשׁוֹקֵי הָאִישׁ יִרְצֶה׃
has favor · the man · legs – not · he delights · the horse · in might · not

10 He delighteth not in the strength of the horse: he taketh not pleasure in the legs of a man.

רוֹצֶה יְהוָה אֶת־יְרֵאָיו אֶת־הַמְיַחֲלִים לְחַסְדּוֹ׃

| desires | ihvh | his fearing - that | the yearning ones – that | to his mercy |

11 The LORD taketh pleasure in them that fear him, in those that hope in his mercy.

שַׁבְּחִי יְרוּשָׁלַם אֶת־יְהוָה הַלְלִי אֱלֹהַיִךְ צִיּוֹן׃

| commend | Jerusalem | ihvh - that | praise | your Elohim | Zion |

12 Praise the LORD, O Jerusalem; praise thy God, O Zion.

כִּי־חִזַּק בְּרִיחֵי שְׁעָרָיִךְ בֵּרַךְ בָּנַיִךְ בְּקִרְבֵּךְ׃

| like – strengthened | bars | your gates | has blessed | your sons | in your nearness |

13 For he hath strengthened the bars of thy gates; he hath blessed thy children within thee.

הַשָּׂם גְּבוּלֵךְ שָׁלוֹם חֵלֶב חִטִּים יַשְׂבִּיעֵךְ׃

| the putting | your borders | peace | fat | wheat | he satisfies you |

14 He maketh peace in thy borders, *and* filleth thee with the finest of the wheat.

הַשֹּׁלֵחַ אִמְרָתוֹ אָרֶץ עַד־מְהֵרָה יָרוּץ דְּבָרוֹ׃

| the sender | his word | earth | swiftly – till | he runs | his speaking |

15 He sendeth forth his commandment upon earth: his word runneth very swiftly.

הַנֹּתֵן שֶׁלֶג כַּצָּמֶר כְּפוֹר כָּאֵפֶר יְפַזֵּר׃

| the giver | snow | like wool | like frost | like ashes | he scatters |

16 He giveth snow like wool: he scattereth the hoarfrost like ashes.

מַשְׁלִיךְ קַרְחוֹ כְפִתִּים לִפְנֵי קָרָתוֹ מִי יַעֲמֹד׃

| one flinging | his ice | like bits | before | his cold | who | he stands |

17 He casteth forth his ice like morsels: who can stand before his cold?

יִשְׁלַח דְּבָרוֹ וְיַמְסֵם יַשֵּׁב רוּחוֹ יִזְּלוּ־מָיִם׃

| he sends out | his speaking | and he melts | he returns | his winds | waters - they flow |

18 He sendeth out his word, and melteth them: he causeth his wind to blow, *and* the waters flow.

מַגִּיד דְּבָרוֹ [דְּבָרָיו] לְיַעֲקֹב חֻקָּיו וּמִשְׁפָּטָיו לְיִשְׂרָאֵל׃

| tells | his speaking | to Jacob | his statutes | and his judgments | to Israel |

19 He sheweth his word unto Jacob, his statutes and his judgments unto Israel.

לֹא עָשָׂה כֵן לְכָל־גּוֹי וּמִשְׁפָּטִים בַּל־יְדָעוּם הַלְלוּיָהּ׃

| not | done | thus | nations - to all | and commandments | they know –in not | praise Ya |

20 He hath not dealt so with any nation: and as for his judgments, they have not known them. Praise ye the LORD.

PSALM 148

ספר תהילים פרק קמח

הַלְלוּיָהּ
praise Ya

הַלְלוּ אֶת־יְהֹוָה מִן־הַשָּׁמַיִם הַלְלוּהוּ בַּמְּרוֹמִים:
in high places　praise he　the heaven - from　ihvh – that　praise

1 Praise ye the LORD. Praise ye the LORD from the heavens: praise him in the heights.

הַלְלוּהוּ כָל־מַלְאָכָיו הַלְלוּהוּ כָּל־צְבָאָו [צְבָאָיו]:
his legions – all　praise he　his angels – all　praise he

2 Praise ye him, all his angels: praise ye him, all his hosts.

הַלְלוּהוּ שֶׁמֶשׁ וְיָרֵחַ הַלְלוּהוּ כָּל־כּוֹכְבֵי אוֹר:
light　stars – all　praise he　and moon　sun　praise he

3 Praise ye him, sun and moon: praise him, all ye stars of light.

הַלְלוּהוּ שְׁמֵי הַשָּׁמָיִם וְהַמַּיִם אֲשֶׁר מֵעַל הַשָּׁמָיִם:
the heaven　from above　which　and the waters　the heavens　his name　praise he

4 Praise him, ye heavens of heavens, and ye waters that *be* above the heavens.

יְהַלְלוּ אֶת־שֵׁם יְהֹוָה כִּי הוּא צִוָּה וְנִבְרָאוּ:
and it was created　commanded　he　like　ihvh　name - that　they praise

5 Let them praise the name of the LORD: for he commanded, and they were created.

וַיַּעֲמִידֵם לָעַד לְעוֹלָם חָק־נָתַן וְלֹא יַעֲבוֹר:
it will pass　and not　he gave – decree　to forever　to time　and he stood them

6 He hath also stablished them for ever and ever: he hath made a decree which shall not pass.

הַלְלוּ אֶת־יְהֹוָה מִן־הָאָרֶץ תַּנִּינִים וְכָל־תְּהֹמוֹת:
deep ones - and all　sea monsters　the earth – from　ihvh - that　praise

7 Praise the LORD from the earth, ye dragons, and all deeps:

אֵשׁ וּבָרָד שֶׁלֶג וְקִיטוֹר רוּחַ סְעָרָה עֹשָׂה דְבָרוֹ:
his speaking　makes　storm　wind　and vapor　snow　and hail　Fire

8 Fire, and hail; snow, and vapours; stormy wind fulfilling his word:

הֶהָרִים וְכָל־גְּבָעוֹת עֵץ פְּרִי וְכָל־אֲרָזִים:
cedars - and all　fruit　tree　hills – and all　the mountains

9 Mountains, and all hills; fruitful trees, and all cedars:

הַחַיָּה וְכָל־בְּהֵמָה רֶמֶשׂ וְצִפּוֹר כָּנָף:
winged　and fowl　creeping things　beasts - and all　the living creatures

10 Beasts, and all cattle; creeping things, and flying fowl:

מַלְכֵי־אֶרֶץ וְכָל־לְאָמִּים שָׂרִים וְכָל־שֹׁפְטֵי אָרֶץ:

earth   judges – and all   princes   to peoples – and all   earth – kings

11 Kings of the earth, and all people; princes, and all judges of the earth:

בַּחוּרִים וְגַם־בְּתוּלוֹת זְקֵנִים עִם־נְעָרִים:

youths –with   old men   virgins - and also   young men

12 Both young men, and maidens; old men, and children:

יְהַלְלוּ אֶת־שֵׁם יְהוָה כִּי־נִשְׂגָּב שְׁמוֹ לְבַדּוֹ הוֹדוֹ

his honor   alone   his name   exalted - like   ihvh   name - that   they will praise

עַל־אֶרֶץ וְשָׁמָיִם:

and heavens   earth – upon

13 Let them praise the name of the LORD: for his name alone is excellent; his glory *is* above the earth and heaven.

וַיָּרֶם קֶרֶן לְעַמּוֹ תְּהִלָּה לְכָל־חֲסִידָיו

his merciful ones - to all   pray   to his people   horn   and he exalts

לִבְנֵי יִשְׂרָאֵל עַם־קְרֹבוֹ הַלְלוּיָהּ:

praise Ya   his near– people   Israel   to sons

14 He also exalteth the horn of his people, the praise of all his saints; *even* of the children of Israel, a people near unto him. Praise ye the LORD.

PSALM 149

ספר תהילים פרק קמט

הַלְלוּיָהּ
Praise Ya

שִׁירוּ לַיהוָה שִׁיר חָדָשׁ תְּהִלָּתוֹ בִּקְהַל חֲסִידִים:
devout ones | in assembly | his prayer | new | song | to ihvh | you sing

1 Praise ye the LORD. Sing unto the LORD a new song, *and* his praise in the congregation of saints.

יִשְׂמַח יִשְׂרָאֵל בְּעֹשָׂיו בְּנֵי־צִיּוֹן יָגִילוּ בְמַלְכָּם:
in their king | they rejoice | Zion – sons | in its maker | Israel | be happy

2 Let Israel rejoice in him that made him: let the children of Zion be joyful in their King.

יְהַלְלוּ שְׁמוֹ בְמָחוֹל בְּתֹף וְכִנּוֹר יְזַמְּרוּ־לוֹ:
to him - they sing psalms | and harp | in drums | in dance | his name | they praise

3 Let them praise his name in the dance: let them sing praises unto him with the timbrel and harp.

כִּי־רוֹצֶה יְהוָה בְּעַמּוֹ יְפָאֵר עֲנָוִים בִּישׁוּעָה:
in salvation | humble ones | he will beautify | in his people | ihvh | his desire – like

4 For the LORD taketh pleasure in his people: he will beautify the meek with salvation.

יַעְלְזוּ חֲסִידִים בְּכָבוֹד יְרַנְּנוּ עַל־מִשְׁכְּבוֹתָם:
their beds – upon | they shout joy | in glory | devout ones | exalt

5 Let the saints be joyful in glory: let them sing aloud upon their beds.

רוֹמְמוֹת אֵל בִּגְרוֹנָם וְחֶרֶב פִּיפִיּוֹת בְּיָדָם:
in their hand | edges | and sword | in their throats | El | high praises

6 *Let* the high *praises* of God *be* in their mouth, and a two edged sword in their hand;

לַעֲשׂוֹת נְקָמָה בַּגּוֹיִם תּוֹכֵחֹת בַּל־אֻמִּים:
people - in not | rebukes | in nations | vengeance | to do

7 To execute vengeance upon the heathen, *and* punishments upon the people;

לֶאְסֹר מַלְכֵיהֶם בְּזִקִּים וְנִכְבְּדֵיהֶם בְּכַבְלֵי בַרְזֶל:
iron | in shackles | and their nobles | in chains | their kings | to bind

8 To bind their kings with chains, and their nobles with fetters of iron;

לַעֲשׂוֹת בָּהֶם מִשְׁפָּט כָּתוּב הָדָר הוּא לְכָל־חֲסִידָיו
his devout ones - to all | he | honor | written | judgment | in them | to do

הַלְלוּיָהּ:
praise Ya

9 To execute upon them the judgment written: this honour have all his saints. Praise ye the LORD.

PSALM 150

ספר תהילים פרק קנ

הַלְלוּיָהּ
praise Ya

הַלְלוּ־אֵל בְּקָדְשׁוֹ
in his holy place   El - praise

הַלְלוּהוּ בִּרְקִיעַ עֻזּוֹ׃
his power   in firmament   praise him

1. Hallelujah! Praise God in his sanctuary! Praise him in the firmament of his power!

הַלְלוּהוּ בִגְבוּרֹתָיו
in his great acts   praise him

הַלְלוּהוּ כְּרֹב גֻּדְלוֹ׃
his greatness   like much   praise him

2. Praise him for his mighty acts! Praise him according to his exceeding greatness!

הַלְלוּהוּ בְּתֵקַע שׁוֹפָר
shofar   in blast   praise him

הַלְלוּהוּ בְּנֵבֶל וְכִנּוֹר׃
and harp   in lyre   praise him

3. Praise him with the sound of the shofar! Praise him with the harp and the lyre!

הַלְלוּהוּ בְתֹף וּמָחוֹל
and dance   in drum   praise him

הַלְלוּהוּ בְּמִנִּים וְעוּגָב׃
and reed pipes   in strings   praise him

4. Praise him with the tambourine and dance! Praise him with stringed instruments and the pipe!

הַלְלוּהוּ בְצִלְצְלֵי־שָׁמַע
hearing - in ringing   praise him

הַלְלוּהוּ בְּצִלְצְלֵי תְרוּעָה׃
alarm   in ringing   praise him

5. Praise him with sounding cymbals! Praise him with loud clashing cymbals!

כֹּל הַנְּשָׁמָה תְּהַלֵּל יָהּ
Ya   you praise   the (high) soul   all

הַלְלוּיָהּ׃
Ya   praise

6. Let every thing that breathes praise the Lord! Hallelujah!